HANDBOOK KEY

LOGICAL COMP...

45 Sentence Unity	46 Faulty Co-ordination	47 Faulty Subordination	48 Overloaded Sentences	49 Choppy Style
50 Comparisons	51 Left Out Words			

CLEARNESS AND ORDER

52 Awkwardness Obscurity	53 Proper Arrangement	54 Dangling Modifiers	55 Reference of Pronouns	56 Parallelism Correlatives
57 Shift in Point of View	58 Mixed Constructions	59 Mixed Imagery	60 Transitions	

EFFECTIVENESS

61 Emphasis by Position	62 Repetition	63 Balance	64 Climax	65 Weak Passive Voice
66 Conciseness	67 Variety			

THE PARAGRAPH

68 Topic Sentence	69 Length	70 Unity	71 Arrangement	72 Concrete Details
73 Appropriate Tone	74 Maturity of Style			

USAGE

75 Glossary				

The Macmillan
HANDBOOK OF ENGLISH

REVISED EDITION

JOHN M. KIERZEK
PROFESSOR OF ENGLISH, OREGON STATE COLLEGE

THE MACMILLAN COMPANY · NEW YORK 1948

Reprinted, June, 1948

Preface

Those who have used the first edition of *The Macmillan Handbook of English* will see at once that this is a new book, completely rewritten, expanded and enriched and, I trust, made more practical and more usable. Like its predecessor, this book is still a rhetoric and a handbook combined. It may be used as either or as both. The first part of the book attempts to give the beginner the sort of helpful, common-sense advice about writing that he needs the most when he is a beginner. The student is introduced to the concept of English as a living and growing language. He is then taken through discussions about grammar as a tool of effective writing, about building good sentences and good paragraphs, to the processes of planning and writing compositions of various kinds and lengths. The first section ends with a discussion of the research paper, the most elaborate and ambitious project which a student will undertake. The material of the second part of the book — the handbook itself — is organized under seventy-five rules. An index and a theme-correction chart help both the student and the teacher to find any rule easily and quickly.

As I wrote in the preface to the first edition, it is difficult for an author to speak of his own work with appropriate modesty and objectivity. Yet every author should be permitted to point out the principle which motivates his work. The principle which I would retrieve from that preface is this: "I wish to explain a point of view which I have tried to keep throughout the book. I have tried to treat the student as a mature person. I have tried to speak to him as one learner would speak to another. A learner must be guided by rules until he knows enough about writing to be superior to rules. If I were learning to skate, or to dance, or to play tennis, I should submit myself to a discipline, knowing well that there is a freedom beyond rules. There is a freedom in writing which comes as a result of discipline. The student will understand, I trust, that although every rule in the book is based on strictly contemporary usage, this usage has been interpreted with discretion and a reasonable conservatism. The rules are the discipline of learning.

"But the student should also see that scattered throughout the book there are numerous references to more comprehensive and scholarly discussions of English usage. These are the invitations to the student to investigate for himself and to decide for himself. These are the open doors through which he may walk — and discover, perhaps, some lifelong interests."

For valuable suggestions in the preparation of the second edition I wish to express my sincere thanks to the scores of teachers throughout the country who have sent in criticisms, and especially to the following: Mr. Arthur A. Adrian, Western Reserve University, Professor Havilah Babcock, University of South Carolina, Professor Oscar Cargill, Washington Square College, New York University, Mr. W. S. Fitzgerald, Duke University, Miss Jane Lawson and members of the English department, University of Washington, Mrs. Dorothy R. Long, University of Texas, Mrs. Elizabeth Brice Wilson, Knox College, and Mr. W. M. Beardshear, assistant city editor of the Denver *Post*.

I also wish to thank those whose student papers or outlines I have used as examples throughout this book: Hallie Ashton, Pat Caven, Lawrence Chapman, Shirley Haag, Marion Jean Kierzek, Audred Roberts (Mrs. Luke Roberts), Pearl Swanson, and Fletcher Walker.

J. M. K.

Contents

CONTENTS

CONTENTS

CONTENTS

CONTENTS

CONTENTS

CONTENTS

CONTENTS

CONTENTS

Part I

THE EXPRESSION
AND COMMUNICATION OF THOUGHT

Writing is like pulling the trigger of a gun: if you are not loaded, nothing happens. — Henry Seidel Canby

Chapter 1

THE ENGLISH LANGUAGE

"Þyslīc mē is gesewen, þū cyning, þis andwearde līf manna on eorðan tō wiðmetenesse þǣre tīde þe ūs uncuð is, swylc swā þu æt swǣsendum sitte mid þīnum ealdormannum ọnd þegnum on wintertīde, ọnd sīe fȳr onǣled ọnd þīn heall gewyrmed, ọnd hit rīne, ọnd snīwe, ọnd styrme ūte; cume ān spearwa ọnd hraedlīce þæt hūs þurhflēo, cume þurh ōþre duru in, þurh ōþre ūt gewīte. Hwæt hē on þā tīd þe hē inne bið, ne bið hrinen mid þȳ storme þæs wintres; ac þæt bið ān ēagan bryhtm ọnd þæt lǣsste fæc, ac hē sōna of wintra on þone winter eft cymeð. Swā þonne þis mọnna līf tō medmiclum fæce ætȳweð; hwæt þǣr foregange, oððe hwæt þǣr æfterfylige, wē ne cunnan. For ðon gif þēos lār ōwiht cūðlīcre ọnd gerisenlīcre brẹnge, þæs weorþe is þæt wē þǣre fylgen."

It is a long road that our English language has traveled since that day more than thirteen centuries ago when the old thane arose and, with the dignity of one good man speaking to another, said to his king, "Now, this is the way it looks to me. . . ." He spoke in the native tongue of the inhabitants of England, a tongue known by scholars as Anglo-Saxon or Old English. This more than any other tongue, in spite of all the intermarriages and all the additions of new blood, is the one important great-ancestor of the English language which you and I speak and write.

The Family of Languages. The position of English in the family tree of Indo-European languages is shown by the table on page 7. English is one of a number of West Germanic languages. The Germanic group of languages is one of a number of groups, all descended from a hypothetical parent language, the Indo-European. All this is true yet highly misleading unless we

3

remember that although English is mainly Germanic in its structure, its vocabulary is only a fourth to a fifth native. More than half of the words in the English language have come to it, directly or indirectly, from Latin. The rest of the words have come from every language on the face of the earth.

The facts concerning relationships between languages have been dug up and pieced together in fairly recent times — recent as compared to the time when the languages themselves broke apart and went their various ways — and dug up and pieced together with a ratiocinative skill that makes a fictional detective look like an infant. No living man has ever heard or seen an actual Indo-European word. The idea that it existed is a hypothesis — a guess with a college education — and yet like most scientific hypotheses it is almost as good as a proved fact. A parent Indo-European language very likely did exist; scholars are even willing to place the home of those who spoke it as somewhere in central east Europe, about where Hungary is at present. A few clues like the existence of words for animals and plants of a temperate European climate, and the absence of any words relating to sea or ocean, gave the philologists their interesting lead.

And as to how language itself originated, your guess is as good as anybody else's. Nobody knows, and at present there does not seem to be any possibility that anybody ever will know. Scholars amuse themselves with ingenious guesses, but they do not pretend that their guesses are hypotheses.

Periods of Linguistic Change. Students of the English language have divided its historical growth into three main periods: the Old English Period, from 450 to 1100; the Middle English Period, from 1100 to 1500; and the Modern English Period, from 1500 to the present time. It must not be assumed, however, that in any one year the people of England stopped speaking one kind of language and began speaking another. The change was gradual, and yet there were definite historical events occurring at the dates mentioned which caused a more rapid change in the language of the people of England. These events were the invasion of England by the Angles, Saxons, and Jutes in 449, the Norman

Conquest in 1066, and the coming of the English Renaissance in 1500.

There were, of course, people in England before 450. The earliest known inhabitants of England were the Britons, a Celtic branch of the Indo-European family, with whom Caesar's Roman armies came into contact in the summer of 55 B.C. Almost a century later the Roman armies of Claudius returned to England and proceeded in earnest to conquer and enslave the native Britons. Four centuries of Roman rule left the natives so thoroughly Romanized and dependent upon their masters that when trouble at home forced the Romans to pull in their armies from their distant colonies, the Britons were helpless against the attacks of their northern neighbors.

According to a later historian (about 730) a British king, Vortigern, called in some Saxon tribes from the mainland of Europe to fight the northern invaders. Unfortunately for the Britons, these liberators, like a less successful self-styled liberator of a later date, quickly took the entire country into protective custody. What Britons survived the wars and massacres retreated westward and northward; a few must have remained, existing as best they could in unhappy servility. First Britons and then Britons and Romans occupied the English land for five hundred years of known history and left practically no trace upon our English language. The real history of our language begins with the Angles, the Saxons, and the Jutes.

The Old English Period. From 449, the legendary date of the first coming of the Saxons to England, to 1066, when William the Bastard defeated and killed the Saxon King Harold at the Battle of Hastings, is a period of 616 years — a time span almost four times as long as the present life span of the great American republic. Many things can happen in 616 years, and many things did happen. England became civilized, prosperous, and largely Christianized. Under the influence of the Christian missionaries and the organized church, schools and monasteries were set up. Politically, the English land was divided up among four important kingdoms, Northumbria, Mercia, Wessex, and Kent, which

5

at various times rose to temporal importance and then declined, as kingdoms do in a space of six hundred years. These kingdoms, too, were visited by trouble of the kind that they had brought upon the Britons. Another Germanic race, the Danes, descended upon the island in raids of growing magnitude over two centuries of time and came close to drawing the final curtain over the first scene of what was to become the great drama of the English-speaking peoples. Instead, they were themselves absorbed by the more stubborn and also more civilized native breed, and although the Danes, like most invaders, were extremely careless about pillaging libraries and burning books, enough of the written language of the Anglo-Saxons survived so that we know pretty well what sort of speech our ancestors used. The language remained predominantly Anglo-Saxon; it is estimated that the Norse [1] additions amounted to less than five per cent of our present vocabulary. More important than additions to the vocabulary was the gradual leveling of many inflectional endings, a language change which naturally takes place when two races speaking different languages try to learn each other's speech.

The Middle English Period. About a century and a half before the end of the Old English Period, another Scandinavian people, the Normans (Norsemen), landed on the Normandy beaches, took over the country, settled down, and adopted the language and culture of the French. In 1066, William, Duke of Normandy, after a tempestuous and unsavory career in his own country, laid claim to the English throne. The Norman Conquest followed his decisive victory at the battle of Hastings. What eventually happened to the language of England can be better understood if one remembers that the Norman Conquest was not a mass migration of one people intent upon displacing another but rather the personal adventure of a dictator grasping for more power and distinction. William the Conqueror proceeded to subdue Anglo-Saxon England from above, killing and replacing the native rulers, confiscating what property was worth taking and parceling it out to his followers, promulgating new laws and

[1] See "The Family Tree of the English Language," p. 7.

```
                                           ⎧ Sanskrit
                              ⎧ Indian     ⎨ Prakrit, etc.
                              ⎪             ⎨ Hindustani, etc.
              ⎧ 1. Indo-      ⎨             ⎩ Gypsy
              ⎪    Iranian    ⎪             ⎧ Old Persian
              ⎪              ⎩ Iranian     ⎨ Zend
              ⎪                             ⎩ Modern Persian, etc.
              ⎪
              ⎪ 2. Armenian
              ⎪
              ⎪              ⎧ Ionic
              ⎪ 3. Hellenic  ⎨ Attic       ⎧ Modern
              ⎪              ⎨ Doric        ⎩ Greek
              ⎪              ⎩ Æolic
              ⎪
              ⎪ 4. Albanian
              ⎪
              ⎪              ⎧ Oscan; Umbrian
              ⎪              ⎪              ⎧ French
              ⎪ 5. Italic    ⎨              ⎪ Spanish
              ⎪              ⎪ Latin        ⎨ Italian
              ⎪              ⎩              ⎪ Portuguese
              ⎪                             ⎩ Roumanian
Indo-European ⎨
              ⎪                             ⎧ Icelandic
              ⎪              ⎧ Norse        ⎪ Danish
              ⎪              ⎪ (North)      ⎨ Swedish
              ⎪              ⎪              ⎩ Norwegian
              ⎪              ⎪ Gothic
              ⎪ 6. Germanic  ⎨ (East)
              ⎪              ⎪              ⎧ High  ⎧ German
              ⎪              ⎪              ⎪       ⎩ Austrian
              ⎪              ⎩ West ⎨       ⎧ Old Saxon
              ⎪                     ⎪       ⎪ Dutch; Flemish
              ⎪                     ⎩ Low   ⎨ Frisian
              ⎪                             ⎩ Anglo-Saxon (English)
              ⎪
              ⎪                 ⎧ Baltic    ⎧ Prussian
              ⎪                 ⎪           ⎩ Lithuanian, etc.
              ⎪ 7. Balto-Slavic ⎨           ⎧ Russian
              ⎪                 ⎪ Slavic    ⎪ Bulgarian
              ⎪                 ⎩           ⎨ Czech
              ⎪                             ⎩ Polish
              ⎪
              ⎪              ⎧ Gallic (old Gaul)
              ⎪              ⎪              ⎧ Irish
              ⎪ 8. Celtic    ⎨ Gaelic      ⎨ Scotch-Gaelic
              ⎪              ⎪              ⎩ Manx
              ⎪              ⎪              ⎧ Welsh
              ⎩              ⎩ Cymric      ⎨ Cornish
                                           ⎩ Breton
```

decrees. In the meanwhile, life went on, with its promise of blood, sweat, toil, and tears; the work was done, crops were grown, trade went on, and the common people continued to speak their native Anglo-Saxon speech. The language of the court and the upper classes was Norman French. The language of the church was Latin, the universal language of that day.

For a time England continued to be trilingual. In the course of time a number of things happened which tended to separate the English people from their neighbors across the Channel. For the rulers it became increasingly more important to be kings of England than to remain dukes of a small French province. Wars with France and Scotland, a break with the Church of Rome, the Crusades, the rise of the middle classes, all tended to foster a sense of national unity and importance. By the middle of the fourteenth century, English, not French or Latin, became the accepted language of the ruling classes, the law courts, and the church. More than that, one dialect of the three which had persisted since the earliest Anglo-Saxon times, the East Midland dialect of London and its governmental agencies, emerged as the leading language of England, a position which it has held to this day. The fact that Chaucer, a Londoner, wrote his popular stories in this dialect helped to establish it.

Naturally, the English that emerged was greatly enriched by additions of Norman French words. As one might expect, most of these words came out of the social, political, and economic life in which the Normans dominated. From the language of government we get such words as *parliament, crown, duke, sovereign;* from the law courts *judge, jury, justice, jail, plaintiff;* from federal life and the life of the higher social classes *castle, count, baron, vassal, liege, war, prison, barber, grocer, tailor, mantle, labor, chamber.* And as an example of the fact that often two sets of names of the same object survived, there is the old joke that whereas the Saxon knew his domestic animals on the hoof as *swine, sheep, cow, calf, ox,* and *deer,* the Norman lord knew them on the table as *pork, mutton, beef, veal,* and *venison.*

By the end of the fourteenth century the language had taken

on a distinctly modern look, as we may see from the following
sample:

> My maister Bukton, whan of Criste our kinge
> Was axed, what is trouthe or sothfastnesse,
> He nat a word answerde to that axinge,
> As who saith: "no man is al trewe," I gesse.
> And therfor, thogh I highte to expresse
> The sorwe and wo that is in mariage,
> I dar not wryte of hit no wikkednesse,
> Lest I my-self falle eft in swich dotage.
>
> I wol nat seyn, how that hit is the cheyne
> Of Sathanas, on which he gnaweth ever,
> But I dar seyn, were he out of his peyne,
> As by his wille, he wolde be bounde never.
> But thilke doted fool that eft hath lever
> Y-cheyned be than out of prisoun crepe,
> God lete him never fro his wo dissever,
> Ne no man him bewayle, though he wepe.
>
> But yit, lest thou do worse, tak a wyf;
> Bet is to wedde, than brenne in worse wyse.
> But thou shalt have sorwe on thy flesh, thy lyf,
> And been thy wyves thral, as seyn these wyse,
> And if that holy writ may nat suffyse,
> Experience shal thee teche, so may happe,
> That thee were lever to be take in Fryse
> Than eft to falle of wedding in the trappe.

Modern English. The year 1500 has been arbitrarily set for the
beginning of the Modern English Period because near that time
two events of superlative importance took place: William Cax-
ton set up his printing press in England in 1476, and England
began to feel the first impulses from the continental European
Renaissance. The history of the English language since 1500 is
one of gradual growth and enrichment, not of violent change,
mainly because no foreign invader has again succeeded in setting
foot on the tight little island. There have been, it is true, "movements," like the swinging of a pendulum, which hurried or
retarded the change. The Elizabethan Age enriched the language

both in flexibility of structure and added vocabulary. The Classical Period, which followed, stressed correctness, conciseness, and simplicity. In the Romantic Period the pendulum swung to the other extreme. In addition to this rhythmic swing from the liberal attitude to the conservative and back to the liberal, there were other influences at work. The simple dignity of the King James Bible of 1611 acted as a brake upon the exuberancy of both Romanticists and Latinists. From time to time some writer rediscovered the virtues of the speech of the common people. England became first a world empire and then the mother country of a world commonwealth of nations, and the speech of the people who inhabited one half of a little island became a world language.

Several other profound influences upon the course which the English language took must be mentioned here. One is the standardizing influence of the dictionaries, the grammars, and the printing houses, which beginning in the eighteenth century set up standards of correctness first in spelling, then in pronunciation and meaning, and more recently in good use. Another is the elevating influence of almost universal education. A third, and now probably the most powerful influence, is that of the radio and the talking motion pictures. The speech of the radio announcer and the newscaster has emerged as the standard speech of the nation today — and tomorrow, it seems probable, of the whole English-speaking world. This leveling influence is so powerful that even at the present day philologists are hard put to it to find distinctions between regional dialects in this country. In a few years, when it will be as easy to pick up a news summary from London or from Melbourne as from New York or Los Angeles, national differences in pronunciation and usage, there is every reason to believe, will gradually tend to disappear.

When one looks back upon the fifteen hundred years which are the life span of the English language, he should be able to discern a number of significant truths. The history of our language has been a history of constant change, at times a slow, almost an imperceptible change, at other times a violent collision between two languages. Our language has always been a living, growing organism; it has never been static. Whether or not every change has been for the best, one does not dare to say. Another significant truth which emerges from such a study is that language at all times has been the possession not of one class or group but of many. At one extreme it was the property of the common, ignorant folk, who used it in the daily business of their living, much as they used their animals or their kitchen pots and pans. At the other extreme it was the ward of those who respected it as an instrument and a sign of civilization, and who strove by writing it down to give it some permanence, order, dignity, and, if possible, a little beauty.

Levels of Usage. It has been customary to divide the living English language of the present day into three main levels of usage, each characterized by certain distinctive practices and conventions. At the top is "formal" English; at the bottom is the vernacular, the spoken language of the uneducated. Between the two extremes is the level of informal writing and colloquial speech. This is a classification that is more convenient than scientifically accurate. It would be more accurate to say that language functions on thirty-three levels than on three. Below the "vulgate" one might place the profane, the vulgar, and the obscene. One might distinguish various important degrees of informality and formality. Furthermore the classification is misleading because from it the student might infer that each level has its own exclusive vocabulary, inappropriate on the other levels. The truth is that the main word stock of each level is appropriate also at the other levels. The uneducated workingman would not say to his wife, "Shoot me the punk, old muff. And lissen, ol' bag, best you mop up your puss an' gussy up your glad rags. The sky-pilot's comin' to put on the nose bag tonight." He would probably say, "Please pass me the bread. And, Mother, don't you think we should dress up a bit tonight? The minister is coming to supper." And that is good conversational English at any level. Such words as *bread, meat, mother, church, prayer, dress, work, sleep,* and thousands of others are the property of all people speaking English at any level. And finally the classification is unfortunate because it tends to obscure the basic unity of standard English and to stress unduly the differences between its varieties.

For there *are* differences. Let us now see how they affect our choice of appropriate language to use for various situations.

Standard English. The differences between varieties of English have often been explained by likening language to clothes. For formal occasions we put on our formal clothes; for a tennis match we dress in sports clothes; for plowing corn or driving a tractor we put on overalls or dungarees. Similarly, we suit our language to the occasion, to the subject, and to our readers or listeners. So far the comparison is good. When we pause to analyze the analogy, we are trapped by the word "formal," which to most people means "tails and white tie," a costume which millions of Americans have never worn, or perhaps never seen worn except by actors on a motion picture screen. And yet every American home which can afford a radio set or a newspaper has been exposed daily to both written and spoken formal English. We must amend our analogy by a further definition of terms, by extending the range of "formal" clothes to include the well-pressed business suit. It is misleading to try to confine the main current of our language to "the cold and lonely heights of formal and highly specialized scientific and scholarly language." [1] The language which we call "formal" — for want of a term with less unfortunate connotations — is far from cold and lonely. It has warmth, strength, beauty, and an infinite range and variety. It is not confined to a few scientific and scholarly treatises. The great body of our literature, from Shakespeare down to the latest book on the international crisis, is written in formal English. It is the language of most books of history, sociology, political science, botany, chemistry — every textbook that you use in college. It is the language of the professions, such as law, medicine, teaching. It is the language of all serious essays, of a good part of all novels and of poems, of radio newscasts and commentaries. Most business letters are written in formal English. So are the news

[1] Arthur G. Kennedy, *Current English*, p. 17.

and editorial sections of most newspapers. As a matter of fact, a good share of the nation's private and public daily work is done with the help of formal English.

What, then, are the distinguishing marks of standard English in its more serious and dignified uses? First, the restrictions upon vocabulary are so slight as to become almost negligible. In contrast to the incredibly vast riches of the "word hoard," as the Anglo-Saxons called it, the inappropriate or unacceptable words are few indeed. Slang and vulgarity, of course, are inappropriate. In more formal situations, most of the words which a modern unabridged dictionary labels as colloquial are inappropriate. There is a general feeling among students that formal English demands only "big" words, bookish words, words with a Latin ancestry. That is not true. The simple, homely, everyday words are as much a part of the vocabulary of formal English as the multisyllabic words. Notice carefully, for instance, the words used in each of the following excerpts — words spoken on occasions as formal and solemn as any in the long and tragic history of mankind:

"With malice towards none, with charity for all, with firmness in the right as God gives us to see the right, let us finish the work we are in, to bind up the nation's wounds, to care for him who shall have borne the battle, and for his widow and his orphans, to do all which may achieve and cherish a just and a lasting peace among ourselves and with all nations."

"And then one of the older men, who agreed with the king, arose and spoke: 'It seems to me, O King, that this present life of man, in comparison with that which is unknown to us, is as if you sat at the banquet table in the wintertime, with your chiefs and your men about you, and a fire burned and the hall was warm, while outside it rained and snowed and stormed. There came a sparrow and swiftly flew through the hall. It came in through one door, and it flew out through the other. Now, so long as he is inside he is not cuffed by the winter's storm, but that is for only a moment, the twinkling of an eye, and at once again he goes from winter back into winter. So this life of man appears but for a moment. What went before it or what comes after it, we do not know. Therefore if this new teaching brings anything more certain or fitting, it deserves to be followed.' "

"I see a book kissed which I suppose to be the Bible, or at least the New Testament, which teaches me that all things whatsoever I would that men should do unto me, I should do even so to them. It teaches me further to remember them that are in bonds as bound with them. I endeavored to act up to that instruction. I say I am yet too young to understand that God is any respecter of persons. I believe that to have interfered as I have done, as I have always freely admitted I have done in behalf of His despised poor, I did no wrong, but right. Now, if it is deemed necessary that I should forfeit my life for the furtherance of the ends of justice and mingle my blood further with the blood of my children and with the blood of millions in this slave country whose rights are disregarded by wicked, cruel, and unjust enactments, I say, let it be done."

"I expect that the Battle of Britain is about to begin. Upon this battle depends the survival of Christian civilization. Upon it depends all our British life, and the long continuity of our institutions and our Empire. The whole fury and might of the enemy must very soon be turned on us. Hitler knows that he will have to break us in this Island or lose the war. If we can stand up to him, all Europe may be free and the life of the world may move forward into broad, sunlit uplands. But if we fail, then the whole world, including the United States, including all that we have known and cared for, will sink into the abyss of a new Dark Age made more sinister, and perhaps more protracted, by the lights of perverted science. Let us therefore brace ourselves to our duties, and so bear ourselves that, if the British Empire and its Commonwealth last for a thousand years, men will still say, 'This was their finest hour.' " [1]

In the second place, standard English on the more formal levels is characterized by orderly structure. The expression and communication of ideas is a planned process, not a spontaneous outpouring. Ideas are grouped and arranged in some logical sequence. There is a serious attempt to show the interrelationship of ideas. As a consequence, the paragraphs tend to be more fully developed than in informal writing; sentences acquire increased complexity as the thoughts they express become more mature.

Third, standard English on all levels is characterized by a scrupulous observance of the accepted rules of grammar. Verbs

[1] From *Blood, Sweat, and Tears*, copyright 1941 by Winston S. Churchill, courtesy of G. P. Putnam's Sons.

are made to agree with their subjects, pronouns with their antecedents. Among those who write for a living, among those who write occasionally, and among those to whom a "talk" to be given before the Rotary Club or the Chamber of Commerce is an event of magnitude, there is a tendency to appeal to an authority, to someone who knows what current usage is. The deference to "correct usage," in the sense of what other writers and speakers are doing, is strong among all users of the language. Grammarians may argue over the question of whether "It is me" is a solecism, a peccadillo, a sign of life in the language, or one of the seven deadly sins. The busy scientist with a radio talk to prepare turns to the author of a handbook, or grammar, or *Webster's New International Dictionary* with the attitude, "I know that you don't make the language, but it is your business to find out what usage is. You are paid for that sort of thing."

And finally, standard English in the more formal situations generally tends toward an impersonal, objective attitude toward the subject matter expressed and communicated. One must not assume that the exclusion of the writer's or speaker's self is a requisite of the formal style. Indeed, some of the finest examples of formal writing are intensely personal in nature. In most cases they are personal because it is the personal element which is the vital substance of what is being said. Subjects in which the personal element is not vital, however, are usually treated objectively. More specifically, the sort of papers, reports, term essays, and discussions which you will write in college for your various courses are usually best treated impersonally and objectively.

Standard English on the Informal Level. Before we begin to examine the characteristics of "informal" English, we must reaffirm the statement that the essential unity of standard English is much more important than the differences among its varieties. One does not stop writing formal English and begin writing informal English as if he were stepping through a door from one room to another.

In some writing traditionally labeled informal, as for instance in those informal essays that are written with skill and good taste, the total extent of informality consists of the attitude of the writer toward his material and toward his reader. You may find in them the same discriminating taste in choice of words, the same respect for present-day standards in grammatical correctness and in usage, the same mature structure as in the best formal writing. The only difference is that the writer frankly and freely interprets his subject through his own personality or through his own likes and prejudices.

From the writing that is informal only in attitude one may move down the scale through a large variety of levels and gradations of informality to writing that is as unceremonious and unconventional as slacks and sweater and a corncob pipe. Much of the writing that you will do in your college composition course will be informal in style and in attitude. In this classification can be included, among others, all of your autobiographical papers and sketches, sketches of persons and places, profiles, personal experiences, discussions of attitudes and likes and dislikes, your reactions to books that you have read, your personal letters, talks before clubs and organizations.

At this point it might be well to examine a few specimens of the informal style. The first one is incidentally an excellent model for you to use when you write your paper on some interesting local custom that you have observed.

[Title] CHRISTMAS PANTOMIME

Surprisingly enough, one of the things about the English least understood by Americans has nothing to do with politics, the Peerage, punting, cricket, or any of the other more somber aspects of English life. It is their astonishing passion for a peculiar form of theatrical entertainment called the Christmas Pantomime.

When I was a little boy in America, I innocently believed that a pantomime was something that happened in dumb-show. I have met Americans in England who wished audibly that that definition still held good. In all fairness I can only say that is because they haven't been here long enough to endure, pity, and embrace. I have myself recoiled from Christmas Pantomimes for years, but must admit that I once saw one that I enjoyed enormously. The English, of course, are brought up on them. They are one of the national traditions, and the English wouldn't be English if they didn't then accept them as a right and necessary facet of the national life.

As many American readers of this will not be quite sure what a Christmas Pantomime is, I shall explain sketchily. It is a musical extravaganza based on one of the more popular fairy tales — Cinderella, The Sleeping Beauty, Puss-in-Boots, Little Red Riding Hood, Aladdin, Jack and the Beanstalk, etc. But the handling must always follow tradition. For instance, the fairies must speak in rhyme; the hero is played by what is always called Principal Boy, who turns out to be a glamorous female star in tights; the principal comedian is called a Dame and becomes a female impersonator for the occasion; and there must always be what is known as the "transformation scene." In the case of Cinderella it comes when she leaves the kitchen and her rags turn to a lovely gown, the pumpkin and the rats turn to a coach and horses — a coach outlined with electric lights, by the way, which is invariably applauded as ecstatically as it was in the days when Thomas Edison first made it possible — and the kitchen scenery, with much bending and creaking and scuffling of stagehands' feet, unsteadily makes way for a snow scene, complete with underrehearsed ballet, which has nothing to do with Cinderella getting to that rather stuffy ball. The most doggedly traditional thing of all, however, is a Harlequinade that comes at the end of the show, which no one ever seems to me to enjoy, but which would cost you social ostracism not to endure.

Any English reader will at once say my description is a little unfair. Well, except for the electric lights on the coach, I suppose it doesn't entirely apply to the more pretentious productions. But at Christmas time in England pantomimes are everywhere — even in some of the neighborhood theaters in outlying districts of London — and many of them have to be as inexpensively put on as possible. Besides, I am speaking as an American, and musical shows over here usually fall short of the standard of slick, lavish production that we manage to maintain in New York.

Pantomimes are primarily for children, and it is a source of wonder to Americans to see the love for them shown by grown-ups. It shouldn't be. After all, grown-up Americans flock to the circus every year and get as ing a kick out of it as any child. Besides, the most popular artists in the English theater go into pantomime, and, although I confess I find it ridiculous to watch a glamorous female star in tights singing a popular sentimental song to Cinderella, I think good comedians may easily be even better in pantomime. The very traditions help them, especially when they play "dames." Those superb clowns, Nervo and Knox, have never been so funny as when appearing as the Ugly Sisters.

Perhaps the strongest pull of pantomime for the grown-up Englishman is the very fact that he has known it all his life. He knows its traditional jokes, such as the "kitchen scene," which is always included and in which the comics invariably run riot with flour and dough. He knows its traditional spectacular effects, and, even when they are rather tinselly and shoddy, he enjoys remembering when he didn't think so. A *very* English Englishman, well on in years, once said to me, "Dear old Panto! Of course I know it's for the kids and all that, but I never miss it. By George, sir, I wish you could have seen Dan Leno as Mother Goose. *There* was a dame for you! No one to touch him to-day, except perhaps George Lacey."

Americans, however, can't have the fun of making such comparisons. They merely see a show that goes on and on for three hours and a half, with comedy scenes that suffer from being overlong, and Principal Boys singing popular songs of the day, and choruses that can't dance like our born jitterbugs, and Demon Kings appearing through obvious trapdoors. And until they've been dragged to a good many pantomimes, through a succession of winters, by enthusiastic English friends, they haven't a chance to develop that familiarity with it that gives the panto germ time to bite them. I recall the bitter comment of one fellow-American who asked me to take him to a pantomime in the winter of '38. I took him to a matinee, hoping the rapture of the children in the audience might deceive him. For three-and-a-half endless hours we sat there, the look of martyrdom on his face deepening each time the squirming urchin on his right kicked him on the knee. He didn't find the jokes funny. He saw no glamor in the rather faded scenery. The singing and dancing suffered, as they always do nowadays, because Hollywood musical films have set a standard for such things with which the theater cannot compete. During the interval I tried to explain to him why the rest of the audience was so obviously enjoying the show. I failed to convince him. And when at very long last the matinee was over, he remarked bitterly, "Well, if the war ever comes, I know now that England will win. Any people who can take *this* kind of punishment will never know when they're beaten."

One of the reasons I like the English is that I've sometimes quoted his remark to them and they've always been highly amused by it. And my principal reason for liking pantomime is that it is one of the few essentially English things left in their theater. Except for the American songs that are dragged into them, the Christmas Pantomimes are as English as Drake's drum. They couldn't happen in any other country in just the same way. Here they are a definite part of Christmas — and many of them run till nearly Easter. They're a part of the English love of familiar things, the national non-resistance to habit. A theater-goer will get as much pleasure, though of another kind, from seeing three different well-known comedians

as the Queen in "Sleeping Beauty" as he does from watching three different eminent actors play Hamlet. With the comedians, of course, the lines
are always different, though the basic situations remain as fixed as the
Tower of London.

Perhaps there's another interesting point here. In "Sleeping Beauty"
the Queen is the chief comedy part, with the King a secondary one.
Royalty and the aristocracy in general are riotously burlesqued. It might
seem odd, when you consider the intense affection the English hold for
their own Royal Family. Yet no one enjoys these burlesques more than
the King and Queen, and each year the two Princesses take part in a pantomime of their own.

I only wish the rest of the English theater would remain as deeply
rooted in the soil as pantomime, for I believe it is losing some of its
English character. Except for panto and an occasional intimate revue, the
musical shows here are often modelled on American patterns, if not actual
importations of New York shows, which are bound to suffer in the transplanting. The English composers, when encouraged to compose at all,
are apt to imitate the American ones. In such matters, as in the case of
British films, the English are prone to distrust their own abilities and
decry their own wares. I wish they'd remember how a little English revue
once crept into New York to try to compete with lavish, spectacular affairs
like the Ziegfeld Follies. It brought with it three people, then unknown
outside of London, named Beatrice Lillie, Gertrude Lawrence, and Jack
Buchanan. The revue was unpretentious, but it had wit and charm and
good taste. And overnight it became the hit of the town, and three well-
loved stars were born. The English theater can do that sort of thing in
a very English way. I only wish they'd trust themselves to do it oftener.
That's why I like pantomimes. I find arid stretches in them, as any American will, but they are English to the core. And like so many of these people,
they are "really very nice when you know them."

— James Dyrenforth, "Through Darkest England with Gun and Camera,"
The Outpost, January, 1945.

What are the characteristics of "informal" standard English?
One notices immediately that informal English is *not* the language
of the uneducated or the unintelligent, or of a lower social class
— if there still *are* social classes. It is rather the English written
and spoken by educated persons in situations where well-bred
ease is more important than dignity and high seriousness. No
part of the vocabulary of formal English is excluded from the

vocabulary of informal English. There is, in addition, a certain freedom permissible in the use of occasional colloquial or slang expressions. Simple, everyday words are perhaps more common than literary, scientific, or technical words. Contractions, like "they're," "can't," "didn't," are used more freely. It is evident, however, that there is in it the same conscientious regard for the conventions of correctness in grammar, in spelling, and in punctuation as in formal English. Sentences, too, are carefully built, and ideas are organized into paragraphs, although in some of the more journalistic types of informal writing both sentences and paragraphs may be shorter.

Here are two other examples of the informal style:

[Title] HIGH JUGGLER [1]

Last week we finally found the small inside room on the third floor of the Hotel Astor where Lew Folds, the juggler who tosses assorted objects around in the prologue of "Carousel," lives, and knocked on the door. Mr. Folds, with whom we had an appointment, shouted to us to come in. We found him in his shirt sleeves, balancing on his chin a white stick at the top of which was a spinning tray. "At your service," he said, and the tray fell off the stick. We had to duck smartly. Keeping a wary eye on our man, who soon began to toy with three Indian clubs, we asked him about the current state of the juggling profession. "There are only about fifteen high-class juggling acts in the U. S. right now," he told us. "That makes it tough to fill the spot I've got in 'Carousel.' The producers must of looked over half a dozen applicants before I turned up with the high tricks they wanted." We asked him to explain high tricks. "That's the kind of juggling," he said, "that you can see plain over the heads of the cast. I toss clubs and balls right up to the overhead lights in 'Carousel' and I also do a little magic. Since it's a period piece, though, I can't use all my stuff. Besides the clubs and balls, I only use a high hat and tray in the show, where I'd ordinarily throw in plates, tambourines, parasols, fans, and a couple other props. I think I hold the American record for bouncing balls — six at one time. I'll show you." Mr. Folds, whose room is strewn with the paraphernalia of his trade, got six balls out from under a pillow on his bed and commenced bouncing them furiously on the rug. "The fellow downstairs may not like this," we suggested. Mr. Folds ignored our remark and said, "This rug is too slow. Come on into the

[1] Permission *The New Yorker*, Copyright, 1945, The F–R. Publishing Corporation.

bathroom." We followed him there and he demonstrated on the tile floor that he is indeed master of big-scale ball bouncing. We congratulated him. "I'm no Rastelli," he said modestly. "*There* was a juggler — stand on one hand, balance three balls with the other, and maneuver something else with his feet. Nobody like him now. He had the most expensive act in the Wintergarten in Berlin in 1925. Of course, he was a third-generation juggler; I'm only a first-generation man."

When we asked Mr. Folds about his career before "Carousel," he responded by handing us a brief autobiographical account of himself written in longhand on Astor stationery. "Put it together to save you time," he said. We ran over the first page of his autobiography while he practiced keeping five balls going overhead. "Born," the manuscript began briskly, "Mura St. Martin, Hungary, Nov. 26, 1906. Came to America at age of 7. Lived in Sarajevo, Bosnia, where my father was mayor. This was the scene of the assassination that started first World War. My father was also newspaper editor of American Hungarian Daily in Cleveland, O., about 1914. Also lived on farm. Worked in stove factory, was also in trucking business and also a welder. Took up dancing for a hobby and turned pro. Teamed with 7 different partners with no success." We inquired about this failure. "I work alone," said Mr. Folds, "I do all right. I work with a girl, right away my heart and duty get all mixed up. It's the Hungarian in me. It was a girl, though, got me into juggling. Mickey Du Vall — God bless her — taught me how to juggle three balls when she was on a bill with me in Rochester in 1939. Took me six months to work up to five balls and three years more to work up to six balls. Then I finally gave up dancing entirely. If I try for seven I'll have to train for about ten more years. Some jugglers figure an even number of objects is harder to handle than an odd number, but I've got as many lumps on my head from dropping three clubs on it as I ever got from dropping four."

Mr. Folds is unique among jugglers in that he arrives onstage in full dress with all his equipment concealed under an opera cape. He has designed a belt to hold his trays, clubs, balls, and parasols. He feels as comfortable, he says, as the average man does in his undershirt. "Funny thing about me in full dress," he remarked. "Everybody thinks I look like Dracula when I get into one — I mean like Bela Lugosi when he's Dracula. One time when I was in Philadelphia, Lugosi was playing there and I went backstage to see if I really did look like him. I talked Hungarian to him and he was real friendly. He looked like me all right, only older, so I figure I must look like him when he was playing Dracula." "Does it bother you?" we inquired. "What the hell?" asked Mr. Folds rhetorically. "It's probably a break. Maybe I'll wind up as the first combination juggler and monster."— From the *New Yorker*, August 11, 1945.

[Title] MOTOR CARS

The motor car is, more than any other object, the expression of the nation's character and the nation's dream. In the free billowing fender, in the blinding chromium grilles, in the fluid control, in the ever-widening front seat, we see the flowering of the America that we know. It is of some interest to scholars and historians that the same autumn which saw the abandonment of the window crank and the adoption of the push button (removing the motorist's last necessity for physical exertion) saw also the registration of sixteen million young men of fighting age and symphonic styling. It is of deep interest to me that in the same week Japan joined the Axis DeSoto moved its clutch pedal two inches to the left — and that the announcements caused equal flurries among the people.

I have long been interested in motor-car design, or the lack of it, and this for two reasons. First, I used to like motoring. Second, I am fascinated by the anatomy of decline, by the spectacle of people passively accepting a degenerating process which is against their own interests. A designer sitting at his drafting board blowing up a mudguard into some new fantastic shape is no more responsible to his public than is a political ruler who is quietly negotiating a treaty for the extension of his power. In neither case is the public in on the deal.

Some years ago car manufacturers maliciously began reducing the size of windows and increasing the size of mudguards, or "fenders" as the young generation calls them. By following no particular principle of design and by ignoring the functional aspects of an automobile, these manufacturers eventually achieved a vehicle which not only was stranger looking than anything which had heretofore been evolved, but which, because it cut off the driver's view, proved itself capable of getting into more scrapes. At first the advantages of this design were not apparent, but it didn't take long before the motor-car industry realized that it had hold of something which, from a commercial angle, was pure gold. Every automobile was intrinsically self-defacing — and sometimes self-destructive — and this soon made the market ever so much brisker.

I shall go into the evolution of this modern car in a little more detail. The way it happened was that a rumor got started (I don't know why) that a motor car should be "longer" and "lower." Now, obviously it was impractical to reduce, to any great extent, the height of a motor car. And it was just as impractical to increase, to any great extent, the length of a motor car. So the designers had to produce an *illusion* of great length and extreme lowness. The first thing they did was to raise the hood, so that the rest of the car would appear lower by contrast. Having raised the hood, they also raised the line of the doors, to carry out the illusion clear to the bitter end. This of course reduced the size of the windows, and the motorist began the long sinking process which was to end, in 1941, in his total immersion. Fenders also had to be raised (you notice that in order to build a "low" car everything was raised). But it was impossible to raise fenders without also enlarging them — otherwise they would rise right up off the wheels. So the designers began playing with new shapes in fenders, and they huffed and they puffed, and they produced some wonderful fenders — fenders which not only were a very odd shape indeed, but which would reach out and claw at everything that came anywhere near them.

Meanwhile wheels had shrunk so small, and tires had grown so big, that the fenders were still further enlarged in a downward direction, so that they would not only be readily bumped, but would scrape along the tops of curbings and culverts and miscellaneous mounds. They also made it impossible for anyone but a contortionist to change tires.

The decrease in the size of windows, simultaneously with the increase in the size of fenders, produced astounding results in the automobile industry. Millions of motorists who had become reasonably proficient in driving their cars without denting them, suddenly lost that proficiency because they no longer could see where they were going (or where they had been), and because the dentable surfaces had been so drastically enlarged. Car owners who were accustomed to keeping a car for six or eight years, found that their modern car was all dented up after a single season of blind flying. So they would trade it in for a new one. Here was a most favorable turn of events for the manufacturer. He wasn't slow in catching on.

The ultimate goal of automobile designers is to produce a car into whose driving seat the operator will sink without a trace. They have very nearly achieved this goal. I know several women whose heads are permanently slanted backward because of neck cramps they have developed trying to peek out over the cowl of a modern super-matic automobile. Incidentally, the steering wheel had been a big help to the designers in producing this type of cramp. If, after the hood had been raised, there still lingered any doubt that the operator's vision had been blocked off, the designer settled it once and for all by moving the wheel up an inch or two till the top of it was exactly on eye level. Even a skinny little steering wheel can cut off about an acre of visibility if properly placed by a skilful designer.

— E. B. White, *One Man's Meat*, Harper & Brothers, New York, 1942. Reprinted by permission of the author and the publishers.

The Vernacular. There is a language below the colloquial level — much more accurately, there is an endless variety of languages — in which the college student has only an academic interest. There have been times in the history of English, in the days before the radio, the airplane, the automobile, the daily newspaper and the weekly newsmagazine, a digest for every pocket, and an education for every child, when there still were social "classes," when rustics spoke dialects and educated persons spoke literary English. Now, the special dialects of small groups, like the special language of jive, of the sub-debs, of racing, of soldiers and sailors, of various occupations, are special, made-to-order vocabularies of people who usually know standard English well enough and use it when the occasion demands it.

That part of this so-called vernacular which seeps into standard English we call slang, a label more convenient than scientifically accurate. There have been many attempts to write entire books in the vernacular, notably James Stevens' *Brawnyman*, Vincent McHugh's *Caleb Catlum's America*, and, in a way, Sinclair Lewis's *Babbitt*, and the result has usually been an illusion — "slightly phony," as one critic remarked — rather than a transcript of actual speech. One of the most delightful stories in what may be called the vernacular is *Anything Can Happen*, by George and Helen Papashvily, from which the following scene is taken:

Naturally when I engaged myself for marriage with Helena Gerbertovna I went right away with heartful of happiness to carry the good news to my friends.

But seemed like they weren't so pleased. Vactangi showed long horse face. Challico sat dark blue in a corner. Even Illarion, practically American himself now, didn't give me any support. Only Dzea shaked my hand and that sadly. "You take a big chance, Bijo, to marry with an American girl." All he said.

"First place," Vactangi pointed out, "American young ladies don't like foreigner names. Now you have to change yours. One Russian, I knew him well, immediately he married American young lady she made him go in court take the name of Gerbert Goover. For honor. Next election Gerbert Goover don't wins. How he feels then, that Russian fellow? Be same with you."

"Main thing," Illarion said, "the American girls I met so far can only cook out of books."

"See. Something else you didn't know," Vactangi said. "Lose the book. Ph-i-i-i-t-t. No eat. You'll starve."

"I can buy another book," I said.

"And what's more," Challico had his turn, "American cooking every day just enough. Two peoples, two steaks. Three peoples, three steaks. Never cooking one extra piece for the pot's good luck. Company comes unexpected they gonna sit hungry. You'll die from shame before you're six months married."

"Yes," Vactangi said, "and after your funeral there won't be any table either. Maybe a cup of tea for who carries your burial box. I won't come."

"Never enjoy the pleasure at mealtime to call in strangers passing on the road to share your table." Challico shook his head. "Won't even be any use to get rich. You'll have a shiny five-hundred dollar, pull-a-button, push-a-button refrigerator and not one extra piece of baloney to keep inside."

"But you don't know the worst that's gonna happen in your house," Vactangi warned. "American young ladies all keep bodguts."

"Helena Gerbertovna has dog," I said. "Irishman setter named Veleike Kneeaz. Comes 'Duke' in English. But that's all."

"Bodguts means writing down moneys before you spending," Vactangi explained. "Suppose you not feeling good, we take for example. You want to stop in Russian Club drink glass of vodka, eat piece herring maybe, for your stomach. You have to write down in bodguts first:

I'm drinking whiskys . . . . . *35¢*
Eating piece herring, too . . . . . *10¢*

"Where you ever knew American young lady to find out such informations?" I asked him.

"That's enough, boys," Dzea said. "If they promised to each other can't help now. Damage is done." He shook my hand again. "Never mind, I stood your friend twenty years, Bijo Gogio, and I don't stop now."

—George and Helen Papashvily, *Anything Can Happen*, Harper & Brothers, New York, 1945. Reprinted by permission.

When a skilled writer sets out to color his writing by using slang, profanity, and what is known as "bad grammar," he does it to produce an effect, a mood perhaps, an impression of reality and genuineness. The following scene is from a book that does use the vernacular very well indeed, although the private first class who after three years in the army is now patiently trying to trim his GI vocabulary to civilian standards might smile a bit cynically at its restraint.

While the doctor and others worked on the bandages and the splint for the shattered arm, the medic with the pencil said:

"What got you, Jack?"

"God, I don't know. It was a tank. Where's the chaplain?"

"You don't need the chaplain, Jack," said the medic. "You're going to be okay. What got you? There weren't any tanks around a while ago."

"It was a grenade," said Jack, his hand still reaching for his face. "Where's the chaplain? God, why do you let me hurt like this?"

"How old are you, Jack?" asked the medic persistently. He had already marked "grenade," because the wounds showed that. It had been a German potato-masher grenade, because the holes in his body looked like bullet wounds, but didn't go clear through him, and they weren't as jagged as shell or mortar fragment wounds. Evidently the German had sneaked up while the boy was down in his hole.

Jack said he was twenty years old, he was a staff sergeant, and he was from Texas.

The questioning seemed heartless at this time, but there is a reason for it. If the patient is able to answer, it distracts him from his pain; and if the information isn't gained here, they have to get it back at the hospital.

Jack had guts. Of course he was scared. He knew he was hurt bad, and it's a shock to anybody to get hit. But when they told him he shouldn't reach for his face, he said okay a little sleepily, because the morphine was taking effect.

"Hold a flashlight," the doctor said to me. "The lantern isn't strong enough."

I grabbed a flashlight and held it on the boy while they worked on him. I thought, "Christ, twenty years old!" I felt like an old man at twenty-three. I looked at the holes which had riddled his right arm and practically severed his little finger, and I looked at the swollen bloody gashes on his leg. I looked at his horribly wounded face and head, and I thought of how twenty minutes ago he was sitting quietly in his hole wondering how soon he could get home.

I handed the flashlight to the medic who had finished filling out the slip, and I went over to the litter and sat on it with my head between my knees and tried to keep from being sick on the floor.

The medic took the flashlight without even a glance, and nobody looked at me. They went right on working. Pretty soon Jack's face was fixed and it didn't look so bad with a neat bandage and the blood washed off. His arm was fixed in a splint and it looked very neat indeed. He was wrapped up in blankets, and the ambulance came up and took him away. He was full of morphine and probably dreaming of home.

"I don't know what we'd do without morphine," the doc said.

I guess I looked a little foolish and white, and I started to open my mouth. I don't know what I was going to say, but the medic who had taken the flashlight turned to me and said:

"It's funny. I handle these guys every night, and some of them are really in awful shape. But last night one came in not hurt half as bad as Jack and I did the same thing you did."

Another medic said, "We keep some medicine to take care of those things."

They brought out a miracle — a half-filled bottle of Pennsylvania Rye. Now I know damned well one of those guys got that bottle in a Christmas package, and I know he could have sold it for a hundred dollars cash anyplace between Florence and Bologna. Or he could have kept it to himself, and nobody would have blamed him. But we all had a slug of rye — the doc with his bloody hands and his eyes which were bantering once more, and the medics who were kidding each other again.

— Bill Mauldin, *Up Front*, Henry Holt & Co., New York, 1945. Reprinted by permission.

The language of these last two selections is appropriate because it is the natural outgrowth of the situations. When slang is used in situations that call for a different sort of treatment, the results are usually stale, flat, and rather painful. Let us look for a moment at Hamlet's soliloquy:

> To be, or not to be: that is the question:
> Whether 'tis nobler in the mind to suffer
> The slings and arrows of outrageous fortune,
> Or to take arms against a sea of troubles,
> And by opposing end them? To die: to sleep;
> No more; and by a sleep to say we end
> The heart-ache and the thousand natural shocks
> That flesh is heir to, 'tis a consummation
> Devoutly to be wished. . . .

Translated into more or less current slang, this is the way Hamlet's soliloquy might read:

To bolt or not to bolt. I'd like the lowdown
On whether it is nervier in the dome
To plug along, though things are not so hot,
Or fly the coop and pass the buck to fate.
To croak; to get a little shut-eye; that
Is one humdinger of a hot idea.
But how can one who doesn't know the ropes
Dope out what happens when one jumps the gun?
Too late for him to stage a comeback then,
Although he gets a rotten deal. Yowsah!
He's up against it till the cows come home.
So when he gives the subject the once over,
Admits he is a dim bulb and all wet,
He finds he has cold feet and lacks the crust
To do his stuff and stage a cagey fade-out.

The Student's Choice. A student of the English language should know something of its history, its forms and varieties, its resources and limitations, so that his attitude toward self-improvement will be realistic. The history of the language has been a history of innumerable changes. It is still a changing language. What *is* the realistic attitude in the face of changes in usage? The common-sense procedure is to ask, "What is being done by the majority of educated men and women at the present time?" It is not sensible, for instance, to use a double negative merely because you know that many great writers in the past have used double negatives. Neither is it sensible to anticipate future changes — to be so progressive that you want to be on the spot to welcome the future when it arrives. If you say, "Sir, I can't see nobody nowhere; I think it was only me and him putting away the goods," your employer will rudely set you right. The standards of the majority must be your standards for the simple reason that you as a college graduate will live among and communicate with those who have these standards.

What these standards are you can discover for yourself by wide reading and by long and careful observation of the practices of educated men and women. That is the way the authors of hand-books, grammars, and dictionaries have found out what current usage is. Some of these men have spent a lifetime doing little else but read, check, analyze, and file examples of usage. Of course you do not have the time or the opportunity for this sort of individual research; you are satisfied to defer to the judgment of those "who are paid to do that sort of thing." That is a realistic attitude, too, but do not give up entirely your research and observation, for that may be fun. Observe current usage in the books that you read; listen to prominent men and women whom you may hear over the radio.

In most of the papers that you will write in college you will make a conscious choice of style, language, attitude, or point of view. Many times, it is true, your choices will be determined for you by the situation. If your instructor in history asks you to write a discussion of the causes of revolutions, you will naturally decide to give him, not a slangy, breezy sketch, but a serious, well-planned and well-constructed essay in standard formal English. It is hard to see that any other decision is appropriate in such a situation. Similarly, a professional writer writing for the *New Yorker* uses the *New Yorker* style; a writer writing for *Harper's* uses a style appropriate for *Harper's*. Either he does this — or his manuscript is returned to him. To that extent he has no choice. But he does choose the language, the style, and the structure appropriate for each situation.

Frequently you will have to decide between a formal and an informal treatment of a subject. A subject like "The Veteran in College" can be handled either with deep seriousness or with a light, perhaps with a humorous touch. It depends on the particular phase of the subject that you decide to use, on the situation, and on the reader for whom you are writing. Your choice, whatever it is, should always consider writing as communication. You are not merely writing — you are writing for someone to read. In the final analysis, perhaps it is the reader, more than anything else, who determines the appropriateness of the choice of language, point of view, and treatment that you make.

The following books dealing with various aspects of the English language — its growth, its various levels of usage, the sources of its vocabulary, etc. — may be found in almost every college library:

Baugh, Albert C., *A History of the English Language*, D. Appleton-Century Co., New York, 1935.

Bradley, Henry, *The Making of English*, The Macmillan Company, New York, 1917.

Curmé, George O., *Syntax*, D. C. Heath & Company, Boston, 1931.

———, *Parts of Speech and Accidence*, D. C. Heath & Company, Boston, 1935.

Fowler, H. W., *A Dictionary of Modern English Usage*, Oxford, 1926.

Fries, C. C., *American English Grammar*, D. Appleton-Century Company, New York, 1940.

Gray, Louis H., *Foundations of Language*, The Macmillan Company, New York, 1939.

Greenough, James B., and George Lyman Kittredge, *Words and Their Ways in English Speech*, The Macmillan Company, 1901, 1923.

Kennedy, Arthur G., *Current English*, Ginn & Co., Boston, 1935.

Krapp, George Philip, *The English Language in America*, The Century Co., New York, 1925.

———, *The Knowledge of English*, Henry Holt & Co., New York, 1927.

———, *Modern English, Its Growth and Present Use*, Charles Scribner's Sons, New York, 1909.

McKnight, George H., *English Words and Their Background*, D. Appleton & Co., New York, 1923.

Robertson, Stuart, *The Development of Modern English*, Prentice-Hall, Inc., New York, 1934.

Smith, Logan Pearsall, *Words and Idioms*, Houghton Mifflin Co., Boston, 1925.

Chapter 2

THE SENTENCE

Grammar: The Tool of Effective Writing. A school superintendent once solemnly admonished a group of English teachers: "We need more useful grammar. We need less useless grammar." What part of grammar is useful? What part is useless? No one can say with absolute certainty. Much of the grammar that you will learn will be useless to you if you make it so. All of it will be useful to you if you study it not for itself but for what it will eventually give you — a greater ease, effectiveness, and interest in your writing. In your study of grammar keep the purpose always in view. The ability to pick out subjects and verbs and modifiers is not a virtue in itself. If you think that you can write well because you can tell the difference between a cognate accusative and an objective predicate, you are like an amateur carpenter who thinks he can build a house because he can distinguish between a plane and a spirit level. Grammar is a tool of expression — rather, a chest of tools. You must learn how to use your tools, but before you can use them you must know what they are.

In the following brief review of grammar you will find numerous cross references to the handbook. These references will help you to understand how a knowledge of grammar is the foundation of correct and effective writing. Let us make this clearer by means of a few examples. How, for instance, can you correct an error like this, "This is strictly between he and I," if you do not know something about pronouns, about prepositions, and about the uses of the objective case? How can a teacher explain that you should punctuate phrases or clauses in a series if you do not know what phrases and clauses are? When a person says, "I done pretty good in the test today," he expresses his thought with absolute clearness — but clearness, as you see, is not enough. How can this person learn, and how can a teacher help him learn, if there is not some understanding of verb forms, of grammatical agreement, of adjectives and adverbs? Grammar is a chest of useful tools, and the names of the parts of speech and the parts of a sentence are the names of the most common and the most useful of them.

The Parts of Speech. The following definitions are condensed and simplified, and therefore open to academic quibbling, but they will serve their present purpose. Study the examples: you will probably learn more from them than from the definitions.

Words are classified according to their function or use in the sentence into what are called parts of speech. Notice that the *use in the sentence* always determines the part of speech to which a word belongs. The parts of speech are nouns, verbs, pronouns, adjectives, adverbs, prepositions, conjunctions, and interjections. If you wish to group these parts of speech according to their functions, you may think of them as follows: nouns and pronouns are *naming* words; verbs are *asserting* words; adjectives and adverbs are *modifying* words; prepositions and conjunctions are *joining* words; interjections are *independents*.

1. A **noun** is a word that names something. It may name an object, a person, a place, or a quality. When a noun names a person, a place, or an object, it is called a concrete noun; when it names a quality or a mental concept, it is called an abstract noun. For the practical value of this information, see sections 36, 39, 40, and 72. Nouns are also classified as proper and common. A proper noun is the official name of some individual person, place, or object; a common noun names any one of a class or kind. Proper nouns are capitalized; common nouns are not. See section 12.

Space, time, society, labor, climate, food, locomotion, the *animals,* the mechanical *forces,* give us sincerest *lessons* . . . whose *meaning* is unlimited. — Emerson.

My *brother Tom* and his *friend, Dick Woods,* stopped in *Detroit* on their *way* to *Minneapolis,* where *Tom* intends to study *engineering* at the *University of Minnesota.*

2. **A verb** is a word that asserts action, being, or state of being. See sections 4 and 7.

Birds *sing.* We *shall be* late. Why *are* you *crying?* I *did* not *think* about you. They *have brought* their relatives. I *am being spoiled* by too much attention. We *should have used* our books. We *shall be standing* by the gate. He *is going to sing* a song.

3. **A pronoun** is a word that takes the place of a noun. Pronouns are classified as personal, demonstrative, relative, interrogative, and indefinite. See section 5.

Personal: I, *you, he, she, it, they, we, them, thee, thou.*
Demonstrative: this, that, these, those.
Relative: who, which, what, that, whoever, whatever, whichever.
Interrogative: who, which, what.
Indefinite: one, none, some, any, anyone, anybody, some one, somebody, no one, nobody, each, everyone, everybody, either, neither, both.

4. An **adjective** is a word that modifies (describes or limits) a noun or a pronoun. The articles *a, an, the,* and the possessive forms of nouns and pronouns, when used to modify nouns, are classed as adjectives. Pronouns have two forms of the possessive: the first form (*my, our, your, her, his, its, their*) when placed before a noun is used as an adjective; the second form (*mine, ours, yours, his, hers, its, theirs*) is used as a pronoun.

Adjective: This is *my* pencil. They did *their* work.
Pronoun: This pencil is *mine.* No work of *theirs* is poorly done.

The place through which he made *his* way at leisure was one of *those* receptacles for *old* and *curious* things which seem to crouch in *odd* corners of *this* town, and to hide *their musty* treasures from *the public* eye in jealousy and distrust. — Dickens.

A *high, clear* flame, *an immense* and *lonely* flame, ascended from *the* ocean, and from *its* summit *the black* smoke poured continuously at *the* sky. — Joseph Conrad.

5. An **adverb** is a word that modifies a verb, an adjective, or another adverb. Occasionally an adverb will modify a phrase, a clause, or a whole sentence. Adverbs express the following relations in a sentence: time, place, manner, degree, affirmation or negation, frequency. See also section 6.

Time: He will come *tomorrow*. They will *soon* be here.
Place: Put it *down*. Come *in*. Leave your dog *outside*.
Manner: He answered *quickly*. I played *better* yesterday.
Degree: You are *very* kind. He is *too* good. They are *rather* dull.
Affirmation or negation: Do *not* go there. *Certainly*, he will return. *Yes*, he is here. *No*, you must *not* see him.
Frequency: She is *always* pleasant. She called *twice*. It rains *often*.

6. A **preposition** is a word used to show the relation between a noun or pronoun, called its object, and some other word in the sentence. Many prepositions are single, short words: *at, by, in, for, from, off, on, up, above, after, around, before, behind, between, below, during, except, over, through, under, until, without.* There are also a number of so-called "group" prepositions: *by means of, in front of, on account of, in place of, with respect to.*

7. A **conjunction** is a word which connects words, phrases, or clauses. Conjunctions are co-ordinating and subordinating. Conjunctions used in pairs are called correlatives. Adverbs used as connectives, either co-ordinating or subordinating, are called conjunctive adverbs.

The chief co-ordinating conjunctions are: *and, for, but, or, nor, yet, both . . . and, not only . . . but also, either . . . or, neither . . . nor.* At the present time, *so* is used as a co-ordinating conjunction in loose, informal writing and in colloquial speech. Its use should be avoided in all writing and in most speech, not because *so* is illegitimate as a conjunction, but because its use produces slovenly, backboneless sentences. Look up "So" in section 75. See also sections 8 and 46.

The following are some of the subordinating conjunctions: *if, although, though, that, because, since, so that, in order that, as, unless, before, than, where, when.*

Correlative conjunctions are: *both . . . and, not only . . . but also, either . . . or, neither . . . nor.*

Some adverbs used as conjunctions are: *how, why, where, while, before, after.* Such connectives as *however, therefore, nevertheless, hence, accordingly,* are often classified as conjunctive adverbs. In modern prose they are commonly used as transitional expressions. There is no profit in quibbling over the question of whether they are transitions or conjunctive adverbs; the only important fact here is that these expressions, in modern writing, are *not* placed at the beginnings of clauses in compound sentences. They are tucked away neatly within the clauses. See section 21 for a discussion of the punctuation which should be used with these transitional expressions.

8. An **interjection** is a word used as an exclamation expressing sudden or strong feeling. Note that an exclamation point is not the inevitable punctuation of an interjection. For mild interjections a comma or a period is sufficient.

Oh! Ah! Bravo! Alas! Dear me! Why!

The Verbals. The English language also has another class of words called verbals, which are formed from verbs and resemble verbs but which are used as other parts of speech. For a more complete discussion of verbals see section 9.

1. **A gerund** is a verbal used as a noun.

Try *hitting* the ball a little harder. [A noun used as the object of the verb *try.*] *Working* in a factory is a valuable education. [The subject of the verb *is.*] I tried to keep him from *asking* too many questions. [Object of the preposition *from.*] His eligibility for office was established by his *having been* so successful as governor. He was proud of *having won* the cup. (Notice the form of the gerund in the last two sentences.)

2. **A participle** is a verbal used as an adjective. See also section 54.

The *shouting* boy ran after the *barking* dog. I put the *broken* dish on the shelf. *Tired* and hungry, he started to walk home. *Having sold* his last paper, Tom returned for a new supply.

35

3. An **infinitive** is a verbal which may be used as a noun, an adjective, or an adverb. The infinitive may be recognized by its sign *to*, which precedes it. Occasionally the sign is omitted.

Wilbur tried *to climb* a tree. [Used as a noun object of *tried*.] Give me a horse *to ride*. [Used as an adjective modifying *horse*.] I did not stop *to ask* his name. [Used as an adverb modifying *did stop*.] There was no meat *to be had* at any price. She seems *to have spent* all of her money. We heard something *drop*. I did not dare *speak* to her about it. (Note that in the last two sentences the sign of the infinitive is omitted.)

EXERCISES

Exercise 1, Parts of speech. In the following sentences name the part of speech to which each word belongs. The sentences are purposely made elementary. You should have no difficulty with this exercise. It is just a preliminary workout.

1. Harry sold his bicycle for thirty dollars.
2. In her arms she carried a large paper parcel.
3. Stealthily the beast crept upon its prey.
4. Sincere praise is welcomed by every student.
5. Lift up your eyes to the hills.
6. Thunder roared and lightning flashed, although no rain fell.
7. What! Are you taking her to this dance?
8. Industry does not always produce success.
9. The Indiana team played a game in Florida.
10. This lunch is mine; his was left on the boat.

Exercise 2, Verbals. Identify the verbals in the following sentences. The verbals are gerunds, participles, and infinitives.

1. The hawk is trying to fly with a broken wing.
2. Look at the quarterback trying to sneak through the line.
3. The grey uniform, faded and mended, hung on his emaciated frame.
4. Having won the set, Doris turned to search for the lost ball.
5. I seem to recall his saying that he was going to write to me.
6. The weeping child seemed unable to control its terrified sobbing.
7. Many of the spectators, having decided that the game was won, were leaving the stands.
8. A barking dog never bites, but no one knows when he will stop barking.

9. The battered shed, having weathered many storms, was in need of repair.
10. All doors having been locked, the frightened girls were forced to *Nom.abl.* spend the night at a neighbor's home.

The Elements of the Sentence. A sentence is a word or a group of words that expresses a thought or feeling. The normal sentence must have two elements — the subject and the predicate. The subject is that about which something is said. The predicate is that which asserts or states something about the subject. The structure of a sentence may be explained by means of a picture or **diagram.**

Time flies.

Potatoes should have been planted.

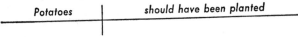

Men, women, and children shouted and screamed.

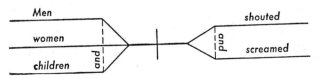

With certain types of verbs a third element is essential to the formation of a complete thought — a complement. There are three main kinds of complements — direct objects, indirect objects, and subjective complements. Less common are the objective complement and the retained object.

1. The **direct object** of a verb denotes that which is immediately acted upon.

She will believe anything.

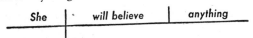

Remove your cap.

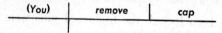

2. The **indirect object** names, without the use of the preposition, the one to whom or for whom the action is done.

Father gave me a dollar.

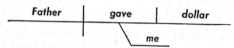

Mr. White taught us mathematics and chemistry.

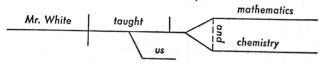

Note that when *to* or *for* are expressed, the substantive following becomes the object of the preposition, as in: Father gave a dollar to me; Mr. White taught chemistry to us; Mother, draw a picture for me.

3. The **subjective complement** refers to the subject and describes or limits it. It may be a noun, a pronoun, or an adjective. It is often called the *predicate substantive* and the *predicate adjective*.

He is an officer.

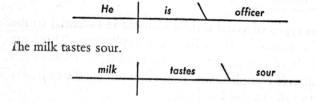

The milk tastes sour.

4. The **objective complement**, used with verbs like *elect, choose, call, appoint* or the like, refers to the direct object.

They elected him their chairman.

5. The **retained object** is used with a verb in the passive voice.

The children were given some candy.

children	were given	candy

EXERCISES

Exercise 1, Subject, verb, complement. In each of the following sentences pick out the subject, the verb, and the complement.

1. Each of the players picked up his cards.
2. At three o'clock in the morning he arose and saddled his horse.
3. Give the dog a bath.
4. Jumping up in confusion, Stella tossed the letter into the fire.
5. Mother, which story have you read him?
6. His face became red, and he threw us a look of hatred.
7. They call their dog Goofy, but the dog is not stupid.
8. Show him every possible courtesy, and he will long remember his visit.
9. He was shown every possible courtesy, but he did not even write us a letter of thanks.
10. Although your roses smell sweet, I cannot enjoy them because I suffer from rose fever.

Exercise 2, Diagrams. Diagram the subject, verb, and complement (if any) in each of the following sentences.

1. Will you do me a favor?
2. We gave the man our tickets.
3. All of his wealth was invested in a Mexican mine.
4. You are looking very happy today.
5. The employer made me a flattering offer.
6. For his evening meal he heated a can of beans.
7. The quarterback is too heavy and slow.
8. The other three boys removed the body from the tracks.
9. Give the car a rub and drive it into the garage.
10. Mother, whom did you call a few minutes ago?

Kinds of Sentences. A group of words having a subject and a predicate, if the group stands as an independent unit, is a sentence. There are, however, dependent groups of this nature (that is, with a subject and a predicate), groups which act as parts of speech. We must therefore have a common name for both types; we call them clauses, or predications, or propositions. If a clause expresses a complete thought, it is called independent or principal. If it does not express a complete thought, it is called subordinate or dependent.

Sentences are divided according to their structure into four classes: simple, complex, compound, and compound-complex.

1. The **simple sentence** is one which contains a single independent clause. A simple sentence may have as subject more than one noun or pronoun and as predicate more than one verb. (See "The Elements of the Sentence," page 37.) It may also have adjectives, adverbs, and phrases as modifiers.

The little old lady smiled sweetly.

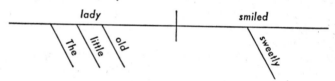

The little boy gave his mother a red rose.

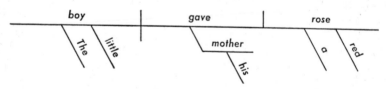

2. The **complex sentence** is one which contains one independent clause and at least one dependent clause. Dependent clauses are used as nouns, as adjectives, and as adverbs. In the following illustrative sentences the dependent clauses are italicized. The grammatical function of each clause is shown by means of the diagrams.

What he told the officers was never revealed. [Noun clause used as subject.]

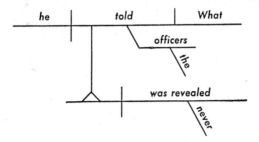

The teacher said *that the answer was correct.* [Noun clause used as object.]

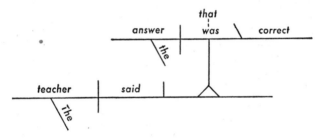

Give it to *whoever calls for it.* [Noun clause used as object of a preposition.]

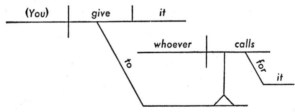

This is the boy *who brought the papers.* [Adjective clause modifying *boy.*]

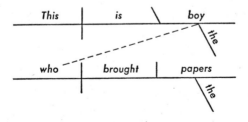

We visited the place *where the first battle of the war was fought.* [Adjective clause modifying *place.*]

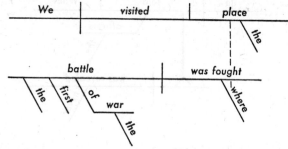

We visited the field *on which the first battle of the war was fought.* [Adjective clause modifying *field.*]

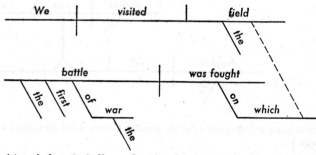

The whistle blew *before the ball was fumbled.* [An adverbial clause of time, modifying the verb *blew.*]

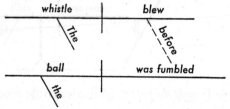

He ran as fast *as he could.* [An adverbial clause of degree.]

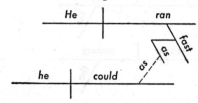

Carol is prettier *than I am*. [An adverbial clause of comparison.]

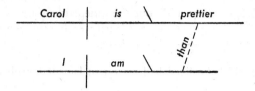

3. The **compound sentence** is one which contains two or more independent clauses.

The performance was poor, but the audience was enthusiastic.

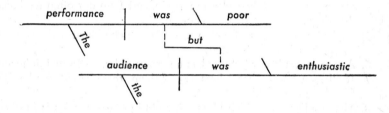

4. The **compound-complex sentence** is one which contains two or more independent clauses and at least one dependent clause. In a diagram of a compound-complex sentence, the diagrams of subordinate clauses are connected with the words they modify as in the diagrams of complex sentences. In the following examples the dependent clauses are in italics.

The boys were discouraged over the tied score, but they smiled *as if the game had been won*.

The senator spoke eloquently in favor of a large navy, but he did not mention the fact *that all of his money was invested in the steel industry*.

The chessboard is the world, the pieces are the phenomena of the universe, the rules of the game are *what we call the laws of nature*.

I know *that entertainments of this nature are apt to raise dark and dismal thoughts in timorous minds and gloomy imaginations*, but for my own part, *though I am always serious*, I do not know *what it is to be melancholy*.

EXERCISES

Exercise 1, Kinds of sentences. Pick out the independent and dependent clauses in the following sentences. Classify each sentence (simple, complex, compound, compound-complex).

1. The time in which he lived had reason to lament his obstinacy of silence.
2. Sorrows are like thunderclouds; in the distance they look black, but overhead they are hardly gray. — Richter.
3. The only good histories are those written by those who had command in the events they describe. — Montaigne.
4. Those slight labors which afford me a livelihood, and by which it is allowed that I am to some extent serviceable to my contemporaries, are as yet commonly a pleasure to me, and I am not often reminded that they are a necessity. — Thoreau.
5. He had a directness of action never before combined with so much comprehension. — Emerson.
6. A man grows better humored as he grows older. — Samuel Johnson.
7. If all men knew what others say of them, there would not be four friends in the world. — Pascal.
8. The rapidity with which ideas grow old in our memories is in direct ratio to the squares of their importance. — Holmes.
9. Men whose minds are possessed with some one object take exaggerated views of its importance, are feverish in the pursuit of it, make it the measure of things which are utterly foreign to it, and are startled and despond if it happens to fail them. — Newman.
10. Style should for this very reason never be subjective, but objective; and it will not be objective unless the words are so set down that they directly force the reader to think precisely the same thing as the author thought when he wrote them. — Schopenhauer.

Exercise 2, Kinds of sentences. Analyze the following sentences in the same manner. These sentences have been purposely simplified, so that if your instructor thinks it worth your time, they may be used for practice in diagramming.

1. Whoever answers my question will receive a prize.
2. Spring is here, and the days are filled with activity.
3. Send home whoever is playing in my garden.
4. The reception was scheduled for eight, but no one came until ten.
5. He said that he could not understand me.

6. This is the boy who took your flowers.
7. If your enemy smiles at you, watch him; if he avoids you, do him a favor.
8. The night was stormy, but a large crowd came in spite of the weather.
9. You speak as if he were your friend.
10. The dean is a woman whom everyone respects.
11. He found the place where he had left his baggage.
12. She wanted to learn how she could become popular.
13. Wisdom is better than rubies.
14. Every dog has his day, but the night belongs to the cats.
15. If I go, will you go?
16. We ate whatever she brought us.
17. George is heavier than his brother.
18. He knew the right time to say nothing.
19. Mere ideals are the cheapest things in life.
20. All is well that ends well.

Phrases. In its general, loose sense, a phrase is any group of words. Thus we say that a man "phrases his thoughts" when he puts them into words, or that he expresses his ideas in "well-balanced phrases" when his sentences are well-built or rhythmical. The word "phrase" in its general sense has its place in the language. In the study of grammar, however, the word refers to one of three kinds: the "verb phrase," which means a verb with all its auxiliaries as opposed to the simple verb, the prepositional, or the verbal phrase. The **verb phrase** is explained in section 9. A **prepositional phrase** consists of a preposition, its object, and modifiers of the phrase or any of its parts. **Verbal phrases** are made up with the verbals: gerunds, participles, and infinitives.

1. A prepositional phrase may be used as an adjective.

The boy *with the books under his arm* is my brother. [The phrase modifies *boy*. Within the phrase is another phrase, *under his arm*, which modifies *books*.]

She married a man *of great wealth*. [Modifies *man*.]

As entertainment it is *without its equal*. [Used as a subjective complement modifying *entertainment*.]

45

2. A prepositional phrase may be used as an adverb.

He plunged *into the pool*. [The phrase is an adverb of place or direction, modifying *plunged*.]

For an hour he played *in the water*. [Both phrases modify *played*. The first is an adverb of time, and the second is an adverb of place.]

Francis was true *to his word*. [The phrase is an adverb modifying *true*.]

3. A prepositional phrase may be used as a noun.

The best time for study is *in the morning*. *On the mantel* would be a good place for it. [The first phrase is used as a noun subjective complement; the second is used as the subject of the verb *would be*.]

The father *of the child* [adjective] watched *from the window* [adverb].

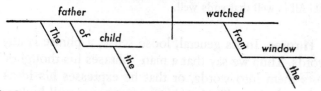

Under the bridge two tramps had built a fire.

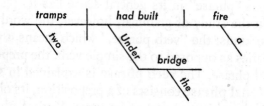

The best time *for study* is *in the morning*.

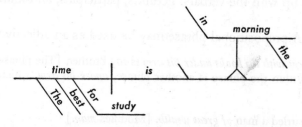

A participial phrase consists of a participle, its complement, if it has one, and any modifiers of the phrase or any of its parts.

It is used as an adjective. A thorough understanding of the uses of participial phrases is of practical importance to any writer because their misuse results in a gross error known as the "dangling modifier." For a discussion of this see section 54.

The boy *now playing center* is a substitute. [The phrase modifies *boy*. The participle is modified by the adverb *now* and it has for its object the noun *center*.]

Frightened by the sudden noise, the deer plunged into the brush. [The phrase modifies *deer*.]

His face, *freshly scrubbed*, shone in the morning light. [The phrase modifies *face*.]

Having given him the required amount, I left the store. [Notice that within the participial phrase there is another participle, *required*, modifying *amount*.]

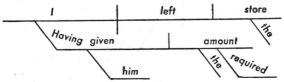

A special kind of participial phrase, called the **absolute phrase,** is made up of a substantive followed by a participle. It differs from the usual participial phrase in that it does not modify any single word in the sentence; grammatically it is an independent element. An absolute phrase cannot become a dangling modifier.

We hunted toward the north, *each taking one side of the ridge*.

Their navy having been destroyed, they were forced to surrender.

The game being over, we returned to our rooms.

A gerund phrase consists of a gerund, its complement, if it has one, and any modifiers of the phrase or any of its parts. A gerund phrase is always used as a noun.

Staying out late at night will not help your reputation. [The gerund phrase is used as the subject of the verb *will help*.]

Harry enjoyed *mowing the lawn*. [Object of the verb.]

You can get the address by *stopping at our house.* [Object of preposition.]

I should call that *violating the spirit of our agreement.* [The phrase is used as an objective complement referring to *that.*]

Hearing that song brings back sad memories to me.

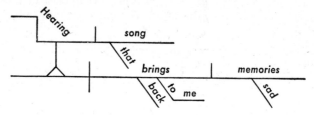

Mary objected to *my telling the story.*

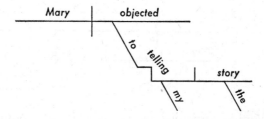

An **infinitive phrase,** like other verbal phrases, may have a complement and modifiers. In addition it may have what is called the assumed subject of the infinitive. The assumed subject of the infinitive is in the objective case. An infinitive phrase may be used as an adverb, an adjective, or a noun.

Tommy did not stop *to pick up his toys.* [An adverb, modifying the verb *did stop.*]

Their attempts *to cut the line* were futile. [An adjective, modifying the subject *attempts.*]

Whether to believe him or to call mother was a real problem for me. [A noun, used as the subject of the sentence.]

We knew *him to be the most hardened gambler of the regiment.* [Notice that the infinitive *to be* has *him* as its assumed subject.]

My orders were *to deliver the guns.*

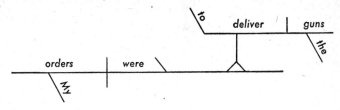

I am happy *to see you again.*

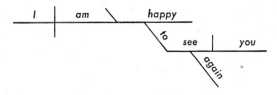

She wanted *me to drive the car.*

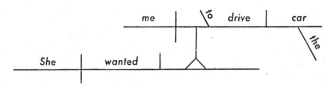

EXERCISES

Exercise 1, Participles. Pick out the participles in the following sentences and tell what word each participle modifies.

1. She gave an apple to the crying child.
2. On the upper shelf are two broken dishes.
3. Being a woman, she could not reply properly.
4. The sound of his voice reached us clearly.
5. He looked under the sagging bed and found a whimpering puppy.
6. He cast his line into the rippling waters.
7. In spite of his warning, I knocked on the closed door.
8. Having finished his breakfast, he went into the garden.
9. The torn and tattered flag hung on the wire, flapping gently in the breeze.
10. Protesting tearfully, the little boy objected to having his face washed.

THE SENTENCE

Exercise 2, Participles and gerunds. Pick out each gerund and participle in the following sentences and tell how each is used.

1. After removing his cap, he politely addressed the smiling landlady.
2. You must collect your scattered papers before closing the door.
3. Wishing for a peaceful world is the same as helping to create one.
4. Having finished reading the themes, the tired professor closed his aching eyes and went to sleep.
5. I shall always remember her loving smile and her dreaming eyes.
6. Wearing a new hat was to her like acquiring a new personality.
7. The war having been won, the returning soldiers began thinking about looking for jobs.
8. As I was examining the battered old wreck, I could not help thinking about the many exciting adventures which I had experienced.
9. Running the half mile requires more endurance than working all day.
10. The man seemed slightly irritated by our obvious discomfort in his evil-smelling cabin.

Exercise 3, Phrases. In the following sentences pick out each phrase and tell whether it is prepositional, participial, gerund, or infinitive.

1. Father advised me not to bet on the game.
2. This is a doctrine dangerous to liberty of opinion.
3. He will try to find relief in his music.
4. To be a radio announcer is my greatest ambition.
5. Against his advice I bet Harold that we would win by three touch-downs.
6. As he was horribly afraid of snakes, he did not try to sleep in the tent.
7. Roger stopped pulling the weeds out of his garden and turned to greet us.
8. We always considered her to be the most brilliant girl in our class.
9. His face, blackened with grime and sweat, was covered with a week's growth of hair.
10. The pounding waves and the whistling winds kept him from sleeping at night.

Dependent Clauses. A dependent clause is distinguished from a sentence in that it does not make complete sense by itself; it depends upon something else in the sentence for its full meaning. Like phrases, dependent clauses are used as parts of speech.

1. A dependent clause may be used as a noun.

As subject of a verb: *What he did at the dance* shocked me greatly.
As object of a verb: Harry thought *that he would not be recognized.*
As subjective complement: This is *where I caught the largest salmon.*
As object of a verbal: Be sure to accept *whatever she offers you.*
As object of a preposition: It depends upon *how many will pay their dues.*
As an appositive: His first argument, *that women are inferior to men,* was easily proved untrue. It has been suggested *that we adjourn.* [See "appositive," section 9.]

2. A dependent clause may be used as an adjective. Adjective clauses are either restrictive or nonrestrictive. See "nonrestrictive," section 9. An important thing to remember in this connection is that restrictive clauses are *not* set off by commas. See section 20b in the handbook.

Restrictive: A teacher *who speaks poor English* is badly handicapped.
    Algebra is the subject *with which I have the most trouble.*
    I shall take you to the store *where I found the linens.*
    That is the precise moment *when you must make your announcement.*
    The reason *why I fainted* is that I was famished.
    Do you know any trick *whereby you can make him confess?*

Nonrestrictive: Our janitor, *who used to be a sailor,* strapped and tied our boxes.
    I am reading *The Loom of Language, which is a fascinating book.*
    It is too late to plant roses in December, *when the ground is usually cold or muddy.*
    He usually gave his tests on Mondays, *when the class was too sleepy to care what happened.*
    The book is *Webster's Collegiate Dictionary, with which you should be quite familiar by this time.*

3. A dependent clause may be used as an adverb to show time, place, cause, purpose, result, condition, concession, manner, or comparison.

Time: You may leave *when the whistle blows.*
    Before you leave the room, close the windows and pull down the shades.

We played cards *until our father returned.*

After you finish your test, hand in your papers.

While Mother entertained her guests, we children played in the orchard.

Place: These men will go *wherever they can find work.*

Cause: I came late *because I was delayed by a wreck.*

As I could not understand the painting, I kept silent.

Since no one volunteered, James finished the work himself.

Purpose: They came to America *in order that they might find religious freedom.*

Result: Every door was locked, *so that it was impossible to leave the building.*

The night was so dark *that we could travel no farther.*

Condition: If you want to go home, I shall call a cab.

Should you find yourself on the wrong trail, return to the starting point.

Children will not be admitted *unless they are accompanied by their parents.*

Concession: Although I did not understand his question, I attempted a reply.

No matter what he says, I shall not be angry.

Manner: Let us sing *as the birds sing.*

Marion Jean looked *as if she were ready for bed.*

Comparison: They are as free *as we are.*

They are not so free *as we are.*

Ralph is older *than I am.*

EXERCISES

Exercise 1, Noun clauses. In the following sentences pick out each noun clause and tell whether it is used as the subject of a verb, as the complement of a verb or verbal, or as the object of a preposition.

1. What he saw in that room must have frightened him terribly.
2. Cover the plants with whatever is convenient.
3. What these people have left behind is full of meaning.
4. This is where I live.
5. Brother Jackson announced solemnly that he did not like modern music.
6. I learned how the tarantula hawk kills its victim and drags it to its tomb.
7. How he disappeared so completely is a mystery to me.
8. Give the message to whoever opens the door.
9. It is not known who the author of this play was.
10. I do not know why I came to college.

Exercise 2, Adjective clauses. Pick out the adjective clauses in the following sentences. Tell what word each clause modifies.

1. This is the book I referred to last night.
2. My brother, who is an ardent philatelist, received a set of coronation stamps.
3. All that I am I owe to my mother.
4. This is the place where the first battle of the war was fought.
5. We met on the day when I entered the academy.
6. The rock from which he leaped is called Suicide Peak.
7. We reached the cabin the minute before the storm broke.
8. That was a side of her character I had not known before.
9. Diamond Lake is the place where we expect to fish.
10. I like to be with Mary, who is a sweet and agreeable child.

Variety in Sentence Patterns. "Style is the man himself," said Buffon, a French naturalist, in his inaugural address before the French Academy. It may be well for you to take this widely quoted definition of style with a bit of prudent distrust. Like many attempts at epigrams, this one is but a half-truth, and you must remember that the other half of a half-truth is a lie. If a man writes as he is, as he has lived, then he who writes in a dull, flat manner has lived a dull, flat life. Conversely, he who has lived a rich, exciting life will write in a rich, exciting manner. Neither statement, as everybody knows, is true. The marine who has fought in the South Pacific, the engineer who has designed bridges of breath-taking beauty, the American sailor who organized the guerilla forces in the Philippines, needs, like as not, the aid of a ghost writer to put his experiences into words. And the author of thrilling yarns of adventure in the South Seas may be an inhibited teacher of English in a small Iowa town. Whatever style is, it is not an unchangeable attribute of personality.

You may take comfort from this fact. To have lived for eighteen years in a small town where nothing ever happens does not sentence anyone to dullness or flatness in writing. Writing, like any other craft, may be learned. Some of the qualities of good writing are stressed so often in this book that they need but to be called to your attention here. The words which you use must be exact, fresh, full of strength and vitality. Picture-making words are better than vague, general words. A fresh point of view will give flavor to your style; humor will lighten it.

In this section, however, we are dealing not with the choice but with the grouping of words. Words, like bricks in a wall, may be arranged either in a dull sameness or in an interesting variety of patterns. Now that we are familiar with grammatical patterns — parts of speech, verbals, phrases, clauses — we shall see how grammar may be used as a means toward a more flexible and pleasing style.

Variety in Structure. The normal order of an English sentence, subject-verb-complement, is so natural, so instinctive, that the untrained writer tends to cast all his thoughts in this one mold. Consider this paragraph from a sketch written by a college freshman:

> Father is an exceptionally calm person. He takes everything as a matter of fact. He is slow and easy-going. It doesn't make any difference what happens, he retains his calmness. He is considerate of other people's feelings. He doesn't try to keep us from making too much noise when he is reading. But this reminds me when he speaks he means business.

Now, quite obviously, no matter how important father is, it is neither accurate nor pleasing to give every detail about him the importance and dignity of a separate sentence. When the writer does recognize a causal relationship between two statements, he indicates the fact by running the two statements together in the same sentence. That sort of error is one of the worst blunders of the immature writer — the run-together sentence. (See sections 1, 2, and 3 in the handbook.) A long string of sentences on the same level results in tedious monotony. Nor is the monotony relieved when a writer, in a helpless gesture toward smoothness and continuity, strings his clauses out with *and's*, *but's*, and *so's*.

If you do not like to be the owner of a monotonous style (and who does?), you have several means of invigorating it. Let us see, first, what can be done with the sentences about father: "Father, a calm, slow, easy-going, matter-of-fact person, does not lose his temper no matter what the provocation." One sentence takes care of five, more effectively, too, than the five did, for the grouping of adjectives in the appositive position is emphatic. Scattered through five sentences, they are lost.

The revised sentences below contain further illustrations of the use of the appositive:

Immature: I have learned how to get along with people. I must try to understand them. I must be patient with them, and I must enjoy being with them.

Improved: Three vital qualities, understanding, patience, and a liking for human companionship, help me to get along with people.

Immature: Father is a congenial sort of person, and he hasn't made an enemy in his life.

Improved: Father, a congenial sort of person, has not made an enemy in his life.

Immature: I have a younger brother who is called Robie. He goes to high school and he is always in mischief. He wears his hair long and is always smiling. He, also, intends to be an engineer like my father.

Improved: My younger brother Robie, a happy, mischievous, long-haired high-school lad, plans to become an engineer like his father.

Immature: I have always wanted to fly. It has been my dream all my life. Now I know it will be soon a reality.

Improved: The desire to fly, a lifelong dream of mine, may soon become a reality in my life.

You see how a change from a clause to an appositive can make a sentence smoother, more compact, more emphatic. A word of caution, however: do not think that an appositive is always better than a clause. Look upon it merely as a resource at your command, to be used for greater exactness in expression as well as for a welcome variety.

Occasionally the thought in a compound sentence is better expressed by a simple sentence with a compound verb:

Awkward: The wise student budgets his time for study, and he prepares his lessons according to a schedule.

Improved: The wise student budgets his time for study and prepares his lessons according to a schedule.

The substance of a co-ordinate clause may often be better expressed in a participial phrase. You must always, however, be on your guard against the danger of subordinating the wrong thought. Ask yourself, "Which is the important thought in my sentence? Which are the supporting details?" In this connection study sections 46 and 47 in the handbook.

Awkward: My decision to enter college came suddenly, and I encountered several obstacles.

Improved: Having made a sudden decision to enter college, I was unprepared for the difficulties which I encountered.

Immature: The inexperienced camper usually sleeps on the ground for several nights, and so he decides that a bed of fir boughs is worth his effort.

Improved: Having endured sleeping on the ground for several nights, the inexperienced camper usually decides that a bed of fir boughs is worth his effort.

Immature: He looks at his teacher. His mind is in a whirl, his mouth is dry, so he makes some worthless answer.

Improved: The confused student stares at his teacher — his brain in a whirl, his dry mouth stuttering some incoherent response.

A similar effect may be produced with gerund or infinitive phrases:

Awkward: Their working hours were shortened. This resulted in more spare time for recreation and enjoyment.

Improved: Shortening their hours of work resulted in more time available for recreation and enjoyment.

Immature: The wife has children which she must clothe. She must take care of them and worry about them. The business woman does not have anybody except herself to whom she is obliged to pay any attention.

Improved: The wife has children to clothe, to care for, to worry about; the business woman has no one to think of but herself.

Wordy: The necessary preparation is simple. You get dressed and pull your old shotgun out of the corner. Then you are ready to start for the duck ponds.

Improved: Having dressed and pulled the old shotgun out of the corner — all the preparation really necessary — the hunter is ready to start for the duck ponds.

Clauses — noun, adjective, and adverb — are a means of relieving the monotony of too much co-ordination:

Immature: Then he went to summer school. There he met many older people. These students really wanted to get something out of college.
Improved: When he attended summer school, he met a number of mature students who were really interested in getting an education.

Awkward: The reason for his failure was plain. In college he had depended upon his fraternity brothers to help him and to keep him at work.
Improved: The plain cause of his failure was that in college he had depended upon his fraternity brothers for help and incentive.

Awkward: My roommate stared at me in unconcealed dismay. She is the chairman of the house scholarship committee.
Improved: My roommate, who is the chairman of the house scholarship committee, stared at me in unconcealed dismay.

Immature: The high-school principal had forgotten to mail my credits to the registrar, so I had to make a special trip to get them.
Improved: As the high-school principal had forgotten to mail my credentials to the registrar, I had to make a special trip to get them.

Awkward: Do not be in too much of a hurry to join an organization. Study its membership before you join.
Improved: Before you join an organization, investigate its membership.

Immature: I have heard stories of the way freshmen were treated, but I have seen no bitter rivalry between classes thus far.
Improved: Although I have heard stories of ill-treatment of freshmen, thus far I have observed no bitter rivalry between the classes.

Variety in Order. You may also relieve a monotonous style by occasionally varying the order of the sentence elements. Here, again, you should keep in mind the fact that variety is a departure from the normal or natural. The normal order of the English sentence — subject, verb, complement — still remains the pattern into which most of your sentences will fall without much effort on your part. In the following examples of various sentence patterns notice the difference in effect. One pattern is not necessarily better than another; it is merely different.

In a home there is love.
There is love in a home.

To be a home, a house must be occupied by a congenial group of people.
A house, to be a home, must be occupied by a congenial group of people.

He recommended to me to keep a full and unreserved journal of my life.
He recommended to me to keep a journal of my life, full and unreserved.

It is very seldom that one is privileged to see such a story-book ending as this game had.
Seldom is one privileged to see such a story-book ending as this game had.

My delicate and fragile dream faded at the sight of her stupid face.
My dream, so delicate and fragile, faded at the sight of her stupid face.

A corsage was delivered at my door just after dinner. It was a huge affair of violets.
Just after dinner, a corsage, a huge affair of violets, was delivered at my door.

Expressed in terms of grammar, the various devices for securing variety in sentence order may be summarized as follows:

1. You may reverse the normal order of subject and verb in a sentence. This device must be used with caution lest it become a mannerism. But an occasional inversion, like one of the following, may be used effectively.

Into their midst stormed the principal.
Straight across his garden raced the terrified dogs.
Over the rail fence and into the brush stampeded the herd of longhorns.
Like a ship under full sail came Aunt Sophronia.

2. You may begin with an adverb or an adverbial phrase.

Seldom do they come back for more.
During the heat of the day he must not leave his post.
In brief interludes of fear he attempts reform.
Narrowly he missed the concrete post.

3. You may put adjectives and participles after the words they modify.

Her voice, low and pleasant, banished my fear.
Her roommate, angry and impatient, threw her hat upon the bed.
To that decision and declaration, generously and faithfully interpreted, I invoke with confidence the approval of the House. — Churchill.

4. You may begin with a clause.

That he lacked physical courage was only too evident.
If you injure your neighbor, better not do it by halves. — Bernard Shaw.
Where there is much desire to learn, there of necessity will be much argu-
ing, much writing, many opinions. — Milton.

5. You may change a clause to an appositive.

The author of the book, a former member of a notorious Chicago gang,
lets his readers infer his social philosophy.
The next morning he decided to tell the truth, a course which should
have occurred to him the day before.
He found himself engaged to three girls at once, a situation fraught with
more danger than glamor.

Parallel Construction. You have just been warned not to use
the same sentence structure repeatedly; now you are to be told
to express similar ideas in similar sentence patterns. This looks
like a contradiction, yet each principle is sound, as a little thought
on your part will show you. All sentences must, after all, be built
to fit the thoughts they express. If several ideas are of equal importance, they properly belong in a series of co-ordinate clauses.
If some of the ideas are less important than others, they should
be given a subordinate position in sentences. The warning against
excessive co-ordination was directed as much against inaccuracy
of expression as against monotony of effect. Parallel structure,
likewise, becomes monotonous when it is carried too far. If it is
used naturally, to fit the thought, it will seldom be overused.
You will not have frequent occasions to say, "To err is human,
to forgive divine," or "You can take a boy out of the country,
but you cannot take the country out of the boy." Even Francis
Bacon, writing in an age when rhetorical mannerisms were fashionable, did not often find it possible to balance phrases as he
did in his essay about studies:

"Reading maketh a full man;
conference a ready man; and
writing an exact man. And therefore

if a man write little, he had need have a great memory;
if he confer little, he had need have a present wit; and
if he read little, he had need have much cunning, to seem to know what
   he doth not."

You can find examples of skillful parallelism in the work of present-day writers, too, and when you run across a balanced sentence you unconsciously say to yourself, "This is good. This has a rhythm and a precision that I like." Notice the different forms of balance in the following sentences:

There is no common faith, no common body of principle, no common body of knowledge, no common moral and intellectual discipline. — Walter Lippmann.

This, in barest outline, is the specific outlook of western man. This, we may say, is the structure of the western spirit. This is the formation which distinguishes it. — Walter Lippmann, "The State of Education in This Troubled Age."

Without information, the imagination is sterile or it produces irrelevant fancies; without imagination, a man is a slave to what is already known; without intelligence, he cannot discipline his imagination or judge what is significant, what not. — Howard D. Roelofs, "In Search of Scientific Method."

It was readily supposed that if reason was an instrument biologically developed to serve the interests of the organism, its pronouncements could never be disinterested; that if truth was relative, nothing could be really true; that if morals varied with the customs of time and place, any custom that got itself established was moral, and one system of morality as good as another; that if ideas were inspired by individual or class interest, the success of an idea in promoting individual or class interest was the only test of its validity. — Carl Becker, "Some Generalities That Still Glitter." From *The Yale Review*, June, 1940. Reprinted by permission.

Abraham Lincoln could use parallel structure with rare skill. Here is his famous letter to Horace Greeley:

Dear Sir:

   I have just read yours of the 19th instant, addressed to myself through the New York *Tribune*. If there be in it any statements or assumptions of fact which I may know to be erroneous, I do not now and here controvert them. If there be in it any inferences which I may believe to be falsely drawn, I do not now and here argue against them. If there be perceptible in it an impatient and dictatorial tone, I waive it in deference to an old friend whose heart I have always supposed to be right.

As to the policy I "seem to be pursuing," as you say, I have not meant to leave anyone in doubt.

I would save the Union. I would save it by the shortest way under the Constitution. The sooner the national authority can be restored, the nearer the Union will be "the Union as it was." If there be those who would not save the Union unless they could at the same time save slavery, I do not agree with them. If there be those who would not save the Union unless they could at the same time destroy slavery, I do not agree with them. My paramount object in this struggle is to save the Union, and not either to save or to destroy slavery. If I could save the Union without freeing any slave, I would do it; if I could save it by freeing all the slaves, I would do it; and if I could save it by freeing some and leaving others alone, I would also do that. What I do about slavery and the colored race, I do because I believe it helps to save the Union; and what I forbear, I forbear because I do not believe it would help to save the Union. I shall do less whenever I shall believe that what I am doing hurts the cause; and I shall do more whenever I shall believe doing more will help the cause. I shall try to correct errors when shown to be errors, and I shall adopt new views as fast as they appear to be true views.

I have here stated my purpose according to my views of official duty, and I intend no modification of my oft expressed personal wish that all men everywhere could be free.

Yours,

A. Lincoln.

As one may suspect, the perfectly balanced sentence is like a four-leaf clover — it is still the three-leaf clovers that fill the hay-mow. Once in a long time we run across a man like Oscar W. Firkins, whose daily class lectures sounded like this:

"Classicism seeks truth, but its care for form, its care for language, its care for dignity, its care for normality and for ethics, cut it off from many truths. The day comes when some truth-lover insists upon telling these untold truths. That day is the dawn of realism.

"Classicism, then, is somewhat restricted on two sides, truth and beauty. Remove the restrictions on one side and you get romanticism; remove them on the other, and you get realism."

But most of us save parallelism for holiday and special occasions, such as seem to require a bit of show and eloquence.

There is, however, a more pedestrian and thoroughly practical occasion for using parallel structure within the sentence. Expressed in terms of grammar — a noun is made parallel with another noun, a gerund with another gerund, a phrase with another phrase, a clause with another clause. Notice how rephrasing the following sentences in parallel form improves their effectiveness:

Awkward: I have learned better manners and how to make myself look better to others. [A noun and an infinitive.]

Parallel: I have acquired better manners and the ability to make myself attractive. [Two nouns.]

Awkward: I have only one suggestion to make: cultivate friends who you think are loyal, have a cheerful disposition, and who are ambitious. [An adjective, a verb, and a clause.]

Parallel: I have only one suggestion to make: cultivate friends who you think are loyal, cheerful, and ambitious. [Three adjectives.]

Awkward: All freshmen assembled in the men's gymnasium for general talks and to give us an idea of the procedure of registration. [A prepositional phrase and an infinitive.]

Parallel: All freshmen assembled in the men's gymnasium to listen to general talks and to learn the registration procedure. [Two infinitives.]

Awkward: During the summer I kept his books, wrote all of his letters, clerk and stock boy, and even managed the store during his vacation. [Three predicates and two nouns.]

Parallel: During the summer I kept his books, wrote all of his letters, acted as clerk and stock boy, and even managed the store during his vacation. [All predicates.]

For a further discussion of parallelism and for an explanation of the error known as the "and which" construction, see section 56 in the handbook.

Euphony and Rhythm. In your study of writing you finally reach a point beyond which grammar will not help you. You must depend upon your feeling for rhythm. Good prose should have a pleasant sound when it is read aloud. It should form patterns of sound — patterns which the reader somehow feels to be an appropriate and harmonious accompaniment of the thought expressed. The selections which are here used to illustrate rhythm are not models which anyone could expect you to imitate. They are merely samples of what can be done with prose. But please do read them aloud.

The first one is from a recent popular novel:

It was a very hot noon, that fatal noon, and coming around the shoulder of a hill Brother Juniper stopped to wipe his forehead and to gaze upon the screen of snowy peaks in the distance, then into the gorge below him filled with the dark plumage of green trees and green birds and traversed by its ladder of osier. Joy was in him; things were not going badly. He had opened several little abandoned churches and the Indians were crawling in to early Mass and groaning at the moment of miracle as though their hearts would break. Perhaps it was the pure air from the snows before him; perhaps it was the memory that brushed him for a moment of the poem that bade him raise his eyes to the helpful hills. At all events he felt at peace. Then his glance fell upon the bridge, and at that moment a twanging noise filled the air, as when the string of some musical instrument snaps in a disused room, and he saw the bridge divide and fling five gesticulating ants into the valley below.

Anyone else would have said to himself with secret joy: "Within ten minutes myself . . . !" But it was another thought that visited Brother Juniper: "Why did this happen to *those* five?" If there were any plan in the universe at all, if there were any pattern in a human life, surely it could be discovered mysteriously latent in those lives so suddenly cut off. Either we live by accident and die by accident, or we live by plan and die by plan. And on that instant Brother Juniper made the resolve to inquire into the secret lives of those five persons, that moment falling through the air, and to surprise the reason of their taking off.

— Thornton Wilder, *The Bridge of San Luis Rey.* Reprinted by permission of A. & C. Boni, publishers.

The second consists of excerpts from two speeches by a great statesman as well as a great orator:

To form an Administration of this scale and complexity is a serious undertaking in itself, but it must be remembered that we are in the preliminary stage of one of the greatest battles in history, that we are in action at many points in Norway and in Holland, that we have to be prepared in the Mediterranean, that the air battle is continuous, and that many preparations have to be made here at home. In this crisis I hope I may be pardoned if I do not address the House at any length today. I hope that any of my friends and colleagues, or former colleagues, who are affected by the political reconstruction, will make all allowance for any lack of ceremony with which it has been necessary to act. I would say to the House, as I said to those who have joined this Government: "I have nothing to offer but blood, toil, tears, and sweat."

We have before us an ordeal of the most grievous kind. We have before us many, many long months of struggle and of suffering. You ask, What is our policy? I will say: "It is to wage war, by sea, land and air, with all our might and with all the strength that God can give us: to wage war against a monstrous tyranny, never surpassed in the dark, lamentable catalogue of human crime. That is our policy." You ask, What is our aim? I can answer in one word: Victory — victory at all costs, victory in spite of all terror, victory however long and hard the road may be; for without victory there is no survival. Let that be realized; no survival for the British Empire; no survival for all that the British Empire has stood for; no survival for the urge and impulse of the ages, that mankind will move forward towards its goal. But I take up my task with buoyancy and hope. I feel sure that our cause will not be suffered to fail among men. At this time I feel entitled to claim the aid of all, and I say, "Come, then, let us go forward together with our united strength."

— Winston Churchill, an address before the House of Commons, May 13, 1940.

What General Weygand called the Battle of France is over. I expect that the Battle of Britain is about to begin. Upon this battle depends the survival of Christian civilization. Upon it depends our own British life, and the long continuity of our institutions and our Empire. The whole fury and might of the enemy must very soon be turned on us. Hitler knows that he will have to break us in this Island or lose the war. If we can stand up to him, all Europe may be free and the life of the world may move forward into broad, sunlit uplands. But if we fail, then the whole world, including the United States, including all that we have known and cared for, will sink into the abyss of a new Dark Age made more sinister, and perhaps more protracted, by the lights of perverted science. Let us therefore brace ourselves to our duties, and so bear ourselves that, if the

British Empire and its Commonwealth last for a thousand years, men will still say, "This was their finest hour."

— Winston Churchill, a speech delivered to the House of Commons, June 18, 1940. From *Blood, Sweat, and Tears*, copyright, 1941, by Winston S. Churchill. Courtesy of G. P. Putnam's Sons.

The third selection was written many, many years ago, but it has lost none of its freshness and power:

A man may read a sermon, the best and most passionate that ever man preached, if he shall but enter into the sepulchres of kings. In the same Escorial where the Spanish princes live in greatness and power, and decree war or peace, they have wisely placed a cemetery, where their ashes and their glory shall sleep till time shall be no more; and where our kings have been crowned, their ancestors lie interred, and they must walk over their grandsire's head to take his crown. There is an acre sown with royal seed, the copy of the greatest change, from rich to naked, from ceiled roofs to arched coffins, from living like gods to die like men. There is enough to cool the flames of lust, to abate the heights of pride, to appease the itch of covetous desires, to sully and dash out the dissembling colors of a lustful, artificial, and imaginary beauty. There the warlike and the peaceful, the fortunate and the miserable, the beloved and the despised princes mingle their dust, and pay down their symbol of mortality, and tell all the world that when we die our ashes shall be equal to kings', and our accounts easier, and our pains and our crowns shall be less. — Jeremy Taylor.

Were Jeremy Taylor alive today, it is barely possible that he might be doing the sort of rhythmical writing that Mr. Norman Corwin does for the radio. The following is a sample:

How much did it cost?
Well, the gun, the half-track and the fuselage come to a figure resembling
    mileages between two stars:
Impressive, but not to be grasped by any single imagination.
High octane is high, and K-rations in the aggregate mount up; also
    mosquito-netting and battleships.
But these costs are calculable, and have no nerve-endings,
And will eventually be taken care of by the federal taxes on antiques,
    cigarettes, and excess profits.
However, in the matter of the kid who used to deliver folded newspapers
    to your doorstep, flipping them sideways from his bicycle,

THE SENTENCE

And who died on a jeep in the Ruhr,

There is no fixed price, and no amount of taxes can restore him to his mother.

His mother sits in a room with a picture tonight, and listens to the clock ticking on the mantelpiece, and remembers, among other things, how he struggled with the barber when he was getting his first haircut, and how she tried to calm him.

And the upstairs tenant in consideration of the news outdoors, says to his wife:

Shall we invite Mrs. Frisch to come up? She's all alone tonight, and it seems sort of a shame.

Well — I have a hunch she'd rather be alone tonight.

Think so?

I don't think she's in a mood to talk or carry on. She probably just wants to be with her thoughts.

Maybe you're right.

And the thoughts of the mother are tall, straight thoughts,

And they burn like candles, quietly and slowly,

And they trail into smoke and are lost in shadows.

And most of the fallen young leave mothers and fathers alive and awake,

And if you wish to assess the cost of beating the fascists, you must multiply the number of closed files in the departments of war, by the exchange value of sorrow, which is infinite and has no decimals.

— Norman Corwin, *On a Note of Triumph.* Reprinted by permission of Simon and Schuster, publishers.

And then descending from the heights we come back inevitably to the mistakes which a writer must avoid — unintentional rhymes, noticeable alliteration, and a succession of harsh or hissing sounds:

We could use the cart and carry Mary and supplies for the expedition.

What equipment does an author need in order to succeed?

Can't you plant alfalfa for forage?

When submission is inevitable, it is vain to complain.

Bring round to the house about an hour from now a half pound of ground round steak.

Weber's unusual musical career extended to the year 1836.

You and I were born to be, but why?

Lack of water caused my eight young larch trees to parch to death.

He stuck a stick through the steak.

66

Chapter 3

THE PARAGRAPH

What Is a Paragraph? A paragraph of exposition or argument is usually defined as a sentence or a group of sentences developing a single, complete idea. You should remember, however, that this definition does not apply to narration or to description. The unit of exposition is the thought or idea. The unit of narration is the incident. The unit of description is the picture. But definitions are of small importance to you except as they help you to write good paragraphs or to read them with greater ease and comprehension. Let us therefore make our definition less formal by adding to it several comments.

Just what is meant by "developing an idea"? Various degrees of development are possible. The same idea may be the subject of a sentence, a paragraph, a group of paragraphs, a chapter, or a book. It all depends on how much the writer wants to say about it. It is quite possible that an idea may be *developed* by a single sentence; on the other hand, it is also possible that another idea may take several paragraphs for an adequate *statement*. There are further possibilities. One idea may be developed by several paragraphs. One idea may be stated in a paragraph of a single sentence, and the various units composing it may be developed in a series of paragraphs following, each unit in a separate paragraph. An idea composed of several subordinate ideas may be stated in the first sentence of a paragraph, the first subtopic developed in the same paragraph, and the other subtopics developed in succeeding paragraphs.

We may therefore revise our first definition by saying that a paragraph is a unit of thought — or, more exactly, a unit of the expression and communication of thought — larger than the sentence and smaller than the section or the chapter. Modern writers and publishers have recognized the need of units of writing larger than the paragraph and smaller than the chapter. These divisions, or sections, are usually composed of the paragraphs discussing one of the main divisions of the theme idea.

Length of Paragraphs. The length of a paragraph depends on several considerations: the thoroughness or completeness with which the writer wishes to develop the topic or idea he is trying to make clear; the class of readers for whom he is writing; and present-day conventions governing paragraph length. Essays written for serious or leisurely study may use more complete development of topics and therefore longer paragraphs. Essays written for hasty reading or for immature minds should use smaller units and therefore shorter paragraphs.

The following analysis, showing the number of words used in a series of paragraphs, will tell you more than an arbitrary rule governing paragraph length. The selections analyzed are fairly representative of contemporary writing of the serious type. One is a popular treatment of science; another is a mixture of autobiography and essay; the third is a magazine article. Compute the average length of these paragraphs, if you wish, but remember that averages will not reveal to you the range and variety of paragraph sizes as accurately as will this analysis.

Number of Words

Sir James Jeans, *The Mysterious Universe,* The Macmillan Company, New York, 1934, chap. 1:

99–106–181–149–141–246–55–100–113–71–289–31–261–168–94–171–199–169–57–64–57–251–100–93–110.

Henry S. Canby, *Alma Mater,* Farrar & Rinehart, New York, 1936, chap. 3:

140–80–80–109–99–61–275–278–219–279–221–117–151–164–77–77–111–338–283–175–266–176–225–177–561.

Number of Words

Nathaniel Peffer, "Is Capitalism to Blame?" *Harper's Magazine*, vol. 170, pp. 549–556 (April, 1935):

141–188–175–324–188–201–213–154–219–150–146–160–224–354–215–215–358–122–378–110.

These figures may be analyzed in another way that should prove helpful to you:

Number of paragraphs below 100 words	15
Number between 100 and 200 words	31
Number between 200 and 300 words	18
Number between 300 and 400 words	5
Number above 400 words	1

The Topic Sentence. A sentence which expresses the central idea of an expository paragraph is called a topic sentence.

A topic sentence may or may not be actually present in a written paragraph. It may be implied or understood. While you are learning to write, however, it is good practice for you to state the central idea of every paragraph in the form of a topic sentence. The practice is an aid to clearer thinking. It is a safeguard against spineless paragraphs. It is good mental discipline. If you write a paragraph without an expressed topic sentence, you must be sure that your paragraph does have a central idea and that your reader will have no difficulty in finding it.

The position of the topic sentence in a paragraph depends on the effect desired. It usually comes first. It may include a transitional phrase, or it may follow the necessary transitional sentence. Placing the topic sentence first has the merit of setting before the reader a guide to the contents of the paragraph. It leads to clearness and directness in writing. The topic sentence may come last in the paragraph. This method may be used when the writer wishes to prepare his reader for the central idea, or to produce an effect of climax. The topic sentence may come both first and last. The entire idea may be repeated by the last sentence, or a part may be stated by the first sentence and a part by the last. And, finally, in some paragraphs the topic sentence appears within the paragraph, whenever the writer is ready for it, usually after a preparation for it by means of examples or details. All of these methods will be made clearer by the sample paragraphs which follow.

How to Write a Paragraph. Since a topic sentence (expressed or implied) is the core of an expository paragraph, it follows that the writing of a paragraph is simply a development of this topic idea to the extent that the writer deems necessary. At the outset, you may be mystified by the term "development." What does it mean? To you, it should mean, in most cases, "make clear." It may also mean "make impressive" or "make convincing." The first quality of good writing, therefore, is *clearness*, the ability to communicate, to convey thought, information, emotions. If you cannot make your reader understand you, nothing else counts. You cannot make him believe you, because he does not know what you want him to believe. How an idea may be made clear and impressive or convincing may be learned by analyzing paragraphs written by professional writers; such an analysis reveals that, basically, all types of paragraph development depend ultimately on the use of specific and concrete details. This principle may serve as your key to good paragraphs — or, for that matter, to good essays and articles. To make a general idea clear to the mind of your reader, arrange and present the evidence which made the idea clear to you.

1. **Development by particulars and details,** the method used in nine out of every ten expository paragraphs written, follows one of the most common processes of thought. We observe a number of details; our minds formulate thoughts which relate these details to one another, which give them a connection, a unity, a meaning. If we write a paragraph in this way, we have a paragraph developed by particulars and details with a topic sentence at the end. We may, however, wish to reverse the process and begin with a general statement. The procedure is not always so simple as this explanation of it, yet the explanation will serve our purpose. The paragraphs quoted below will help to explain the method.

Let us begin with a brief analysis of the substance of the first paragraph:

Transitional word: other
Topic idea: conventions concerning safe driving at intersections
Details: passing another vehicle
      example: a large truck
   consideration for pedestrians
   approaching at high speed
     dangers: fright to pedestrian
         collision from the rear

There are other conventions concerning safe driving at intersections that cannot be omitted from a discussion of this kind. [Topic sentence.] You should never pass another vehicle, particularly a large truck, at an intersection. As you pass, your view to the right is cut off, and the truck driver may be waving a motorist to pass in front of him and into your path. Show consideration for pedestrians by stopping for a traffic signal behind the crosswalk, so that people on foot do not have to walk around your machine. A dangerous practice is to approach your corner at high speed, depending on your brakes to bring you safely to a sudden stop. To do so frightens pedestrians who do not know that you can stop and are not sure that you intend to. In addition, the driver coming up from the rear may not have brakes as efficient as yours, and he may crash into you. [155 words]

— Curtis Billings, "Rules of the Road," *The Atlantic Monthly*, vol. 154, p. 341 (September, 1934). Reprinted by permission.

The next paragraph begins with a transitional sentence, which shows the connection between this paragraph and what the author has said before. Here are the details he uses to develop his topic idea:

range of fears: from skepticism to deep pessimism
fear of decline of capitalism
fear of war
concern over the revival of brutality
belief that democracy is bankrupt
    turn to rule of proletariat, or
    welcome of totalitarian rule
flight from reason to pure emotionalism
weariness of a trading civilization
comment on these fears

What, if anything, does literature show to be the prevailing time-current of the thirties? *I believe it to be fear, although fear is too strong a word for its quiet margins, and panic would better describe some of its hurrying tides.* [Topic sentence.] This fear is sometimes conscious, sometimes subconscious. It ranges from a skeptical inquiry into the possible disintegration of culture as we have known it, to the deep pessimism of convinced alarm. Sometimes the writer is inspired by what he may call the decline of capitalism. Sometimes the underlying fear is of war. Sometimes, and very commonly, the writer is concerned with the revival of the brutality of more desperate ages. Sometimes the unrest which spreads through a book is a reflection of the author's belief that democracy is bankrupt; sometimes jubilantly or fearfully he hails the rise of the proletariat, or the reappearance of the strong arm and submission to the state. More subtle is what has been recently called the flight from reason toward pure emotionalism, where men are encouraged to exchange their liberties for the joys of being the most powerful of animals. Again, this fear is only the weariness of a trading civilization, such a weariness as may have overcome the initiative of the Byzantines. Any of these fears, skepticisms, distrusts may be justified or unjustified. The fear remains. [223 words]

— Henry Seidel Canby, "The Threatening Thirties," *The Saturday Review of Literature*, vol. 16, No. 4, p. 3 (May 22, 1937). Reprinted by permission.

In the next paragraph the first half of the opening sentence is a transition; the second half is the topic sentence. You should notice the various sorts of words, phrases, or sentences that writers use as connections between sentences.

When I first began going down beneath tropical waters in my diving helmet, *I found myself re-living the cave-man's evolution.* Whether the nearest coral was warm buff or primuline yellow was quite subservient to the fact that it might shelter a lynx-eyed octopus, and until I learned to know better, the sight of an approaching shark sent messages to portions of my brain far other than the seat of appreciation of color and beauty. It was necessary to get used to the strange costume, the complete submergence under water, and the excitement of a new world of unknown life. [99 words]

— William Beebe, *Beneath Tropic Seas*, G. P. Putnam's Sons, New York, 1928. Reprinted by permission.

In the following paragraph, developed by particulars and details, the topic idea is not specifically stated in a topic sentence, but the first and fourth sentences together come close to being the topic sentence.

I came to Cross Creek with such a phobia against snakes that a picture of one in the dictionary gave me what Martha calls "the all-overs." I had the common misconception that in Florida they were omnipresent. I thought, "If anything defeats me, sends me back to urban civilization, it will be the snakes." They were not ubiquitous as I expected, but I saw one often enough to keep my anxiety alive. A black snake actually ran at me, and a chicken snake thrust his face into mine from a pantry shelf. These were harmless, I knew, but none the less revolting. I took my first faltering steps of progress through sheer shame. In a section where the country women possess great physical fearlessness, I felt feeble-minded to find myself screaming at sight of a king snake that asked nothing more than a chance to destroy the rats that infested the old barn. I forced myself to stand still when I saw a snake in the weeds of the neglected house yard, at least long enough to determine its non-venomous nature. The only poisonous reptiles in Florida, I knew, were the rattlesnake and the cottonmouth moccasin, which I had already seen with horror, and the coral snake, which I did not know.   [212 words]

— Marjorie Kinnan Rawlings, *Cross Creek*, Charles Scribner's Sons, New York, 1942. Reprinted by permission.

Particulars and details are used in paragraphs of characterization, as in the following brilliant example:

Physically he [James Otis] was a large man — "a great Leviathan." He had a short neck, bold, narrow eyes, and a big, eloquent mouth which looks, in his portrait, capable of taking in all the liquor credited to him and giving forth the fiery speeches. An obscure little lawyer of the moment, John Adams, said he "is extremely quick and elastic, his apprehensions as quick as his temper. He springs and twitches his muscles about in thinking." Friends said he was "rough, hasty, loved good cheer." But his enemies called him "rash, unguarded, foul-mouthed," or even "a rackoon" or "filthy scunk." And how he could talk! The wildness and magic (sometimes boredom) of his talk must have swept the Masonic lodges even as it swept through the diaries and letters of his contemporaries. It varied from dreams of a perfect British Empire uniting the whole peaceful world in bonds of love, with God over all, to dirty (and not very funny) stories, but it never stopped.   [164 words]

— Esther Forbes, *Paul Revere and the World He Lived In*, Houghton Mifflin Company, Boston, 1942. Reprinted by permission.

That a recipe for ice-box rolls can be as pleasant to read as the rolls are to eat may come as a surprise to many.

We have a wonderful recipe in these parts for ice-box rolls, whose yeast-rising dough may be prepared in advance, kept in the icebox, and brought out to be raised and baked when needed. [Topic sentence.] It is perhaps exceptional or local only in that we bake it by preference in a Dutch oven with live coals for heat. Cast iron is so superior for cooking utensils to our modern aluminum that I not only cannot grieve for the pioneer hardship of cooking in iron over the hearth, but shall retire if necessary to the back yard with my two Dutch ovens, turning over all my aluminum cookers for airplanes with a secret delight. The Parker House in its hey-day could not have made rolls as good as those we make on camps in the Dutch oven. I make the rolls a trifle larger than is usual and tuck them in lightly in their buttered iron nest. I put on the heavy cover and set the oven with its three short legs either within faint warming distance of the camp fire, or out in the sun. The heat for baking, when they have risen and are ready in an hour or so, must be handled as carefully as a munitions plant handles its powder. Too little heat in baking means pale wan doughy rolls, and too much means rolls of charcoal. Only experience teaches the number and depth of hot glowing oak coals both under the oven and on the lid. When properly done, the rolls are light as feathers, done to a great flakiness, hazel-nut brown, and of a flavor achieved under no other circumstances. [273 words]

— Marjorie Kinnan Rawlings, *Cross Creek*, Charles Scribner's Sons, New York, 1942. Reprinted by permission.

2. **Development by examples or typical instances** does not, like development by particulars and details, take the idea apart to see what it means. It uses examples of the working of the general idea stated in the topic sentence. Let us assume, for instance, that you have just written: "An unpromising performance in college often leads to unusual success in later life." You feel that your reader will say, "Oh, is that so? It does not seem reasonable." You meet his disbelief by supplying a few examples. "There is Dr. Blank, the great cancer specialist. There are Generals White and Brown, brilliant leaders both of them, who stood near the bottom of their class at West Point. Then there is H. V. Jones, the head of the Blank Steel Corporation." You

have made your point, and your reader is more receptive to your idea.

You will find examples used constantly in books of every kind and in magazine articles. Some kinds of writing naturally call for the use of examples. In other types, the example is used occasionally in combination with other methods.

Examples are of two kinds, the general and the specific. In the following selection, which is typical of a great deal of informative writing, both kinds are used extensively. Notice in this section quoted that examples, whether general or specific, often need explanatory comment or interpretation.

What has caused these people to leave established homes and risk the dangers of an unknown land? [Transition, referring to what has been just said and setting up the topic sentence of the next section.] Three main reasons underlie population movements: economic, political, and religious. [Topic sentence of entire section.]

The economic motive has been the principal cause of most of the great migrations. [Topic sentence of paragraph.] Peoples in early times, lacking food and pasture lands, sought more productive regions. [General example.] Tribes which increased rapidly in population were forced to expand beyond their original boundaries in order to have living room. [General example.] After the Industrial Revolution, men moved from European villages to the new factory towns, hoping to secure better economic opportunities. [More specific example.] Others left backward countries, such as the Balkan and eastern European lands, to seek their fortune in the New World. [Specific.]

The political motive for migration was often mixed with the economic. [Topic sentence.] Migrations sometimes took the form of armed invasions. [General.] Warlike groups, greedy for more territory and power, invaded lands occupied by other tribes. [More specific.] It will be recalled how Cortez and his Spaniards, in their desire for gold, conquered the inhabitants of ancient Mexico. [Most specific of series.] Often the vanquished groups were forced to move on to less desirable land which was unoccupied or undefended. [General.] The American Indian, for example, was pushed farther and farther from his "happy hunting grounds" as the white man filled up the empty spaces of North America. [Specific example.] Oppressed people in Old World despotisms often fled to new lands in search of political freedom. [General.]

Religious persecution has also been a motive for countless migrations. [Topic sentence.] The Huguenots, at the end of the seventeenth century, were driven out of France because their Protestant beliefs conflicted with those of the Catholic French king. [Specific example.] The Pilgrim Fathers, familiar characters in colonial history, are an example of a group that sought freedom from religious, as well as political, oppression. [Specific example.] Missionary enterprise also stimulated migration.

— Harry Elmer Barnes and Oreen M. Ruedi, *The American Way of Life*, Prentice-Hall, Inc., New York, 1942. Reprinted by permission.

The example may be extended or brief; a single example may stand as a paragraph, or a short paragraph may be loaded with examples.

They came by every means imaginable — on foot, carrying bundles and babies; in wheelbarrows and sedan chairs; on Chinese junks, poled or pulled upstream with bamboo poles by sweating manpower. They came in carts, on donkeys or horses, or with the modern speed of steamers, automobiles, and trimotored planes.   [49 words]

— Walter C. Lowdermilk, "China Fights Erosion with U. S. Aid," *The National Geographic Magazine*, vol. 87, No. 6, p. 641 (June, 1945).

Often a topic sentence can be developed only by examples. It is hard to imagine any other method used in the following paragraph:

One other general group of French borrowings has been mentioned, that composed of words standing for the usages and the conventions of polite society. [Topic sentence.] Too much can easily be made of a contrast between "homely" Anglo-Saxon and "polished" French ideas in Middle (and Modern) English; nevertheless, to some extent this contrast does hold good. It has often been pointed out that vigor and sincerity rather than grace and finish are characteristic of the "Anglo-Saxon tradition" in literature. In language, the words standing for courtly and graceful ideas are similarly more likely to be of French than of native origin. *Courtliness* and *grace* themselves belong here, as do such kindred terms as *chivalry* and *honor.* The French introduced more polished table manners, and words pertaining to eating, like *dinner, supper* (though the homelier *breakfast* remained), *table, fork, plate*, and *napkin;* also, various ways of preparing food for the table, like *boil, broil*, and *roast*, as well as the names of different kinds of food. French, too, are the general names for clothes — *apparel, costume, dress*, and *garment* — as well as most of the specific ones dealing with the kinds of dress, their styles and materials: *brassière, décol-*

leté, voile, chemise, and *lingerie* are a few recent examples of such words. The earliest words relating to art are French — *art* itself, and *beauty, color, design, ornament,* and *paint* — and so are the more specialized terms of such a field as architecture (for example, *aisle, arch, chancel, column, pillar, porch, reredos,* and *transept*). Some of the humbler occupations, like those of the *baker, fisherman, miller, shepherd,* and *shoemaker* have kept their native names; but many others, especially the more skilled trades and those that brought their practitioners into contact with the upper classes, have French designations: the words *barber, butcher, carpenter, grocer, mason, painter,* and *tailor* are typical.   [305 words]

— Stuart Robertson, *The Development of Modern English*, Prentice-Hall, Inc., New York, 1934. Reprinted by permission.

3. **Development by definition** again makes use principally of details and examples. A definition is written in answer to an implied question: What do you mean by this? In what sense are you using this or that word? What — to use an example — is a good sport? You explain by analyzing the qualities of sportsmanship (particulars and details), or you say that June Guesser, who sincerely congratulates her winning opponent in a tennis game, is a good sport (an example). What do you mean by "courage"? You may say that courage is a quality that differs from daring, valor, or audacity in that it is more rational, quiet, and considered (contrast and elimination), or you may say that Private William Dean, who volunteered as a human guinea pig in the fight against yellow fever, showed more true courage than Private Kulpinski, who received a medal for dragging a wounded sergeant to safety in the battle of the Ardennes Forest (contrasted examples).

A definition may be scientifically precise or informally loose; in length it may range from a single sentence to an entire book. It may use definitive statements, examples, contrast, analogy, the historical development of the meaning — in fact, any or all devices that seem useful and appropriate. In the first of the following two definitions analogy is used freely. In the second, a "good sport" is defined first by what he is and second by what he does.

Truth, — which is a concept conforming to reason, experience, and knowledge, — is the breath of the poet, the vision of the artist and prophet, the quarry of the scientist, the haunted house of the fundamentalist, the bone of contention between bone-headed contenders, the toy of the careless, the *bete noire* of the politician, the elixir of life to the sage, and the embalming fluid for fools. It is the weapon of offense against ignorance, and the offensive weapon of the prejudiced. Truth is the voice of God speaking to the inner ear of man.   [94 words]

— Reverend Myron Lewis Morley, "What Is Truth?" *The Forum*, vol. 78, p. 614 (October, 1927). Reprinted by permission.

A Good Sport is a combination of a hero, a martyr, and a humorist, with a deep sense of justice in acknowledging the rights of others at the cost of his own disadvantage and discomfort, relieving the harsh realities in life's drama with the brighter and warmer color of good fellowship and generosity without spoiling the comedy through self-love and false susceptibility. He can smile when it rains on a picnic day, laugh at a joke about himself, shake hands with a man who inadvertently knocks him down with his car, forgive the friend who marries the girl he loves, and die on the battlefield for his country with a smile on his lips.   [114 words]

— O. F. Page, "What Is a Good Sport?" *The Forum*, vol. 77, p. 243 (February, 1927). Reprinted by permission.

The following definition written by a college freshman uses analogy and contrast:

Simple courage is like a narrow channel between two rocks in a stream: there the water flows with a deceptive smoothness; it does not fume and froth; it wastes no energy by boiling and foaming while it flows through the narrow space. It makes no big show of going through, but there is more actual force in it than in an equal amount of "white water." The courageous person does his job with as little fuss as possible, and as efficiently as he can without deliberately attracting attention; the daring person will usually play to the grandstand even though there is no grandstand to play to. Since he wants some publicity, he does things in a spectacular manner. The physical and moral bravery may be exactly the same in daring as in courage, but the one is innately more showy than the other.   [143 words] — From a theme written by a college freshman.

4. **Development by comparison or contrast** likewise involves the use of particulars, details, or examples. Comparison is telling what a thing is like. Usually the more familiar thing or idea is used to explain the less familiar one. If you were to explain the game of badminton, for instance, you could show how it was

similar to tennis, the more familiar game. In what ways is piloting a plane like driving a car? How are Canadians like their friends in the United States? Contrast, on the other hand, is telling what a thing is not like. How does college football differ from professional football? How does the American way of living differ from the Oriental way? How does democracy differ from communism? How does propaganda differ from news? These are typical subjects which invite treatment by contrast, not in paragraphs alone but also in entire essays or articles.

Tolerance is that state of mind which regards truth as being always relative and never absolute. It arrives at opinions, but never reaches conclusions; it entertains persuasions, but avoids convictions; it ignores verdicts but courts facts. Tolerance indicates an intellect hitting on all six; it mirrors a mind mellow with good humor. It loves light and laughter, and hates nothing, save intolerance. It is the Nirvana of the dreamer, but Pandemonium to the doer. Tolerance first visions the plan. But in the end Intolerance does the job.   [87 words]
— Dwight T. Scott, "What Is Tolerance?" *The Forum*, vol. 77, pp. 749–750 (May, 1927). Reprinted by permission.

When one meets a stranger, to make a favorable impression he brings forth his manners, a set of actions prescribed for the occasion. Should this same person meet an old friend, he would adopt no superficial airs but instead act naturally and exemplify the true spirit of courtesy. Courtesies are the doors which open into a man's soul, revealing his true nature; manners are the shades drawn across the windows of the soul in the attempt to frustrate the gaze and inspection of others. When a man thinks he is being watched, he uses manners, but if he knows he is unobserved he is courteous. Manners are assumed; courtesy is natural. Manners are obvious; courtesy is subtle. The distance between the two is the distance between East and West, but the point of their separation is imperceptible. Actions remain manners so long as they are performed consciously, but when they become instinctive they are courtesies. A youth of twelve at a party is embarrassed. He had been told at home that he must remember his manners. The same youth at eighteen is courteous under similar circumstances, but at a formal dance he remembers his manners. At twenty-five the boy has become a man of courtesy. Before his thirtieth year he marries. From two years after his marriage until his death this man will have manners, because he has a wife who will not let him forget them. Have you ever passed a florist's window and noticed the flowers there? They are very pretty but they are so showy and so obviously displayed that they seem insincere. Manners, too, may look pretty, but they are so noticeable that they leave the impression of artificiality. High upon the snow-covered slopes of the Alps there grows a hardy flower of indescribable beauty. It is rarely noticed, because it blends so perfectly with its surroundings that one must search diligently to be rewarded with a glimpse of its beauty. This is courtesy, enduring, beautiful, and blending into human nature itself so completely that it is unobserved.   [342 words] — Written by a college freshman.

5. **Development by repetition** implies more than mere restatement. It implies a change, a modification of the idea to make it more exact or more specific. The process of restatement usually requires the use of supporting details.

6. **Development by analogy** is used by a writer when he wishes to make something clear by comparing it with something from a different, and to the reader a more familiar, field of experience. Literature as well as popular speech is full of analogies. Life, wrote Shakespeare, is "a tale told by an idiot"; it is a "bowl of cherries," says the popular-song writer. Life is "a narrow vale between the mountain peaks of two eternities." It is "an empty dream," "a fleeting breath," "a short summer." All these, when expanded by supporting details, are analogies.

Similar to the analogy is the illustration or the anecdote or even the figure of speech. James Russell Lowell, speaking of Wordsworth, said: "Even where his genius is wrapped in clouds, the unconquerable lightning of imagination struggles through, flashing out unexpected vistas, and illuminating the humdrum pathway of our daily thought with a radiance of momentary consciousness that seems like a revelation." In his essay on "Rousseau and the Sentimentalists" he used this anecdote:

There is an old story in the *Gesta Romanorum* of a priest who was found fault with by one of his parishioners because his life was in painful discordance with his teaching. So one day he takes his critic out to a stream, and, giving him to drink of it, asks him if he does not find it sweet and pure water. The parishioner, having answered that it was, is taken to the source, and finds that what had so refreshed him flowed from between the jaws of a dead dog. "Let this teach thee," said the priest, "that the very best doctrine may take its rise in a very impure and disgustful spring, and that excellent morals may be taught by a man who has no morals at all." It is easy enough to see the fallacy here. Had the man known beforehand from what a carrion fountain-head the stream issued, he could not have drunk of it without loathing. Had the priest merely bidden him to *look* at the stream and see how beautiful it was, instead of tasting it, it would have been quite another matter. And this is precisely the difference between what appeals to our aesthetic or to our moral sense, between what is judged of by the taste or by the conscience.   [218 words]

In analyzing paragraphs to learn the methods used by professional writers, you must not be confused by a possible complexity of paragraph structure. A writer may use these methods singly or in various combinations, and the combinations may be intricate. It is not always possible to pick out a sentence and say, "This is example; this is definition." Frequently you will find several methods used in the same sentence. At times you may even find that example, analogy, or definition is used to make clear, not the topic idea, but a subordinate idea. Remember also that some of the words or even sentences in a paragraph must do other things than develop the topic idea. They may be used to relate the topic idea to ideas that came before it or that may come after it, or to establish connections between the subordinate ideas in the paragraph.

The following paragraph begins with a topic sentence. The first half of the paragraph is an example. Then after a comment on the example, the author repeats his topic idea, briefly suggests other examples, and finally concludes with an instance of the recognition of the truth of his central thought. The last sentence should emphasize to you the fact that examples often need to have their pertinence or application interpreted if they are to be effective.

The [honor] system works, of course, only in those colleges which have sufficient social solidarity to ensure that any offender will promptly be "sent to Coventry" by undergraduate sentiment. [Topic sentence.] One of the two violations of the code which occurred during my years at Princeton was in an examination in one of my own courses. I had left the room as soon as the papers were distributed, and there were no longer any "proctors."

But a boy was seen to cheat, was reported by his classmates to the undergraduate "honor committee," and told to leave Princeton forever that afternoon. I knew nothing about it until Dean Murray announced at our next faculty meeting that Mr. X, on recommendation of the student committee, had severed his connection with the college. Only those professors who have taught under the humiliating police system and then under the honor system can understand the happy difference made in relations between professors and students. Yet without the requisite social solidarity the system is doomed to failure. It worked admirably at Williams, for example, and at many other of the smaller institutions. Some of us made a futile effort, many years ago, to persuade the Harvard authorities to try it, but even Dean Briggs, generous and idealistic as he was, was not to be convinced that the scheme was workable at Cambridge. There are, alas, too many "Untouchables" in every great university, as Briggs knew sadly well, and you cannot send a boy to Coventry if he lives in Coventry already. [252 words]

— Bliss Perry, *And Gladly Teach*, Houghton Mifflin Company, New York, 1935, p. 131. Reprinted by permission.

Effective use of concrete examples gives the following paragraph its cumulative force. The first two sentences are transitional. That transitions are a part of writing from the very first plan or outline of an essay may be seen by examining the paragraphs that preceded the one here used. "I am not referring to direct physical contact" is Mr. Gunther's beginning of one paragraph. "Nor do I mean to discuss the psychological effects of Chicago crime" starts the next paragraph on its way. The third paragraph brings us closer to his announcement of the subject: "Nor do I mean to elaborate on the larger political issues." What we have called a transition, then, is really the announcement of the subject of the rest of the essay. A topic sentence follows, repeated with more specific application, and then made clear and convincing by a piling up of example after example.

What I am after is something newer, more intimate, and more definite. I mean racketeering. *Crime is affecting the Chicago citizen in a new fashion.* [Topic sentence.] A system of criminal exploitation, based on extortion, controlled by hoodlums, and decorated with icy-cold murder, has arisen in the past five or six years, to seize the ordinary Chicagoan, you and me and the man across the street, by the pocket-book if not the throat. Crime is costing me money. It is costing money to the taxi-driver who took me to the office this morning, the elevator boy who lifted me ten stories through the steel stratifications of a great skyscraper, the waiter who served me my luncheon, the suburban business man who sat at the next table. Very few persons, in Chicago or out of it, realize that the ordinary citizen is paying liberal tribute to racketeers. This tribute is levied in many ways. The ordinary citizen pays it, like as not, whenever he has a suit pressed and every time he gets a haircut; he may pay it in the plumbing in his house and the garaging of his car; the very garbage behind his back door may perhaps mean spoils for someone.   [201 words]

— John Gunther, "The High Cost of Hoodlums," *Harper's Magazine*, vol. 159, p. 530 (October, 1929). Reprinted by permission.

The following is an excellent example of a paragraph of definition. Notice how carefully and how exactly the authors specify the sense in which they will use the term "virtues," and then, because in defining virtues they had to use two other disputable terms, how most of the paragraph becomes an attempt to clarify these two terms.

I shall define virtues as those mental and physical habits which tend to produce a good community, and as vices those that tend to produce a bad one. [Topic sentence.] Different people have different conceptions of what makes a community good or bad, and it is difficult to find arguments by which to establish the preferability of one's own conception. I cannot hope, therefore, to appeal to those whose tastes are very different from my own, but I hope and believe that there is nothing very singular in my own tastes. For my part, I should judge a community to be in a good state if I found a great deal of instinctive happiness, a prevalence of feelings of friendship and affection rather than hatred and envy, a capacity for creating and enjoying beauty, and the intellectual curiosity which leads to the advancement and diffusion of knowledge. I should judge a community to be in a bad state if I found much unhappiness from thwarted instinct, much hatred and envy, little sense of beauty, and little intellectual curiosity. As between these different elements of excellence or the reverse, I do not pretend to judge. Suppose, for the sake of argument, that intellectual curiosity and artistic capacity were found to be in some degree incompatible, I should find it difficult to say which ought to be preferred. But I should certainly think better of a community which contained something of both than of one which contained more of the one and none of the other. I do not, however, believe that there is any incompatibility among the four ingredients I have mentioned as constituting a good community; namely, happiness, friendship, enjoyment of beauty, and love of knowledge. [283 words]

— Bertrand and Dora Russell, *Prospects of Industrial Civilization*, "Moral Standards and Social Well-Being," D. Appleton-Century Company, New York, 1923, pp. 161–162. Reprinted by permission.

Concrete details, a number of examples, and an interesting analogy form the substance of the following paragraph:

I suppose the truth is that Americans are really more kindly and more sensitive and more vulnerable than English people, with the result that their manners are more unreliable. Social life in America is not smooth. It is jerky, turbulent, changeable. The social climate is an April climate. Clouds rush up, storms break, the skies clear again, all in the course of an evening party. As I have said elsewhere, one is reminded of children. Observe a children's party. The youngsters to begin with are on their best behavior, but presently they grow excited, boisterous, rows begin, tears are shed, and so on. Self-control, an iron self-discipline, an invincible quiet under provocation are not striking characteristics of the American. If he is annoyed he loses his temper. If he is amused he shouts with laughter. If she is jealous she shows it. Indeed, Americans almost always show their feelings too much for perfect manners. Good manners demand that one should ignore one's personal feelings and, if they are disagreeable, that one should hide them. [174 words]

— Mary Borden, "Manners," *Harper's Magazine*, vol. 160, p. 81 (December, 1929). Reprinted by permission.

Three paragraphs where one would produce the same effect — that may be your comment on the following selection. You are quite right, and yet when Galsworthy chose to make the subtopic the unit of paragraph structure he was doing what modern writers do frequently. There are two reasons for using this method of grouping ideas: one is that the writer may want to set off, to emphasize, to point to each topic separately; another is that the writer may wish to break up a forbiddingly large block of solid print. Notice that the topic sentence not only expresses the general idea but also forecasts the structure.

Now, in writing plays, there are, in this matter of the moral, three courses open to the serious dramatist. [Topic sentence.] The first is: To definitely set before the public that which it wishes to have set before it, the views and codes of life by which the public lives and in which it believes. This way is the most common, successful, and popular. It makes the dramatist's position sure, and not too obviously authoritative.

The second course is: To definitely set before the public those views and codes of life by which the dramatist himself lives, those theories in which he himself believes, the more effectively if they are the opposite of what the public wishes to have placed before it, presenting them so that the audience may swallow them like powder in a spoonful of jam.

There is a third course: To set before the public no cut-and-dried codes, but the phenomena of life and character, selected and combined, but not distorted by the dramatist's outlook, set down without fear, favour, or prejudice, leaving the public to draw such poor moral as nature may afford. This third method requires a certain detachment; it requires a sympathy with, a love of, and a curiosity as to, things for their own sake; it requires a far view, together with patient industry, for no immediately practical result.   [Total: 223 words]

— John Galsworthy, *Candelabra*, "Some Platitudes Concerning Drama," Charles Scribner's Sons, New York, 1933, pp. 3–4. Reprinted by permission.

Development by the use of contrast, particulars and details, repetition or restatement, and citing results is illustrated in the following paragraph.

We went to science in search of light, not merely upon the nature of matter, but upon the nature of man as well, and though that which we have received may be light of a sort, it is not adapted to our eyes and is not anything by which we can see. [Topic sentence.] Since thought began we have groped in the dark among shadowy shapes, doubtfully aware of landmarks looming uncertainly here and there — of moral principles, human values, aims, and ideals. We hoped for an illumination in which they would at least stand clearly and unmistakably forth, but instead they appear even less certain and less substantial than before — mere fancies and illusions generated by nerve actions that seem terribly remote from anything we can care about or based on relativities that accident can shift. We had been assured that many troublesome shadows would flee away, that superstitious fears, irrational repugnances, and all manner of bad dreams would disappear. And so in truth very many have. But we never supposed that most of the things we cherished would prove equally unsubstantial, that all the aims we thought we vaguely perceived, all the values we pursued, and all the principles we clung to were but similar shadows, and that either the light of science is somehow deceptive or the universe, emotionally and spiritually, a vast emptiness.   [223 words]

— Joseph Wood Krutch, *The Modern Temper*, Harcourt, Brace & Company, New York, 1929, pp. 68–69. Reprinted by permission.

Here is a paragraph developed inductively with the topic sentence at the end:

On the whole, the Fathers of the Republic believed that war was principally a wicked trade of princes and tyrants, and that the United States, by keeping out of the brawls of Europe, might steadily enjoy peace as a national blessing. If, being practical men, they took into account the possible recurrence of war and made ample provision in the Constitution for defense, they did it with reference to the chances of life, not in praise of war as a manly exercise. By and large, the creed of peace, scorned by feudal aristocracies as the craven ethics of commercial huckstering, became a kind of national tradition, although nearly every generation after the establishment of independence passed through an armed conflict. Even while condemning pacifists privately as weaklings, cowards, and near-traitors, President Roosevelt never publicly exalted war as a virtue in itself but only when waged for a "righteous" cause. President Wilson branded it as an evil and called on the nation to help him "end war." *It is not surprising, therefore, that some haziness exists in the American mind on the subject of armed combat and its uses in world economy.*   [191 words]

— Charles A. Beard and William Beard, *The American Leviathan*, 1931, pp. 754–755. By permission of The Macmillan Company, publishers.

The next two paragraphs, both of them developed largely by particulars and details, are good examples of scientific writing.

Looked at in its broad implications, the law of gravitation was important, not so much because it told us why an apple fell to the ground, or why the earth and planets moved around the sun, as because it suggested that the whole of Nature was governed by hard and fast laws. [Topic sentence.] For instance, to the ancients comets had been fearsome portents of evil, of famines or pestilences, of wars or the death of kings; seen in the light of Newton's work, they became mere inert chunks of matter, following their predestined paths as they were dragged about in space by the gravitational pull of the sun. Clearly, their motions could have nothing to do with the deeds or misdeeds of men. In the same way, darkness spread over the earth at an eclipse of the sun, not because the gods were angry with men, but because gravitation had pulled the moon into a position in which it temporarily shut off the sun's light — a position to which it had been pre-destined from the beginning of time. The tyranny of superstition and magic was broken, and Nature became something to study, not some-thing to fear. Man began to see that he was free to work out his own destiny without fear of disturbance from interfering gods, spirits, or demons.   [218 words]

— Sir James Jeans, "Man and the Universe," from *Scientific Progress*, 1936, pp. 15–16. By permission of The Macmillan Company, publishers.

We of these later days, living in the narrow temperate zone surrounding our sun and peering into the far future, see an ice-age of a different kind threatening us. [Topic sentence.] Just as Tantalus, standing in a lake so deep that he only just escaped drowning, was yet destined to die of thirst, so it is the tragedy of our race that it is probably destined to die of cold, while the greater part of the substance of the universe still remains too hot for life to obtain a footing. The sun, having no extraneous supply of heat, must necessarily emit ever less and less of its life-giving radiation, and, as it does so, the temperate zone of space, within which alone life can exist, must close around it. To remain a possible abode of life, our earth would need to move in ever nearer and nearer to the dying sun. Yet, science tells us that, so far from its moving inwards, inexorable dynamical laws are even now driving it ever farther away from the sun into the outer cold and darkness. And, so far as we can see, they must continue to do so until life is frozen off the earth, unless indeed some celestial collision or cataclysm intervenes to destroy life even earlier by a more speedy death. This prospective fate is not peculiar to our earth; other suns must die like our own, and any life there may be on other planets must meet the same inglorious end.   [249 words]

— Sir James Jeans, *The Mysterious Universe*, 1934, pp. 14–15. By permis-sion of The Macmillan Company, publishers.

When a scientist sets out to write an interesting definition, he produces a paragraph like this one. Notice again that definition depends on the use of concrete details.

Proteins are bodies of complicated composition and structure which play a fundamental part in animal life. [Topic sentence.] They are essential con-stituents of muscle and nerve, skin and hair and wool: the values of our foods are related to protein-content, since the body's store must be con-tinually replenished. We have long known that carbon, nitrogen, oxygen, hydrogen, sulphur, and other atoms are elements of the protein molecule, and that its molecular structure must in some ways be very variable, whence its name. Only recently we have acquired new information about the general plan, mainly from our X-ray studies, and it is extremely curious and interesting. Every protein molecule has a backbone or central framework, consisting of an atomic chain in which carbon and nitrogen atoms recur with perfect regularity, two of the former to one of the latter. The chain cannot be pulled into a straight line because the two links that join each atom to its neighbors in the chain make with each other an invariable angle. This angle, which can be measured with great exactness, as can also the distance between each pair of atoms, is rather more than a right angle. Although there is this element of rigidity the chain as a whole can be crumpled up because any part of the chain can turn around the link that connects it to the remainder, as if the link were an axle. It is the shortening of the protein chains in this way which constitutes the contraction of our muscles, or the shrinking of a textile fabric. All animal movements are produced by the contraction and extension of muscular fibre, and directed by way of nerves, in which also protein is the important constituent. [284 words]

— Sir William Bragg, "The Progress of Physical Science," from *Scientific Progress*, 1936, pp. 70–72. By permission of The Macmillan Company, publishers.

The following is a paragraph developed by analogy, showing you the usefulness of this method in explaining abstruse scientific concepts.

Roughly, one might say that the atoms correspond to the members of the engineer's structure and the electrons to the rivets which hold the members together. With a little greater license one might compare the energy-quanta to the exertions of the workmen who insert or remove the rivets. In these terms the construction or alteration of the engineer's design is a fairly close analogue to physical and chemical operations, such as the melting of wax or the growth of a plant in the rays of the sun. Bonds are broken and reformed, and energy-quanta are derived from the radiant light and heat. [102 words]

— Sir William Bragg, "The Progress of Physical Science," from *Scientific Progress*, 1936, pp. 50–51. By permission of The Macmillan Company, publishers.

The following paragraph, "Diagnosis of an Englishman," should challenge you to attempt a similar diagnosis of an American — or a Southerner, a Texan, a New Yorker, whichever commands your loyalty. The central thought — or impression — of this paragraph is clear enough, but to put it into an adequate summarizing sentence is not easy. Try it.

The Englishman must have a thing brought under his nose before he will act; bring it there and he will go on acting after everybody else has stopped. He lives very much in the moment because he is essentially a man of facts and not a man of imagination. Want of imagination makes him, philosophically speaking, rather ludicrous; in practical affairs it handicaps him at the start; but once he has "got going" — as we say — it is of incalculable assistance to his stamina. The Englishman, partly through his lack of imagination and nervous sensibility, partly through his inbred dislike of extremes and habit of minimising the expression of everything, is a perfect example of the conservation of energy. It is, therefore, very difficult to come to the end of him. Add to this his unimaginative practicality, and tenacious moderation, his inherent spirit of competition — not to say pugnacity — a spirit of competition so extreme that it makes him, as it were, patronize Fate; add the sort of vulgarity that grows like fungus on people who despise ideas and analysis, and make a cult of unintellectuality; add a peculiar, ironic, "don't care" sort of humour; an underground humaneness, and an ashamed idealism — and you get some notion of the pudding of English character. It has a kind of terrible coolness, a rather awful level-headedness — by no means reflected in his Press. The Englishman makes constant small blunders; but few, almost no, deep mistakes. He is a slow starter, but there is no stronger finisher, because he has by temperament and training the faculty of getting through any job he gives his mind to with a minimum expenditure of vital energy; nothing is wasted in expression, style, spread-eagleism; everything is instinctively kept as near to the practical heart of the matter as possible. He is — to the eyes of an artist — distressingly matter-of-fact; a tempting mark for satire. And yet he is at bottom an idealist, though it is his nature to snub, disguise, and mock his own inherent optimism. To admit enthusiasm is "bad form" if he is a "gentleman"; and "swank," or mere waste of good heat, if he is not a "gentleman." England produces more than its proper percentage of cranks and poets; this is nature's way of redressing the balance in a country where feelings are not shown, sentiments not expressed, and extremes laughed at. Not that the Englishman is cold, as is generally supposed in foreign countries — on the contrary he is warm-hearted and feels strongly; but just as peasants, for lack of words to express their feelings, become stolid, so does the Englishman, from sheer lack of habit of self-expression. The

Englishman's proverbial "hypocrisy" — that which I myself have dubbed his "island Pharisaism" — comes chiefly, I think, from his latent but fearfully strong instinct for competition which will not let him admit himself beaten, or in the wrong, even to himself; and from an ingrained sense of form that impels him always to "save his face"; but partly it comes from his powerlessness to explain his feelings. He has not the clear and fluent cynicism of expansive natures, wherewith to confess exactly how he stands. It is the habit of men of all nations to want to have things both ways; the Englishman wants it both ways, I think, more strongly than any; and he is unfortunately so unable to express himself, *even to himself*, that he has never realized this truth, much less confessed it — hence his "hypocrisy." [582 words]

— John Galsworthy, *Candelabra*, "Diagnosis of an Englishman," Charles Scribner's Sons, New York, 1933, pp. 57–59. Reprinted by permission.

Unity, Order, and Transitions. A paragraph may be used for a transition from one subject to another. It may recapitulate or summarize what has been said, announce the next topic, and indicate the plan of treatment which is to follow, or it may state simply that the writer has finished one idea and is about to begin another. Paragraphs of transition are usually short.

Before turning to the medical advances of the present century, let us just briefly recapitulate the changes that have been mentioned above. [Topic sentence.] We have seen medicine emerge from a period of magic and religion to a stage where disease came to be accepted as a phenomenon of nature. Following this there came a time when the structure of the body was investigated; this led to the further stage in which clinical signs and symptoms and anatomical structures of diseased organs were correlated. Ultimately, the present era arrived, when the experimental method was seriously applied to the study of the body, with the result that big strides were made not only in knowledge of the actions of many organs, but also of the causes of many diseases. There were still, however, at the beginning of the present century, many diseases which had been distinguished as entities but about which we knew little or nothing as to causation or treatment, and, although this is still the case, the work of the last thirty years has helped to fill in many blanks. [179 words]

— Edward Mellanby, "Progress in Medical Science," from *Scientific Progress*, 1936, pp. 116–117. By permission of The Macmillan Company, publishers.

A paragraph is a unit of structure, dealing with one topic or subtopic. It is obvious, therefore, that the inclusion of material not related to the central idea violates paragraph unity and makes the paragraph confusing and ineffective. The best safeguard of unity in a paragraph of exposition is still the topic sentence, expressed or implied.

Frequently the topic sentence can also be made the best safeguard of a logical, effective arrangement of parts in a paragraph. If the writer, for example, says, "In our foreign policy our nation must take one of three courses," you expect him to continue by specifying each of these courses in turn. If he begins, "Light can be thrown on this subject by tracing the development of the meaning of the word *propaganda*," you expect him to use the historical order. In other words, a topic sentence is not only a statement of the central idea but also, at times, an indication and a forecast of arrangement.

The writer of a paragraph should use the order which best fits his material and his purpose. If he is explaining a process, he should use the order of happening, usually called the chronological order. If he begins with a general statement, he should proceed from the general to particulars. If he wants to build up to a conclusion, he should go from particular details to his general statement. In some paragraphs, especially in short ones, it does not matter what order is used. The writer's common sense will usually warn him against gross confusion.

The ideal paragraph has often been defined as one in which each sentence grows so naturally out of the one before it that the reader *feels* the natural, logical growth of the paragraph idea. It is pointless to quibble over the question whether such a paragraph is any closer to the ideal than the one which is liberally sprinkled with connective words. Good paragraphs may be written either with or without connecting links or transitions. When two ideas are set side by side, the mind naturally assumes that the ideas are related. Not many paragraphs, however, are so simple that the ideas in them may be stacked like bricks in a pile. If a writer is building a wall, instead of piling bricks, he may need to work out a complex pattern, and — to extend the analogy — he may find it necessary to use mortar.

The mortar which holds the bricks of thought together in a paragraph may be one of several kinds. Assuming that the thoughts have been properly arranged, they may be further tied to each other by conjunctions, by transitional or directive words or expressions, by pronouns, by repetition of key words, and by parallel structure. Among transitional or directive expressions are such words and phrases as *moreover, therefore, consequently, for example, for instance, however, as a result, nevertheless, on the other hand, similarly, first, second, third, in conclusion, that is, that is to say, on the contrary, conversely*. This list is by no means complete. Pronouns (*this, that, these, those, his, her, its*, etc.), as you can readily see, carry the reader's mind back to their antecedent. Repetition of key words similarly serves to remind the reader that what is being said is not entirely new but a continuation of what has already been mentioned. These repeated words may be called echo words. Parallel structure carries the thought along, since the reader rightly assumes that ideas expressed in parallel form are parallel, that is, that they are similar and closely related.

Whatever has been said about connectives within a paragraph applies to connectives between paragraphs, except that here the connecting links may occasionally be longer. As within paragraphs, the links may be words or phrases; frequently these are the opening parts of the topic sentences. More rarely the topic sentence is preceded by an entire sentence of transition, and still less frequently the transition is paragraphed by itself.

But, again, your best method of learning how to use connectives is to analyze paragraphs written by experienced writers. There follow three demonstrations: one is a direct, straightforward exposition of observed details, arranged in chronological order; the second deals with ideas; the third is an unusual example of repetition and parallelism.

Not all spiders spin webs, and of those that do, the best spinners are usually the females; frequently the males make only temporary

Transition from preceding paragraph.

"bachelor diggings," or dwell in the nests of the female. There are probably as many kinds of web as there are species of spiders that spin. The simplest sort is the delicate hidden trap made by the common house spider and called "cobwebs." A much finer web is made by the grass spider, who spins a filmy platform with a funnel-shaped hideout at the back; generally there is a vertical cobweb above this which serves to catch flying insects who then tumble into the "parlor" below, where they stick fast and are soon greeted by the little hostess who darts out from the funnel.

But the finest type of all, the height of spider art, is the orb web, built on the principle of spokes banded by circumferential lines. Some are suspended horizontally, some vertically, some at an angle. These are made by many kinds of spiders, all over the world, but the commonest orb-weaver is the so-called garden-spider. Anybody with time and patience can watch the building of an orb web. True, most spiders are shy ladies and prefer to work at night, but if you will locate such a web by day, and take a flashlight out after dark, you may watch the spinstress on the job. It is well, though, not to shine the light directly on the web. The tricks of her trade are a guild secret.

The other day I had my first chance to watch a spider spinning in daytime. Her name was Miranda, according to my scientific books, and she was black with yellow bands. This particular specimen was a young female, hence she was still slender, not having lost her figure from egg-bearing, and her long slim legs were still handsomely clad in the black-and-yellow bands that denote youth in this species.

She had already built two sides of her triangular framework, of the heavy tough thread

---

Annotations (right margin):

Reference to "spinners."
Ref. to "kinds."

Ref. to "kinds."

Pronoun.

Ref. to "kinds of web" above.
Ref. to "orb web."

Refers to kinds of "orb web."

Repeats words.
Connective.

Connective.
Refers to "spinstress."
Transition: refers to last idea of previous paragraph.
Pronoun "her."
Refers to "Miranda."

Transitional clause.

spiders use for that purpose. At the moment she was starting to make the third side. To do this she climbed back up the perpendicular line she had spun, all the time reeling out a new line, anchored at the base of her perpendicular line and held away from the old one with her hind legs. It looked like thread hanging from the needle of a woman sewing, as she laboriously made her way to the top, then walked down the inclined plane of the other completed side of her triangle. She did not walk upright, like a tight-rope walker, but slung herself underneath the wire, like a tree sloth inching along. When she got to the end she stopped, and reefed in her slack that she had been carrying and spinning, until it was taut. Then she fastened it to the twig from which she had started, with a little dab of mucilage-like matter from her glands, and so the third side of her triangular loom was complete.

Here she took a rest, and well she might. She had now to solve the problem of making the radial lines, or spokes, of her wheel. To do this she walked out to the middle of the top side of her triangle, made fast there the beginning of a line, and let herself down to the lower side, where she fastened the end of the line she carried. Then she crawled back up and located the center, by what capacity to measure distance we can only guess. This was to be the hub of her wheel. Here she fastened a new line, which she carried free as she climbed to the top of her triangle, crawled a way along the top of her frame, took in her slack line, and fastened it. Now she had a radius, or, counting the two halves of her first diametrical lines, she now had three radii. And, going back each time to the center, she laboriously built one radius after the other.

Adverbial phrase.

Pronoun.

Pronoun.

Clause refers to idea in preceding sentence. Adverb.

Adverb, tying this with last fact of preceding paragraph. Infinitive and pronoun.

Adverb "then."

Pronoun "this." Adverb.

Adverb

Conjunction.

But not in regular succession. Oh, no, our little lady welder is too smart for that. She does not wish to put too many stresses on one side of the frame at once. Instead, she built first on one side, then on another, then to the right of center, then to the left. After that she rested, built a little hub, a sort of damask platform, her future headquarters, and began to fill in more radii, working now on one side, now on the opposite, as a man tightens nuts on an auto wheel.

Contrast — by using the last half of the last sentence of the preceding paragraph as the transition. Transitional adverb. Phrase.

When she had nineteen radii in place, Miranda stepped slowly around just outside her hub, forefeet on one radius, hindfeet on another, pacing off the angles between them. At first she was satisfied. Then she found one angle that was twice as wide as it should be. Quickly she filled it in with a twentieth radius; that seemed to be the number that pleased her. Perhaps Miranda could count, but even if not she could do something much more wonderful — she could measure angles, about eighteen degrees in this case, far more exactly than I could do it without a graduated scale! She was, indeed, an able engineer.

Clause referring to substance of preceding paragraph. Phrase. Adverb.

Pronoun.

Pronoun.

Miranda now took another rest. Her body, if not her head, was tired. The human head is the seat of thought. But who can say where the instincts (which replace thought in the lower animals) reside? Who can say where they come from, how they are handed down? The art of weaving by spiders descends, primarily, on the distaff side, from mother to daughter. But presumably Miranda never saw her mother weave a net, and she could not have learned by imitation if she had. Her first bit of workmanship was as good as any she will ever make. And Miranda, in her turn, will never see her children as anything but eggs. Yet she will hand on her

Adverb "now." Reference to "rest." Repetition of "head." Conjunction. Repetition of phrase.

Conjunction.

Pronoun. Conjunction and phrase. Conjunction.

95

exquisite craft to them with the very chromosomes of her reproductive cells.

Her rest over, Miranda began to weave outward from the hub a spiral band, in the nature of a scaffolding to brace the radii for the stresses she is about to put on them. She gave the spiral four and a half turns. — Reference to previous uses of "rest." / Pronoun.

Then, walking deliberately out to the end of one of the lower radii, she began for the first time to spin a sticky stuff; I could see it come gushing from her glands, glistening like dew. It is elastic, too, so that it will not snap; indeed, the victim who gets into its toils will merely entangle himself more with every exertion. Miranda lays a few bands of it on the bottom half of the web, a few bands at the top. Then she goes to the bottom again and builds more concentric lines of what is, in essence, so much sticky fly-paper. Thus, working her way to the center, Miranda encounters the spiral scaffolding and begins to tear it out, as a tailor tears out basting threads. She does not want to leave this nice, dry escape ladder for any fly to use! As fast as she removes it she replaces it with the sticky loops. But she stops well short of the hub, her personal living quarters. — Adverb. / Adverb "too." / Adverb. / Adverb. / Pronouns. / Pronouns. / Repetition. / Conjunction and pronouns.

At last the little miracle is finished, the toil of four and a half hours, counting brief rests. It is the most complex structure built by any living creature. A bird's nest is clumsy beside it, and the vaunted comb of the honeybee monotonous and simple in comparison. The spider web is the work of a little engineer without diploma, of a geometrician who never heard of Euclid, of a weaver whose design never falters. — Phrase. / Pronoun. / Pronoun.

— Donald Culross Peattie, "Spider Silk — Wonder-stuff of Nature," *Nature Magazine*, vol. 38, No. 6, pp. 290–291 (June–July, 1945). Reprinted by permission.

The next selection illustrating the use of transitions employs more repetition and parallel structure than the preceding one.

It is my purpose to consider the type of justification which is available for belief in doctrines of religion. This is a question which in some new form challenges each generation. It is the peculiarity of religion that humanity is always shifting its attitude towards it. *[Introduction. Statement of objectives. Pronoun. Restatement.]*

The contrast between religion and the elementary truths of arithmetic makes my meaning clear. Ages ago the simple arithmetical doctrines dawned on the human mind, and throughout history the unquestioned dogma that two and three make five reigned whenever it has been relevant. We all know what this doctrine means, and its history is of no importance for its elucidation. *[Topic sentence and transition. Rep. of "religion." Echo-word. Pronoun and rep. of "doctrine."]*

But we have the gravest doubt as to what religion means so far as doctrine is concerned. There is no agreement as to the definition of religion in its most general sense, including true and false religion; nor is there any agreement as to the valid religious beliefs, nor even as to what we mean by the truth of religion. It is for this reason that some consideration of religion as an unquestioned factor throughout the long stretch of human history is necessary to secure the relevance of any discussion of its general principle. *[Conjunction. Rep. of words "doctrine," "religion." Echo-word. Phrase. Rep. of word.]*

There is yet another contrast. What is generally disputed is doubtful, and what is doubtful is relatively unimportant — other things being equal. I am speaking of general principles which are entirely unsettled. If we do not know what number is the product of 69 and 67, we defer an action presupposing the answer, till we have found out. This little arithmetical puzzle *[Sentence. Parallel structure. Repeated later. Pronoun.]*

97

can be put aside till it is settled, and it is capable of definite settlement with adequate trouble.

But as between religion and arithmetic, other things are not equal. You use arithmetic, but you are religious. Arithmetic of course enters into your nature, so far as that nature involves a multiplicity of things. But it is there as a necessary condition, and not as a transforming agency. No one is invariably "justified" by his faith in the multiplication table. But in some sense or other, justification is the basis of all religion. Your character is developed according to your faith. This is the primary truth from which no one can escape. Religion is force of belief cleansing the inward parts. For this reason the primary religious virtue is sincerity, a penetrating sincerity.

Conjunction.
Rep. of words.
Rep. of phrase.
Parallel structure.
Conjunction.
Parallel structure.

Conjunction.

Pronoun.

Phrase.

A religion, on its doctrinal side, can thus be defined as a system of general truths which have the effect of transforming character when they are sincerely held and vividly apprehended.

Transitional and summarizing paragraph.

In the long run your character and your conduct of life depend upon your intimate convictions. Life is an internal fact for its own sake, before it is an external fact relating itself to others. The conduct of external life is conditioned by environment, but it receives its final quality, on which its worth depends, from the internal life which is the self-realization of existence. Religion is the art and the theory of the internal life of man, so far as it depends on the man himself and on what is permanent in the nature of things.

Rep. of word.

Parallel structure.

Repetition of "external" and "internal."

This doctrine is the direct negation of the theory that religion is primarily a social fact. Social facts are of great importance to religion, because there is no such thing as absolutely independent existence. You cannot abstract society from man; most psychology is herd

Pronoun.
Repetition.
Repetition.

psychology. But all collective emotions leave untouched the awful ultimate fact, which is the human being, consciously alone with himself, for his own sake.

Conjunction.

Religion is what the individual does with his own solitariness. It runs through three stages, if it evolves to its final satisfaction. It is the transition from God the void to God the enemy, and from God the enemy to God the companion.

Repetition of idea.
Pronouns.

Thus religion is solitariness; and if you are never solitary, you are never religious. Collective enthusiasms, revivals, institutions, churches, rituals, bibles, codes of behavior, are the trappings of religion, its passing forms. They may be useful, or harmful; they may be authoritatively ordained, or merely temporary expedients. But the end of religion is beyond all this.

Repetition of words and idea.

Repetition. Pronoun. Parallel structure.

Accordingly, what should emerge from religion is individual worth of character. But worth is positive or negative, good or bad. Religion is by no means necessarily good. It may be very evil. The fact of evil, interwoven with the texture of the world, shows that in the nature of things there remains effectiveness for degradation. In your religious experience the God with whom you have made terms may be the God of destruction, the God who leaves in his wake the loss of the greater reality.

Pronoun.
Adverb.
Conjunction.
Repetition of "good," "evil."

Repetition of "the God."

In considering religion, we should not be obsessed by the idea of its necessary goodness. This is a dangerous delusion. The point to notice is its transcendent importance; and the fact of this importance is abundantly made evident by the appeal to history.

Phrase.

Pronoun.
Repetition.
Pronoun.

— Alfred North Whitehead, *Religion in the Making*, 1926. By permission of The Macmillan Company, publishers.

THE PARAGRAPH

Fourscore and seven years ago our fathers brought forth on this continent a new nation, conceived in Liberty, and dedicated to the proposition that all men are created equal.

Now we are engaged in a great civil war, testing whether that nation, or any nation, so conceived and so dedicated, can long endure. We are met on a great battlefield of that war. We have come to dedicate a portion of that field as a final resting-place for those who here gave their lives that that nation might live. It is altogether fitting and proper that we should do this.

But, in a larger sense, we cannot dedicate — we cannot consecrate — we cannot hallow this ground. The brave men, living and dead, who struggled here, have consecrated it, far above our poor power to add or detract. The world will little note nor long remember what we say here, but it can never forget what they did here. It is for us, the living, rather, to be dedicated here to the unfinished work which they who fought here have thus far so nobly advanced. It is rather for us to be here dedicated to the great task remaining before us — that from these honored dead we take increased devotion to that cause for which they gave the last full measure of devotion; that we here highly resolve that these dead shall not have died in vain; that this nation, under God, shall have a new birth of freedom, and that the government of the people, by the people, for the people, shall not perish from the earth. — Abraham Lincoln.

Connects with "now" in second par.
Repeated later.

Words repeated: "nation," "dedicated," "that war."
Pronoun.
Pronoun. Repetition.
Pronoun. Repetition.

Pronoun.
Conjunction. Phrase and rep. Pronoun.
"here" + "this ground." Repetition.

"here" + "this ground."
"they" + "brave men."

Parallel structure and repetition.
Ref. to "brave men" above.
Pronouns.
Pronoun and repetition.
Ref. to "Liberty" in first sentence.

EXERCISES

Exercise 1. In one of your textbooks (history, sociology, economics, psychology) find examples of paragraphs developed entirely by examples, by analogy, by comparison and contrast, by particulars and details. Bring these to class and be prepared to analyze them for the class. Point out the topic sentence, if there is one, in each of the paragraphs. Point out the transitional phrases or sentences in each of the paragraphs. Find one paragraph which is entirely transitional.

Exercise 2. Bring to class examples of the following:

a. a paragraph with a topic sentence at the end.
b. a paragraph beginning with a transitional sentence.
c. a paragraph used as a transition between two topics of an essay.
d. a paragraph summarizing a section of an essay or chapter.

Exercise 3. In one of your textbooks find several paragraphs of definition. What other methods are used to develop these paragraphs?

Exercise 4. Point out the errors in the following paragraph. Where does it violate unity? How could the topic sentence be improved? Can you improve the arrangement of the material? Where can you add transitions to improve the smoothness of the paragraph?

Football is a nationally known game to all Americans. A football field must be one hundred yards long, thirty yards wide, and it must be marked off in ten-yard divisions. The game football requires a great deal from its players. It requires co-ordination, stamina, quick thinking, and courage. Most people think that courage has little to do with football. This is where they are mistaken because when a player is afraid of getting hurt he is of little value to the team. Stamina is a big factor in football. If a player becomes fatigued in the first quarter then he is of little help to his teammates. If he is continually getting hurt then again he is of little value. Injury is due mostly to the fact that an athlete is not in the best possible condition. In order that an athlete be in good condition he must have stamina. Football requires a great deal of co-ordination of the entire team and the quick thinking of every single man. It requires that each player know what he is supposed to do on each play, how to do it and the correct time to do it. If every man does his job right on each play then every play would be a touchdown, but of course this is impossible.

Rewrite the paragraph after you have analyzed its errors. Improve the diction and sentence structure, too, but keep to the central thought, only vaguely realized in this paragraph, that football requires of its participants certain qualities of character.

Exercise 5. Try to determine which method of paragraph development is called for by each of the following topic sentences.

a. In peace, no less than in war, there are many occasions for heroic conduct.
b. Life is like a walk through the streets of a strange village.
c. My life thus far has been a flight from fear.
d. Let us explain, before we proceed further, exactly what we mean by a "totalitarian state."
e. College English courses are very different from high-school English courses.
f. The new secretary's first day at the office is a succession of ludicrous mistakes.
g. The farm home was a scene of quiet and dignified beauty.
h. I have never understood why brains in a girl should be looked upon as any more her special accomplishment than her beauty.
i. A coed who cuts classes is like a girl who buys a pair of nylon stockings and then throws them under the counter when the salesman is not looking.
j. The recent World War amply demonstrated that indifferent success in college does not always predict indifferent success in life.

Exercise 6. Write a paragraph with a topic sentence which forecasts the structure of the paragraph. Here are a few suggestions:

a. The profession of law demands three important qualities of mind — the ability to analyze ideas, an interest in people, and patience with details.
b. Since I came to college I have learned four vital truths about living happily in a group of girls.
c. The husband shortage is likely to affect my life in three ways.
d. I can see four vital flaws in the theory of a communistic society.

Exercise 7. In the following paragraph insert transitions where you think they are necessary:

A boy's social education begins at the moment he becomes conscious of the existence of girls. [Topic sentence.] They have seemed like pals to him or perhaps just nuisances. He begins to realize that girls are a trifle different from the boys he plays with. He begins to take new pride in his personal appearance. Not long ago he liked to tease girls for interminably combing their hair; now he painstakingly trains a wave in his own sun-bleached locks. He polishes his shoes without being nagged, and his clothes lose some of their appearance of being slept in. His manners improve. He takes pride in knowing how to ask for a second helping at the table. He even opens a door for a girl. He practices complimenting his sisters. He suddenly becomes so shy that he is barely able to speak to girls of his own age. His shyness soon leaves him, and he realizes that girls are good companions.

Exercise 8. Read Galsworthy's "Diagnosis of an Englishman," page 89, and then write a similar diagnosis of the inhabitant of your own state or section of the country. Begin by making a long list of the qualities which you intend to use as details of your development; group these by putting together those that seem similar. Galsworthy's diagnosis is worth studying for its transitions. Look it over again with this in mind, and then try to imitate his device of tying thoughts together by constantly repeating key words and echoing ideas previously used.

Exercise 9. In a single paragraph try to give an informal definition of one of the following: loyalty, religion, courtesy, swing music, jazz, radicalism, a liberal education, a practical education, the good neighbor policy. In your paragraph use definitive statements, particulars and details, examples, and analogy. In the margin at the left of your paper label each device as you have used it.

Exercise 10. Write a paragraph which depends largely on contrast. Here are a few suggested subjects:

a. discipline and freedom
b. freedom and anarchy
c. the liberal and the conservative
d. democratic and representative government
e. the "movie" West and the real West
f. what "progressive" education is not
g. what religion is not
h. what the small town is not
i. courtesy and manners
j. sentiment and sentimentality

The Précis (Summary or Digest). A précis is a condensed version of a longer composition. Its essential qualities are clearness, simplicity, good English, and faithfulness to the original in thought and emphasis. The précis is sometimes said to differ from the abstract and the summary, but the distinction, if it exists except in theory, need not worry the student who is primarily concerned with the training in accurate thinking and expression which précis writing will give him. The popularity of summaries and digests any student can verify for himself by turning to his monthly copy of *The Reader's Digest;* the importance of knowing how to write a good digest he *will* verify for himself when he meets his next "essay type" final examination. To write a good summary, the student must first master the thought of the original. He must train himself to get at the heart of the selection he is reading. No lazy, half-awake reading will do.

The length of a précis, or digest, will depend to a certain extent on the thought content of the original. Some writing is pithy and compact; it may be cut down but it can scarcely be boiled down. Other writing is diffuse. It will bear a reduction in words without a corresponding loss in content. It would be foolish to assume that any piece of good writing did not lose by being trimmed down to a fourth or a third of its original size. It loses, first of all, the many details which give it its life and meaning; then it loses its personality, its distinctive flavor. It may lose other things, too. Despite all this, the occasions in a college student's life when he has to boil down a chapter or a lecture to a single paragraph are many. The amount of boiling down must depend on the demands of the occasion.

ORIGINAL

The reactionary policy of Tz'ŭ Hsi thus proved worse than a failure, and henceforth the somewhat chastened Empress Dowager tried to make amends by restraining anti-foreign agitation and introducing Europeanizing reforms. The traditional classical education of Chinese officials was modified and some attention given in the schools to natural science, European history, political economy, and modern languages. A commission was sent abroad to investigate the political institutions of the West, and Chinese students were encouraged to attend universities in Europe and America.

These reforms were not radical enough to satisfy the growing party of "Westernizers" among the younger generation of Chinese intellectuals, many of whom by this time had studied abroad and all of whom were coming to believe that Chinese regeneration depended upon getting rid of the Manchu dynasty and its conservative bureaucracy. The leader of the party was Sun Yat-sen, a man of humble origin who had been trained in medicine and had become a Christian and who, though compelled to live in exile, exerted a tremendous influence on the formulation and propagation of a revolutionary program of nationalism, republicanism, and political and social democracy. In 1908 the almost simultaneous deaths of the Dowager Empress Tz'ŭ Hsi and the puppet Emperor Kuang Hsü served to quicken the revolutionary agitation of Sun Yat-sen and his radical following, for the succeeding Emperor, Hsüan T'ung, was only an infant.

In vain the conservative régime at Peking made concessions to the radicals, sanctioning provincial assemblies in 1909 and convoking a National Assembly in 1910. The followers of Sun Yat-sen refused to compromise with the existing government and in October 1911 rose in arms against it. Ambitious military chieftains, including the powerful Yüan Shik-kai, refused or delayed to obey the orders of the court to suppress the rebellion, and very soon the revolutionaries were in possession of several important cities and provinces. In December 1911 a provisional republican government was established at Nanking, with Sun Yat-sen as President, and in the following February the boy-Emperor Hsüan T'ung abdicated and the Manchu dynasty ceased to rule.   [344 words]

— Carlton J. H. Hayes, *A Political and Cultural History of Modern Europe*, 1939. By permission of The Macmillan Company, publishers.

PRÉCIS (OR SUMMARY)

After the failure of the reactionary policies of China's Dowager Empress Tz'ŭ Hsi, some attempts were made at educational and social reforms. These reforms did not satisfy the younger Chinese intellectuals, who, under the leadership of Sun Yat-sen, agitated for the removal of the bureaucratic Manchu dynasty. In 1908 the deaths of the Dowager Empress and the Puppet Emperor resulted in concessions to the radicals. These concessions were not enough; the followers of Sun Yat-sen started a revolution, which culminated in December, 1911, in the establishment of a republic with Sun Yat-sen as president.   [94 words]

EXERCISES

Exercise 1. Study the following summaries. Judge them by these standards:

1. Has the essential thought of the original been preserved?
2. Has any important part of the thought been omitted?

3. Have the author's ideas been given the same relative importance, or emphasis, as in the original?
4. Does the summary preserve the point of view of the original?
5. Is the summary expressed in good English?

Be specific in your criticisms. Do not say merely that the thought of the original has been changed; tell what ideas have been left out or slighted, what ideas have been given a prominence not found in the original.

ORIGINAL

It is a great point then to enlarge the range of studies which a University professes, even for the sake of the students; and, though they cannot pursue every subject which is open to them, they will be the gainers by living among those and under those who represent the whole circle. This I conceive to be the advantage of a seat of universal learning, considered as a place of education. An assemblage of learned men, zealous for their own sciences, and rivals of each other, are brought, by familiar intercourse and for the sake of intellectual peace, to adjust together the claims and relations of their respective subjects of investigation. They learn to respect, to consult, to aid each other. Thus is created a pure and clear atmosphere of thought, which the student also breathes, though in his own case he only pursues a few sciences out of the multitude. He profits by an intellectual tradition, which is independent of particular teachers, which guides him in his choice of subjects, and duly interprets for him those which he chooses. He apprehends the great outlines of knowledge, the principles on which it rests, the scale of its parts, its lights and its shades, its great points and its little, as he otherwise cannot apprehend them. Hence it is that his education is called "Liberal." A habit of mind is formed which lasts through life, of which the attributes are freedom, equitableness, calmness, moderation, and wisdom; or what in a former discourse I have ventured to call a philosophical habit. This then I would assign as the special fruit of the education furnished at a University, as contrasted with other places of teaching or modes of teaching. This is the main purpose of a University in its treatment of its students. — Cardinal Newman.

PRÉCIS (OR SUMMARY)

1.

Cardinal Newman says that a University must have a large number and variety of studies. Even if a student can take only a few courses, he will gain by association with professors and students in other departments. He will gain a point of view and a habit of thought which will stay with him through life. I do not agree with Newman, for I think that a student in a professional school can also get the point of view of professors whose courses he does not take.

2.

The special advantage of a University, as a place of education, is in its range and variety of studies, wherein many learned men, each interested in his own field, learn to co-operate and to understand one another's point of view. In such an atmosphere of learning the student profits, too, in that he becomes acquainted with the general field of knowledge and learns the relative importance of the separate studies. He thereby acquires a philosophical habit, which consists of freedom, broad-mindedness, moderation, and wisdom. It is in producing this habit of mind that a University differs from other places of teaching.

3.

In a University, as contrasted with other places of education, there are many professors and courses. These professors have different interests, but by associating with each other they acquire an understanding and a respect for each other's point of view. The result is a more favorable atmosphere for getting a more liberal education.

Exercise 2. Write a summary of each of the following selections. Make each summary a single, well-organized paragraph.

It had formerly been widely held that if only the masses of mankind could be put in school and taught to read and write, they would become custodians as well as products of "enlightenment," that they would be equipped to appreciate and secure the benefits of peace, liberty, and democracy. It had accordingly been a central aim of the Era of Enlightenment, and one of its outstanding achievements, to promote popular and secular education. So far as the promotion of public education was concerned, there was no reaction after the war [World War I]. On the contrary, it was now pressed more vigorously and more universally than ever before. Under dictatorships, as in democracies, earnest and largely successful efforts were made to give everybody a schooling and to expose everybody to the supplementary instruction of newspapers, cinemas, and radios. Yet the results of all this educational endeavor were not quite in keeping with "enlightened" hopes. While the least literate nation in Europe submitted to a Communist dictatorship, the most literate stampeded to the Nazi dictatorship of Hitler. Apparently, literacy of itself did not predispose anybody to anything. It merely enlarged the opportunities for propaganda. And, in the dawning new age, expanding education became frankly and boastfully propagandist.

— Carlton J. H. Hayes, *A Political and Cultural History of Modern Europe*, 1939. By permission of The Macmillan Company, publishers.

The increased momentum of American life, both in its particles and its mass, unquestionably has a considerable moral and social value. It is the beginning, the only possible beginning, of a better life for the people as individuals and for society. So long as the great majority of the poor in any country are inert and are laboring without any hope of substantial rewards in this world, the whole associated life in that community rests on an equivocal foundation. Its moral and social order is tied to an economic system which starves and mutilates the great majority of the population, and under such conditions its religion necessarily becomes a spiritual drug, administered for the purpose of subduing the popular discontent and relieving the popular misery. The only way the associated life of such a community can be radically improved is by the leavening of the inert popular mass. Their wants must be satisfied and increased with the habit of satisfaction. During the past hundred years every European state has made a great stride in the direction of arousing its poorer citizens to be more wholesomely active, discontented, and expectant; but our own country has succeeded in traveling farther in this direction than has any other, and it may well be proud of its achievement. That the American political and economic system has accomplished so much on behalf of the ordinary man does constitute the fairer hope that men have been justified in entertaining of a better worldly order; and any higher social achievement, which America may hereafter reach, must depend upon an improved perpetuation of this process. The mass of mankind must be aroused to still greater activity by a still more abundant satisfaction of their needs, and by a consequent increase of their aggressive discontent.

— Herbert Croly, *The Promise of American Life*. Published by The Macmillan Company.

No one who has worked a farm would suggest that there is some one simple solution to the problem of mechanizing agriculture. All too often in the past we have concluded that since there was one big farm problem there must be one big solution. If the answer to the problem we are facing here must be reduced to one generality, that would not be a specific program, but a method of approach to the whole problem. This would go far beyond the narrow concept of efficiency. It would be rather an application of vigorous imagination to the actual needs of a various and resourceful people.

An idea so general has meaning only when you bring it down to cases. Very well, here is Case One. It is found in a relatively prosperous farming area with medium to large-size farms. During the past few years prices have been good. Everyone has money in the bank; a few have considerable sums. After the war it is not going to be necessary to make any major changes in the local farm setup. Unlike many of the most prosperous farm regions today, this particular one is not faced with the problem of returning grain land to grass, or drastic reduction of herds, or abandonment of heavy capital expenditures for big war production. One man who has one of the smaller farms has made enough profit to buy three thousand dollars' worth of war bonds. He knows, however, that under average conditions his land will not produce enough economically to give his family a decent standard of living. He has a son in the tank corps. The boy never cared much for farming, but ever since they bought their first tractor he spent every possible minute tinkering with the machinery. That is why he is a mechanic in the Army today. Some day he is coming home.

His father decides to invest his savings in big farm machinery when machinery is available. His neighbors would like to have the use of a field ensilage harvester, a combine, a manure-loader, a chain saw to cut cord wood in the winter, a pickup baler. No one of them can buy machines like these for himself. But a father and son doing custom work with such heavy tools will have plenty of work in the neighborhood the year around. For the returning soldier there will be a job with machines he knows how to work and likes. For his father there will be a good use for his savings and a chance to earn a good, steady income.

That is one way of solving the problem for farms that are too small to support heavy machinery costs alone. It does not have to be a father-and-son combination. A young man returning from the Army might be able to borrow enough money to establish himself in this business. A group of them might form a company in highly concentrated farm areas. The essential elements are sufficient capital, a knowledge of machinery and farm conditions, and a neighborhood in which the machinery can be used profitably. The difficulty with this solution is that there are too few areas in which all three of these elements are present. It would be no major part of the solution to the general problem of mechanizing agriculture.

Case Two has a wider application. Here the farms are smaller. Most of the farmers have been making a fair living, but no one has saved up enough to buy the tools that a custom-work farm business would require. The greatest asset of this community is the fact that the farmers have learned to work together. During the machinery shortages and labor shortages of wartime they got into the habit of helping one another out of a jam. When a neighbor's hay was down and black thunderheads were gathering in the west, the man across the road and his friend down at the fork brought their side-delivery rakes, hay-loaders, and teams and put the hay in the barn before the three-day rain started. They had supported a milk producers' co-operative for years. They had had experience in working out community solutions to their problems. Most important, they understood that working together meant giving up small individual advantages to gain the big benefits.

It is natural for farmers with such background to solve the machinery problem co-operatively. A group of them meet and decide that by contributing a few hundred dollars each they can buy the most essential heavy tools. That will give them a start on a co-operative machinery pool. The machines will be owned co-operatively, and the directors of the co-operative will determine how they are to be used. As capital accumulates from payments for the use of the machines, expenses can be met and new tools bought. As in the first case, it will be easy to find competent operators from among the young men returning from the war with the essential skill they gained from their experience with the machines of battle.

— Ayers Brinser, "Don't Plow Us Under," *Harper's Magazine*, vol. 190, No. 1141, pp. 668–669 (June, 1945). Reprinted by permission of the author and *Harper's*.

Before it is very long, I am of opinion that you will both think and speak more favorably of woman than you do now. You seem to think that from Eve downwards, they have done a great deal of mischief. As for that lady, I give her up to you: but since her time, history will inform you that men have done much more mischief in the world than women; and, to say the truth, I would not advise you to trust either, more than is absolutely necessary. But this I will advise you to, which is, never to attack whole bodies of any kind; for, besides that all general rules have their exceptions, you must unnecessarily make yourself a great number of enemies, by attacking a corps collectively. Among women, as among men, there are good as well as bad; and it may be full as many, or more, good than among men. This rule holds as to lawyers, soldiers, parsons, courtiers, citizens, etc. They are all men, subject to the same passions and sentiments, differing only in the manner, according to their several educations; and it would be as imprudent as unjust to attack any of them by the lump. Individuals forgive sometimes; but bodies and societies never do. Many young people think it very genteel and witty to abuse the clergy; in which they are extremely mistaken: since in my opinion, parsons are very like men, and neither the better nor the worse for wearing a black gown. All general reflections, upon nations and societies, are the trite, threadbare jokes of those who set up for wit without having any, and so have recourse to commonplace. Judge of individuals from your own knowledge of them, and not from their sex, profession, or denomination. — Lord Chesterfield, *Letters to His Son.*

The regulations of streams by storage reservoirs is really an imitation of what nature is able to accomplish by the forests. Forests at the sources of the streams are veritable storage reservoirs, and without them no artificial remedy can be either adequate or permanent. Erosion destroys reservoirs, and must be controlled if reservoirs are to succeed. This can be done only by conserving or restoring the forests. The forest cover alone can reduce the amount of sediment carried by water, and make possible the permanent improvement of inland waterways. To check erosion by reforestation, work must begin in the highlands, because there the slopes are the steepest, the rainfall greatest, and the action of frost most considerable, and therefore the process of erosion is most rapid and the results most destructive. — Gifford Pinchot.

The only difference between organisms which annually produce eggs or seeds by the thousand, and those which produce extremely few, is, that the slow-breeders would require a few more years to people, under favorable conditions, a whole district, let it be ever so large. The condor lays a couple of eggs and the ostrich a score, and yet in the same country the condor may be the more numerous of the two; the Fulmar petrel lays but one egg, yet it is believed to be the most numerous bird in the world. One fly deposits hundreds of eggs, and another, like the hippobosca, a single one; but this difference does not determine how many individuals of the two species can be supported in a district. A large number of eggs is of some importance to those species which depend on a fluctuating amount of food, for it allows them rapidly to increase in number. But the real importance of a large number of eggs or seeds is to make up for much destruction at some period of life; and this period in a great majority of cases is an early one. If an animal can in any way protect its own eggs or young, a small number may be produced, and yet the average stock be fully kept up; but if many eggs or young are destroyed, many must be produced, or the species will become extinct. It would suffice to keep up the full number of a tree, which lived on an average for a thousand years, if a single seed were produced once in a thousand years, supposing that this seed were never destroyed, and could be insured to germinate in a fitting place. So that, in all cases, the average number of any animal or plant depends only indirectly on the number of its eggs or seeds. — Charles Darwin.

Chapter 4

THE PROCESS OF PLANNING AND WRITING

Selecting an Appropriate Subject. Many of the papers which you will write in college will be on subjects chosen or prescribed by the occasion or by some person, such as your instructor in a course in history, or political science, or sociology. Some of your papers will be summaries or reports based on assigned reading. Some will be more or less brief discussions in answer to examination questions. Such situations as these will place their own limitations upon what you will say, how you will organize your material, and what attitude you will adopt toward your material.

Frequently, however, especially in a course in English composition, you will be given a broad or general subject, which you must narrow down to a usable topic, or a type of writing to experiment with, such as a personal essay, a profile, a narrative sketch, or a pattern of structure to imitate. The choice of specific subject will be left to you. The suggestions which follow are designed to help you explore the various resources at your command. If you do not need this help, no harm has been done. The suggestions are here; you may turn to them if you feel the need of help, or you may use better ideas of your own.

It is too often true, however, that many students spend twice as much time wondering what they should write about as they do in actual writing. There is a story about W. Somerset Maugham, the English novelist and playwright, which is apropos. He once urged a young friend of his to try his hand at writing a book. "But I haven't anything to write about," objected his friend. "My boy," replied Mr. Maugham, "that is the most inconclusive reason for not writing that I have ever heard." Very true. The world is full of people who have nothing to say and who say it at great length. Theirs is an ancient art. Who among us has not coveted it at times — yearned for the power to summon words, many words, and to command them to do our bidding: On the other hand there is the story of the New England farmer who was locally famous as a trainer of sheep dogs. "How do you do it?" inquired a lady. "I can't train my dog to do a single trick." "Well," replied the farmer, "first you have to know more than the dog." To the inexperienced writer it is a comfort to know more about something than does his reader.

Everything that you know has come to you, in one way or another, through personal experience. You have learned by living, by doing things, by going to school, by reading, by observing, and by listening. As a convenient grouping of subjects about which you know something, through the fact that you have lived, read, observed, and listened, let us try the following:

1. Home and family
2. School and college
3. Work
4. Sports and games
5. Hobbies and amusements
6. Friends and social life
7. Religion and morals

Now let us try narrowing these general subjects to something more specific and usable.

The Autobiographical Sketch. Instead of writing a narrative account of your life, listing in chronological order such items as when you were born, who your parents were, where you went to school, where you lived, etc., tell about the development of some one important interest or attitude in your life. Tell about the development of your interest in music, about your religious life, about your attitude toward democracy or toward a life work. On the following page is a plan which some students have used successfully:

[Title] TOWARD SUNLIT UPLANDS

I. Earliest ideas about God and heaven
   A. Influence of home training
   B. Influence of Sunday School
II. The influences of church membership
   A. Social activities
   B. Music and ceremony in church ritual
III. Tempering influences of books and friends
IV. More mature concepts
   A. The restraining hand of habit
   B. Disturbing effects of scientific study
   C. Period of spiritual uncertainty
   D. Broadening perspectives

The following paper, written by a college student, illustrates one method in which the "development of an attitude" may be handled.

[Title] NOVEMBER SEVENTH, NINETEEN FORTY–FOUR

November 7, 1944. It was a dark day in the Willamette Valley. The skies, cloudy and dull, showed promise of rain by night. It was about three o'clock as I started on my way over to Precinct 11 to place my little "✕" in the square that favored my candidate. As I walked along through the autumn leaves, I wasn't thinking so much of the political aspects of this election, as of what this day meant in my own life. In the past I had done my thinking and my arguing on politics; now I was confident that my way of voting was the right way.

As I neared the school yard where the precinct voting headquarters were located, I came across a group of first- and second-graders fighting. One of them, a tiny, poorly-dressed child from the wrong side of town, had downed her little brother. The other youngsters were pelting her with hard walnuts gathered from the trees near by. I couldn't help looking back then to my first day of school and to the small, red-haired little boy who stood crying on the front steps of the schoolhouse. Even then he was afraid of what the world had to offer him. I couldn't help wondering if he might somehow have known that the world wasn't going to be particularly kind to him. What he is now and where he is, I don't know. I don't think I want to know. Even before he completed junior high school, he had spent several months in the Boys' Training School at Woodburn.

This little red-haired boy was my first contact with the poor, or as they grew to be known, "the kids from down in the hollow." As I look over those years of high school and grade school, I wonder just how much we were all affected by the political and economic status of our country. In the early thirties, I recall the days when my father would come home bearing the news of the loss of another staff member or the further cut in salaries. Because I was young, it didn't affect me particularly. Most of the talk was in big words about sabbaticals and leaves of absence. I learned to know that the words meant someone else had gone and later I knew that these words meant that these same people wouldn't come back.

About that time politics and political debate became the center of national attention and I followed the talk of Roosevelt and the New Deal plans. He was to be the man who would lead us out of the depression brought about by Hoover and the Republicans. Later our friends talked about the alphabet era, or the manner in which Roosevelt created alphabetical agencies whenever he wanted to do away with some form of social menace. Yes, I heard their talk, but I watched, too, the rise of these letter organizations. Each summer I traveled through the parks and along the highways sheltered by forest lands preserved by young men known by the letters CCC. I met men and women who created murals and similar works of art through the WPA organization. Many of these men and women I had known when jobs were scarce and their living had been lean. This new life didn't look so wrong to me.

Through my junior-high-school teachers and their friends I heard the taunts of "He's just an unemployed bum." They wouldn't have listened if I could have argued with them, but to me these men weren't bums. They had been unemployed just because there was no work for them.

The talk of politics dropped off a bit in those first years of Roosevelt's administration, and we all watched the rise of the air-machine age. We listened far into the night to the tales of the great Hindenburg disaster, but we didn't worry much about what was happening in Asia between those two Oriental countries, China and Japan. About that time some people began to warn us of the importance of Japan's belligerence, but we passed it off as the idle play of some faraway brown-skinned folk we knew little about.

There was a slight flurry of Landon buttons after about four years of political silence, but the country wasn't willing to change. During the next four years I thought little of national trends, for getting ahead in the new world of ninth, tenth, and eleventh grades took up my time. Mine was a world of high-school parties, committee meetings, and friendly bull sessions. Then came my senior year of high school. I had tired of high-school activities and was just waiting for the time when I could enter into that world of gilt and frills known as college. Little did I know then that the talk of the fourth term would change to echoes of war in Europe and college boys leaving behind them the old jalopy out in front of the frat house, and the sweet smells of perfume and the misty tulle of the girl friend's newest formal.

These were the thoughts that passed through my head as I walked up to cast my vote on November 7 of the year 1944. By then there were no more college days such as I had known that first year. There were only a lot of boys in uniform stopping for a while in the shelter of a college campus. There were some who thought that by voting for the newest candidate they could bring forth a house cleaning in Washington and perhaps a new life. And then there were others like myself who were casting their ballots in hopes of bringing that Utopia so many of us want — a "lasting peace." In my heart I was hoping to break this long and endless period of waiting. I wanted a chance to go back and take the girl, her little brother, and the red-haired kid by the hand and lead them into a world where no one would be known as "that kid from down in the hollow."

Another interesting method of treating autobiographical material is to concentrate on the development of your dominant trait of character or personality. First, analyze yourself and your nature. Are you an introvert or an extrovert? Are you normally happy, gloomy, irritable, friendly, lonely, timid? What has made you the way you are? Write a paper in which you explain yourself. The following are a few suggestions for thesis sentences that you might use:

1. For eighteen years I have lived with fear.
2. My life has been dominated by the fact that I am an only child.
3. It is a tragic thing that a girl's personality can be moulded by the fact that she wears thick glasses and has a bad complexion.
4. I am the child of divorced parents.
5. All my life I have never been allowed to forget that my parents were born in Europe.

The Autobiographical Incident. If you choose to write about some interesting experience of yours, you should discard the obvious possibilities, such as the automobile accident, the trip to the mountains, the boating accident, the big fire downtown.

Much more effective is some apparently minor incident, so written that it acquires importance in the telling. The following is an example of an autobiographical incident handled in this way by a student in college:

[Title] PRELUDE TO BEAUTY

I had no idea for what purpose she had come, or how long she would stay. I only knew that the sight of her delighted me tremendously. From the first she appealed to me as no other mature woman had done. She was a striking woman, forceful without hauteur, and when she relaxed at her desk, I saw that she was beautiful without beauty.

She did not review the dull lessons of our former teacher, but offered us a project of fascinating proportions. She was a craftsman, I said to myself, who loved her craft.

She asked us to write of our birthplaces. Ashamed of the fact that mine was a farmhouse, I wrote of Myrtle Point, a town in which my grandparents lived. For thirty minutes she watched us impersonally, while pens scratched feverishly at twenty desks. Of the papers that she read, mine, which had never pleased the regular teacher, she praised for an eloquence prompted only by a loving heart and a pair of observant eyes.

It was the first praise I had had since I entered a graded school. But it was compensation enough for the shabby dress, tight braids of hair, coarse stockings, and thick shoes which were right enough for little girls but not good for young ladies who wanted the favor of their teachers and the respect of their classmates. Such a windfall of approval made me eager to do another theme for this remarkable teacher. I resolved to do something even better, and more bona fide than "My Birthplace." Before going to bed that night I had ready my new theme, "Our Farmhouse at Sundown."

In the morning, so eager was I to return to school, I awakened before daybreak. Although I felt much too grown-up for such a juvenile costume, Mother insisted that I wear my blue rubberized raincape and storm rubbers. I reached the schoolhouse before the doors were unlocked, but protected my theme from the gusty, frail rain by waiting in the play-shed.

The janitor and two of my classmates approached this shelter. "I suppose you youngsters know your teacher was killed on her way to school this morning." With his long-handled rake the janitor prodded a shelf of sodden leaves.

"Not Miss Rigdon?" I murmured.

"Yep." More prodding of leaves. More gusts of rain on the play-shed roof. "A car got her, an ottermobile."

In common with all desolate figures, I asked only to be left to myself. After school, I eluded Bertha and Wilhelmina in order to walk home alone.

As I pushed toward the west, I left the last mist of the rain behind. Standing on the summit of Reservoir Hill, I saw the cup-like valley fill up with a golden light the overflow of which touched my very feet and glossed with gold my rubbers and the hem of my raincape. I began to descend the hill, finding every blade of grass, every thread-bare leaf filmed with a rainbow. I looked at the sky and could not describe it. Yet over the wooden bridge into our barnyard I saw the colored vapors drift and assemble until a frail cathedral of light had risen straight above the lower pasture bars. I swallowed audibly. This was sorrow. This was grief. This was the pain of a beauty too great to bear.

I thought to myself — the artisans of heaven are building a mansion for one that I love.

It surprised me to recall how brief a time I had known Miss Rigdon. Yet in one day I was certain that I had made and lost a friend.

As the sky darkened and the cathedral melted into blackness, my raincape rustled around my ankles. In my heart were two admonitions: I must hurry; I must reach home before the storm. I repeated to myself the beautiful words which I had discovered: the artisans of heaven are building a mansion for one that I love. I liked the sound of them, but I didn't know why. In a short time I would repeat them to my mother. If they were beautiful, she would know.

But when I reached home, Mother was plucking clothes from the line — muslin underwear, billowing nightgowns, sheets, pillowcases, tablecloths.

"Hurry and help me," she directed, "before it rains."

I wanted to tell her about the cathedral, about the death of Miss Rigdon, but I couldn't speak. Perhaps she would laugh if I said I had just seen the artisans of heaven building a mansion for someone that I loved.

I was just a bit suspicious of the words myself. Mere words shouldn't give one such an unreasonable joy. But I loved them, oh how I loved them. That night, until I went to sleep, I held those words in my mouth like the bread of some strange communion. Finally, long after the house was still, I choked on the fumes of a sulphur match, lifted a yawning lamp-chimney, and with a shaking hand scrawled softly in my school notebook: Today I watched the artisans of heaven build a mansion for one that I love.

Interpretations of Home and Friends. You can always find
material for descriptive and expository papers in your home life

— anything from short profiles of your father or your mother to longer discussions interpreting your family life in terms of its relation to American democracy. Here are the main headings of a sentence outline for a five-paragraph interpretation handed in by a college freshman:

[Title] THIS IS AMERICA

I. Mine is just a plain, ordinary, middle-class American family.
II. Mom is a typical American mother — only more so.
III. Dad is a happy Irish American garage mechanic, proud as sin of his son in the service and his daughter in college.
IV. Howard and I, the kids of the family, are just like fifty million other American youngsters.
V. Our family life has been a healthy, normal life, worth cultivating and worth fighting for.

If you care to use this idea, you can easily adapt it to suit your own material. Or you can take a single brief incident out of your home life and make it interesting and significant. This is how one college freshman told about going home for the first vacation:

[Title] GOING BACK

It was nine thirty Wednesday night as our taxi turned the familiar corner by the church and stopped before my home. The block was surrounded by parked cars, and mellow light from the large windows of the main auditorium of the church displayed their beautifully colored story pictures for the people on the streets. These lights meant home to me. These cars meant friends, and companions, and song. Here were people I knew and loved; here were people who sang, and let me sing with them; here I had been taught, rebuked, congratulated, chided, encouraged; here were people and affairs that I missed at school.

I knew that it was just about time for the threefold Amen which would close this choir practice, and as I raced up the stairs to Mother, I knew that I wanted to sing those last eight measures again. I knew that I wanted to sing in the choir. You can sing at the dinner table at school or with a group of girls in your room, but nothing compares with the music sung by a church choir.

My eyes smarted with tears as I realized what my words would tell Mother — I wanted to go to other people before I went to my family!

Yet, as I told her, we both knew that this was not true. I had not sung in the choir for six months, and had heard the familiar voices only twice since school began in the fall. Mother remembered those stormy nights when we lived at the Clarendon house, and I had spent my last bus tokens to go to choir practice. Mother remembered those days when colds made it impossible for me to sing, yet I had gone to choir practice to learn the music just in case I was well on Sunday. How could she forget those dull Saturday mornings when I completely monopolized the air with my practice on the third line of the fourth page? Mother had not forgotten those evenings when the younger choir members had taken possession of her living room to harmonize "just for fun" or to practice for a concert. Mother knew the eagerness and anxiety I felt as I asked her to forgive me.

The church door emitted the same old complaining squeak and closed with the familiar thud as I entered through the side entrance. I skipped the third step, as I remembered its noisy creak, and tiptoed through the side wing and around to the rear of the main auditorium. My heart was pounding and I could hardly get my breath. I felt silly! Why should I be so excited and frightened? Did I really know these people? Would they understand this crazy visit? How would they react to it? Everything came at once. There were the new members; I wanted to meet them. There was the new choir director; I wanted to meet her. There was a small matter concerning the treasurer's account which I needed to check with the president. At least I had a practical reason for this sudden appearance.

I slipped quietly into the last pew and folded my hands to keep them from shaking. Familiar heads started and then nodded friendly greetings. Old friends smiled and new faces peered quizzically into the shadows at the back of the room. I fought the knowledge that the new director could feel nothing but annoyance toward the stranger who disrupted the attention of her singers. Instead, I relaxed into a comfortable feeling of hominess.

"They certainly need some good sopranos, and the basses need several deeper and older voices. But the war has changed all this, too. If only those few who are left could feel the strong sense of duty and faithfulness which Mrs. Roth expresses through her attendance and her voice. A choir needs people who feel it their obligation to give their utmost when they are singing the praises of God, but Mrs. Roth expresses hers too loudly for the rest of the choir. If she were twenty years younger, her volume might add greatly to the quality of the singing, but she isn't, and her voice tells the story."

These were my conscious thoughts. A deeper meaning was voiced by my subconscious as I walked home in the cold night.

"I hadn't appreciated the enjoyment and relaxation those choir hours had given me during the past years. I had not understood how much I loved that type of music and those words. They had to be taken from me before I learned how highly I valued them."

Occupations. The profession you expect to enter after you leave college, the work you have done during your vacations, or the job that you have while you are attending college — all have material for many interesting discussions. Here are two or three suggestions.

If you have ever worked at a serious job anywhere, plan a descriptive paper which will give the reader a vivid, detailed picture of your first day on the job. Use a narrative framework on which to hang your details. Use word pictures constantly; give your impressions of the appearance of the place, pictures of people as types and as individuals, sense impressions of sounds and smells.

If you have decided on your life occupation, you may write a serious analytical discussion of your chosen profession. The following scheme may give you a few hints as to how to treat your subject.

[Title]   ENGINEERING IS MY LIFE

I. Opportunities in the profession of engineering
   A. Industrial
      1. Reconstruction of war-torn countries
      2. Development of backward countries
      3. Transportation
         a. Railroads
         b. Ocean transportation
         c. Air transportation
         d. Highways
      4. Chemistry
         a. Plastics
         b. Textiles
   B. Public service
      1. Reclamation projects
      2. Governmental projects
   C. Broadening experiences of travel

II. Desirable personal qualities
  A. Interest in scientific processes
  B. Love of outdoor life
  C. Creative imagination
  D. Capacity to grow
III. Necessary preparation for the profession
  A. Adequate professional training
  B. Vital need of wide cultural training
    1. Thorough training in writing and speech
    2. Command of some foreign language
    3. The social sciences
    4. Psychology
    5. Wide reading
IV. The personal satisfactions in the profession
  A. Assurance of a lifelong job
  B. Association with interesting people
  C. Constant variety of work
  D. Satisfaction of doing something for mankind

The following short essay deals almost entirely with preparation for a certain occupation or profession. It should give you a few ideas on how to develop your own subject.

[Title] TEXTILES

The more I have thought over the problem of education in preparation for work in the textile industries the more hesitation I feel in attempting to give advice. The difficulty is that the requirements are so varied according to the particular position to be filled. The qualities and the training demanded of a chief executive are quite different from those which are called for in departmental supervision or in management of production and yet they are all related. However, in order to reach the top it is necessary to pass successfully through the other stages and so we must evidently prepare for mill work as a fundamental requisite upon which to base promotion. Here we face a real perplexity. If we first train ourselves to be good, practical, technical mill men and don't round out and broaden our minds we may succeed in becoming valuable aids without ever being able to qualify for promotion to the higher places even when in the course of time the opportunity arrives. The truth is that preparation is a lifelong affair and that as we pass through each grade we must be expanding our understanding and our ambitions and equipping ourselves to comprehend and to master the requirements of the next.

In actual life we shall find that this broadening process, or shall I call it habit, is not a thing that can be taken up at some convenient time in the future when we feel that we want to make a move. It has to be established early in life before we are cramped by the routine and burden of daily toil.

I am taking it for granted that our purpose is to train youth for the top of the profession or at least so to train it that it will have a chance at reaching the top and, therefore, I am going to be strenuous about this matter of providing a broad base of culture, vision, and general fitness for the highest positions.

With the great growth and evolution of industry, business administration has come to be something quite different from being merely the big boss. To be the head of a great industrial organization has become a real profession and one which calls for a more varied training and as great abilities as any other. The modern textile industrial leader must have a technical foundation, a good understanding of mechanics, and, if possible, of chemistry. He must understand style and fashion and maintain contact with the sources of style and fashion. He should be, if not an artist, at least one who has artistic appreciation. He must be something of a sociologist and a psychologist and know how to lead and to command. He must be an economist and a financier. He must be in touch with and take his place in public affairs, watch politics and governmental processes. He must be a man of the world and have the ability to represent his organization adequately before the world. He will often be called upon to speak upon a wide range of subjects.

If he starts life with a narrow outlook and a limited vision he will never catch up. If, in his riper years, he is to measure up to these tests he must begin with his eyes and his spirit open.

If possible he should go to college and while there he should fill himself with those things which he will find it hard to obtain in the outside world. That is to say, he should avail himself of this one opportunity to become a cultivated gentleman. Fill himself with history, with literature, with psychology, and with the languages (living and dead). He should have a grounding in physics and chemistry.

When he has graduated from this course in mental development he can specialize in some one of the sciences as well as in some technical course. What he wants is an education plus specialized training. He must not fall into the common error of thinking that a specialized training is an education. If he reverses this order and satisfies himself with a technical education he will find out when it is too late that he is handicapped if not crippled.

The main thing is that he should take this course seriously and not look upon this great chance as a four years' postponement of work with social life and athletics as the main issues.

Travel is a wonderful educator if it is intelligent travel done with eyes open and mind at work. Mere touring either in foreign lands or at home is usually time half wasted. The most interesting and usually the most pleasant travel is that done with some business purpose and when possible with some business contact with the countries visited. More than half of the value of travel is in seeing and meeting new people and in absorbing their points of view and their philosophies. Time spent in school and college in learning the languages will pay big dividends when the time comes to travel. A very fine finish would be a course in one of the European textile schools. This would serve the double purpose of completing the technical education and making the command of the language become a vital thing.

All of the foregoing does not make an education, but it is a good preparation for an education which must be obtained in the university of life.

When the young man is ready for it he should go into the mill and work, labor with his hands and look the world in the face. Learn to know and to understand and to respect the other laborers and gain their respect and confidence and then never miss a chance to observe and study what is going on. Always ask questions of all sorts of people. Beat them at their own game, and promotion will take care of itself.

— Charles Cheney, "Textiles," from Edward L. Bernays, *An Outline of Careers*. Reprinted by permission of Edward L. Bernays.

The Profile. A profile is a short biographical sketch which depends for its effect on a few well-chosen, vivid facts and details. The subject of a successful profile need not be famous — or notorious; as a matter of fact, the writer of a profile often takes some totally obscure person and tries to make the reader feel that that person is worth knowing. On the other hand, many profiles, like some of those in the *New Yorker*, are of celebrities. You may take your choice.

As an example of a typical short *New Yorker* profile, read pages 20–21.

Write a profile of one of your college teachers (not the one who will read it, please!), one whom you know fairly well. Select one whom you like and admire. Go to the library and consult some local "who's who" in education or science for background facts. Then organize your profile on the basis of a number of the following divisions.

I. An interview, in which you introduce your subject and give us a quick picture of his appearance.
II. A glimpse of him at work, in class or in his office.
III. A cutback to the facts about his career, education, etc.
IV. His dominant traits.
V. A typical classroom performance (your big scene).
VI. What others say about him.

You need not use all of these divisions, but if you want to compress, remember that I, III, and V are pretty essential. The others are expendable.

If you want to do a more ambitious biographical piece, one that will take you to some of the reference books in the library, try writing a biographical sketch of 1. the author of the book you are reading; 2. a pioneer of your locality; 3. the man who represents you in Congress; 4. a well-known scientist who is connected with your college or university. Be careful to give all your borrowed information in your own words!

Discussions Based on Reading. If your instructor wishes you to write a formal "book report," he will probably give you explicit directions to follow.

A more informal paper of another kind, however, has possibilities. Assume that you are going to recommend a book which you have enjoyed reading by discussing three or four reasons why you liked it. Do not attempt to criticize or judge it. This sort of paper is entirely interpretation. First ask yourself why you liked the book — because of its humor, its philosophy, its unusual characters, because it took you to new lands, thrilled you with action, revealed to you the secrets of the human mind, or whatever the reasons were. In your opening paragraph or two give us briefly the facts about the book, the author, perhaps the type of book it is. It may be necessary to summarize the contents of the book very, very briefly. Then in a paragraph apiece present your two or three reasons for liking the book. Many professional reviews fall into this pattern, as you may see from the following.

[Title] *RICKSHAW BOY*, BY LAU SHAW

When Happy Boy, the rickshaw puller who is the protagonist of Lau Shaw's excellent novel, has all but lost his faith in himself and in human decency, he is suddenly released from a part of the evil that has plagued his life, and he reflects:

> Evil men would all meet with evil, and come in the end to die: the soldiers who stole his rickshaw; Madame Yang, who starved her servants; Tiger Girl, who had cheated and oppressed him; Fourth Master, who despised him; Sun, the detective who had swindled him of his money; the Second Wife, Ch'en, who had made a fool of him; and Madame Hsia, who had seduced him — all were doomed, all must die. Only Happy Boy — the loyal, simple, honest Happy Boy — would go on living, would live forever!

That this passage is written not without its share of irony is made plain when Happy Boy shortly after finds his hopes for the future shattered. But it is also a fair summary of the content of this novel, which is both a lively picture of city life in contemporary China and a record of the endurance of a virtuous man.

In the company of Happy Boy, the reader learns a great deal about rickshaw pulling. He learns what it is to run along the broad avenues and through the twisting alleys of Peking in the teeth of a winter wind and in the suffocating dusty heat of midsummer. He wanders through the city's parks on holidays, looking at the big white dagoba and the ornamental lakes. He sees life in tea-shops and private homes and stinking hovels; he learns to fear bicycles, chauffeurs, and policemen; he understands the worth of a hot cup of tea after a long run and the pleasures of a good belch after a meal of meat balls. But the reader learns all this without any feeling of coming into contact with the exotic or the picturesque, and though the book has something of the fascination of a novel of roguery, it has the added value of communicating an admirably strong sense of the real.

Even more vividly revealed than the city are the characters. There is Tiger Girl, her girlhood long since spent, who preys on Happy Boy's manhood. There is Little Lucky One, with whom Happy Boy falls in love. There is old Master Liu, Tiger Girl's father. In his youth he bought and sold women, but now he is a "reformed" character and he grudgingly gives the men who rent his rickshaws a free meal on his sixty-ninth birthday. There is Kao Ma, the Ts'ao family's very practical amah. She lends small sums of money at high rates of interest and only on the best security. And there is Madame Hsia, who puts on a delicate pink smock and pale green trousers to stimulate Happy Boy's passions. In a rather different vein, there is Mr. Ts'ao, a professor who has picked up some notions of Socialism from reading William Morris and who tries to do what he can for the poor. The ironic touches in the author's treatment of him suggest that he is in part a self-portrait.

In harmony with both scene and character is the vigorous, pungent language, particularly that used in the conversations. For once in a novel set in China, the characters of the street speak as they would in everyday life, and Evan King has been able to preserve in English most of the flavor of the original phrases. Occasionally a colloquial idiom loses something because of a too literal translation.

Alive and colorful as all this is, it is the nature of Happy Boy himself that gives the novel its depth. Born in the country and orphaned at an early age, Happy Boy comes to Peking, bringing with him as his only guides the maxims on which he has been raised. He puts his faith in the classic virtues of honor, ambition, loyalty, and integrity. That the maxims often appear to be proved false puzzles and discourages him, but he persists doggedly in following them. He hardens under the impact of experience and he grows desperate when he is in the clutches of Tiger Girl, but he still listens to "the frail voice that calls one to the way of virtue." He runs head on into public treachery and personal vice. Both passive and aloof at first, he eventually begins to feel a little for his fellows, who, like himself, are the helpless victims of social disorder, and he expresses his feelings (much to the relief of at least one reader) not by mouthing political platitudes but by sharing his cigarettes and buying another round of drinks. Only after he has been defeated time after time does he act. That the outcome of his rescue of Little Lucky One from prostitution is left somewhat obscure is of little importance. The simple fact of his acting is the climax of the story.

— A review by John J. Espey, in the New York *Herald Tribune Weekly Book Review*, July 29, 1945. Reprinted by permission.

Directions, Processes, Organizations. The "how to do it" literature of America is impressive in extent but pitifully unimpressive in literary quality. More than a generation ago Stewart Edward White wrote a "how to do it" theme on "Making Camp," which remains the one dependable example when one is in a hurry to find something better than the usual directions in a cook book or a manual of dressmaking. The ability to give accurate directions is extremely important, however, and should be cultivated strictly for its pedestrian, unliterary virtues. Here are a few suggestions that you may find useful:

1. Take two points rather far apart in your city, such as your home in the suburbs and a downtown theater. Write a short paper of directions in which you tell a total stranger to the city how to reach your home by starting from the point downtown. Do *not* once use any of the directions of the compass — north, east, south, west — in your explanation. Depend entirely on an accurate record of landmarks and distances.

2. Explain to an unmechanical friend how to start and drive a farm tractor. Do not use a single technical term without explaining it in clear, untechnical language.

3. Tell one of your younger friends what he is to do to register in college. Take him from one building to another, and explain every step of the procedure in words that he cannot fail to understand.

You have in this book two interesting "process" papers — one a short paragraph giving a recipe for ice-box rolls, page 74, the other a longer explanation of how a spider weaves a web, page 92. Read both before you attempt a process explanation of your own. Try explaining the entire process without once resorting to the imperative or the "impersonal you." Here are a few suggestions:

1. The V-Mail Letter	11. Taming a Wild Animal
2. Making a Blueprint	12. Delivering Newspapers
3. Life-saving Blood	13. One Issue of the College Paper
4. Making an Enlargement	14. Making Christmas Cards
5. Making a Bird-feeding Station	15. Learning to Swim
6. How to Sail a Boat	16. Training a Dog
7. How to Use a Fly Rod	17. Redecorating a Room
8. The Outdoor Fireplace	18. How to Model Clothes
9. An Informal Dinner Party	19. Operating an Elevator
10. Transplanting Wild Flowers	20. The "Hello" Girl's Day

An explanation of an organization calls for somewhat more extensive treatment than an explanation of a process. It is a particularly effective device for practicing outlining techniques, as you must be careful that your divisions are co-ordinate and that they are mutually exclusive and not overlapping. Here are a few topics that you may use:

1. The Red Cross
2. Your Fraternity or Sorority
3. The College You Are Attending
4. The Induction Center
5. The Boy Scouts of America
6. The 4-H Clubs
7. Camp Fire Girls or Girl Scouts
8. A Consumers' Co-operative
9. The County Fair
10. A Business Organization

"Local Color" Articles. America's literary renaissance after the Civil War began when writers realized that their own communities were worth writing about. Since that time the literature of "local color" has piled up until now its bulk — and probably its importance — exceeds that of any other type. Every section of America, every state, every city has its stories, poems, novels, and essays of praise or interpretation. The supply of good material is apparently inexhaustible.

You may treat the available "local color" material in various ways. For instance, you may choose to write an article based on reading in the library and, perhaps, on a few interviews. A project of this sort will be fairly ambitious, an article, let us say, of two thousand words or so. The article should be accompanied by an outline.

1. You may investigate the history of your community and write a paper on some interesting phase of it, such as a. the pioneer days, b. the coming of the railroad, c. the rivalry for the county seat, d. Civil War days, e. the founding of the college, etc.

2. You may investigate local science — geology, botany, etc. — and write an article on a. the geologic structure of the region, b. the birds of the region, c. the characteristic vegetation, etc.

3. You may look up the lives and achievements of some of the local celebrities and tell about their work.

There are undoubtedly unusual and interesting customs in your home community that can be explained in readable articles or essays. For a model illustrating this sort of paper read "Christmas Pantomime," pages 16–19.

Then there is always one's home community, a subject of infinite possibilities. One good way of treating this subject, a way which has been tried successfully by many students, is to begin with a personification of your home town, which you will use as the dominant theme of your whole analysis. Then organize your essay on the basis of five or six of the following topics:

1. Cultural opportunities
2. Industrial or business problems
3. Relation to democracy
4. The world of the adolescents
5. Adequacy of the school system
6. Politics
7. Plans for the future
8. Tribute to beauty: parks, homes, etc.
9. Recreation
10. Post-war reconstruction
11. Relation to surrounding communities
12. What the people live on

What do we mean by personifying a town, a city, or a community? Well, here is the way Dorothy Canfield Fisher began this sort of essay:

Everybody knows that New York State is a glowing, queenly creature, with a gold crown on her head and a flowing purple velvet cloak. The face of Louisiana is as familiar — dark-eyed, fascinating, temperamental. Virginia is a white-haired, dignified *grande-dame* with ancient, well-mended fine lace and thin old silver spoons. Massachusetts is a man, a serious middle-aged man, with a hard conscientious intelligent face, and hair thinned by intellectual application. And if I am not mistaken, Pennsylvania is a man too, a well-dressed business man, with plenty of money in his pockets and the consciousness of his prosperity written large on his smooth indoor face and in his kindly calculating eyes.

These State countenances are familiar to all of us, and many more; but back of this throng of affluent, thriving personalities, quite conscious of their own importance in the world, stands one, known to fewer Americans, lean, rather gaunt compared to the well-fed curves of the others, anything but fine, aristocratic, or picturesque. Yet the little group of mountaineers who know the physiognomy of Vermont from having grown up with it have the most crabbed, obstinate affection and respect for their State, which they see as a tall, powerful man, with thick gray hair, rough outdoor clothes, a sinewy axman's hand and arm, a humorous, candid, shrewd mouth and a weather-beaten face from which look out the most quietly fearless eyes ever set in any man's head.

— From *These United States*, edited by Ernest Gruening, published by Liveright Publishing Corporation. Reprinted by permission.

And here is the beginning of a 1500-word characterization written by a college freshman — a characterization which, by the way, called forth violent disagreement from other students whose homes were in the same town:

Capitol City, the hub of the State, is also the county seat of Marion County, having a population of 36,000. It is the home of all but two of the state institutions. Its principal industries are the growing of long-fiber flax and hops. It is an old city, as old as the days of Jason Lee and his Methodist mission of 1834, born out of the red mountains and the green earth of the Willamette valley. Here the purple-blue Polk hills in year-round dusk watch over a rain-filled river, and the sky broods with its burden of windy storms from the Pacific coast. Capitol City is old and lovely and quiet, a city of tall trees and spaced homes and wide streets. It is an old woman, who once had been a laughing girl who fought Indians and lighted bonfires in the pioneer trails, but who now sits gently, closing her eyes to the rest of the world and drawing her skirts over to cover her defects.

The Radio Talk. One of the popular present-day forms of writing is the radio talk, a tailored-to-measure informational article that demands careful organization, clear structure, a simple vocabulary, and a constant awareness of the interests and the intellectual capacities of the listeners. If you write one that you will actually speak over your college radio, you must read it aloud, time its length, and then rewrite it and trim it down carefully to fit the time that is allotted you. Just for practice, it may be fun to write a talk to fit five minutes, or ten minutes, or fifteen minutes. This sort of practice is the finest discipline in writing that you can give yourself.

For a subject, take some scientific development of current interest, such as the use of atomic energy, the discovery of penicillin, the treatment of neuropsychosis, read up on it in the library, and then adapt your technical material to your audience. The following is an excellent example of this sort of talk.

[Title] ARE THE PLANETS HABITABLE?

Ever since it was known that the planets were bodies more or less like the earth, people have asked: "Are there living things on them too?" This is a hard question, but by pooling the resources of most of the sciences, we can make a pretty good answer.

First, let us consider life on our earth for a bit. Our world would not be habitable if it did not have water on it. All living things are absolutely dependent on water. We digest our food, for example, only when it is dissolved in water in our stomachs. Moreover, this water must be liquid — neither ice nor gaseous water vapor, but ordinary liquid water. Many living things — such as the inner bark of trees — can survive being frozen and thawed out again; but nothing grows while it is frozen. And no living thing can stand having the water boiled out of it. Hence the temperature on a habitable planet must be above freezing part of the time, and below the boiling point all the time.

Light is necessary too. Practically all the food in the world is produced by green plants. These are the most marvelous laboratories in the world. Plants take in simple raw materials, carbon dioxide gas from the air and water with some things dissolved in it from the ground, and build up out of these, as they grow, all the complex substances of which they themselves are made, and some of which serve as food for animals. The plants get the energy required for this process from sunlight.

The waste product of the green-leaf laboratories is oxygen gas, which is turned back into the atmosphere. There is good reason to believe that the vast store of oxygen in the air has all been put in by plant life during the long course of geological time. Without plants, there would be no food for us animals to eat, nor oxygen-containing air for us to breathe.

There is, however, another geological process which takes oxygen out of the air. Most of the igneous rocks, which, like lava, have come up melted from below, contain a good deal of incompletely oxidized iron. As these rocks are "weathered," that is, broken down and carried off by rain and streams, the iron in them combines with more oxygen, taken from the air, and the originally black or gray rocks give rise to red or yellow sand, mud, or clay.

This is a one-way process, and one might fear that there might ultimately be no oxygen left in the air. But it works so slowly that there is no cause for alarm for a great many hundred million years to come.

If we inquire whether other planets are habitable, we must then try to find out whether their temperatures are suitable for life, whether they have water and atmospheres on them, and, if so, whether oxygen and carbon dioxide are present in these.

As for the composition of the atmospheres, certain gases, if present in them, absorb light of particular wave lengths. We therefore study the planet's light with a spectroscope — an instrument which can tune out and separate different wave lengths of light many hundreds of times more powerfully than your radio can separate two stations of nearly the same wave length. And with this sensitive device we can find whether or not oxygen, carbon dioxide, and water vapor are present in any considerable quantity, and, if so, can estimate their amounts.

Electrical heat-measuring devices can be made so sensitive that, when attached to a great telescope, they can measure the heat of a single candle 400 miles away. By measuring the heat from a planet with such equipment, it is possible after a good deal of calculation, to get a pretty close estimate of the temperature of its visible surface.

Measures of planetary heat show that Mercury, which is the nearest planet to the sun, has a noonday temperature of about 600 degrees, as measured on the Fahrenheit scale used in ordinary thermometers. For the remoter planets, Jupiter, Saturn, Uranus, Neptune, and Pluto, the temperatures range from 180 degrees to 300 degrees below zero. All these planets are evidently uninhabitable by any form of life known to science. The Moon, which we can observe in great detail, shows no trace of atmosphere or water, and must therefore also be a dead world.

This leaves for consideration only Venus and Mars. Venus is the least satisfactory planet to observe. She is surrounded by an atmosphere so hazy that it hides her solid surface. There is a large quantity of carbon dioxide in her atmosphere, but too little oxygen or water vapor to measure. The maximum surface temperature is probably about that of boiling water. This indicates strongly that there is no life on Venus. It is, however, very interesting to note that, except for the higher temperatures, conditions on Venus are decidedly similar to the theoretical picture of what our earth was like before life started on it.

Turning finally to the one remaining possibility, we find that Mars has a thin atmosphere, so that we can see the surface clearly. The planet has seasons like our own, and the heat measures indicate that, in the tropics, the temperature rises above freezing (to about 50 degrees) every day and falls below freezing every night. At the poles, the maximum temperature in summer is also about 50 degrees; the winters must be very cold.

White caps form at the poles of Mars every winter, and shrink almost to nothing in summer. This immediately suggests snow, and the temperatures confirm this beyond reasonable doubt. Hence there is water on Mars. The polar snows are, however, probably only a few inches thick, for spectroscopic observations show that there is little water vapor in the atmosphere. They indicate, too, that there is at present very little oxygen on Mars — not over a thousandth part of the amount above an equal area on earth. But there is strong reason to believe that there once was oxygen there, for most of the surface has the characteristic yellow-red color of weathered, oxidized material. There is nothing like this color on any other of the planets. The Moon, for example, which has no atmosphere, does not have a single red or yellow patch on it.

Mars, then, matches closely the theoretical picture of a planet in a late stage, when rock weathering has used up almost all the oxygen of the atmosphere. The darker parts of its surface show seasonal changes and are large and greener in summer than in winter. They probably represent surviving vegetation; but it has not been proved that some other explanation may not be possible. Whether animal life ever existed on Mars and whether it has been able to survive is at present beyond our finding out.

Outside the system composed of our sun and its circulating planets, there was no evidence for the existence of other planets till within the last three years. Recent precise photographic observations, however, show that several of the nearest stars have invisible companions, revolving about them, which can be detected because their attraction causes the bright stars to move in slightly wavy curves. The smallest of these companions are certainly dark bodies, and may fairly be called planets. We can find small companions of this sort only if they belong to some one of the few hundred stars which lie nearest to the sun. Among the many millions of remoter stars, there are very likely great numbers of them. Though the conditions for habitability are fairly stringent, there may well be thousands or more of habitable worlds among them.

Thus, in our own sun-planet system, there are only three possibly habitable bodies — Venus, the earth, and Mars. Life is in full blast on the earth; and has probably existed, and may still exist, on Mars. That is, life has scored twice out of three tries. It is therefore reasonable to suppose that, within the vast expanse of the universe, there may be very many other bodies which are actually the abodes of life.

With Mars at its nearest, a spot about eight miles in diameter would just be visible with a 100-inch telescope under ideal conditions, and a spot one-half as big with a 200-inch. There is obviously no hope of seeing individual animals. Inhabitants could be detected only if they were intelligent enough to construct large-scale engineering works.

Unfortunately we have to observe Mars through the ocean of air above our heads. This is always turbulent, and so the rays of light which fall on different parts of the telescope mirror are slightly but irregularly deviated, blurring the image, and it is not possible to see the finest details clearly enough to be certain what they are like.

A larger telescope collects more of this trouble, and the 200-inch is likely to be too big to give the best view of Mars. It was built for other purposes.

Even if we could observe with it often, under perfect conditions, it would be very hard to find out whether any queer things we saw on Mars were artificial, and the problem appears to be practically insoluble.

It is hardly reasonable to suppose that on all habitable worlds, life is in the same stage of evolution as on earth today. On some there may be only primitive forms; on others there may be living creatures far surpassing mankind in intelligence and character. What these forms of life, high or low, may be we have no way at all of finding out. The variety of living things, past and present, on our planet is vast. The material possibilities of life probably outrun the human imagination. Our race has possessed intellectual and moral capacities for something like a thousandth part of the time in which life has existed on earth, and the possibilities in this field presumably transcend our present powers of thought.

— A radio talk by Dr. Henry Norris Russell, one of a series, delivered by American scientists, on the New York Philharmonic-Symphony Program, sponsored by the United States Rubber Company. Reprinted by permission.

Personal Essays. Although the personal essay has been ridiculed or gently sniffed at by writers who are quivering to be on their way from where they are to where they are not, it is still a favorite with many writers and readers. Perhaps the decadence of the personal essay is a part of our restless civilization. It requires calmness of spirit, repose, and the ability to enjoy the flavor of life. Essentially, the personal essay is a discussion not of a subject but of a writer's attitude toward a subject. Its tone should be pleasant, easy, well-bred, never violent or argumentative.

For an example of the humorous personal essay read E. B. White's "Motor Cars" (from *One Man's Meat*), reprinted on pages 22–23 of this book. And below is an example of a personal essay written by a college freshman:

[Title] PENCIL TRACKS

A returned paper without the instructor's written criticism, no matter how good the grade may be, is like a drink of cold lemonade without any sugar in it. Nothing in the world is so disappointing; nothing leaves the student with such a flat feeling as does the search through the essay, the history report, or whatever the paper may be, for the note of praise or criticism which is not there. It is like cracking a nice large hazel nut and finding the shell empty.

They are such personal things — confidential words from the instructor to the student, which no one else may see or hear, unless the student chooses to show them to a pal. They mean a great deal more to him than the grade-mark up in the right-hand corner of the paper. Personally, I should rather receive a grade of C on a paper if it was accompanied by a note from the professor who graded it, than a nice big, red A without the note.

It doesn't make much difference where these notes are written, just so they are there. I have found them scattered here and there, at the top of the page, along the margins, and between the lines, all over my papers from one end of the page to the other. It is real sport hunting them, one that arouses a good deal of enthusiasm, especially when the hunter can be quite sure the end of the search is going to bring him the prize he is hoping for, a note which tells him what was good and what was bad in his paper.

It doesn't make much difference, either, to what racial class these notes belong. Whether they are red, green, blue, or just plain lead-gray, they accomplish their purpose just as efficiently as if they were written in gold.

Sometimes they are exceedingly difficult to decipher, owing to the fact that they tumbled into their places so fast they were slightly jammed and crowded into their corners; but they are there, and they tell the student everything he wants to know, frankly, quickly, and decisively just when he wants to know it the most.

There is no doubt about it. He likes to see them smile; but if they frown, he knows something he has written is all wrong and he'll have to get busy and make it right. How much easier it is to do that when those little notes keep repeating their message to him over and over again until he has satisfied their demands.

Some of them make the student's ears burn with their twinging, biting sarcasm. They arouse his anger, and he swears he'll "make the prof eat

137

those words yet." He reads them again and again until their meaning has been seared into his soul. It hurts; but he'll never again forget to cross his *t*'s or dot his *i*'s.

Then, of course, there are the prim, neatly written, fine exhibitions of penmanship that the student finds at the end of his paper, exactly three lines below the last line of his own writing. They are carefully indented, standoffish paragraphs of exposition. Very worthy, they are, as they would have the reader know. For my part, however, I prefer the scrawly ones perched intimately over the left ear of one of my phrases, or stepping on the toes of a flowery adjective.

No matter how they look, where they are, nor what they say, those confidential notes, in search of which the student eagerly scans his paper, are welcome. Without them, a grade of A-plus could not be perfect.

Occasionally, in the midst of carefully thought-out, well-organized, and well-documented research papers, a student is moved to do something different, like the following "theme" on Mother's Day which a college student handed in:

[Title] SHE MAKES THE BEDS

She makes the beds: she is in league
  With him who sends the boon of sleep.
She shakes the pillows, smooths the sheets,
  And when the evening shadows creep,
Who seeks his bed may shake away
  The cerements of his fatigue.
Oh, she who makes the beds each day
  Is of a quaint and godly league.

The patchwork quilt my mother made
  Is prayerful as a church in Lent.
Log cabins, stars, and bleeding heart
  Spring where her shining needle went.
The goose that pillows us in down
  A goodly, golden egg once laid —
Or so I dreamed it as I slept
  Beneath the quilts my mother made.

She makes the beds: how fair a task.
  I wonder will I do it well
Who have the formula and all
  To cast the same mesmeric spell.

> Will I bestow beloved sleep
>> With beds well-made on those who ask
> No greater boon than sleep at night —
>> I make the beds: how fair a task.

Or, as one student did, a college girl might be inspired to compose a charming "so sorry" note and give it to the instructor the day after she had cut class to spend a day shopping in the big city:

[Title] GIRL ON AN ESCALATOR

> If I could be,
> Like you, all loveliness,
> Impetuous, and brightly spun,
> And delicately gowned for ecstasy,
> I too would wind a bun
> Of honeyed hair against my head,
> And teeter on each tread
> Impatiently; and also, I confess,
> I'd spring ahead a step or two
> Unwilling to be carried, much less
> Thrust mechanically,
> As if I were a bit of milkweed in the breeze,
> A sea-gull on the sea,
> A poplar for chilly winds to seize.
> Oh, if I had the loveliness of you,
> The wit to fill each step with secret glee,
> I'd be, I'd seek, I'd do
> A thousand things, unheard of now.
> But then I have no plaint:
> God made me for a saint.
> Even these stairs
> Are heaven bent. My hands and brow
> Are plain
> And spent with pious prayers.
>
> But oh what loveliness just sped ahead:
> God, let me be a pagan when I'm dead.

Planning the Paper. The planning of your paper begins when your instructor tells you that you are to write, let us say, an eight-hundred-word theme on some local custom, on some new development of science, on the author of the book you happen to be reading — whatever the particular subject may be. You begin by thinking in terms of the space which you have to fill, just as the professional writer begins to plan when his editor asks him to write a five-hundred-word filler on a new grass for shady lawns, a two-thousand-word article on a new hybrid corn, or a six-thousand-word article on the commercial uses of radar. You begin to think in terms of space to fill and readers to interest. What do you have to say that is new, that has not been said over and over again, and, most important at the moment, that can be effectively said in eight hundred words? This process of thinking in terms of a limited space to fill is what in academic language is called "limiting the subject."

Let us restate the principle by taking a specific subject. Let us say that you are interested in antiques, a general subject about which many books have been written. You know something about antiques because your mother and your older sister have several cupboards filled with early American glass. You too have a few choice pieces as the beginning of a collection. Your subject is already beginning to limit itself. What can you tell your reader — in eight hundred words — that is not old and general? Your answer may be the natural result of your own experiences: you decide to give point and direction to your article by concentrating on a single objective, on the idea that an amateur collector of glass develops through three stages. State this objective in the form of a "thesis" or summarizing sentence: "An amateur collector of early American glass develops through three stages: first, he buys everything in sight; second, as his knowledge and taste grow, he discards all except a few of his choicest pieces; third, he begins to see that the pleasure of owning a few perfect things is worth more than a large collection. There you have a target to shoot at, a rough plan of operations, and some idea of the ammunition you are going to use. Up to this time most of your planning has been done in your head. Now jot down your main ideas on a sheet of paper, write down under each main head a few of the details as they occur to you, and you have a working plan. You are ready to begin writing.

You will probably change your plan as you proceed, but that is what every writer must do. Changes will improve your finished product as long as you keep to your main objective and your first general plan. Your paper will have direction, purpose, organization, and clearness.

Here are two examples of plans for thousand-word themes:

[Title] THREE MORE LAPS TO GO

Thesis: I report progress in my two objectives in coming to college: to learn a trade and to acquire a certain amount of culture.

TOPIC OUTLINE

   I. My reasons for coming to college:
- A. To learn a trade
- B. To learn how to live

 II. My reasons for wanting to learn a trade
III. My progress in secretarial science
IV. My progress in culture and discipline
- A. To find an ideal of beauty and culture
- B. To learn mental discipline
- C. To find my relation to the world I live in

[Title] MORE BUSHELS

Thesis: The process of cross-pollination of corn, which is adding much to the world's supply of food, requires a careful and exact technique.

TOPIC OUTLINE

   I. Natural pollination by air
 II. Importance of cross-pollination
III. Artificial pollination:
- A. Inspecting the corn field every day
- B. Placing glycine bags over new shoots
- C. Observing the shoots through glycine
- D. Using paper bags to catch pollen
- E. Shaking pollen over the corn silk
- F. Keeping records of pollination

IV. Fixing a strain by "selfing"

Every paper written needs a plan, although some plans spend their life cycles in the heads of the writers without ever emerging on paper in the form of outlines. The experienced writer may plan almost subconsciously; some writers say that they do all their outlining in their heads, whereas many others say that they write out elaborate outlines on paper. But the inexperienced writer has everything to gain by using paper and pencil to record and clarify the planning that goes on in his head. Even when a paper is written offhand, as the outpouring of an inspired idea, an outline of the finished paper is an excellent check for organization and logic. If there are flaws in the product of your inspiration, the outline will reveal every one of them.

The Formal Outline. Most of the longer papers — term papers, research papers, essays, articles, reports — that you will write in college will call for outlines, either topic or sentence. There is a third type, called the paragraph outline, which consists of a series of sentences each one summarizing the thought of a paragraph. That type will be illustrated later. In the topic and the sentence outlines, the heads and subheads do not necessarily match the paragraph divisions of the finished paper.

There are a number of conventions governing the formal outline which the student should observe.

1. The parts of the outline, heads and subheads, should be labeled by alternating figures and letters as follows: I, II, III, etc., A, B, C, etc., 1, 2, 3, etc., a, b, c, etc. Periods, not dashes, should be placed after these numbering figures and letters.

2. No punctuation is needed after the topics in a topic outline. In a sentence outline, each sentence should be punctuated in the conventional manner.

3. The heads in any series should be of equal importance. That is, the heads numbered I, II, III, IV, etc., should actually be divisions of the whole paper; heads numbered with capital letters should be co-ordinate divisions of heads numbered with Roman numerals; and so on.

4. Whenever possible, co-ordinate heads should be expressed in parallel form, that is, in a given series, nouns should be made

parallel with nouns, adjectives with adjectives, and so on. But although parallel structure is desirable and logical, clearness and directness should never be sacrificed on the altar of strict parallelism. There are times when nouns and gerunds can live side by side in a formal outline.

5. In a topic outline, all heads and subheads must be topics. In a sentence outline, all heads and subheads must be sentences. Sentences should not run over from one head to another.

6. Each head and subhead should be as specific as it is possible to make it in an outline. Vague topics and sentences are bad because they tend to hide flaws in the logic or organization of the outline.

7. Using such headings as "I. Introduction, II. Body, III. Conclusion" is unnecessary and undesirable. Such divisions do not indicate correctly the structure of most essays or articles. Many papers written by students are too short for a formal introduction or conclusion. In most long papers the conclusion is simply the main topic which the writer wants the reader to hear about last — for reasons explained elsewhere. Separate introductions are used more often than separate conclusions in essays of six thousand words or more, but in the outline it is better to use a topic which tells what is said in the introduction than to use the vague "Introduction" itself.

8. Since an outline represents a grouping of parallel parts, it should never have a single subhead under any head. A single subhead can usually be combined with its head with benefit to the logic and organization of the outline.

The conventions of outlining are illustrated in the following two outlines, one a topic outline and the other a sentence outline, both of which were prepared by a freshman student in English composition. The research paper itself was about 4300 words in length.

[Title] OUR ENEMY THE TERMITE

Thesis sentence: The termite, an interesting insect of social habits, whose life philosophy is "eat to live and live to eat," must be better understood if we are to protect ourselves against its destructive appetite.

TOPIC OUTLINE

   I. Life history of a termite
      A. Relation to other insects
      B. The subterranean, and the dry- or damp-wood termite
      C. The cycle of its life
  II. Distribution throughout the world
      A. Termites in the United States
         1. Distribution
         2. Food
      B. Interesting termites in other countries
         1. The African termites
            a. What the mound looks like
            b. What goes on inside
         2. Species in Hawaii, Central and South America, and the Antilles
 III. Social organization
      A. The workers
      B. The soldiers
      C. The reproductive adults
         1. Colonizing flight
         2. Courtship and pairing
         3. Reproduction
      D. The queen
  IV. Destructiveness
      A. The termite's method of destruction
      B. The extent of damage
         1. Cost of actual damage
         2. Cost of prevention
      C. Damage to stored materials
      D. Damage to wood structures
   V. Methods of control
      A. Proper construction of buildings
         1. Treatment of wood with creosote
         2. Plating
         3. Insulation
      B. Buildings most likely to be attacked
      C. The signs of infestation
      D. Protection after the house is built

A sentence outline is similar in organization to a topic outline. It differs from a topic outline in that every topic and every sub-topic is translated into a complete sentence. This sentence states the central idea of each head or subhead. The sentence outline has two advantages over the topic outline: (1) it forces the writer to study his material carefully so that he has something specific to say for each head and subhead, and (2) much more than the topic outline it is able to convey information to the reader. The topic outline merely states the topics about which the writer intends to say something; the sentence outline actually summarizes what he has to say.

[Title] OUR ENEMY THE TERMITE

SENTENCE OUTLINE

I. The termite, erroneously called the white ant, lives a highly socialized life, the purpose of which is eating.
   A. The nearest relative of the termite is the cockroach, the nearness being a matter of several million years.
   B. Termites fall into two main classes: the subterranean termite and the dry- or damp-wood termite.
   C. From an egg, termites hatch into soldiers, workers, or reproductive adults, each type with its predestined work.
II. Termites are to be found in almost every part of the world.
   A. There are fifty-four species in the United States.
      1. Termites are found in all the states except two.
      2. American ermites eat deadwood tissue and convert it to soil.
   B. There are many interesting termites in other countries.
      1. Termite mounds are thick in the grasslands of Africa, the paradise of termites.
         a. The mound has chambers, nurseries, and incubating rooms.
         b. Life in the mound is the most elaborate form of planned communistic economy found in the world.
      2. Hawaii, Central and South America, and the Antilles have new and interesting species of termites.
III. The social classes in a termite colony are the workers, the soldiers, and the reproductive adults.
   A. The most numerous type, the saw-tooth worker, is the destructive member.
   B. The soldiers have large heads and jaws, which they use to protect the colonies.
   C. There are three types of female reproductive forms, the "queens," of the termite race.

      1. Annually the termites swarm, allowing the adults to start new colonies.

      2. The male follows the female constantly, keeping contact with his feelers, until males and females are in pairs.

      3. The queen, after fertilization, lays thousands of eggs a day

   D. The queen is imprisoned in a chamber of her own where she lays eggs and has the workers take care of her.

IV. Vast harm and destruction has been caused by the termite.

   A. The termite bores from within and eats the inside of the wood.

   B. Estimates have been made of the cost of termite appetite.

      1. The annual damage in this country may run as high as fifty million dollars.

      2. The cost of prevention measures another seven million dollars.

   C. Termites destroy and spoil a variety of stored goods.

   D. The damage done to wooden structures is much greater than the damage to other materials.

V. Termite control consists of both prevention and cure.

   A. Damage by termites can be prevented by proper construction of buildings.

      1. A good wood preservative is creosote.

      2. Copper rolled plating is an excellent way of preventing termite damage.

      3. Wood placed directly on the foundation should be insulated by means of some material between the wood and the foundation.

   B. The buildings most likely to be attacked are those with direct contact with the ground — a situation which the termite understands as an invitation to the banquet.

   C. Signs of infestation can be detected in annual swarms, earth-like tunnels, and sagging beams.

   D. A termite-infested house should have all weakened beams removed and replaced with chemically treated wood.

The paragraph outline is a numbered succession of paragraph summaries. As a device for tightening up paragraph structure it is useful to the writer, but it is not one of the conventional formal outlines usually required with long papers.

The following is a paragraph outline of pages 746–752 in volume 2 of Hayes' *A Political and Cultural History of Modern Europe:*

[Title] THE LEAGUE OF NATIONS

PARAGRAPH OUTLINE

1. The World War gave impetus to the pre-war propaganda for some kind of world league.
2. The idea was the most important of Woodrow Wilson's plans.
3. The different ideas about what kind of league to have resulted in a compromise embodied in a "Covenant."
4. The structure of the League, as provided by the Covenant, consisted of an Assembly, a Council, a Secretariat, and an associated Court.
5. Of the several purposes of the League, the most important was to prevent war.
6. Articles ten to seventeen of the Covenant made provisions for the various steps which should be taken to preserve the peace.
7. The Covenant did not actually forbid war, only "illegal" war.
8. The Covenant specified sanctions to be taken against recalcitrant members and neutrals.
9. The League was to take positive steps to organize for peace through its central agencies and through the Court.
10. Secret treaties were prohibited as leading to wars.
11. The Covenant made provision for revising treaties.
12. The Covenant aimed at doing away with competitive armaments.
13. In addition to its functions as a peacemaker, the League was given the task of putting into effect the peace treaties of 1919–1920.
14. The League was charged with promoting humanitarian co-operation.
15. Associated with the League were the International Labor Conference and an International Labor Office.
16. In its plan to become the cornerstone of world peace, the League invited all nations to become members.

EXERCISES

Exercise 1. (Before you do this exercise, reread the "conventions governing the formal outline" on pages 142–143.) Note the faults in the following outline. Are the four main heads parallel? What can the writer say under "Retail dealers" that he has not already said under the first two heads? Would not the dealers utilize both advertising and decorations? Are the two subheads under "III. Santa Claus" co-ordinate?

Rewrite the outline.

THE PROCESS OF PLANNING AND WRITING

[Title] COMMERCIALIZED CHRISTMAS

TOPIC OUTLINE

Thesis: Christmas is growing more commercialized each year.

   I. Advertising
      A. Newspapers and magazines
      B. Billboards
  II. Decorations
      A. Natural sources
      B. Artificial sources
 III. Santa Claus
      A. Universal symbol of Christmas
      B. Attraction for children
 IV. Retail dealers
      A. Merchandise
      B. Payments

Exercise 2. Point out the faults in the following outline. What faults do you find in the statement of the thesis? What error in division do you notice? Are there any heads that are not parallel?

Rewrite the outline.

[Title] LEARNING TO SKATE

TOPIC OUTLINE

Thesis: Ice skating is the fastest sport in the world and is being enjoyed by more and more people every day.

   I. Preparation
      A. Building up confidence
      B. Forgetting all fear
  II. The process of learning
      A. The first tentative try
         1. The disastrous results
      B. Effects on one's nerve
      C. The second attempt
      D. One's confidence is bolstered by success.
 III. The results
      A. Reward for one's patience
      B. Love for the sport

Exercise 3. Point out the faults in the following outline. What are your comments on the thesis sentence? The outline itself is pretty bad. First, point out the errors in co-ordination and parallelism. Then try to select three or four of the topics that you could use for the main divisions. Arrange the others under these heads. Restate each head and subhead in correct form.

[Title] THE IMPOLITE PERSON

TOPIC OUTLINE

Thesis: There are certain things that are very unpleasant in the world today.

    I. Social etiquette should be corrected
   II. The poorly mannered individual
  III. Etiquette discussed
       A. Little favors
       B. Result
   IV. The "de-lifer"
       A. Life of the party
       B. Sad mistake
    V. How to acquire good manners
       A. Smile
       B. Be agreeable
       C. Be cheerful
       D. Our resolution

Exercise 4. Study and analyze the following two outlines. Make your own criticisms of each one. Rewrite one of them.

[Title] AS THE TWIG IS BENT

SENTENCE OUTLINE

Thesis: My life has been dominated by the fact that I am a college professor's daughter.

    I. Many things are taken for granted because I am a college professor's daughter.
       A. A restraining hand is placed upon my impulses.
       B. I am destined to live in a town where all my actions are known and where I have to live up to my father's standards of respectability.
       C. It is taken for granted that I graduate with honors from the college in my home town.

II. There are several advantages resulting from being a professor's daughter.
  A. I have had frequent opportunity for travel.
  B. I have had a permanent home town.
  C. I have had a few of the sharp stones removed from the long road to an education.
III. Only a girl who loves a quiet life should choose to be born into a professor's family.

[Title]   ONE OF THREE

SENTENCE OUTLINE

Thesis: Being reared with a brother and sister has kept me from becoming a spoiled brat.
  I. My brother and sister have helped me to develop several desirable traits.
  II. I have learned to be considerate of others.
    A. Thoughtfulness is learned through experience.
    B. I learned to want my brother and sister to share my happy experiences.
      1. An only child cannot see the effects of his behavior.
III. My college life is happier because of my early training.
    A. Being happy with a variety of roommates.
    B. "Difficult" teachers do not worry me in the least.

Exercise 5, Limiting the subject. Practice cutting down a general subject to a phase of it suitable for a paper of eight hundred or a thousand words. After each general subject write a statement of the narrowed subject as in the examples given below.

General subject	*Limited subject*
World peace	What is a pacifist?
Athletics	How to throw the javelin
Life on a farm	Feeding the threshing crew
College traditions	The fraternity initiation
Reading for recreation	
Horses	
Life in a big city	
The veteran in college	
Careers for women	
Nature	
Modern music	

Exercise 6, The thesis sentence. It will be useful to you to form the habit of stating the objective or the central idea of your paper in a single sentence. Study the examples given below and then write thesis sentences for each of the subjects given.

Subject: Reading for recreation
Thesis: My recreational reading so far has been an escape to a world of wonder, mystery, and romance.

Subject: A good teacher
Thesis: A good teacher is one who knows that his students are more important than his courses.

Subject: Trout flies
Thesis: Four of the most popular trout flies used by fishermen in my locality can easily be tied by any amateur fisherman.

Subject: "Dont's" for the popular girl
Thesis: The popular college girl must not assume that popularity need not be deserved or worked for.

Subjects for analysis:
    Respect for the law
    Neglected courtesies
    The intelligence of a dog
    Education for leisure
    Early marriages

Exercise 7. The statement of each of the following subjects indicates the major divisions of a short paper on that subject. Construct topical outlines for each of the subjects, giving each main head several subheads. Do not make the outlines too elaborate.

    Four college traditions I could do without
    Three reasons for studying a science
    Four characters of fiction I should like to meet
    Three arguments in favor of student self-government
    Three reasons why I like this book

Beginning the Paper. Every writer faced with the task of setting his ideas down on paper is conscious of the overwhelming importance of an effective beginning. It is like first meetings — the first interview with your employer, the first introduction to your mother-in-law. There is something terrifying about it simply because it must be got over with first. In writing, students spend entirely too much time getting started.

"The best way to begin is to begin. Do not write introductions. Just plunge in." All this is sound advice but not very helpful to the beginner. One might as well tell him to learn how to dance by plunging in — some persons do dance that way — or to play contract, or to swim. After all, one must know what he is to do after he plunges in. Another bit of advice, a trifle more helpful, is, "Just write down anything about your subject. Keep going until you get well into your first main topic. Then in revision cross out the first two paragraphs."

There are, however, a number of specific devices which a writer may use to introduce his subject appropriately and interestingly. After he has experimented with a few of them, he will no doubt invent variations of his own.

1. Begin by specifying the phase or aspect of the subject to which you intend to limit your discussion. In formal papers, such as the research article, this sort of beginning is often a help to both writer and reader. The announcement of the subject need not be stiff and artificial. Notice how easily the introducing is performed in the following specimen:

When foreign notables arrive in America, they at once declare — having been previously primed — "I think your women are wonderful." When newsworthy celebrities arrive in England, for "women" they substitute "police." Being a Crusader at heart, I now propose to risk probable mayhem and possible assassination, and write about English women.

Naturally I can't generalize about them to any great extent. Believing, as I emphatically do, that no two human beings are exactly alike, I can't describe any one English woman as typical of them all. I have met a considerable number of them, representing many walks of life, and they have various characteristics in common. I have observed many others as well, whom I haven't met — in that way that one observes one's fellow-creatures in buses, and trains, and shops, and theaters, etc. — and on occasions such as the Aldershot Tattoo, where people congregate in tens of thousands, I have seen a great many more. And so I suppose I am qualified as much as, and certainly no more than, any other casual observer to write about them.

— James Dyrenforth, "Through Darkest England with Gun and Camera," *The Outpost*, June, 1945.

2. Begin with an incident, real or imagined, out of which the discussion arises, or which illustrates the point of the discussion.

A puff of wind comes down the street. An old newspaper stirs in the gutter, jumps up on the sidewalk, spirals up to second-story height and flaps about there for a moment; then, with a new burst of energy, it sweeps upward again, and when you last see it, it is soaring high above the roof tops, turning over and over, blinking in the sunlight.

The wind has picked up a piece of paper and blown it away. What of it? A generation ago, in philosophical discourse, one might have chosen this as an example of an event completely void of significance, completely chance. But not in the air age. The tiny occurrence demonstrates an important fact concerning the air ocean — one that is only now becoming the practical knowledge of practical airfaring men: there are winds which blow neither east nor west, neither north nor south, but in the third dimension: straight up.

— Wolfgang Langewiesche, "Winds That Blow Straight Up," *Harper's Magazine*, August, 1945. Reprinted by permission of the author.

Some years ago when I was the dinner guest of a famous club in Boston, the chairman of the evening introduced me in the following words: "Our guest tonight is an economist. I need hardly remind you, gentlemen, of the large part played in our life today by our economists. Indeed, it has been calculated that if all the economists were laid out in a line, end to end, starting at the Mexican border, they would reach —" The orator paused impressively and added: "nowhere."

That, I may say, was a few years ago. What was a genial joke then is a plain fact now. In my opinion that is exactly where economics stands. At a time when the world is in danger of collapse from the dilemma of wealth and want, the economists can shed no light, or rather only a multitude of cross lights that will not focus to a single beam — in place of a lighthouse, wreckers' signals, or at least, fireworks, elaborate and meaningless.

How has this come about? What has happened to our economic science?

— Stephen Leacock, "Lost in the Jungle of Economics," *New York Times Magazine*, August 20, 1939. Reprinted by permission.

3. Begin with some fact or series of facts related to your subject which shows the importance or the timeliness of your subject.

The nation of Canada is a triumph of politics over race, geography, and economics. The Canadian political system has held together two diverse peoples and cultures under almost unbearable strains. It had dammed up and diverted into its chosen channels the natural economic currents of the North American continent. It has created a single economic system of entirely diverse elements always in active conflict with one another. It has made Canada one of the world's three chief traders, given it the world's second highest living standard, enabled it to become, with a population of less than twelve million, the fourth fighting power among the United Nations. Since Canada is the closest neighbor and friend of the U. S., since it stands poised at the crossroads of the world between the U. S. and its great allies, Britain and Russia, the system that makes Canada possible at all should be worth a U. S. examination.

— Bruce Hutchison, "In Canada It's Different," *Fortune*, August, 1945. Reprinted by permission.

Four and a half million American farmers have put 13 million bushels of seed corn into the ground this year. If all of it were placed in one field, that 95,000,000-acre field would be about the size of the state of California. During the fall and early winter the farmers will harvest a crop of some three billion bushels — enough to fill a freight train stretching half way around the world. It is our greatest crop by any measurement — acreage, bulk, or value. The corn crop is usually worth about as much as our cotton, wheat, and oats crops combined.

But the story of our corn crop is richer and more exciting than any mere list of statistics. To begin with, it is a mystery story. No one knows for certain how corn originated or what its botanical ancestors were. Corn is an orphan among grains, belonging to no known family. As if to make up for this, corn has attached itself so devotedly to man that for unnumbered centuries it has depended on man's help for its very survival.

— Kurt Steel, "Revolution in the Corn Belt," *Harper's Magazine*, August, 1945. Reprinted by permission of the author.

4. Begin with a general observation about your particular subject and then show how it is applicable to the particular phase of the subject that you intend to discuss.

The English, I begin to realize, have only one thing wholly in common with us Americans: we both suffer from that incurable complaint called human nature. It takes us quite differently, in most respects, but the root trouble is the same. For instance, consider the matter of class distinctions. On paper, of course, we Americans haven't any such thing, whereas the English have a well-defined class system which has endured for centuries and has become one of those traditions to which they'll cling till Doomsday. I don't believe that the English people who bother to analyze it consider it ideal. In fact, I've heard many of them pick it to pieces. But it has been with them for a long while, and they won't change it until they can find something better. In subtle ways, Time and the social revolution that is spreading throughout the world are changing it for them. But it is bound to be a longer and slower process here than in most countries, because resistance to change is one of the strongest links in the chain of English character. . . . Long before William the Conqueror, kings rewarded men who helped them keep their uncertain thrones by giving them titles, for which they charged a useful fee, and land, which wasn't necessarily theirs to bestow. The land brought wealth, which gave aristocrats their real power, and the vast majority of common folk stood in awe of it just as human beings have done since the days of Atlantis.

— James Dyrenforth, "Through Darkest England with Gun and Camera," *The Outpost*, November, 1944.

5. Begin with a question or a series of questions, the answers to which will constitute your article or essay.

Visiting a television studio gives the impression of looking directly into the future. The newest and most shining gadget of science — breathtaking in its implications — is about to emerge into everyday reality. What forms will television entertainment take? What new crafts and skills will it require in writing, acting, costuming, scene designing, lighting and directing? How will it relate itself to the other arts of the theater — from which will it draw and upon which will it improve?

—T. R. Carskadon, "Report on Television," *Theatre Arts Monthly*, June, 1937. Reprinted by permission.

6. Begin by setting up something to knock down (the "straw man" beginning), such as a current notion, a tradition, a theory that you intend to show is wrong.

Just as too many English people still believe that all American cities are composed of skyscrapers, and that our population is largely made up of cowboys, Indians, gangsters, movie stars, and a vast number of millionaires, so too many foreigners have been deceived by the sporting prints and picture the average Englishman as going about in hunting attire, riding furiously to hounds, and then changing into tweeds and a Sherlock Holmes cap and shooting pheasant and grouse all over the place. As a matter of fact, except in certain less populous districts, very few Englishmen ever see a fox outside of a zoo or a pheasant that isn't lying naked and forlorn on a butcher's counter.

— James Dyrenforth, "Through Darkest England with Gun and Camera," *The Outpost*, October, 1944.

EXERCISES

Exercise 1. The following are the opening paragraphs of papers written in a course in freshman English. Criticize each one. Does it serve to attract the reader's interest? What device has the author used in his introduction? Is his device honest and legitimate?

1. [Title] VATICAN CITY

Have you ever heard of a station master with no train to call, or a guard with nothing to do but to tend three eagles every day? Yes, these positions actually do exist. They exist in a place where the noon hour is three hours long. All this happens in the smallest and strangest state in the world — Vatican City.

In this paper I shall introduce my reader to . . .

2. [Title] THEATER NUISANCES

The long-forgotten item, theater etiquette, has and is becoming more and more extinct every day and every year. The theater is not a place for a vigorous workout, a place for sleep, or a place for a general get-together but a place for quiet relaxation and educational activity. Now we shall proceed to enumerate some of the common theater nuisances who make a motion picture a disagreeable event.

3. [Title] CONFESSION OF THE CAREFREE

It is all right to commend the straight and narrow path as a mode of life, but a straight and narrow mind is another matter. Children brought up under a strict parental discipline are supposed to be sober, industrious, and virtuous. I have always suspected that there was a flaw in this pious assumption. I do not base my suspicion on the fact that ministers' sons are traditionally wild young hellions. Perhaps their wildness seems wilder by contrast with their background. I do know, however, that in my own case the freedom which my broad-minded parents have always granted me has made me, if not industrious or virtuous, a much more serious girl than the average person of my age.

4. [Title] A MATTER OF CONSCIENCE

There is an old story about the little boy who was saying his evening prayers during a thunderstorm. "O Lord," he pleaded, "please give us less noise and more light." For many years most discussions of the place of the conscientious objector in wartime have generated more noise and heat than light. Before we can decide his place in an unfriendly world, we should try to see more clearly who he is. Is he a physical coward or a moral hero? Is he an enemy of society or one of its martyred leaders?

5. [Title] AN ENJOYABLE CUSTOM

"Can you come to the smorgasbord tonight with me?" asked Roy. "What on earth is that?" I asked. "Why, it's the Norwegian way of saying, 'Come on over for dinner this evening,' " he replied.

The Norwegian people are probably the most generous, good-hearted people in the world. They love to eat. They are particularly fond of good pastries and meats. Their houses are immaculately clean and well kept. The Norwegian families are, as a whole, rather large, and everyone is gay all of the time. Their main occupation is fishing.

Their national custom which I shall describe is their custom of setting out a table of delicacies called the "smorgasbord."

Exercise 2. Select a subject that you want to use for your next essay. Write four beginnings for it. With the help of your instructor pick out the most successful one and use it in writing your paper.

1. Begin by using an imagined incident which illustrates the point of your paper or out of which a discussion of your subject may seem to arise.
2. Begin with evidence of the importance or the timeliness of your subject.
3. Begin by stating your purpose in writing.
4. Begin with a question or a series of questions.

Writing the Paper. After you have thought your subject through, worked it over in your mind, laid out your general plan and supplied as many details as you could, you will probably want to write it rapidly without pausing too often to ponder over the perfect sentence or the exact word. Write rapidly if that is the way you write naturally. Write slowly and carefully if slow and careful writing is your best method. Among professional writers no two work alike. Some write fast and revise slowly, changing words and phrases, crossing out and rewriting, copying the revised manuscript and then rewriting again, sometimes as many as fifteen times. Some chisel out every word in creative agony in their first draft — and never revise.

If your preliminary planning has been done carefully, most of the technical aspects of writing, such as preserving the unity of effect, using the right order of presentation, and giving the parts the right proportion, will have been taken care of. There is a stronger probability that your materials will have unity, order, and proportion if you keep the general principles somewhere in the back of your mind as you plan. For that reason they are here summarized.

Unity means oneness. It means aiming at a target instead of merely shooting in the air for the sake of the noise. It means having a definite objective, which you have stated in your thesis sentence. It means adapting your subject to fit the space at your disposal and to impress the readers for whom you are writing. And finally it means excluding everything which might take the reader's attention from the main idea.

The order in which you present your material to your reader will depend partly on what you have to say and partly on the sort of reader you are addressing.

If you are telling how something is made, how a game is played, how a system grew or developed in the course of time, you will naturally use the order of happening, called the chronological order. In discussions like the following the chronological order is inherent in the material: how to clean a rifle, how to organize and manage a formal dance, how to prepare for a final examination, how to operate a bulldozer, the history of tennis, the development of consumers' co-operatives, learning how to tap-dance. When a subject does not naturally call for this order, you can often achieve a clearer presentation by changing your approach so that you can use the order of time.

If for any reason you think it wise to keep from your reader the central thought of your discussion until you have reached the end, you may use the inductive order. This order is adapted to compositions in which a number of instances, facts, or observations all lead to a single general statement. It is useful where it is necessary to prepare the reader's mind for a new idea by the massing of evidence. For instance, if you are advocating the adoption of an honor system in your school, you may get a more favorable reaction from your readers if you convince them first that a system of strict, paternalistic supervision has resulted in widespread dishonesty. If you are urging the establishment of teen-age night clubs, you can begin by picturing first the existing undesirable conditions.

If you can divide your subject into several parts of equal importance, you may indicate the division in your opening paragraph and then discuss the parts one by one in the selected order. For convenience, we shall label this order the order of enumeration. "Communism differs from socialism in four important aspects," you begin. "Before the Diesel engine can be used in light motor cars, automotive engineers must solve the following three problems." "The comments of those veterans who are not interested in more free education fall into three general groups." You can see from these examples how a considerable number of subjects will adapt themselves to this sort of treatment. You must remember, however, that a formal enumeration of parts implies a serious and formal treatment of the subject. The lighter, more informal subjects should be handled more informally.

If your subject is an organization, or a complicated piece of machinery, or an idea hard to grasp, you may start with the simple elements of your subject and gradually proceed to those more difficult to understand. You may call this order "from easy to hard," if you wish, or "from known to unknown."

If you are dealing with a subject in which the topics may be arranged in the order of increasing importance, it may be effective to use the order of climax.

And finally, there is the method of division — the method used in perhaps ninety-eight per cent of all expository essays, papers, articles, and books. It is a simple method and a good one. In his process of planning the writer says to himself, "Now, I have a certain number of main facts or ideas to give to my reader in the time and space that I have for all this. There doesn't seem to be much difference in their importance; there doesn't seem to be any reason why one should come first and another last." If there is a topic which seems more important than the others, that topic should be placed last, because that is the position of advantage and importance. It has the same advantage in an essay that the last speaker has in a debate or in an oratorical contest — that the last contestant has in any contest. What is said last should make the strongest impression on the reader's mind.

Proportion. The amount of space that you give to each of the topics in your paper will depend on what you have to say and on your purpose in writing.

In general, certain things are unimportant. Long, rambling beginnings, formal conclusions, and digressions from the central idea should be severely pruned or grubbed out entirely.

As for the rest, the principle is simple. Keeping in mind the old rule of "an interesting beginning and a strong ending," you will give relatively more space to the important topic which you have saved for the end of your paper. That is the fact or idea that you want to stress, both by placing it at the end and by saying more about it. You may, of course, introduce your last topic by some such phrase as, "And, finally, the most important —," but telling your reader that an idea is most important is not the same as making him think and feel that it is. For this you need concrete details. You need evidence. And you also need a certain amount of time for the idea to sink into his mind.

Substance: Use of Details. To reach the mind of your reader, to make him understand and to persuade him to accept emotionally, you must be specific and concrete. Generalities will not touch him. An essay on the need of international understanding and co-operation may get a reader's passive mental agreement, but a concrete picture of it in a little novel called *A Bell for Adano* will reach his heart too. A lecture on man's inhumanity to man is one thing; a newsreel showing the inside of a concentration camp, especially if your brother is there, is something very different. Your outline consists of a series of generalities. It is the skeleton of your paper, with the emotional appeal, the personality, and the warmth of a skeleton. You must cover the skeleton with living flesh. Explanations, specific details, instances, illustrations, concrete examples — out of these you build your finished essay.

The substance of definitions or explanations of a process is obvious enough. Essays of fact are simple, too — if you know enough facts. If not, you will get the facts you need, or take another subject. But even facts need to be interpreted, clarified, or made to appear as significant as they have a right to be. Your real problem is to be found in writing discussions of ideas and opinion. Here your best procedure is to muster for your reader the evidence out of which your general idea or opinion came into existence. Take, for instance, a general subject like "College grades." You, to the surprise of your instructor, undertake to defend the system of grades, by showing that it is not an artificial system found nowhere but in schools, but a valuable preparation for the realities of the workaday world. One of your general ideas is that it resembles, in a milder form, the grading that every student receives from his fellow students. "Just what do you mean by that?" asks your reader. "What gave you that idea?" That is it. What gave you the idea? "Well," you reply, "I've noticed. . . . The men at my fraternity house discussing Ted Jones, the new freshman from my town . . . brilliant, but. . . . Blackballed him. It was something he said about communism. Or the way the girls talk about each other's gowns after a dance. Or the way they label a fellow . . . you're a playboy or a grind or a crud." Put material like that into your paper, and your reader will react as you did. Your next general idea is that grading in college will prepare the graduate for the inevitable grading he will get from his employer. "From the very first day," you will explain, "the employer grades his man. That man is an 'A' worker, the employer will think. He'll bear watching; we need 'A' men. That other man is doing 'C' work; he's competent enough, but uninspired, without enthusiasm. That last fellow we hired is an 'F.' And the grades are recorded, not, as in college, at the end of the term or at the end of the year, but with the weekly pay envelope. An 'A' means a raise in salary or a promotion; an 'F' means dismissal." Put this into your theme. That is what we mean by substance.

The following are a few illustrations of the principles discussed in this chapter.

ORDER OF ENUMERATION (OPENING SECTION)

To seek for the real differences between the Chinese and the western civilizations is to seek for certain characteristics that run through their histories. To notice only the differences of modern times and assume these to be fundamental, as though they appeared all at once, would be the grossest absurdity. Such unique differences as that the West has experimental science, an industrial revolution, a world market and parliamentary government and the East does not, did not appear by accident or all at once. Three fundamental differences have lasted in unbroken tradition at least since the Chou and Tsin dynasties in the East, and ancient Greece in the West, and have interacted to produce the respective civilizations as they now exist.

These three aspects of diverse development are in sense of values, in social organization, and in mode of existence.

— Y. L. Chang, "How Chinese and Western Civilizations Differ," *Asia and the Americas*, July, 1945. Reprinted by permission.

ORDER OF ENUMERATION (THE PARTS NUMBERED)

The first requirement for an accountant is analytical power. Perhaps the best illustration of what we mean by analysis is found in the attempt to distinguish two things absolutely familiar to everyone — running and walking. Everyone can tell whether another person is walking or running; yet few people can quickly analyze the two gaits. The difference is not in speed, for the same person can walk faster than he may sometimes run; nor is it in the length of step, for he can take longer steps in walking than he may sometimes take in running; nor is it in the pitch of the body, nor in the bend of the knee, nor in the height of the step, nor in the violence of exertion, nor in various other apparent but unimportant things. It lies in a single factor or element in one gait that is not in the other. Analysis of the two gaits discovers it.

A person who does not find delight in studying things in such fashion, picking them to pieces, finding the relations of their parts, and then comparing them with other things, is not cut out for an accountant. An accountant must have what we call the philosophic mind, a mind which finds pleasure in discovering what things really are as contrasted with what they appear to be.

The second requirement for an accountant is a knowledge of business practice and experience, for otherwise he will not know what facts about business need study and record, and will not know what light such study and record can throw on the future conduct of the business. If, for example, he does not know that in certain trades it is customary to allow large discounts for early payment of bills, he will not be trustworthy in calculating how much a firm in that business is likely to collect on sums owed it. If he does not know that certain chemicals collect moisture from the atmosphere, he will not be trustworthy in interpreting in terms of value reports of quantities of chemicals on hand in terms of weight. If he does not understand manufacturing processes, he will not direct the bookkeepers so that their records can be used to show whether this or that process is more or less economical than another.

The third requirement is imagination, — the last thing people usually think of as a requirement, or even a virtue, in an accountant. One of the purposes of accounting is to serve as a guide for the future. The records of the past must be so clear, and must be so clearly interpreted (as a historian interprets the facts of history so that they may help us in solving problems of the present and the future), that the policy of the business may be intelligently directed largely on the basis of the information that the accounting gives.

— William Morse Cole, "The Profession of Accounting," from Clayton H. Ernst's *What Shall I Be?* D. Appleton & Co., Inc., New York, 1928. Reprinted by permission of D. Appleton-Century Co.

(Notice in this selection the use of details to build up and clarify the general statements: a skillful use of analogy in the first paragraph, of concrete examples in the third.)

SHARPENING THE AX

An ax of stone was probably one of the most prized possessions of the ancient man. He guarded it jealously, and any attempt to appropriate or injure the tool was cause enough for a fight. Such is the attitude of the woodsman of today. His ax is a prized tool whether it is used to fall eight-foot Douglas firs of Western Washington or to make his bed more comfortable by removing roots from the campsite or cutting boughs for a mattress. To nick the razor-like edge of the shining blade is a major tragedy, a calamity which is announced to all in sulphurous but eloquent words. If the damage is done by the owner of the ax, he will usually pause toward the end of his broadcast to set about restoring the ruined edge.

The character of the work that the chopper is doing has much to do with the manner of sharpening the ax. If he is clearing brush, he wants the sharpest, thinnest edge that steel will take without buckling or turning when it strikes a flinty piece of vine maple; if he is doing heavy chopping, such as undercutting a large tree preparatory to falling it, he still wants the thin blade; but if he is chopping knots or tough limbs, he wants a thicker, sturdier edge that will not chip or break in the hardest of cedar knots or the most stubborn of fir limbs. The woodsman knows exactly how thin his ax may be because he has experimented to see just how much steel will stand.

As he is a western man, the woodsman uses the double-bitted ax. Everyone knows that Paul Bunyan originated this straight-handled, double-edged tool. He did it because the single-bitted ax simply would not stay sharp long enough to permit any work to be done. So, to offset this handicap as much as possible, Paul designed an ax with a head that tapered, or flattened, to an edge on both sides of the handle. Since both edges were to be used, the handle had to be adaptable to either position of the head; the straight handle was the ideal solution. By using this new ax, Paul managed to make the edges last for about fifteen minutes. This might seem a bit fast for chopping, but when a person realizes that the best Scotchman or Irishman in the woods could not keep up when Paul was working steadily, it seems reasonable enough.

But get back to our woodcutter with the nicked ax. He has, by this time, set his ax rigidly with the handle and bits in a horizontal plane. It must be rigidly fastened, and he knows it because many gashed fingers have resulted from the unexpected movement of a loose blade. The ax is clamped in a vise if one is available. If not, it is probably driven into a cut of a large log so that the handle and bits are in that horizontal plane about waist high or a little higher. Then with a file he carefully cuts the metal down until the nick has disappeared. In this filing he will not form a dubby, blunt edge just to get rid of the nick, but he will carefully bring it to a keen, thin edge. He will remove the metal back to a point about two and a half inches back from the edge toward the center of the bit. Working from this point, he will shear off the metal in a sort of oval form which will have the corners of the ax for the ends, and the edge and a curve from the corners through the point for the sides of the oval. When one side is satisfactorily trimmed down, the other side gets similar treatment. This insures the perfect balance of the ax. Then holding the ax in the most convenient position, either on his knees or standing with the handle between his knees, he finishes the job with a whetstone. It is this final touch that removes the feather edge left by the file and makes the ax as sharp as a razor. It is this finish that enables him to slice a three-inch sapling at one stroke. But this completes only one of the two bits.

The ax is again fastened horizontally with the other blade in position to be filed. Usually this other blade will be sharpened to cut the harder materials. This means that the edge will not be as thin as the other. Instead of working away from the edge for a distance of two and a half inches, he works only about an inch inward from the edge. This makes a thicker edge that will stand the shattering effect of tough knots. By working on both faces and finishing with the whetstone as before, he achieves an edge that is not to be despised for any general work. It will split wood much better than the thinner edge, but it will not cut quite so easily. On the other hand, it will not chip or nick as readily as the thinner blade.

But since an ax is an ax, and it represents hard work, I think that I prefer the thinner blade, and I'll take my chance on chipping it. Anything that will lighten the labor of driving steel into wood is worth investigating.

— From a student paper.

USE OF DETAILS

The Carmel is a lovely little river. It isn't very long but in its course it has everything a river should have. It rises in the mountains, and tumbles down a while, runs through shallows, is dammed to make a lake, spills over the dam, crackles among round boulders, wanders lazily under sycamores, spills into pools where trout live, drops in against banks where crayfish live. In the winter it becomes a torrent, a mean little fierce river, and in the summer it is a place for children to wade in and for fishermen to wander in. Frogs blink from its banks and the deep ferns grow beside it. Deer and foxes come to drink from it, secretly in the morning and evening, and now and then a mountain lion crouched flat laps its water. The farms of the rich little valley back up to the river and take its water for the orchards and the vegetables. The quail call beside it and the wild doves come whistling in at dusk. Raccoons pace its edges looking for frogs. It's everything a river should be.

— From *Cannery Row*. Copyright 1945 by John Steinbeck. Reprinted by permission of The Viking Press, Inc.

But Mulan was a child of Peking. She had grown up there and had drunk in all the richness of life of the city which enveloped its inhabitants like a great mother soft toward all her children's requests, fulfilling all their whims and desires, or like a huge thousand-year-old tree in which the insects making their home in one branch did not know what the insects in the other branch were doing. She had learned from Peking its tolerance, geniality, and urbanity, as we in our formative years catch something of the city and country we live in. She had grown up with the yellow-roofed palaces and the purple and green-roofed temples, the broad boulevards and the long, crooked alleys, the busy thoroughfares and the quiet districts that were almost rural in their effect; the common man's homes with their inevitable pomegranate trees and jars of goldfish, no less than the rich man's mansions and gardens; the open-air tea houses where men loll on rattan armchairs under cypress trees, spending twenty cents for a whole afternoon in summer; the enclosed teashops where in winter men eat steaming-hot mutton fried with onion and drink *pehkan* and where the great rub shoulders with the humble; the wonderful theaters, the beautiful restaurants, the bazaars, the lantern streets and the curio streets; the temple fairs which register the days of the month; the system of poor man's shop credits and poor man's pleasures, the open-air jugglers, magicians, and acrobats of Shihshahai and the cheap operas of Tienchiao; the beauty and variety of the pedlars' street-cries, the tuning forks of itinerant barbers, the drums of second-hand goods dealers working from house to house, the brass bowls of the sellers of iced dark plum drinks, each and every one clanging in the most perfect rhythm; the pomp of wedding and funeral processions half-a-mile long and official sedan chairs and retinues; the Manchu women contrasting with the Chinese camel caravans from the Mongolian desert and the Lama priests and Buddhist monks; the public entertainers, sword swallowers and beggars, each pursuing his profession with freedom and an unwritten code of honor sanctioned by century-old custom; the rich humanity of beggars and "beggar kings," thieves and thieves' protectors, mandarins and retired scholars, saints and prostitutes, chaste sing-song artists and profligate widows, monks' kept mistresses and eunuchs' sons, amateur singers and "opera maniacs"; and the hearty and humorous common people.

— Lin Yutang, *Moment in Peking*, The John Day Co., New York, 1939. Reprinted by permission.

I walked for a mile and a half along the water's edge of our many-miled invasion beach. I walked slowly, for the detail on the beach was infinite.

The wreckage was vast and startling. The awful waste and destruction of war, even aside from the loss of human life, has always been one of its outstanding features to those who are in it. Anything and everything is expendable. And we did expend on our beachhead in Normandy during those first few hours.

For a mile out from the beach there were scores of tanks and trucks and boats that were not visible, for they were at the bottom of the water — swamped by overloading, or hit by shells, or sunk by mines. Most of their crews were lost.

There were trucks tipped half over and swamped, partly sunken barges, and angled-up corners of jeeps, and small landing craft half submerged. And at low tide you could still see those vicious six-pronged snares that helped snag and wreck them.

On the beach itself, high and dry, were all kinds of wrecked vehicles. There were tanks that had only just made the beach before being knocked out. There were jeeps that had burned to a dull gray. There were big derricks on caterpillar treads that didn't quite make it. There were half-tracks carrying office equipment that had been made into a shambles by a single shell hit, their interiors still holding the useless equipage of smashed typewriters, telephones, office files.

There were LCTs turned completely upside down, and lying on their backs, and how they got that way I don't know. There were boats stacked on top of each other, their sides caved in, their suspension doors knocked off.

In this shore-line museum of carnage there were abandoned rolls of barbed wire and smashed bulldozers and big stacks of thrown-away life belts and piles of shells still waiting to be moved. In the water floated empty life rafts and soldiers' packs and ration boxes, and mysterious oranges. On the beach lay snarled rolls of telephone wire and big rolls of steel matting and stacks of broken, rusting rifles.

On the beach lay, expended, sufficient men and mechanism for a small war. They were gone forever now. And yet we could afford it.

We could afford it because we were on, we had our toe hold, and behind us there were such enormous replacements for this wreckage on the beach that you could hardly conceive of the sum total. Men and equipment were flowing from England in such a gigantic stream that it made the waste on the beachhead seem like nothing at all, really nothing at all.

But there was another and more human litter. It extended in a thin little line, just like a high-water mark, for miles along the beach. This was the strewn personal gear, gear that would never be needed again by those who fought and died to give us our entrance into Europe.

There in a jumbled row for mile on mile were soldiers' packs. There were socks and shoe polish, sewing kits, diaries, Bibles, hand grenades. There were the latest letters from home, with the address on each one neatly razored out — one of the security precautions enforced before the boys embarked.

There were toothbrushes and razors, and snapshots of families back home staring up at you from the sand. There were pocketbooks, metal mirrors, extra trousers, and bloody, abandoned shoes. There were broken-handled shovels, and portable radios smashed almost beyond recognition, and mine detectors twisted and ruined.

There were torn pistol belts and canvas water buckets, first-aid kits, and jumbled heaps of life belts. I picked up a pocket Bible with a soldier's name in it, and put it in my jacket. I carried it half a mile or so and then put it back down on the beach. I don't know why I picked it up, or why I put it down again.

Soldiers carry strange things ashore with them. In every invasion there is at least one soldier hitting the beach at H-hour with a banjo slung over his shoulder. The most ironic piece of equipment marking our beach — this beach first of despair, then of victory — was a tennis racket that some soldier had brought along. It lay lonesomely on the sand, clamped in its press, not a string broken.

Two of the most dominant items in the beach refuse were cigarettes and writing paper. Each soldier was issued a carton of cigarettes just before we started. That day those cartons by the thousand, water-soaked and spilled out, marked the line of our first savage blow.

Writing paper and air-mail envelopes came second. The boys had intended to do a lot of writing in France. The letters — now forever incapable of being written — that might have filled those blank abandoned pages!

Always there are dogs in every invasion. There was a dog still on the beach, still pitifully looking for his masters.

He stayed at the water's edge, near a boat that lay twisted and half sunk at the waterline. He barked appealingly to every soldier who approached, trotted eagerly along with him for a few feet, and then, sensing himself unwanted in all the haste, he would run back to wait in vain for his own people at his own empty boat.

— Ernie Pyle, *Brave Men*, Henry Holt & Co., New York, 1944. Reprinted by permission.

EXERCISES

Exercise 1. Select a number of subjects which can be developed by using the chronological order. Construct an outline for your paper. The following are subjects which may be used. Others will readily suggest themselves to you.

1. An issue of the college newspaper
2. How to bind a book
3. Learning to skate
4. Make your own Christmas cards
5. How to train a dog
6. Delivering your morning paper
7. How to explore the city
8. Prepare for inspection
9. Fishing
10. Getting married
11. Making a dress

Exercise 2. Make a list of five subjects which can be best presented by using the inductive order. Use two reasons for selecting subjects: *1.* you wish to prepare your reader for an idea to which he is naturally antagonistic; *2.* you wish to use a number of concrete instances so as to prepare his mind for a generalization.

Exercise 3. Plan a sketch of some place, such as a town, a summer resort, a college, etc., which you can write in imitation of John Steinbeck's characterization of the Carmel River.

1. My home town isn't very large, but it has everything that a little town should have.
2. Our farm is like thousands of other farms, but it is everything that a farm should be.
3. Few people have ever heard of the little village which I call my home, but it has everything that a village should have.

Exercise 4. Reread Lin Yutang's characterization of Peking. Write a characterization of your own home town in imitation of it.

Exercise 5. Reread Ernie Pyle's picture of the invasion beach in Normandy. Write a descriptive sketch of some scene in which you try to get your effect by piling up concrete details.

The Ending. In the writing process, stopping is much simpler than starting. In a short paper, after the writer has discussed the last phase of his topic adequately, no literary device surpasses the finality of lifting the pen from the paper or pulling the paper out of the typewriter. The short essay, sketch, article, or discussion has no room for summaries or formal conclusions.

In an article of several thousand words, a quick restatement of the thesis idea is effective. If a summing up of the central idea is inconvenient, the reader's mind should be directed to some important thought related to the main subject, not to a subordinate detail. An analysis of the expository essays in one issue of *Harper's Magazine* (August, 1945) reveals these principles in action:

1. John Fischer, in "Odds Against Another War," restates his main thesis.

If we and the Russians together can learn this lesson — if we can learn to behave with the responsibility and restraint of true Super-Powers — we may in time build a real peace of mutual confidence instead of an armed truce.[1]

2. Wolfang Langewiesche, in "Winds That Blow Straight Up," takes the reader back to his opening incident. (See p. 153.)

That's the dynamite packed in the puff of wind which picks up a piece of paper.[1]

3. Roy A. H. Thompson, in "What's Happening to the Timber," restates and summarizes his main thesis.

The day of low lumber prices and apparently unlimited supply is almost over. When businessmen and home builders demand vast quantities of

---

[1] All selections from *Harper's Magazine* reprinted by permission of the authors and of *Harper's Magazine.*

lumber for the post-war housing boom, they probably will have trouble getting it and the prices may provide an unpleasant shock. And at that point, the nation may finally decide to do something about its forests.[1]

4. James Rorty and N. Philip Norman, in " All the Food That's Fit to Eat," end with an explanatory comment and a summary of their main thesis.

Throughout this survey we have adopted conservative estimates and have tried to err on the side of understatement. Some of these promising developments may be stopped by practical difficulties, some by vagaries of consumers' taste; others may be stifled in trade pressures. Even so, the prospect of a postwar flood of good food is real enough to afford the American housewife a good deal of satisfaction.[1]

5. Kurt Steel, in " Revolution in the Corn Belt," ends with a summarizing comment on what he has written.

The Aztecs believed that the corn plant was a direct gift to mankind from the gods. They may not have been so far wrong, at that.[1]

The rest of this issue of *Harper's* consists of fiction, narrative articles, and special departments. The principles of expository writing do not apply, except incidentally, to those types of writing.

[1] *Ibid.*

Chapter 5

WRITING THE RESEARCH PAPER

The Use of the Library. The purpose of this section is to give you information helpful to you in getting books from your library and in getting information from books and periodicals which ordinarily cannot be taken out of a library.

The starting point for your exploration of the library is, logically, the card catalogue. This is a collection of cards listing every book, bulletin, pamphlet, or periodical which the library owns. The cards are arranged alphabetically according to authors, titles, and subjects. In other words, every book is listed on at least three separate cards. You can therefore find a book if you know the author's name, or the title, or the subject with which it deals. Magazines and bulletins are usually listed by title; that is, the card catalogue will tell you whether or not the library possesses a certain magazine or series of bulletins. For detailed information about the contents of these periodicals or bulletins you will have to consult other guides.

Let us examine a typical library card (see p. 173).

1. 341.6–B977 is the call number, according to the Dewey Decimal system.

2. "Butler, Nicholas Murray, 1862–" tells you the author's name, last name given first; the date of his birth; and that at the time this card was made out he was still living.

3. "The path . . . 1930" tells you the title of the book and the subtitle; the author's name, written in the natural order; the place of publication; the name of the publisher; and the date of publication.

341.6   **Butler, Nicholas Murray,** 1862–
B977
      The path to peace; essays and addresses on peace and its making, by Nicholas Murray Butler ... New York, London, C. Scribner's sons, 1930.

xiii, 320 p. 19^{cm}.

1. Peace. 2. Renunciation of war treaty, Paris, Aug. 27, 1928. 3. International law and relations.   i. Title.

30—28072

Library of Congress   JX1952.B83

——— ——— Copy 2.

Copyright A 29303   [31p5]   341.6

4. The fifth line tells you that the book has thirteen pages numbered in Roman numerals and 320 pages numbered in Arabic numerals, and that the height of the book is 19 centimeters.

5. The next two lines give you the subject references under which the book may be found listed in the card catalogue. You will find the book listed under: peace; renunciation of war treaty, Paris, Aug. 27, 1928; international law and relations; and under the title.

6. "Library of Congress" and "——— ——— Copy 2" tell you that the Library of Congress has two copies of the book.

7. "JX1952.B83" is the Library of Congress cataloguing symbol.

8. "30—28072" is the order number used by librarians in ordering cards.

9. "[31p5]" is the key to the printing of the card.

10. "341.6" is the class number under the Dewey Decimal system.

11. "Copyright A 29303" is the Library of Congress key to the copyright of the book.

The card just examined is an author card. A title card is just like an author card, except that the title is typewritten at the top.

PE1075   Modern English in the making.
M3

McKnight, George Harley, 1871–

Modern English in the making, by George H. McKnight ... with the assistance of Bert Emsley ... New York, London, D. Appleton and company, 1928.

xii p., 1 l., 590 p. front., illus., pl., facsims. 21^{cm}.

1. English language—Hist. 2. English language—Grammar, Historical. i. Emsley, Bert, joint author. ii. Title.

28—23547

Library of Congress   PE1075.M3

—— —— Copy 2.

Copyright A 1054337   [35u2]

The descriptive line, "xii p., 1 l., 590 p. front., illus., pl., facsims. 21^{cm}." (see card above), tells you that there are twelve pages numbered in Roman numerals, one leaf printed on one side only, 590 pages of print, a frontispiece, illustrations, plates, and facsimiles. This specimen card also shows you that books

HC103 U. S.–Economic conditions
B57

Bogart, Ernest Ludlow, 1870–

... Economic history of the American people, by Ernest Ludlow Bogart ... New York, London [etc.] Longmans, Green and co., 1930.

xii p., 1 l., 797 p. illus. (maps) diagrs. 22$\frac{1}{2}$^{cm}. (Longmans' economics series)

"First edition."
"Bibliographical note" at end of each chapter.

1. U. S.—Econ. condit. 2. U. S.—Indus.—Hist.

30—28303

Library of Congress   HC103.B57

—— —— Copy 2.

Copyright A 29217   [33z3]   330.973

are catalogued under the name of a joint author. All the other information you should be able to interpret for yourself.

A subject card (see bottom of p. 174) is an author card with the subject typed, usually in red, above the author's name at the top.

Call Numbers. A "call number" is a symbol or group of symbols used by libraries to designate any particular book. The call number for any book is placed in the upper left-hand corner of the card-catalogue card, on the back cover of the book, and usually on the inside cover as well. Books are arranged on shelves according to their call numbers. Call numbers usually consist of two parts: the upper part is the classification number, and the lower part the author and book number.

For the ordinary undergraduate, a knowledge of the systems used in devising call numbers is relatively unimportant. To satisfy a natural curiosity on the part of many students and to make library work a little more interesting, the following brief explanation is given.

Two systems of classification are used by libraries in this country: the Library of Congress system and the Dewey Decimal system.

The Library of Congress system, found more frequently in college than in public libraries, uses the letters of the alphabet, followed by Arabic numerals or additional letters, as the basis of its classification.

A General works
B Philosophy — Religion
C History — Auxiliary sciences
D History and topography (except America)
E and F American history
G Geography — Anthropology
H Social sciences
J Political science
K Law
L Education
M Music
N Fine arts

P   Language and literature
Q   Science
R   Medicine
S   Agriculture — Plant and animal industry
T   Technology
U   Military science
V   Naval science
Z   Bibliography and library science

The Dewey Decimal system, devised by Melvil Dewey, uses a decimal classification for all books. The entire field of knowledge is divided into nine groups, with an additional group for general reference books. Each main class and subclass is shown by a number composed of three digits. Subdivisions of these classes are designated by numbers after a decimal point. In the following table the subdivision is shown under the class of natural science.

000 General works
100 Philosophy
200 Religion
300 Sociology
400 Philology
500 Natural science
     510 Mathematics
     520 Astronomy
     530 Physics
     540 Chemistry
     550 Geology
     560 Paleontology
     570 Biology
     580 Botany
     590 Zoology
600 Useful arts
700 Fine arts
800 Literature
900 History

The Reference Library. The reference library consists of all the general works, such as encyclopedias and dictionaries, and collections of pamphlets, bibliographies, guides, maps, pictures, and the like, which are to be consulted for some specific information rather than to be read in their entirety. Reference books ordinarily cannot be taken from the library. The following list of reference books should be a starting point for your explorations of the reference room of your library. Get acquainted with these books. Find out where they are shelved. Examine them, and examine others like them that you find on the shelves.

In the following list, the date given is usually the date of the latest revision. In this changing world, the date of publication may be very important in a reference book.

THE GENERAL ENCYCLOPEDIAS

Encyclopaedia Britannica, 24 vols., Encyclopaedia Britannica Co., Chicago, Illinois.

Since 1940 the *Britannica* has been kept up to date by continuous revision. Hence a date is necessary with a reference to any printing or revision of this work since 1940. The fourteenth was the last numbered edition. No more numbered editions will be published.

The *Britannica* — owned, edited, and published in the United States, in spite of what its name might suggest — is an exhaustive work. The articles, written by 3,700 contributors from 62 different countries, cover almost every field of human knowledge. The more important articles are signed with the initials of the authors; the index to the initials is found in each volume. The subjects are arranged alphabetically; a general index of 500,000 references is found in volume 24. There are bibliographies, over 17,588 illustrations, 700 maps, and many figures and diagrams.

Encyclopedia Americana, 30 vols., Americana Corporation, New York.

Like the *Britannica*, the *Americana* is now kept up to date by continuous revision. Hence the date is necessary with any reference to it.

The articles in the *Americana*, usually shorter than in the *Britannica*, are written by authorities in the various fields. The more important articles are signed in full. The whole field of knowledge, from ancient to modern times, is treated. The various aspects of modern life — business, industry, science, government, literature, music, biography — are dealt with in reliable and compact essays. The historical studies are excellent. Like the *Britannica*, it has bibliographies, illustrations, and maps. The index is in volume 30.

New International Encyclopaedia, 25 vols., Dodd, Mead and Co., New York, 1922 (sup., 2 vols., 1925; 2 vols., 1930); distributed by Funk and Wagnalls.

Although the *New International* is written from the American point of view, it is really international in scope. The 75,000 articles cover a wide field. Good bibliographies, maps, illustrations, and reading courses are included. The articles are unsigned, but the table of contents of each volume gives the authors of the more important articles. The *New International* has not been revised recently.

A student using the *Britannica*, the *Americana*, and the *New International* should also consult the annual supplements, the *Britannica Book of the Year*, the *Americana Annual*, and the *New International Year-Book*, for additional information.

THE SPECIAL ENCYCLOPEDIAS

The Catholic Encyclopedia, 17 vols., Robert Appleton Company, New York, 1907–1922 (vols. 16–17 published by the Encyclopedia Press).

Although this work deals primarily with the accomplishments of Roman Catholics, its scope is rather general. The signed articles are arranged alphabetically. It is useful not only for subjects relating to the Catholic Church but also for subjects relating to medieval literature, history, art, and philosophy.

The Jewish Encyclopedia, 12 vols., Funk and Wagnalls, New York, 1925.

This work contains articles (signed by initials) dealing with the history, traditions, customs, literature, and accomplishments of the Jewish people from the earliest times to the present.

Bailey, L. H., ed., Cyclopedia of American Agriculture, 4 vols., The Macmillan Company, New York, 1907–1909.

Signed articles are grouped under four heads: vol. 1, farms; vol. 2, crops; vol. 3, animals; vol. 4, farm and community. Bibliographies and illustrations are included.

Hastings, James, ed., Encyclopaedia of Religion and Ethics, 13 vols., Charles Scribner's Sons, New York, 1908–1928.

This work contains signed articles on various religions, systems of ethics, philosophies, religious customs and practices, persons important in religious history, and places famous because of religious associations.

Monroe, Paul, ed., Cyclopedia of Education, 3 vols., The Macmillan Company, New York, 1925.

This work contains articles dealing with various educational systems, noted educators, and colleges and universities.

Munn, Glenn G., Encyclopedia of Banking and Finance, 2 vols., Bankers Publishing Company, New York, 1935; 1 vol., 1937.

This is a manual of terms relating to banking, money, credit, trusts, foreign exchange, insurance, markets, securities, and the like.

Seligman, Edwin R. A., and Alvin Johnson, eds., Encyclopaedia of the Social Sciences, 15 vols., The Macmillan Company, New York, 1930–1935 (reprinted in 8 vols. in 1937).

The articles about sociology, political science, economics, ethics, philosophy, education, etc., are prepared under the sponsorship of ten national learned societies. Good bibliographies and an index are included.

THE YEAR BOOKS

The World Almanac and Book of Facts, The New York World-Telegram, New York, 1868 to date.

This is the most widely used of the year books. It gives summarized and tabulated information about everything of importance that happens in the fields of science, finance, politics, medicine, sports, literature, current affairs, etc.

Britannica Book of the Year, Encyclopaedia Britannica Co., Chicago, 1938 to date.

This is the annual supplement to the *Encyclopaedia Britannica*. The date of each volume is the date of publication. The volume itself is a record of the events of the previous year.

The American Year Book, now published by Thomas Nelson & Sons, 1910 to date.

The articles for this year book are prepared under the direction of representatives of 45 national learned societies. They are classified under such headings as science, history, American government, etc. The articles are signed.

The Americana Annual, Encyclopedia Americana Corporation, New York, 1923 to date.

This is the annual supplement to the *Encyclopedia Americana*.

The New International Year Book, now published by Funk and Wagnalls, New York, 1907 to date.

This is the annual supplement to the *New International Encyclopaedia*.

Statesman's Year-Book, The Macmillan Company, London, 1864 to date.

Information about governments, industries, resources, etc., is given by countries, the British Empire being listed first, followed by the United States and then the other countries in alphabetical order.

Economic Almanac, National Industrial Conference Board, New York, 1940 to date.

This is an annual volume, a "handbook of useful facts about business, labor, and government in the United States and other areas."

BIOGRAPHICAL DICTIONARIES

Dictionary of National Biography, 22 vols., Oxford University Press, London, 1921–1922.

This contains biographies of famous persons of the British Empire who are no longer living.

Dictionary of American Biography, 21 vols., Charles Scribner's Sons, New York, 1928 to 1943.

Prepared under the auspices of the American Council of Learned Societies, this is the American equivalent of the *Dictionary of National Biography*. This work contains the biographies of more than 15,000 men and women who have made some special contribution to our national life. Each biography is written by a recognized authority.

Current Biography: Who's News and Why, H. W. Wilson Company, New York, 1940 to date.

This is published monthly, with six-month and annual cumulations.

Webster's Biographical Dictionary, G. & C. Merriam Company, Springfield, Mass., 1943.

This is a pronouncing biographical dictionary of over 40,000 names. It includes living persons.

Who's Who, A. and C. Black, Ltd., London, 1849 to date.

This is an annual publication containing compact biographies of prominent living Englishmen and a few famous persons of other nations.

Who's Who in America, A. N. Marquis Company, Chicago, 1899 to date.

This is published every two years. It gives brief biographical sketches of famous living persons in the United States.

DICTIONARIES AND BOOKS OF SYNONYMS

New English Dictionary, 10 vols. and sup., Oxford, Clarendon Press, 1888 to 1933.

This dictionary, also called the *Oxford Dictionary, Murray's Dictionary, N.E.D.,* and *O.E.D.,* is not for general use. Its purpose is to give the history of every word in the English language for the last 800 years. It contains many quotations illustrating meanings of words in various periods and full discussions of derivations and changes in meanings and spellings.

New Century Dictionary, 3 vols., The Century Company, New York, 1927–1933.

This is based on the original *Century Dictionary* in 12 volumes, which was published in 1911.

Webster's New International Dictionary, 2nd ed., G. & C. Merriam Company, Springfield, Mass., 1934 to date.

This edition, published after ten years of preparation, is an entirely new book. It is the dictionary almost universally appealed to as the final authority in spelling, meaning, pronunciation, derivation, and usage. It is kept up to date by means of a new words section.

New Standard Dictionary, Funk and Wagnalls, 1935 to date.

This one-volume unabridged dictionary is kept up to date through changes and additions with every printing.

The Roget Dictionary of Synonyms and Antonyms, G. P. Putnam's Sons, New York, 1931.

This is *Roget's Thesaurus*, revised and modernized, and completely rearranged in form. The revision is a decided improvement. Words are listed in dictionary order. The most important entries are followed by synonyms grouped as nouns, verbs, adjectives, and adverbs. Less important words are followed by a few synonyms and a reference to a major group.

Webster's Dictionary of Synonyms, G. & C. Merriam Company, Springfield, Mass., 1942.

This is a dictionary of discriminated synonyms with antonyms and analogues and contrasted words. Its purpose is to provide users with "the means of making clear comparisons between words of a common denotation and to enable them to distinguish the differences in implications, connotations, and applications among such words, and to choose for their purposes the precisely suitable word."

Allen, F. Sturges, Allen's Synonyms and Antonyms, Harper & Brothers, New York, 1938.

The words, in alphabetical order, are followed by synonyms and antonyms but not by definitions. Usage labels, such as *affected, archaic, colloq., formal, obs.*, etc., are helpful.

Crabb, George, Crabb's English Synonyms, Harper & Brothers, New York, 1934.

The words, in alphabetical order, are arranged by first word of groups of synonymous words, with explanations and examples of use. There are cross references and an index.

Fernald, James C., English Synonyms and Antonyms, Funk & Wagnalls, New York, 1938.

Under key words are synonyms and antonyms and correct use of prepositions, followed by discussions of differences between synonyms. There are questions for study and an index in part 2.

Fowler, H. W., A Dictionary of Modern English Usage, Oxford, Clarendon Press, 1926.

Although this is neither a dictionary nor a book of synonyms, it is an invaluable aid to every person who is interested in writing correctly. No description can do justice to the wit and scholarship that went into the making of this little book. The index is the flower of true British reticence.

GAZETTEERS AND ATLASES

In a world of quickly changing national boundaries, atlases are out of date almost as soon as they are printed. Most of the following, however, are kept up to date by frequent revisions. Look for the date on the book that you are using.

Rand McNally Commercial Atlas and Marketing Guide, Rand McNally & Co., Chicago.

This contains information about population, transportation, products, manufacturing, markets, steamship lines, and railroads. The maps are large, and there is a good index.

The New World Loose Leaf Atlas, C. S. Hammond & Co., New York.

Hammond's New World Atlas, Doubleday, Doran & Co., Garden City, New York.

The Times Survey Atlas of the World, The Times, London.

Encyclopaedia Britannica World Atlas, Encyclopaedia Britannica Co., Chicago.

LITERATURE

Cambridge History of English Literature, 15 vols., Cambridge University Press, 1907–1927.

The chapters are arranged by periods and famous authors, each chapter being written by a specialist in that field. The bibliographies have been brought up to date in the *Cambridge Bibliography of English Literature*, 1941.

Cambridge History of American Literature, 3 vols., The Macmillan Company, New York, 1933 (originally 4 vols., G. P. Putnam's Sons, New York, 1917–1921).

This is similar in arrangement and plan to the *Cambridge History of English Literature*.

LITERARY QUOTATIONS

Bartlett, John, Familiar Quotations, 11th ed., Little, Brown & Co., Boston, 1937.

The quotations are arranged chronologically by the date of the author's birth. There is an index of authors in the front. The quotations are indexed by important words in the back of the book.

Hoyt, J. K., Hoyt's New Cyclopedia of Practical Quotations, Funk and Wagnalls, New York, 1922.

The quotations are arranged alphabetically by subjects, and then by authors under the subjects. Quotations represent English and foreign languages, both ancient and modern. The book is well indexed.

Stevenson, Burton, The Home Book of Quotations, Dodd, Mead & Co., New York, 1934.

About 50,000 quotations are arranged alphabetically by subjects. The authors are indexed, and quotations are listed by important words in each quotation.

Mencken, H. L., A New Dictionary of Quotations on Historical Principles from Ancient and Modern Sources, Alfred A. Knopf, New York, 1942.

The academic title belies the interesting nature of this book. The quotations are arranged under subjects. In most cases, authors' names and titles of works are given in full. Quotations are dated whenever possible. There is no index.

MYTHOLOGY AND ANTIQUITIES

Peck, Harry T., Harper's Dictionary of Classical Literature and Antiquities, American Book Company, New York, 1897.

This work deals with Greek and Roman history, literature, mythology, geography, biography, etc. The arrangement is alphabetical, with cross references.

Smith, Sir William, A Dictionary of Greek and Roman Antiquities, 2 vols., John Murray, London, 1890–1891.

This is primarily for the classical scholar.

Gayley, Charles M., Classic Myths in English Literature and Art, Ginn and Company, Boston, 1911.

This is a popular handbook.

Hamilton, Edith, Mythology, Little, Brown & Co., Boston, 1942.

This is an attractive modern presentation of Greek, Roman, and Norse myths, written with good taste and exact scholarship. There are complete genealogical tables and a comprehensive index.

INDEXES TO PERIODICALS AND NEWSPAPERS

In the reference room of the library you will also discover a number of guides and indexes which will enable you to find material published in magazines and newspapers. Although a little of the material which was originally published in magazines may be available in book form, most of it will never be republished. Some of it is too recent to be published elsewhere. Since in the study of any current question you must go directly to magazines and newspapers, you must acquaint yourself with the following guides:

Poole's Index to Periodical Literature, 1802–1881; supplements: 1882–1886, 1887–1891, 1892–1896, 1897–1901, 1902–1906.

This guide indexes about 590,000 articles in 12,241 volumes of 470 different American and English periodicals. To be able to use it intelligently, you must know that: it is a subject index only; it has no author entries; all articles having a distinct subject are entered under that subject; articles having no subject, like poems and stories, are entered under the first word of the title; no date is given, only volume and page, but not inclusive paging; the periodicals indexed are principally of a general nature.

Readers' Guide to Periodical Literature, 1900 to date.

This is a monthly publication, with annual and permanent cumulated volumes. Its special features are: the entries are under author, title, and subject; it gives volume, inclusive paging, date; it indicates illustrations, portraits, maps, etc.; it indexes book reviews up to 1904; it has a list of 597 books in the second and third cumulated volumes.

Public Affairs Information Service, 1915 to date.

This indexes periodicals, books, documents, and pamphlets relating to political science, sociology, and economics. It is the best source for last-minute information on problems in these fields. It is issued weekly, with bimonthly and annual cumulations.

Agricultural Index, 1916 to date.

This is a subject index, issued nine times a year and cumulated annually, except that every third year a three-year cumulation is published instead of the annual volume.

Experiment Station Record, 1889 to date.

This is a record and digest of current agricultural literature, so complete that it serves as an index to periodical, bulletin, and report material on the subject.

Dramatic Index, 1909 to date.

This is an annual subject index to all articles on drama, the theater, actors and actresses, playwrights, and plays in about two hundred English and American periodicals.

The Education Index, 1929 to date.

This is an author and subject index. The field covered is obvious from the title.

The Art Index, 1929 to date.

This is an author and subject index.

Index to Legal Periodicals, 1908 to date.

This is an author and subject index, issued quarterly with annual cumulations.

Quarterly Cumulative Index Medicus, 1927 to date (Index Medicus, 1879–1926).

This is an author and subject index. It is a complete guide to more than 1,200 periodicals in the field of medicine. It indexes books, pamphlets, theses, as well as periodical articles.

Engineering Index, 1892–1906.

Engineering Index Annual, 1906 to date.

This is a classified subject index from 1906 to 1918, and an alphabetical index from 1919 to date.

Industrial Arts Index, 1913 to date.

This is published monthly with annual cumulations. It is a subject and title index.

International Index to Periodicals, 1907 to date.

This consists of current issues and cumulations in annual and permanent volumes. It is an author and subject index. The *International Index* deals with more scholarly journals than does the *Readers' Guide*. It is the best guide to articles in the foreign languages, especially in German and French.

New York Times Index, 1913 to date. ✓

This is a monthly index of the pages of The New York *Times*, with annual cumulations. The references, arranged according to subject entries, are to date, section, page, and column. It may be used as an index to any daily newspaper over the United States, since the same news stories will probably be found in all daily papers on the day they appear in the *Times*.

The Research Paper. The research article, often called the investigative theme or the term paper, is an exposition which aims to present the results of careful and thorough investigation of some chosen or assigned subject. You will no doubt have occasion to write term papers based on laboratory experiments, or on questionnaires, or on your own critical reactions to something you have read; papers of that sort are organized and written like any other expository theme. The information given here applies primarily to papers based on published material. The problems treated here are those you will meet when you begin your investigations in a library.

The writing of a research paper is justified partly through what you produce and partly through the training you get in the process of writing it. If you produce a good paper, it will be, in one sense, a real contribution to knowledge. The paper may serve a reader by giving him in easily accessible form information which he would have difficulty in finding for himself. It may clarify or evaluate ideas and opinions. It may assemble and organize available materials as a basis for further investigations or for a new and original interpretation.

But the more immediate value, the one you will recognize and appreciate at once, lies in what it will do to you. You will become acquainted with the resources of your library. You will learn how to find information in books, periodicals, pamphlets, documents, and bulletins. You will learn how to take adequate and usable notes. You will get practice in assembling and organizing materials. Your thinking will be stimulated because you will have to reason from your assembled facts and because occasionally you will have to weigh contradictory opinions. And, finally, your judgment will be sharpened through practice in selecting and adapting material for some specific class of readers.

Since a research paper aims to gather and interpret facts for the use of some specific reader, it must be accurate, clear, and interesting. It must be accurate not only in the facts selected and presented but also in the emphasis given to different facts. The information must be based on the most recent studies. Clearness is partly a matter of understanding the purpose of the research and partly a matter of organization and composition. A good, though simple, outline helps to assure clearness. Adequate understanding of the subject matter usually results in greater clearness, since no writer can explain what he himself does not understand. A wide reading in the selected field is an aid to clearness, since it helps the writer to select and reject material wisely. Interest comes, first of all, from subject matter which is in itself interesting to the reader. Not even the most bungling writer can spoil that entirely. But interest may, and usually must, come from other sources — a new point of view, a new interpretation, the flavor of the writer's personality, a lively and enthusiastic attitude. A research paper should not — must not — be dull.

Choosing the Subject. As soon as the research paper is assigned, many students will almost instinctively ask themselves: "Now what subject do I know something about?" A major in English will want to investigate some author or literary movement. A student of forestry will want to write on conservation. A student of home economics will want to write on nutrition or antique furniture. In some ways this attitude is commendable; in other ways it is a mistake. A student should indeed be interested in the subject of his investigation, but his interest may as well bring the thrill of exploring a field entirely new to him. His choice of a field, however, must be limited by certain practical considerations. He cannot take a subject which is too technical for his understanding. No matter how far he explores into strange fields, he must never undertake to explain what he does not fully understand himself. Furthermore, he must limit himself to the resources of the college library. Since the project is designed to be the means of learning how to use library material, information secured by interviews, or through experiments, or from personal experiences, should be submitted only as a supplement to information found in the college reference library.

The following list of subjects should include something that will interest almost any student.

1. Atomic bombs
2. The San Francisco conference
3. Tanks and tank warfare
4. Aircraft carriers
5. Battleships
6. Transport planes
7. Substitutes for rubber
8. Women in factories
9. Allergy
10. Dirigibles
11. Migratory birds
12. The Smithsonian Institution
13. Blood plasma
14. Stratosphere flights
15. The electric eye
16. The Burma road
17. Statehood for Alaska
18. Modern India
19. Soil conservation service
20. Tabloids
21. Social security
22. The U. S. Public Health Service
23. Diego Rivera
24. Modern American painting
25. The Olympic games
26. Archery

CHOOSING THE SUBJECT

27. National Geographic Society
28. Metropolitan Museum of Art
29. Virus diseases
30. Plastics
31. The new Poland
32. Psychoanalysis
33. Psychoneuroses
34. New metals
35. Sulphathiazole
36. Cellulose acetate
37. Modern Turkey
38. Artificial fever
39. Irish Free State
40. The resources of Alaska
41. The defense of Alaska
42. The McGuffey Readers
43. Dust storms
44. American Medical Association
45. Winston Churchill
46. Chiang Kai-shek
47. The American Bar Association
48. Butterflies
49. Bee culture
50. Modern Arabia
51. The Mayan civilization
52. Plant hormones
53. Paul Cézanne
54. Deep-sea explorations
55. Gargoyles
56. Plans for world peace
57. Greenland
58. The Coast Guard
59. Locusts
60. Truffles
61. Frozen foods
62. Freedom of speech
63. Chinchillas
64. Boulder Dam
65. The French in Canada
66. Vitamins
67. Modern American music
68. American antique furniture
69. Modern China
70. The Suez Canal
71. Unemployment insurance
72. The Cossacks
73. Ultra-violet rays
74. Old age pensions
75. The Isle of Man
76. The Danube River
77. Penicillin
78. The Jewish State
79. Problem children
80. The Russian constitution
81. Automobile accidents
82. Colonial architecture
83. An efficient kitchen
84. New anesthetics
85. Education of the feeble minded
86. Substitutes for silk
87. The Vatican
88. Vaudeville
89. Experimental colleges
90. New uses for aluminum
91. Veterans' organizations
92. Progressive education
93. New bactericides
94. Flood control
95. Television
96. Transport planes
97. New automotive fuels
98. Model homes
99. Earthquakes
100. New kinds of glass
101. Prefabricated houses
102. South of the border
103. The Atlantic Charter
104. Some famous newspapers
105. The Basques
106. Government housing projects
107. Dust diseases
108. The Good Neighbor Policy
109. Weather forecasting
110. Religion in Soviet Russia

139

111. Microfilms
112. Dmitri Shostakovich
113. Lemmings
114. Pan Americanism
115. Socialized medicine
116. Documentary films
117. Schools in Soviet Russia
118. The Soviet army
119. Highway illumination
120. Modern treatment of burns
121. Wood preservation
122. The Soviet theater
123. Color blindness
124. Adult education
125. Social reforms in Britain
126. Yugoslavia
127. Military courses in colleges
129. Airplane models
128. Post-war education
130. Industrial diseases
131. The career of Masaryk
132. Technicolor
133. Animated cartoons
134. Artificial precious stones
135. Test pilots
136. Baldness
137. Palestine
138. Bird banding
139. Our foreign policy
140. Rocket ships
141. Chemical gardening
142. Old coins
143. The poetry of Carl Sandburg
144. The little theater
145. Grand opera in English
146. Proletarian literature
147. Negro poets
148. Professional football
149. Censorship of motion pictures
150. The symphony orchestra
151. The poet laureate of England
152. The novels of Willa Cather

153. Expressionism in the theater
154. The copper industry
155. Cryptography
156. Economic planning
157. Electron microscopes
158. Flying boats
159. Gliders
160. Commandos
161. The work of Luther Burbank
162. The poetry of Amy Lowell
163. Famous Shakespearean actors
164. Helicopters
165. Minorities in India
166. Spiders
167. Advertising over the radio
168. Some recent inventions
169. College graduates and business
170. Careers for college women
171. Radar
172. American folk songs
173. Modern stage lighting
174. The Bank of England
175. Air travel
176. The mechanized farm
177. Free verse
178. Modernistic architecture
179. Literature of the small town
180. The American ballet
181. Sinclair Lewis as a social reformer
182. Utopias
183. Dictators
184. Termites
185. Television
186. The G-men
187. Igor Stravinski
188. American dance orchestras
189. The career of Gershwin
190. Strategy in football
191. Consumers' co-operatives
192. Racketeering

193. The TVA
194. Control of poliomyelitis
195. Shakespeare in motion pictures
196. Tap dancing
197. Development of color films
198. Swing music
199. Famous motion picture directors
200. World peace

Limiting the Subject. After you have indicated your general field of interest, you will, with the help of your instructor, select some part or aspect of it that can be effectively presented in the given space and time. If you are interested in literature, you may decide to write about Carl Sandburg. In a paper of about three thousand words you cannot tell everything about Sandburg. You may, however, choose to tell about his stories for children, or his glorification of industry, or his championship of the common man. Or if you are interested in the subject of industrial diseases, you might select some one disease, such as silicosis. In choosing your subject, always remember that you cannot narrow or limit a subject by excluding from it essential details. A research article should be interesting. Interest comes from the concrete details, the examples, or the imaginative touches that you can give your writing.

Before you make your final decision, it might be well for you to spend an hour or two browsing around in the library. Look in the card catalogue. Check through some of the periodical indexes to find out the extent of the published material in your field. Notice in what types of periodicals your information is found, and make a preliminary check, either through the general card catalogue or through a special index of periodicals, to see which of the sources are available in your library. After you have done that, you are ready to begin collecting your bibliography.

The Bibliography. A bibliography is an alphabetized list of books, articles, bulletins, or documents relating to a given subject or author. Bibliographies may be classified as either complete or limited.

A true bibliography consists of all the references relating to a given subject. It has nothing to do with the number of sources available in any given library or the number actually consulted in the preparation of any given research article. It is simply a directory. Like a city directory or a telephone directory, it is there to be consulted but not necessarily read from cover to cover when one wishes to locate an address or find a telephone number.

Most bibliographies are limited. The extent of the bibliography you will prepare will depend on the time you have or on the assignment made by your instructor. You should, however, attempt a fairly adequate guide to your subject. You should list many more references than you expect to use. Some of them will be worthless to you in your particular project; others you will not be able to get in your library. Always expect a certain amount of wastage of your materials. And, finally, remember that your bibliography is a convenience for your reader as much as an acknowledgment of the sources you have consulted.

If your instructor asks for only the sources actually used in the preparation of the paper, hand them in properly alphabetized and typed on a separate sheet of paper. This sort of limited bibliography is usually placed at the end of a research paper.

Bibliography Cards. Use 3 × 5 note cards for your bibliographic references, a separate card for each reference. Adopt a definite form for entries on your cards. Your bibliographic entries should be clear, uniform, complete, and accurate. Remember that three items of information are necessary for every reference: the author's name, the title, and the facts of publication. If you cannot find the author's name, start with the second item. In making out your cards, translate the forms used by guides to periodicals into more generally understood forms. Although you will find references in which Roman numerals are used, it is better for you to use Arabic numerals exclusively. The present tendency — and a welcome one — is to avoid Roman numerals altogether in all kinds of references. Never abbreviate the names of periodicals. Label the volume number and the page numbers, so that you will always know what each number stands for; use *vol.* for *volume* and *pp.* for *pages*.

It is unfortunate that bibliographic forms have not been standardized as completely as have the parts of an automobile. For your convenience, two widely used forms are given in this handbook, an older form, sometimes referred to as the "Chicago style," and a newer, simplified form. You may use the one which your instructor recommends. See section 18 for examples of each form. The two forms are also given side by side in the specimen bibliography on pages 200–202.

The following detailed directions are for the simplified form. It is simple, usable, compact, logical, and practically foolproof.

REFERENCES TO ENCYCLOPEDIAS

For references to encyclopedias, copy:

1. The author's name, last name first, if you can find it (put a comma at the end of the line).
2. The title of the article (put quotation marks around it and a comma after it).
3. The title of the encyclopedia (underline it); the year or edition; the volume number; the pages (put a period at the end).

---

(5)

Thomas, Albert,

"The International Labor Organization,"

Encyclopaedia Britannica, 14th ed., vol. 12, pp. 517–520.

As soon as you have made out a card, give it a number. Write this above the line at the top — in the left-hand corner. This is your "code number" which you will use in the process of gathering notes and writing your theme. Instead of putting down the entire reference, or a shortened form of it, on each note card and on the first draft of your research paper, you will put down the "code number" of the reference, with an exact page reference to the material you are using. This system will save you a great deal of useless copying of references; at the same time it is more accurate than any system of abbreviations that you could invent. Of course, when you copy the final draft of your paper, you will refer to the code numbers of the cards you have used, and copy, in correct form, every footnote according to the directions on pages 203–204. It does not matter what number you give to any card just so that you do not repeat numbers.

REFERENCES TO BOOKS

For references to books, copy:

1. The author's name, last name first, exactly as it appears in the card catalogue (put a comma at the end of the line).
2. The title of the book (underline it to indicate italics and put a comma at the end of the line).
3. The publisher, the place and date of publication (put a period at the end).
4. The library call number (copy it in the upper left-hand corner).

---

(23)

PE1075
M3   McKnight, George Harley,

          Modern English in the Making,

          D. Appleton and Co., New York, 1928.

REFERENCES TO MAGAZINE ARTICLES

For references to magazine articles, copy:

1. The author's name, last name first (if the article is unsigned, begin with the title).
2. The title of the article (in quotation marks).
3. The name of the magazine (underline it); the volume (use Arabic numerals); the pages; the date (in parentheses).

Punctuate this as you punctuated the reference to a book or to an encyclopedia: a comma after the author line; a comma after the title line; a period at the end. Every bibliographic entry thus becomes a single unit, divided into three parts by commas, closed with a period.

For example, let us assume that you find in the *Readers' Guide* a reference like this one:

POUND, Arthur
    Industrial America: its way of work and
       thought.   Atlan. 157:121-8, Ja '36

On your card the reference will appear, without confusing abbreviations and symbols, like this:

```
 (16)
 ------------------------------------------------

   Pound, Arthur,

   "Industrial America: Its Way of Work and
   Thought,"

   Atlantic Monthly, vol. 157, pp. 121-128
   (January, 1936).



```

REFERENCES TO GOVERNMENT BULLETINS

For references to government bulletins, copy:

1. The author's name (if the article is signed).
2. The title of the article (in quotation marks).
3. The publication (with correct references to volume, number, series, pages, date, and publisher).

Students in land-grant colleges and universities may have occasion to use the card catalogue of the United States Department of Agriculture (the USDA catalogue), which indexes all bulletins and magazines published by that department. Here is a sample card from the USDA catalogue:

HORSE–JUDGING

Reese, Herbert Harshman.
   ... How to select a sound horse. [By] H. H. Reese ...
Washington [Govt. print. off.] 1917

    27p. illus. 23ᵐ. (U. S. Dept. of agriculture. Farmers' bulletin 779)

    i. Horse [Judging] i. Title.

                                       Agr 17–332.

Library, U. S. Dept. of Agriculture   1A84f   no. 779

In using this catalogue remember that the facts of publication are all within parentheses in the descriptive line.

The reference to the same bulletin appears in the following form in the *Agricultural Index:*

How to select a sound horse. H. H. Reese. il
   Farmers' B   779:1–26   '17

On your card this will appear as shown below. Why use the USDA catalogue when the same references may be found in the *Agricultural Index?* The *Agricultural Index* was started in 1916; the USDA catalogue covers the whole range of publications of the Department of Agriculture. It is, moreover, arranged according to a subject classification, so that the student working with some one subject will find all his references conveniently grouped in one place.

The bibliography card shown here should give you a key to the form that may be used for every kind of bulletin or pamphlet. Remember that three items are necessary for a complete reference: the author's name, the title, and the publisher. You will have no difficulty with the first two. If the article is unsigned,

---

(38)
_____

    Reese, Herbert Harshman,

    "How to Select a Sound Horse,"

    Farmers' Bulletin, No. 779, pp. 1-26 (1917),
    United States Department of Agriculture.

---

start with the title. For the third item get the name or title of that particular bulletin or series of bulletins, the number or numbers used to identify it, the date of publication, and the institution responsible for the publication. Verify every abbreviation by turning to the index of the guide you are using. Remember that a publisher may be a person, a department of a school, a college or a university, a department of state or national government, a business or industrial concern, a religious organization — in fact, the possibilities are infinite.

REFERENCES TO NEWSPAPERS

In copying references from the *New York Times Index* you must supply the year from the date of the volume you are using. The following references were taken from the 1944 volume.

> **MENTAL Diseases and Hygiene. See also** Veterans, subheads US — Gen, S 18,22 in 2d S 1 par and US — World War II, S 18
>
> Lr on ed on mil use of term psychoneurosis, S 6, 18:6
> Maj Gen Hershey on draft rejections for mental deficiency, S 18, 19:3

On your bibliography card the last of these references would appear as follows:

```
(15)
-----------------------------------------------

  "Major General Hershey on Draft Rejections
  for Mental Deficiency,"

  The New York Times, September 18, 1944,
  p. 19, col. 3.
```

Final Form of the Bibliography. Bibliography cards are for your own use. You need not hand them in unless your instructor asks for them. In spite of this, you should follow either the Chicago Press form or the Simplified form exactly down to the last period. If you do, you will memorize the correct forms so that mistakes in your final bibliography or your footnotes will be impossible. Make out your cards in ink as you find your references. Do not copy a list of references on a sheet of paper and then type your bibliography cards. That procedure is a waste of time. The purpose of using cards is to save you time and useless work. You may have noticed that the models show the lower third of the card blank. That space is for your comments on the value, the timeliness, or the thoroughness of your source. These comments are in no sense notes on reading. They are simply your estimate of the importance of the book, article, or bulletin, an estimate arrived at as a result of your preliminary examination of your source material. For example, your comments might be "Out of date," or "Accurate but brief," or "Too general."

If you are handing in an extensive bibliography of fifty to a hundred and fifty items, you should classify your references under the following heads: 1. General reference works; 2. Books; 3. Periodicals and bulletins (which may be subdivided into "signed" and "unsigned" articles, bulletins, and newspaper reports).

If your bibliography consists of only ten to twenty sources actually consulted in the preparation of your paper, no classification is usually necessary. Alphabetize both signed and unsigned items in the same list.

When you alphabetize, simply take your bibliography cards, spread them out on a table, and rearrange them in the proper order. Alphabetize unsigned articles according to the first letter of the title, disregarding *a, an,* or *the.* In typing, start your entry at the margin on the left. Use single space between the lines of each reference if it runs over a single line, and use double space between references. Begin the run-over lines of each reference about a half an inch to the right of the margin.

The following is a sample bibliography using the Simplified form:

THE NEUROPSYCHIATRIC CASUALTY

BIBLIOGRAPHY

(General Reference Works)

Evans, William A., "Neurosis," The World Book
Encyclopedia, 1941 ed., vol. 12, p. 4897.

White, William A., "Psychiatry and War," Encyclopedia Americana, 1944 ed., vol. 22, pp. 731-
732.

(Books)

Adler, Alfred, Problems of Neurosis, The Cosmopolitan Book Co., New York, 1930.

Brown, Junius Flagg, The Psychodynamics of Abnormal Behavior, McGraw-Hill Book Co., New
York, 1940.

———————————, Psychology and the Social Order,
McGraw-Hill Book Co., New York, 1936.

Brown, William, Suggestion and Mental Analysis,
University of London Press, London, 1923.

Fisher, Vivian Ezra, and Joseph V. Hanna, The Dissatisfied Worker, The Macmillan Co., New
York, 1931.

Murray, Henry A., and Others, Explorations in
Personality, Oxford University Press, New
York, 1938.

(Magazine Articles, Signed)

Deutsch, A., "Mental Hazards of Sea War," Science
Digest, vol. 13, pp. 59-60 (February, 1943).

Farrell, M. J., and M. B. L. Ray, "Will the
Battle-shocked Come Home Cured?" Woman's
Home Companion, vol. 71, p. 33 (April,
1944).

Freeman, Walter, "Wartime Neuroses," Hygeia, vol. 20, pp. 492–493 (July, 1942).

Painton, F. C., "There Is No Such Thing As Shell Shock," Reader's Digest, vol. 43, pp. 59–63 (October, 1943).

Van De Water, M., "Soldiers Wounded in Mind," Science News Letter, vol. 45, pp. 262–263 (April 22, 1944).

(Magazine Articles, Unsigned)

"Fighters Often Get Guilt Neurosis Which Psychiatry Can Easily Cure," Newsweek, vol. 23, p. 68 (May 29, 1944).

"Hypnosis Urged for Speed-up Treatment of War Neurosis," Science Digest, vol. 11, pp. 48–49 (April, 1942).

"Spit It Out, Soldier," Time, vol. 42, p. 60 (September 13, 1943).

"War Neurosis Effects," Science News Letter, vol. 42, p. 134 (August 29, 1942).

"War Neurosis Must Be Cured by Prompt Treatment," Science Digest, vol. 12, p. 58 (July, 1942).

(Newspaper Articles)

"Letter on Education on Military Use of Term Psychoneurosis," New York Times, September 6, 1944, p. 18, col. 6.

"Major General Hershey on Draft Rejections for Mental Deficiency," New York Times, September 18, 1944, p. 19, col. 3.

In the sample bibliography reproduced above you may notice that (1) when an author is represented by more than one work, his name is given for the first entry, but in subsequent entries a line, about an inch in length, is used instead of his name; (2) when a book or article has two authors, the second name is given in the normal order; (3) when three or more authors are responsible for a book, the name of only the first author is used, plus "and Others."

The following sample bibliography shows the "University of Chicago Press" style. Some authorities recommend this style with one change — substituting Arabic for Roman numerals.

White, William A. "Psychiatry and War," Encyclopedia Americana, XXII (1944), 731–732.

Adler, Alfred. Problems of Neurosis. New York: Cosmopolitan Book Co., 1930.

Brown, Junius Flagg. The Psychodynamics of Abnormal Behavior. New York: McGraw–Hill Book Co., 1940.

————————. Psychology and the Social Order. New York: McGraw–Hill Book Co., 1936.

Fisher, Vivian Ezra, and Joseph V. Hanna. The Dissatisfied Worker. New York: Macmillan Co., 1931.

Murray, Henry A., and Others. Explorations in Personality. New York: Oxford University Press, 1938.

Deutsch, A. "Mental Hazards of Sea War," Science Digest, XIII (1943), 59–60.

Farrell, M. J., and M. B. L. Ray. "Will the Battle–shocked Come Home Cured?" Woman's Home Companion, LXXI (1944), 33.

"War Neurosis Effects," Science News Letter, XLII (1942), 134.

"War Neurosis Must Be Cured by Prompt Treatment," Science Digest, XII (1942), 58.

Most scientific journals have their own special variations of bibliographic forms.

Footnotes. Footnotes have several uses. Although, in the main, you will use them to identify and acknowledge the material which you have used in the body of your paper, you should know that they may also be used to define some term used in the text, to give additional information that does not fit into the text, or to explain in detail what has merely been referred to in the text.

To indicate to the reader that a footnote is being used, place an Arabic numeral immediately after and a little above the material referred to. Do not put a period after the number, either in the text or with the footnote at the bottom of the page. Place the same number before the footnote at the bottom of the page. The styles used in numbering footnotes vary. Either you may number all your footnotes consecutively from the beginning to the end of your paper or you may begin numbering with number one on each page. The second style is the more common. Do whatever your instructor asks you to do.

The following are the usual conventions regarding the use of footnotes:

1. Complete information about the source referred to must be given in the first reference to that source (author, title, all facts of publication as in the bibliography). After that, if there is no danger of confusion, a note consisting of author's last name, the title, and the page reference is sufficient.
2. When a list of sources used has been handed in with the paper, it is usually acceptable to abridge all references, including the first reference to any item, to author, title, and page. Be sure to consult your instructor before you use this style.
3. The footnote follows the same order as the bibliographic entry — author, title, facts of publications — except that the author's name is given in the normal order.
4. Any part of the source which is given in the text of the essay need not be repeated in the footnote. For example, if the author has been mentioned, only the title and the facts of publication need be given in the footnote.

To avoid copying the same footnote several times, you may use the following abbreviations (see also section 18b):

1. *Ibid.*, for *ibidem*, meaning "the same" or "in the same place," to show that the footnote refers to the same work, as the footnote immediately preceding. It should be followed by a page reference if the source is the same but the page is different. The author's name is not used with *ibid.*

2. *Op. cit.* (from the Latin *opere citato*, meaning "in the work cited") is ordinarily used after the author's name. It means that the reference is to that author's work which has already been mentioned in the footnotes. The author's last name is sufficient if there is only one author by that name; if more than one author of the same name is being used in the references, the initials of each must be used. *Op. cit.* cannot be used when more than one work by the same author is among the references. The correct title must be repeated in each reference.

Assuming that the bibliography on pages 200–201 is being used, let us illustrate the correct use of footnotes.

First mention of a book: [1]

[1] J. F. Brown, *The Psychodynamics of Abnormal Behavior*, McGraw-Hill, New York, 1940, p. 132.

Succeeding reference is to the same page of the same book: [2]

[2] *Ibid.*   *Loc. cit.*

A different reference intervenes: [3]

[3] Henry A. Murray and Others, *Explorations in Personality*, Oxford University Press, New York, 1938, p. 231.

Brown, op. cit., p. 174.

There is a reference to a magazine article: [4]

[4] A. Deutsch, "Mental Hazards of Sea War," *Science Digest*, vol. 13 (Feb., 1943), p. 60.

Now we wish to go back to the book by Murray and others: [5]

[5] Murray, *op. cit.*, p. 168.

We have another book by J. F. Brown: [6]

[6] J. F. Brown, *Psychology and the Social Order*, McGraw-Hill, New York, 1936, pp. 102–104.

After this we must repeat the title of either of his books: [7]

[7] Brown, *Psychodynamics of Abnormal Behavior*, p. 57.

Notes on Reading. It is assumed that before you begin to take notes you have collected a fairly adequate bibliography. Take your bibliography cards with you to the library. Look up a few of the most promising of your references. You might start with the encyclopedia articles. Your purpose is to make a preliminary exploration of your field. Read for general information. Do not take notes, but indicate on your bibliography cards the merits or weaknesses of the sources you examine. While you are exploring, make a note of the most important topics that seem to be related to your particular project. These topics, properly arranged, will become your first rough outline. They will be the headings you will use on your note cards when you begin taking notes.

When you go to the library to begin work, you must have with you a generous supply of note cards. The 3 × 5 library or filing cards, like those you used for your bibliography, are most convenient. Larger cards may be used. If possible, get cards that have a space at the top marked off by a red line. This space you will use for your notation of the exact source from which you are taking your information.

After your preliminary exploration of your field you will be ready to construct a topical outline of your paper. This topical outline is to be based partly on what you have learned about your subject and partly on what any intelligent and mature person would want to be told if he were reading an article about your subject. Let us now experiment with two subjects. The first is "The Little Theater." You and I both know something about it. There is probably a little theater on the campus of our university. We have attended performances of plays there. What do we want to know about it? Or let us say, what is there that *can* be told about it in an hour's lecture? A few pertinent and interesting facts about, first, its origin and history; second, the leaders in the movement; third, some of the most famous little theaters; fourth, its influence on the professional theater; fifth, its value to the community; sixth, the opportunities it gives to unknown artists. Let us reduce these to outline topics:

THE LITTLE THEATER

1. Origin and history
2. Leaders in movement
3. Famous theaters
4. Influence on professional stage
5. Value to community
6. Opportunities to unknown artists

These topics will be the headings under which you will gather your notes. As soon as you have found a book or article on which you are ready to take notes, copy in the space above the red line the code number of that reference from your bibliography card. After the code number write the exact page reference to your material. Let us suppose that your reference is an article in *Theatre Arts Monthly*. The number of your bibliography card to this article is 27. Write 27 in the upper left-hand corner of your note card. Just below the red line write one of the topics from your list. Fill the card with notes from that article relating to that topic.

Our next subject will be more technical — it will be "Diesel Engines." What do we know about Diesel engines? Well, we have read something about a mysterious passenger car equipped with a Diesel engine; we know that it burns crude oil; we know a few other things, most of them more or less indefinite. Here is what we should *like* to know:

DIESEL ENGINES

1. Principles of structure
2. Advantages over other types
3. Difficulties to be overcome
4. Relation to fuel supply
5. Use in light passenger cars
6. Use in heavy trucks

As we read more extensively we may wish to modify our outline; that is part of the plan. The preliminary outline is just that — preliminary or experimental, subject to modification. But it will give us a guide for our note-taking.

Now as to the form which your notes should take: let us remember that although you will not take perfect notes, you can save much unnecessary waste by following a few well-defined principles. Here they are:

1. Take notes in the form of a condensed summary. Get what is essential and get it accurately, but do not waste words.
2. Do not copy your material in the form of direct quotations, unless you mean to use exact quotations in your paper. If you copy the exact words of the original, enclose them in quotation marks.
3. Let your first unbreakable rule be "One topic to a card." Do not include in your notes on the same card material relating to two or more topics. You may have as many note cards as you wish relating to the same topic, but you must label each card and give the exact source of your notes on each card.
4. Let your notes be so accurate and so complete that they will make sense to you when they become cold.
5. Use headings or topics which represent actual divisions of your outline, as closely as it is possible for you to anticipate the outline you will use. Avoid the unnecessary and confusing multiplication of topics and subtopics.
6. And, finally, remember that every note card must have three pieces of information:
   a. The exact source of your material.
   b. The heading or topic which shows where your information belongs.
   c. The information itself.

Your first attempts to take notes on your reading may result in a few scattered entries and much wasted time. But you will soon discover that your English composition course has taught you more than merely how to write a few themes. You begin to realize that at least half its value lies in what it has taught you about reading. You have learned to organize themes so that their contents may be comprehended by your reader easily, quickly, without confusion, without wasted effort. Those who write books, chapters, essays, or articles employ the same principles of writing that you have learned — so that *you* may get the information you want, easily, quickly, without confusion, without wasted effort. In a book you examine first the table of contents, the index, the chapter headings, and the topics of the minor divisions. In an essay or article you look for a formal statement of plan or purpose at the beginning of the selection. Then you glance through the essay, reading a topic sentence here, another one there, until you come to what you want.

You will also learn to use other signs indicating the value of your source. Look at the date of publication to see if it contains information recent enough for your purpose. In some fields, such as chemistry and medicine, information even a few months old may be highly misleading or absolutely worthless. Investigate the author, too. Is he an authority in his field? What is his reputation for scholarship or for honesty? If you are examining an article in a magazine, let the reputation of the magazine help you to determine the reliability of your author. Above all, beware of the mistake so often made by too many people — the mistake of assuming that anything in print is necessarily true.

The Outline. The outline is the literary architect's set of blueprints from which he builds his essay. That you know already. You know also that the common-sense method of beginning your planning is to ask yourself the same questions which your reader would ask if he had the chance to question you instead of merely reading what you have prepared. Your essay should satisfy your reader's legitimate questions. Put yourself in his place. Ask his questions. The answers to his questions should give you most of the main topics that you should discuss in your paper. Additional topics may have to be added, and some topics that at first appeared to be essential may have to be deleted as you work into your subject, but your main outline will probably remain much as it was at the beginning.

To show how this method of planning operates in actual practice, let us examine a number of preliminary outlines constructed in a freshman English composition class. Each student in the class asked five questions which he would like to have answered if he were reading an article on a given subject. These sets of questions were collected by the instructor, discussed briefly, and then assembled with the help of the class. Here are a few samples:

GRAND OPERA IN AMERICA

1. What are some of the most famous grand opera companies in America?
2. What is the organization of a typical grand opera company?
3. Who were some of the greatest singers produced in America?
4. What were some of the notable performances in America?
5. How does American grand opera compare with European?
6. What has been the success of grand opera in English?
7. What is the outlook for the future of American grand opera companies?

(TOPICS)

1. Survey of background
2. Organization of typical company
3. Outstanding singers
4. Notable performances
5. Comparison with European
6. Grand opera in English
7. Outlook for the future

RHODES SCHOLARSHIPS

1. How, when, and for what purpose were they established?
2. What is the method of selecting candidates?
3. What courses may a Rhodes scholar study at Oxford?
4. What opportunities for travel do these scholarships offer?
5. How does an Oxford education compare with the education a man can get at a good American university?
6 How good is the record made by American scholars at Oxford?

(TOPICS)

1. Origin and nature
2. Method of election
3. Opportunities at Oxford
4. Education through travel
5. Comparison with American universities
6. Record made by American scholars

MILITARY TRAINING IN AMERICAN UNIVERSITIES

1. When and under what conditions was it established?
2. What is the purpose of military training in state universities?
3. How efficient is this training?

4. Does it tend to teach the militaristic attitude?
5. Is it necessary as a measure of self-defense?
6. How strong is the sentiment against compulsory training?

(*TOPICS*)

1. Origin and history
2. Purpose
3. Efficiency of training
4. Dangerous influence
5. Need for self-defense
6. Sentiment against compulsory training

Beginning with the first tentative division of the main subject into parts, or topics, you will expand and elaborate — and change where necessary — until you have a workable plan. Keep the details out of your plan; details belong in your finished manuscript. The following is an example of an outline which began with an interest in the general field of psychology. The field quickly narrowed to "Psychoanalysis," and then to the special problems surrounding the treatment and cure of battle-shocked soldiers. It is not a perfect outline; it is rather the sort of outline which the average college freshman should be able to construct and use.

THE NEUROPSYCHIATRIC CASUALTY

SENTENCE OUTLINE

I. The characteristic behavior of the battle-shocked soldier is shown in many different ways.
  A. In the midst of battle, a soldier may stand up in a stupor trance.
  B. He may have a psychic wound, such as blindness or a paralyzed arm.
  C. He feels that he is isolated in the darkness.
    1. Every semblance of security is gone.
    2. The whole world is hostile, and nothing can make it right again.
  D. He frequently weeps or throws a fit of temper.
  E. He sees battle scenes and dreams about them at night.
II. Every man has a breaking point where he reaches the limit of his endurance.
  A. Normal minds will break but will not stay broken.

B. The condition may be due to an early cause.

C. Exhaustion is the result of strain and fatigue of battle.

D. The physical, emotional, and mental processes are in disbalance.

    1. There is a conflict between the sense of duty and the desire to escape.

    2. The subconscious mind chooses symptoms which will incapacitate the individual.

E. A psychic wound is touched off by an intense emotion.

III. Psychiatrists have classified neuroses in five classes.

  A. The anxiety type is characterized by a nervous breakdown.

  B. The hysteria type is marked by the loss of the use of a body part or a sense organ.

  C. The mental deficiency type is not normal in the first place and is hard to cure.

  D. The psychopathic personality is the bluffer, the fourflusher.

  E. The blast concussion injures body tissues.

IV. The early treatment of the N–P is very important.

  A. New methods are being put into use.

    1. The Army is building up its preventive program.

      a. Potential psychiatric casualties are screened out.

      b. They are taught simple exercises in relaxation and thought control.

    2. Casualties should be treated as near the front lines as possible.

    3. Sedation is the first and most important step.

    4. Treatment also consists of sleep, food, warmth, and reassurance.

    5. Drugs and hypnotism are used to quiet nerves.

    6. A patient is purged of his problems by acting them out on a stage.

  B. There is an urgent need for facilities to take care of the N–Ps.

    1. Clinics are needed to help in fitting the soldier back to normal life.

    2. A small percentage of cases that need help get it.

    3. New York City has six clinics to take care of the 135,000 rejected and discharged men so far in the war.

  C. Facts concerning the effectiveness of the treatment are very encouraging.

    1. The rate of discharge is fifty per cent below that of the first World War.

    2. Eight out of ten men, if treated soon enough, will go back into the fight.

    3. Some may return to combat duty in a few hours.

V. The N–P will have many problems to face in becoming adjusted to civilian life.
  A. Employers, friends, and relatives show curiosity about and distrust of a man labeled as neuropsychiatric.
  B. He feels that he is stigmatized by discharge for mental condition.
  C. If he is given a break, he can work out his own problem.
  D. He should get back to work as soon as he is ready.
  E. Employers must be educated to the needs of the N–P.
    1. He should be kept active at pleasant work.
    2. He cannot take responsibility at first.
    3. He should be kept away from sudden, crashing noises.
    4. Employers should rely upon his former work record.
  F. Friends and family must give their sympathy and understanding.
  G. The following are the ways in which his family may help.
    1. They should not argue the imaginary issue which brought on the violent outbreak.
    2. They should pay no attention to angry words.
    3. They should force him, gently but firmly, to make use of his self-control.
    4. They should let him be by himself during his moods of depression.
    5. They should pretend not to notice his violent reactions.
    6. They should treat him as if he were well.

The Finished Paper. When you have most of your material on note cards, you should plan an interesting beginning or introduction to your research paper. One good way to catch the reader's interest is to begin with some fact or incident of unusual importance or significance, or to explain why your subject is timely or vital. Next you may give briefly the extent and limits of the field covered in your research. By that time you are ready for a transition to a discussion of the first major section of your subject.

The following are the first two pages of a sixteen-page paper written by a student in a freshman English course:

THE NEUROPSYCHIATRIC CASUALTY

At the beginning of World War II, a gunner on a battleship fell flat on his face before a

single shot had been fired and was picked up stone
blind, with not a mark on him, nothing wrong with
his optic nerve, nothing organically wrong anywhere.[1] This incident exemplifies one of the many
thousands of neuropsychiatric casualties which
have occurred in World War II. In the first World
War these cases were known as victims of shell
shock. The men were called "yellow" and were isolated from their units in the hope that they would
give up their notions and return to their units
rather than endure their disgrace. As one might
guess, very few recovered, and now the veterans'
neuropsychiatric hospitals are crowded with this
wreckage of war.[2]

Now we know that these men suffer from the
most frightful kind of injury that war can inflict.[3] Four or five men out of every ten men
discharged are mentally or emotionally unfit.
Twenty-five thousand casualties come home every
month.[4] Some of these men will be cured before
they return home; others will be discharged and
returned to the United States to be treated.

Our biggest problem will be to help these
mentally stricken men to adjust themselves back to
normal civilian lives. We must know how to act
toward these men when they come back to our fami-

----

[1]M. J. Farrell and M. B. L. Ray, "Will the
Battle-shocked Come Home Cured?" Woman's Home
Companion, vol. 71 (April, 1944), p. 33.

[2]F. C. Painton, "There Is No Such Thing As
Shell Shock," Reader's Digest, vol. 43 (October,
1943), p. 60.

[3]Ibid., p. 62.

[4]M. Van De Water, "Soldiers Wounded in
Mind," Science News Letter, vol. 45 (April 22,
1944), p. 262.

lies and how to take care of them. By a thorough understanding of their behavior and reactions and the causes of their mental difficulties, we can better understand the methods of treatment, and thereby we can learn what can be done to help them.

The characteristic behavior of the battle-shocked soldier is shown in many different ways. In the midst of explosions and flying bullets, a soldier may suddenly stand up and walk away from the battle. He walks as if he were asleep; his eyes are vacant; his knees are weak. His gun trails behind him.[1] This stupor state, very much like amnesia, is the most common condition of the shocked soldier in World War II. The hysterical outbursts common in the first World War are less common and less effective as a defense mechanism, because there are no rear lines, no safety anywhere.[2] Other common symptoms are shattered mind and nerves, or a paralyzed limb. The casualty may be blind or mute.[3] Sometimes a soldier will show blind confusion and panic, terror, or rage.[4] Often a soldier will fall into a stupor two or three days after the actual danger is past.[5] The mental casualty feels that he is deserted by everything that is protective or kindly. Officers, soldiers, friends, and buddies become impo-

----

[1]Farrell, op. cit., p. 49.

[2]"War Neurosis Must Be Cured by Prompt Treatment," Science Digest, vol. 12 (July, 1942), p. 58.

[3]Farrell, loc. cit.

[4]A. Deutsch, "Mental Hazards of Sea War," Science Digest, vol. 13 (February, 1943), p. 60.

[5]"War Neurosis Must. . . ," loc. cit.

tent in the face of enemy fire. He is helpless
and alone in a vast darkness; he is a picture of
heart-breaking insecurity. He is convinced that
the whole world is his enemy and that nothing can
make it right again.

Chapter 6

LETTER WRITING

A letter is, in a sense, a theme, governed by the same laws of writing that govern every other kind of composition. It must be clear, well organized, coherent. It must be correct in spelling, grammar, and punctuation. And it should be interesting. Interest in a letter, as in other forms of composition, can be created by concreteness, by originality, by vitality. But a letter is also governed by certain other laws, or conventions, of usage, which the letter writer cannot ignore without serious penalty. Since everyone has occasion to write letters — personal letters, business letters, informal or formal social notes — the college student should know the correct usage in the different types of letters.

These are the parts of a letter:

1. The heading.
2. The inside address.
3. The salutation or greeting.
4. The body of the letter.
5. The complimentary close.
6. The signature.

For each of these parts usage has prescribed certain set forms. These forms must not be ignored or altered, especially in business letters. Conformity is a virtue here, not originality.

The Heading. The parts of a heading, written in the following order, are the street address, the name of city or town, the name of the state, the date. A letterhead takes the place of a typed address. On paper with letterheads, the writer types the date, either directly under the letterhead or flush with the right-hand margin of the letter.

[*Letterhead*]

March 20, 1938

(or)   March 20
1938

(or)   20th
March
1938

On paper that does not have a letterhead, the writer types the heading at the right according to one of the following forms:

327 East Walnut Street
Glendale, California
March 20, 1938

327 East Walnut Street,
Glendale, Calif.,
March 20, 1938.

Department of English
Oregon State College
Corvallis, Oregon
February 24, 1938

The first and third examples show the block form with open punctuation. The second example shows the indented form with closed punctuation.

The Inside Address. In a business letter the inside address is the address of the person written to. In a personal letter the inside address is usually omitted. It may, however, be written at the bottom of a personal letter, in the lower left-hand corner. The first line of the inside address should be flush with the left-hand margin of the letter. One of the following forms may be used, but the style should be the same as in the heading. Either the block form or the indented form should be used throughout the letter.

Dr. Claudius Pochelu
235 East Hortense Street
New Ulm, Minnesota

Miss Dorothy L. Anderson,
   1740 University Avenue,
     Glendale, California.

In a business letter it is always correct to use a personal title with the name of the person addressed. The use of a personal title is correct even when a business title follows the name. A business title should not precede the name. Correct personal titles are: Mr., Mrs., Miss, Dr., Professor, Messrs. The business title may follow the name of the person addressed if the title is short, or it may be placed on the line below it if the title is long.

Professor Henry M. Jones, Secretary
Shattuck Alumni Association

Dr. Howard Olson
Superintendent of Schools

Mrs. Cornelius Blank, Chairman
Finance Committee, Women's Club

Miss Helen Throckmorton
Chairman, Council of Teachers of English

The Salutation. The following forms are correct for business and professional letters:

Dear Sir:
Dear Madam:
Gentlemen:
Mesdames:
My dear Sir:
My dear Madam:
Dear Mr. Jackson:
My dear Miss Blank:
Ladies and Gentlemen:
Dear Professor Potts:

In personal letters the use of *Sir, Madam, Gentlemen,* and *Mesdames* suggests an inappropriate formality. Correct forms which may be used are:

Dear Mr. Howard:
Dear Miss Brown:
My dear Chambers:
Dear Jack,

For correct usage in addressing government officials and other dignitaries, see *The Secretary's Handbook*, pp. 271–306.

In personal letters either a colon or a comma is correct after the salutation. The comma is probably more generally used than the colon. In both business and personal letters, *My dear Mr. Howard* is more formal than *Dear Mr. Howard; My dear Sir,* than *Dear Sir.*

The Body of the Letter. The composition of business letters is a subject much too complex to be discussed here. A good letter obeys the principles of good writing. It should be clear, direct, coherent, dignified, and courteous. A student who can write a good class paper should be able to write a good business letter. The following are good guides to the various types of business letters.

Hotchkiss, George Burton, and Edward Jones Kilduff, *Advanced Business Correspondence*, Harper & Brothers, New York, 1935.
Saunders, Alta Gwinn, *Effective Business English*, The Macmillan Company, New York, 1936.
Taintor, Sarah Augusta, and Kate M. Monro, *The Secretary's Handbook*, The Macmillan Company, New York, 1937.

The Complimentary Close. Correct forms for business letters are:

> Yours truly,
> Very truly yours,
> Respectfully yours,
> Yours very truly,
> Sincerely yours,
> Yours sincerely,
> Cordially yours,

It is now considered bad taste in business letters to use a participial phrase, such as *Hoping for an early answer* with the complimentary close. A comma after the complimentary close is the usual punctuation, but if punctuation is omitted after the salutation, it may also be omitted after the complimentary close. In ordinary formal business letters *Yours truly*, or *Yours very truly*, is the accepted form; in business letters between men who are familiar with each other *Yours sincerely* and *Cordially yours* are used.

The Signature. The form of the signature may depend upon certain special conditions which will be discussed later, but for the ordinary person it is correct to sign a letter as he would sign a check. If possible, he should write his name legibly. Since a legible signature is impossible for many persons, it is desirable to type the name under the signature.

Some of the conventions which govern the form of a signature are:

1. Neither professional titles, such as *Professor, Dr., Rev.*, nor academic degrees, such as *Ph.D., LL.D., M.A.*, should be used with a signature.
2. An unmarried woman should not sign herself as Miss Laura Blank, but she may place *Miss* in parentheses before her name if she feels that it is necessary for proper identification.
3. A married woman or a widow signs her own name, not her married name. For example, *Diana Holoday Brown* is her own name; *Mrs. George Brown* is her married name. She may place *Mrs.* in parentheses before her signature, or her married name in parentheses under it.
4. When a secretary signs her chief's name to a letter, she may add her own initials below the signature.

Invitations, Acceptances, Regrets. An informal invitation should be written in an easy, natural, and cordial manner.

> 1520 East 34th Street
> May the fifth

My dear Mrs. Fowler,

Will you and Mr. Fowler dine with us on Saturday, May the fourteenth, at seven o'clock? We shall probably drive out to the Oasis to dance afterwards. We shall be very glad if you are able to come.

> Sincerely yours,
> Beatrice W. Scott

Dear Mrs. Fowler,

Mr. Scott and I shall be greatly pleased if you and Mr. Fowler can come to an informal dinner at our apartment on Saturday, May the fourteenth, at seven o'clock. If you feel like dancing afterwards, we shall drive out to the Oasis for an hour or two.

Sincerely yours,
Beatrice W. Scott

1520 East 34th Street
May fifth

My dear Mrs. Scott,

Mr. Fowler and I are delighted to accept your very kind invitation to dine and dance with you on Saturday, May the fourteenth, at seven o'clock. We are looking forward to seeing you again.

Sincerely yours,
Marion Fowler

46 West Clinton Avenue
May sixth

My dear Mrs. Scott,

Mr. Fowler and I regret exceedingly that we are unable to accept your invitation for dinner on Saturday, May the fourteenth, as unfortunately we have another engagement for that evening.

Sincerely yours,
Marion Fowler

46 West Clinton Avenue
May sixth

Formal social notes are written in the third person. No abbreviations are used. Dates and hours are written in full. The following examples will serve for ordinary invitations, acceptances, and regrets. For correct forms in engraved invitations and announcements it is usually better to depend upon the stationer.

Mrs. Prentiss requests the pleasure of Miss Roxbury's company at dinner on Friday evening, May the thirteenth, at seven o'clock.
620 Monroe Street,
    May the fifth.

Miss Roxbury accepts with pleasure the kind invitation of Mrs. Prentiss to dinner on Friday evening, May the thirteenth, at seven o'clock.
1224 Franklin Road,
    May the sixth.

Miss Roxbury regrets that she is unable to accept the kind invitation of Mrs. Prentiss to dinner on Friday evening, May the thirteenth, at seven o'clock.
1224 Franklin Road,
  May the sixth.

Faults to Avoid.

1. Do not omit pronouns, prepositions, and articles where they are grammatically necessary. If your letter should begin with *I* or *we*, begin with *I* or *we*.

    Bad: Received your letter yesterday.
          Am writing to you in reply . . .
          Have not heard from you . . .
    Right: I received your letter yesterday.
          I am writing to you . . .
          I have not heard from you . . .

2. Do not close a letter with a sentence or a phrase introduced by a participle.

    Bad: Hoping to hear from you soon . . .
          Hoping for an early answer . . .
          Thanking you again for your past favors . . .
          Trusting to hear from you by return mail . . .

3. Do not write *yours*, *your favor*, or *your esteemed favor* for *letter*.

    Bad: In reply to yours of the 20th . . .
          Your esteemed favor at hand, and in reply . . .
          In reply to yours of the 15th . . .

4. Avoid certain trite and stilted expressions frequently used in business letters.

    Bad: In reply would say . . .
          Yours of the 10th inst. received . . .
          And contents thereof noted . . .
          Your valued favor . . .
          And oblige, Yours truly . . .
          Enclosed please find . . .

EXERCISES

Exercise 1. Write a letter to a friend who lives in your home community explaining to him the value of the course you are now taking in your college.

Exercise 2. Write a letter to your college newspaper in which you correct a wrong impression produced by a news story which has appeared in the paper. Make your letter courteous, dignified, and logical.

Exercise 3. Write a letter to your dean in which you request permission to take your final examinations several days before the scheduled period. Give your reasons clearly and convincingly.

Exercise 4. As secretary of a student organization, write a letter to the members urging them to pay their dues.

Exercise 5. You plan to work at one of the national parks during the summer. Write a letter of application. Apply for some position that you could fill. Give adequate information about yourself and your qualifications.

Exercise 6. Write to a friend asking him to accompany you on a fishing and camping trip.

Exercise 7. Write to your hostess thanking her for the pleasant time you have had at her home. She is your roommate's mother.

Exercise 8. A man for whom you worked last summer owes you thirty dollars. Write him a letter that will induce him to pay what he owes you.

Exercise 9. You have been asked to tell what you think of some acquaintance who has applied for a position as teacher in the public schools. Write a letter in which you convey a favorable impression. Be specific.

Exercise 10. You forgot a conference you had scheduled with your English teacher. Write a note of apology.

Part II

A HANDBOOK
OF WRITING AND REVISION

THE SENTENCE FRAGMENT

1. Do not write part of a sentence as if it were a complete sentence.

A grammatically complete sentence must have a subject and a predicate. It must convey the meaning intended and give the reader a sense of completeness. A group of words lacking a subject or a predicate or a complete thought but used as a sentence is called a *sentence fragment*. Placing a period after a sentence fragment is called a *period fault*. The most common types of sentence fragments are subordinate clauses, verbal phrases, prepositional phrases, appositives, and parts of a compound predicate.

The fragment is the affliction characteristic of only the first few papers written in a composition course, because sentence sense is something that is easily and quickly mastered. It must be mastered quickly, moreover, if you are to progress to more vital matters related to good writing. If you do not know what a sentence is, refer to pages 37–43 and study the definitions, the examples, and the diagrams which you find there. It might be well for you to work the exercises which deal with sentences, clauses, and phrases.

Fragment: It happened two years ago, but it seemed like yesterday. *Probably because of the impression it left on me at the time.* [This is a subordinate clause.]
Complete: It happened two years ago, but probably because of the impression it had left on me, it seemed as if it had happened yesterday.

Fragment: Our time was taken up with lectures, placement examinations, and social functions. *All of these being very important.* [This is a participial phrase, of the special type called the absolute phrase. See page 47.]

Complete: Our time was taken up with lectures, placement examinations, and social functions. All of these were very important. [Change the participle to a verb.]

Fragment: After I had shaved and dressed, I strolled down into the lobby of the hotel. *Hoping but not expecting to meet Jane there.* [Participial phrase.]

Complete: After I had shaved and dressed, I strolled down into the lobby of the hotel, hoping but not expecting to meet Jane there. [Add the phrase to the main part of the sentence.]

Fragment: Food supplies are low, and starvation is imminent. *Especially in the industrial districts of Germany.* [Prepositional phrase.]

Complete: Food supplies are low, and starvation is imminent, especially in the industrial districts of Germany. [Add the phrase to the main part of the sentence.]

Fragment: Five species of bears live in Alaska. *The polar, the black, the grizzly, and two exclusively Alaskan species, the kodiak and the glacier bear.* [Appositive.]

Complete: Five species of bears live in Alaska — the polar, the black, the grizzly, and two exclusively Alaskan species, the kodiak and the glacier bear. [Add to the main part of the sentence. For the correct punctuation to be used with an appositive see section 20h.]

Some good writers use the sentence fragment occasionally in order to produce special stylistic effects. Others have developed the use of sentence fragments into an irritating mannerism. The fact that a good writer uses an occasional incomplete sentence does not necessarily justify its use by an inexperienced writer. Although a fragment may at times be used effectively, it is better for you to avoid it altogether until after you have mastered the possibilities of the complete sentence. After that you may experiment with confidence in the results.

The point is that a sentence fragment used for effect may be good, but one written through ignorance is almost sure to be bad.

Modern literary custom, as well as ordinary common sense,

sanctions the use of certain types of fragments as complete sentences. In some of these either the subject or the predicate is understood; in others no amount of ingenious interpretation will supply a missing subject or verb. We must accept them for what they are — sentence fragments correctly punctuated as sentences.

a. The command.

Right: Come.
        Open a window.
        At once!
        Please!

b. The question.

Right: Too early?
        Not here yet?
        At the top of the page?
        How much?

c. The exclamation.

Right: Splendid!
        How terrible!
        Well done!
        What a man!

d. Bits of dialogue.

Right: "Stop now? Glad to. Terrible heat, isn't it?"

        "Impossible!" he objected. "Can't trust him. Never pays his bills. Never works. Never saves a cent. Just like his dad."

        "How old are you?"
        "Sixteen. Why?"
        "Look young for your age, don't you?"

The following rules will call to your attention the faults most frequently committed by students:

1a. Do not write a dependent clause as a complete sentence.

Remember that a dependent clause begins with a subordinating conjunction, such as *although, when, if, as if, because.* The

229

presence of a subordinating conjunction at the beginning of a group of words should set you on your guard. The main clause may follow the subordinate, of course, but you should be positive that it does follow.

Fragment: I let Ranger Bill pay for the coffee. *As I did not want him to know I carried a hundred dollars in my pocket.*

Complete: Because I did not want Ranger Bill to know that I carried a hundred dollars in my pocket, I let him pay for the coffee. [Putting the clause at the beginning produces a more compact sentence.]

Fragment: Their right halfback was edging in closer to the line. *Which was being ripped to pieces by our attack.*

Complete: Their right halfback was edging in closer to the line, which was being ripped to pieces by our attack. [Leave the clause next to the word it modifies.]

1b. Do not write a phrase (verbal or prepositional) as a complete sentence.

Remember that the verbals — infinitive, gerund, participle — are dependent forms of the verb. They cannot serve as predicates of complete sentences. Prepositional phrases also are dependent elements. See pages 35–52.

Fragment: I left school in time for the important work on the farm. *Repairing fences being the one labor I missed.* [Participial phrase.]

Complete: I left school in time for the important work on the ranch, missing only the labor of repairing fences. [Notice that the correction also improves the point of view of the sentence.]

Fragment: To quit school now would be to disappoint my parents. *To destroy the faith they had in me.* [Infinitive phrase.]

Complete: To quit school now would be to disappoint my parents, to destroy the faith they had in me. [Simply add the phrase to the sentence.]

1c. Do not write an appositive phrase as a complete sentence.

Guard against this fault especially when the phrase is introduced by such words as *namely, for example, such as,* and the like. For the correct punctuation with an appositive see section 20h.

Fragment: His first bark is just a friendly warning. *Just a reminder to be careful.* ["Reminder" is the appositive of "warning."]

Complete: His first bark is just a friendly warning, just a reminder to be careful.

Fragment: I have found one phase of college life truly stimulating. *Namely, my contacts with my fraternity brothers.* ["Contacts" is in apposition with "phase."]

Complete: I have found one phase of college life truly stimulating, namely, my contacts with my fraternity brothers.

Fragment: My work in a CCC camp taught me several important virtues. *Such as self-reliance, honesty, and loyalty.*

Complete: My work in a CCC camp taught me several important virtues, such as self-reliance, honesty, and loyalty.

1d. Do not write a sentence in which a part of the thought is left uncompleted.

Some fragments are written because the writer has not taken the trouble to think; others are written because the writer has carried over into writing the exclamatory mannerisms of very informal speech. The following examples will make the points clear.

Fragment: Unexpectedly I dropped in on her daughter. *Just a friendly call, no party.* [The writer of this was making note jottings, not sentences. Rewritten, this might read, "I intended this to be just a friendly, informal call."]

Fragment: *Too many stems and leaves mixed with the hops* and you have to pick them over.

Complete: If the picker has too many leaves and stems with the hops, he must pick them over.

The following sounds like something from a love story published in one of the "love and suffer" magazines, which go in for this sort of thing.

Undesirable: I looked at the backs of the couple sitting on the bench under the hawthorn tree. They had nice shoulders. His broad and black. Very strong too. Hers slim and straight. A cheap fur around her neck.

Undesirable: A *moment of carelessness* and your car will be skidding in the gravel or plunging into the ditch.
Complete: A moment of carelessness on your part may send your car skidding in the gravel or plunging into the ditch.

A sentence of this sort is permissible if the punctuation indicates a sharp break in the thought.

Permissible: A moment of carelessness — and your car is skidding in the gravel or plunging into the ditch.
Incomplete: Silent and lifeless, bleak desolation describes the desert of Arizona.
Complete: Silent, lifeless, bleak, and desolate — these words describe the deserts of Arizona.

EXERCISES

Exercise 1. Some of the following are complete sentences. Some are fragments. If a sentence is complete, underline its subject once and its verb twice. If the group of words is a clause, draw a circle about its subordinating conjunction. If it is a verbal phrase, draw a circle about the verbal.

1. Although the Russian delegates attracted much attention.
2. The kind of work being of no special importance at the moment.
3. When he was at last gradually converted to a vegetarian diet.
4. Her efforts to be kind having been misinterpreted.
5. With a deep sigh he paid his bill and went out the door.
6. Both talk about their adventures to the point of exhaustion.
7. Both the children having learned something from defeat.
8. Which would involve us in new difficulties.
9. The matter having been argued in several faculty meetings.
10. Which of the two courses do you recommend?

Exercise 2. In some of the following word groups you will find sentence fragments. Whenever you find a fragment, write before it the number of the rule (1a, 1b, 1c) which tells what type of fragment it is. Then make whatever corrections are necessary.

1. Then the German armies broke through our lines at the Ardennes Forest. Just when the world was expecting an easy victory. 1a

2. The deck canvas and the rest of the boat are painted. The colors ~~being~~ of your own selection.

3. The spirit of nationalism was growing rapidly in several countries, Especially in Italy, Germany, and Spain.

4. These radical groups had long demanded certain concessions. Such as cultural freedom and a certain amount of self-government.

5. Success or failure in wheat farming depends, to a large extent, on rainfall. Over this, as I soon learned, not even the most scientific farmer had much control.

6. These men began to write in a new style. To which, to distinguish it from the old realism, the name of "naturalism" was given.

7. I registered for a course which included English literature, social science, sewing, archery, and golf. Believing that a broad, cultural education would be best for me.

8. Herbert Spencer, in his *Principles of Ethics*, developed a new theory: That with the process of evolution there is a corresponding growth of the moral sense in man.

9. His knowledge of dancing, as I suspected, ~~being~~ confined to the waltz and the two-step.

10. Being a clerk has taught me to be patient. To be an attentive listener as well as to keep up a conversation.

Exercise 3. In each of the following sentences place a period at the spot indicated by the parallel bars. Then reword the fragment which you have thus split off from the sentence so that it too is complete.

1. Unfortunately, he had several expensive habits // such as gambling, collecting antique furniture, and lavish entertaining.

2. The estimated coal area of Alaska is twenty thousand square miles // the most important deposits occurring near the Bering River and near Matanuska.

3. The elections returned most of the Conservatives to Parliament // certainly too many of them to leave the Liberals with much hope for a speedy change in policy.

4. At three o'clock we were told to clean up the surgery and to sterilize the instruments // although both of us were so tired that we seemed to be moving in a trance.

5. He realized with increasing clarity the superficial character of his own mind, and that the struggles in other men's minds meant nothing // that he had existed without realizing that it seriously mattered to anyone what men believed in.

THE COMMA SPLICE

2. Do not run two sentences together with only a comma between them.

The comma splice, like the sentence fragment, is assumed to be an infallible sign of illiteracy. Although the error may be more often the result of carelessness than of ignorance, it is serious enough to deserve your attention. Avoid it in one of the following ways:

1. By using a period to separate the sentences, if the sentences are felt as separate thoughts.

Wrong: Cross-cut saws are used to cut the boards to the correct length, these saws are set in a table with the saw sticking out of the top.

Right: Cross-cut saws are used to cut the boards to the correct length. These saws are set in a table with the saw sticking out of the top.

Wrong: Nothing about the woods was a mystery to him, he was a living and talking nature book.

Right: Nothing about the woods was a mystery to him. He was a living and talking nature book.

2. By using a semicolon instead of a comma, if the sentences are close enough in thought to be combined into a compound sentence.

Wrong: I knew that my brother would not be late, he was the most painfully punctual man I have ever known.

Right: I knew that my brother would not be late; he was the most painfully punctual man I have ever known.

Wrong: From 100,000 seedlings Burbank chose four to be kept, the rest he destroyed.

Right: From 100,000 seedlings Burbank chose four to be kept; the rest he destroyed.

3. By inserting a co-ordinating conjunction after the comma.

Wrong: Don Morris is a very plausible man, he has no real depth of character, he cannot be trusted.

Right: Don Morris is a very plausible man, but he has no real depth of character. He cannot be trusted.

4. By subordinating one of the two independent statements.

Wrong: To give him the chairmanship would be unwise, he has had no practical experience in student politics.

Right: Because he has had no practical experience in student politics, it would be unwise to give him the chairmanship.

Wrong: I was not asking Mother if I could go, I was telling her I was going and when I would get back.

Right: Instead of asking Mother if I could go, I informed her that I was going and when I would be back.

Note, however, that usage sanctions the comma in compound sentences which consist of three or more clauses that are short, parallel in form, and closely connected in thought. The practice of using the comma in short sentences of two clauses, without a co-ordinating conjunction, although fairly common in journalistic writing of less than professional caliber, is still frowned upon in more serious and permanent writing.

Acceptable: I came, I saw, I conquered.
He protested, he blustered, he stormed.
The leaves are turning to gold, squirrels are fattening, hunting time is near.

Warning: Guard against the comma splice in sentences of dialogue. When two complete co-ordinate clauses are separated by a dialogue tab, like "he said," use a period or a semicolon, not a comma.

Right: "No one remembers the good things I have done," she complained; "no one ever does."
"I'm sorry, sir," he said. "I didn't know that you wanted it."

THE RUN–TOGETHER SENTENCE

3. Do not run two sentences together with no mark of punctuation between them.

The sentence fragment, the comma splice, and the run-together sentence are probably all symptoms of the same infirmity — carelessness rather than ignorance of what constitutes a sentence. If you know what a sentence is, do not let slovenly carelessness mar your writing. After all, your writing is judged not by the knowledge you have but by the knowledge you use. If you do *not* know what a sentence is, go back to pages 39–43 and ponder over the explanations and the examples which you find there.

Run-together: He knows nothing about the problems of workingmen he never had to work for a living.

Unified: Since he never had to work for a living himself, he knows nothing about the problems of workingmen. [By running his sentences together, the writer indicated that the second statement was somehow a justification for the first. Subordination indicates correctly what the writer felt.]

SUPPLEMENTARY EXERCISES

Sections 1, 2, and 3 of the handbook deal with what is usually called "sentence sense," that is, the ability to recognize and to write complete and unified sentences. If you do not have this "sentence sense," you must go back to the elementary drill of sentence analysis or diagraming.

Exercise 1. In the following exercise each sentence begins with some element before the subject. Look for the subject and the verb of the *main* clause. Underline the subject once and the verb twice.

1. Being without funds, the provisional government announced that it was assuming an inactive state.
2. After the ratification of the treaty, the minister retired from public life.
3. The monsoon rains having set in, progress up the Burma coast was slow.
4. Late that evening, after the noises of battle had receded inland, the entertainers began to set up a makeshift stage.
5. Glancing quickly over his shoulder, he caught sight of a crawling figure in the tall grass.
6. The bridge being down, there was no object in hurrying the trucks along the highway.
7. Following a brief parley with the sentry, one of the men was allowed to enter the bombed cathedral.
8. Among his most tolerant critics is a man who dislikes every kind of modernistic music.

9. Still, boys being only boys, the desire to revolt against authority was strong in them.
10. As far as anybody has been able to discover, homesickness is not a fatal sickness.

Exercise 2. Correct each of the following sentences by subordinating one of the principal elements.

1. My favorite sport is basketball it is the one sport in which I excel.
2. To him studying was only a minor detail, all that counted was the football games, the pretty girls, and the social life.
3. The new stadium will be finished this summer it will be the largest structure of its kind in the Middle West.
4. Unfortunately I do not like to write themes I have never had much practice in writing.
5. We drove through Texas last summer the heat was at its worst then.

Exercise 3. Correct each of the following sentences by the use of either a semicolon or a period.

1. He worked fourteen hours a day, it was his work that he loved.
2. My father jerked at the window it would not budge.
3. You must start at the bottom and work up, the only job where you can start at the top is digging a well.
4. Reformers come and go, the poor are always with us.
5. Some of the girls will be toasting marshmallows others will be trying to harmonize one of the latest song hits.

Exercise 4. Correct each of the following sentences by using subordination of a rank below that of a subordinate clause (a phrase or an appositive).

1. In the line were several older men, some were reading newspapers, others were just patiently standing.
2. Two virtues every dog trainer must have they are patience and gentleness.
3. The world does not owe any person a living. Nor any institution.
4. Waldron was registering for a course in engineering, he had been a mechanic in the ordnance corps.
5. Dean Warrington believes that character rests on loyalty. Especially on loyalty to one's ideals.

Exercise 5. Correct each of the following by the method most appropriate to the thought. Be able to explain what method you have used in each correction.

1. Mr. Turner will act as our financial adviser; he has had some experience in banking.
2. Clothes make the man, this proverb is not always true.
3. The wheat fields look brown and parched, we have had no rain since April.
4. One day a tramp appeared at the back door, Mother and Father were away I was so terrified that I just stared at him.
5. The urge to travel is perennial; it will overcome all obstacles.
6. Captain Conners directed the athletic program at our camp he had been a star football player at West Point.
7. Medicine or surgery I did not even consider I could never stand the sight of blood.
8. I was being shoved toward the door. But all the time getting closer and closer to the little piece of paper which would admit me to the game.
9. Few things are so exhilarating as to know that your team is the best. That it is not surpassed by any other team in the country.
10. They work for very little salary, what they want is experience.

SUBJECT AND VERB

4. Make the verb agree in number and person with its subject.

Do not use a plural verb with a singular subject nor a singular subject with a plural verb. Nouns and pronouns have two "numbers," singular and plural, that is, one or more than one. Pronouns are said to have three persons: *I, we* are first person; *you* is second person; *he, she, it, they* are third person. Nouns are considered to be in the third person. (See section 5.)

Right: He doesn't smoke (*not* he don't smoke). We were robbed (*not* we was robbed). They weren't interested (*not* they wasn't interested).

4a. Do not let yourself be confused by a plural word that intervenes between a verb and its singular subject.

Wrong: The *babble* of so many shrill voices *are* irritating and confusing. [Note that *voices* cannot be the subject because it is the object of a preposition and therefore in the objective case.]

Right: The *babble* of so many shrill voices *is* irritating and confusing.

Wrong: A complete *list* of his plays *are given* in the appendix. [*Plays* is not the subject because it is the object of the preposition *of*.]
Right: A complete *list* of his plays *is given* in the appendix.

Wrong: *One* of his most unpleasant characteristics *are* his arrogance, his inability to see another person's point of view. [The subject is not *characteristics*, which is the object of a preposition.]
Right: *One* of his most unpleasant characteristics *is* his arrogance, his inability to see another person's point of view.

4b. Do not let the addition of *as well as, together with, with, in addition to, except,* and *no less than* to the subject influence the number of the verb.

Right: *Marion Jean*, as well as the boys, *enjoys* fishing.
My *purse*, together with my gloves and keys, *was taken* from my locker last night.
The humblest *workman*, no less than our wealthy manufacturers, *is affected* by the new tariff.
A *canteen* of water, in addition to the usual supplies, *is* to be taken on the trip.
Our whole system of representative government, no less than a few dishonest politicians, is on trial today.

4c. Use a plural verb with a compound subject joined by *and*.

Students rarely make mistakes in the number of the verb when the sentences are short and simple and when the verb immediately follows the subject.

Right: A *horse* and a *cow are* in the pasture.
Courage, loyalty, and *service constitute* his code of life.

They are usually led into error in long sentences under the following conditions:

1. When the subjects follow the verb.

Wrong: In this file *was listed* every *breach* of discipline and every *peculiarity* of the student's character.
Right: In this file *were listed* every *breach* of discipline and every *peculiarity* of the student's character.

2. When the sentence is a question.

Wrong: How *has* this *money* and the later government *appropriations increased* the culture of the United States and, to a certain extent, that of the whole world?

Right: How *have* this *money* and the later government *appropriations increased* the culture of the United States and, to a certain extent, that of the whole world? [Money and appropriations have increased.]

3. When the subject and the verb are separated by other groups of words.

Wrong: Recent studies reveal that the *quality* and the *amount* of medical services which people receive *depends* upon the income of the patient.

Right: Recent studies reveal that the *quality* and the *amount* of medical services which people receive *depend* upon the income of the patient. [Quality and amount depend.]

When several singular subjects, however, represent the same person or thing, or when they form one collective idea (see also the second part of section 4i), a singular verb is correct.

Right: Our *friend* and *benefactor has come.* [Same person.]
The *long* and *short* of it *is* that I have no money. [Like "the sum and substance," this is an idiomatic expression always used in the singular.] The *secretary* and *treasurer is* Helen Thornton. [If it were two persons, it would probably be "the secretary and the treasurer."]

Notice also that when each of several singular subjects is considered separately, the singular verb is used.

Right: Many a rascal and fool has prospered in times of public distress. The trifler, the athlete, the waster is not the typical college student.

4d. When subjects are joined by *neither — nor, either — or, not only — but also,* make the verb agree with the nearer subject.

The verb actually must agree with each subject, but as the subjects are considered singly, the verb is expressed with the nearer subject and understood with the other.

Wrong: Neither the *twins* nor their *nurse are* ready.
Right: Neither the *twins* nor their *nurse is* ready.

Wrong: Either *Margaret* or her *sister are* coming with us.
Right: Either *Margaret* or her *sister is* coming with us.

When the subjects differ in person, it is also correct to make the verb agree with the nearer subject, but it is often better to recast the sentence so as to avoid an awkward situation.

Right: Either *Margaret* or *I am* going with you.
        Not only your *agent* but *you* also *are* responsible to the purchaser.

Right: Either Margaret is going with you or I am.
        Not only is your agent responsible to the purchaser, but you are also.

4e. Use the singular form of the verb after *each*, *every*, *each one*, *everyone*, *everybody*, *anybody*, *nobody*, *either*, and *neither*.

Since these words are singular, they are also the antecedents of singular pronouns. See sections 5h and 55f.

Wrong: *Each* of the men *have contributed* something valuable to the discussion.
Right: *Each* of the men *has contributed* something valuable to the discussion.

Wrong: I know that *either* of the candidates *are* well *qualified.*
Right: I know that *either* of the candidates *is* well *qualified.*

Wrong: Neither *have accomplished* anything remarkable.
Right: Neither *has accomplished* anything remarkable.

Wrong: Neither *have done* what *they were going* to do.
Right: Neither *has done* what *he was going* to do.

Note in this connection that *either* and *neither* are here used as pronouns, whereas in section 4d their use as disjunctive conjunctions was explained. In a sentence like "Either one will do," *either* is used as an adjective modifying *one*.

4f. In *there is* and *there are* sentences, make the verb agree with the subject that follows it.

Wrong: There *is* always two *sides* to everything, the right side and the wrong side.

Right: There *are* always two *sides* to everything, the right side and the wrong side.

Wrong: There *is*, if I am not mistaken, a *man* and a *dog* under that tree.

Right: There *are*, if I am not mistaken, a *man* and a *dog* under that tree.

4g. With a collective noun use a singular verb when the group it names is regarded as a unit, and a plural verb when the noun is regarded as indicating the individuals of the group.

In your choice of verbs and pronouns to go with collective nouns you must depend on consistency as your guiding principle. Once you have spoken of a group as a single unit, you cannot, without some logical explanation, refer to it in the plural. See also section 5i.

Consistent: The band are taking off their heavy overcoats. They are assembling in front of the speaker's stand.

After a short rest period, the class proceeds with its work.

Inconsistent: The choir files in and take their places.

The large crowd which was watching the game rose as one man and threw their caps in the air.

4h. Make the verb agree with its subject, not with its subjective complement.

If the difference in number between subject and subjective complement produces an awkward sentence, rewrite the sentence.

Wrong: His chief *worry are* his devoted but imprudent disciples.

Right: His chief *worry is* his devoted but imprudent disciples.

Wrong: The *reason* for my late theme *are* the many interruptions that kept me from my work.

Right: The *reason* for my late theme *is* the many interruptions that kept me from my work.

Better: My theme is late because I was frequently interrupted in my work.

4i. Use a singular verb when the subject of the sentence is a title, the name of a book, a clause, or in general a group of words expressing a single thought.

Right: Stones of Venice is one of Ruskin's most famous books.
Amy Lowell's *Lilacs* is my favorite poem.
The *Times* is a reliable newspaper.
Everybody for himself and the devil take the hindmost is apparently the code by which he lives.

This rule applies to verbs used with nouns expressing quantity, distance, time, amount, etc., when the subject is felt to be a unit.

Right: Twelve years is a long time to spend in exile.
Three hundred words is a good length for a paragraph.
Thirty miles is a day's journey in these hills.
Fifteen divided by three equals five.

4j. As a general rule, use a singular verb with nouns that are plural in form but singular in meaning.

When in doubt as to whether a noun is singular or plural in meaning, consult a good dictionary. Under the suffix *-ics*, *Webster's New International Dictionary* gives us the following helpful information: "As denoting a scientific treatise or its subject matter these plural forms are now construed as singular; but forms in *-ics* denoting matters of practice (gymnastics, tactics), activities (athletics), qualities (acoustics), are usually construed as plurals; but the presence of a complementary noun in the singular often causes such a form to be construed as a singular; as, dramatics is his hobby."

Usually singular: news, economics, measles, ethics, physics, mathematics, gallows, mumps.
Usually plural: gymnastics, tactics, athletics, acoustics, tidings, scissors, riches, trousers.
Either singular or plural: headquarters, politics, alms, means.

Right: The *news was received* with loud applause.
Mathematics is my favorite study.
Athletics are his ruin.
Ethics deals with the problem of moral duty.

With *none* use a singular verb if the meaning intended is singular, and a plural verb if the meaning is plural.

Right: *None are* so arrogant as those who have never suffered misfortune. Rumors of a peace offer spread rapidly, but *none* of the correspondents in the city *was* able to trace them to their sources.

4k. Use a plural verb with a relative pronoun referring to a plural antecedent.

The use of a singular verb in this construction is now widespread on the colloquial level. For the sake of training the ear, however, you should cultivate the formal agreement between subject and verb.

Formal: She is one of those women *who believe* that carrying matches is a sign of moral turpitude.

Colloquial: I am one of those husbands *who likes* to have his meals on time.

If you have difficulty in understanding this construction, rearrange your sentence so as to begin with *of:*

Richard is one of those boys who never study until the day before the final examination.

Of those boys who never study [Could you well say "boys who never studies"?] until the day before the final examination. Richard is one.

EXERCISES

Exercise 1. In each of the following sentences underline each subject once and each verb twice. If you are able to pick out the subject and verb of a sentence, most of your troubles with agreement will disappear.

1. Hidden under the cushions of his car was found a package of counterfeit bills.
2. A carrier, as well as a number of escort ships, was lost in the attack.
3. In the beginning there were three divisions taking part in the battle.
4. The true cause of his frequent outbursts of temper was his sense of inferiority.

5. With returning veterans crowding the campuses, there is even greater need to worry about an adequate staff.
6. Hard work, as well as games and dances, is a part of college life.
7. As he was leaving, a statement of the reasons for his dismissal was handed to him.
8. The colonel, as well as the junior officers, was present.
9. Neither wants to offend the other.
10. A list of the regulations is posted in the office.

Exercise 2. Correct the errors in each of the following sentences. Tell what rule applies.

1. The news you brought to us are indeed distressing.
2. The object of these exercises are to develop your speed and agility.
3. The house, as well as the barns in which the fire started, were burned to the ground.
4. Did you say that the scissors was lying on the desk?
5. The purpose of my frequent questions are to keep you alert.
6. Physics are one of my most difficult studies.
7. A record of his losses were found among his private papers.
8. Now all that remains are charred walls and smoking timbers.
9. The acoustics of the new auditorium is very poor.
10. Enthusiasm and willingness to work is very necessary.

Exercise 3. Some of the following sentences contain errors. Some are correct. Point out each mistake that you find, correct the sentence, and tell what rule applies.

1. There is no one who does their work more carefully than he.
2. The whole course of events are largely determined by the weather.
3. The music starts, and in marches the bridesmaid, the best man, the bride and the groom, each taking his place before the fireplace.
4. People should realize that the words they use in ordinary conversation tells others more about them than do the clothes they wear.
5. Upon the wisdom of the planners rest the opportunity of the different nations to develop their own forms of government.
6. A few final words sends the culprit back to his room.
7. In this part of the boat are the motor and other mechanical equipment.
8. The jury has reached a verdict in the case, but the judge is not pleased with its work.
9. There has been many changes in our manner of celebrating the Fourth of July.
10. College was one of those distant dreams which was suddenly becoming true.

PRONOUNS

5. Be careful to use the right form of the pronoun.

Both nouns and pronouns have "cases" and "persons." In English there are three cases, the nominative (subjective), the possessive, and the objective. There are also three persons: the *first* person indicates the speaker; the *second* person indicates the one spoken to; the *third* person indicates the one spoken about. Nouns change form only for the possessive case (See section 23), and, except in rare constructions, they are generally considered to be in the third person. Pronouns, however, usually change their forms for person, number, and case, and thereby cause the student of the English language numerous difficulties.

The forms of the personal pronoun are shown in the table below:

	First Person	Second Person	Third Person		
	Masculine or feminine		*Masc.*	*Fem.*	*Neuter*
SINGULAR NUMBER:					
Nominative:	I	you	he	she	it
Possessive:	my, mine	your, yours	his	her, hers	its
Objective:	me	you	him	her	it
PLURAL NUMBER:					
Nominative:	we	you	they		
Possessive:	our, ours	your, yours	their, theirs		
Objective:	us	you	them		

The archaic or poetic forms *thou, thy, thine, thee,* and *ye* do not belong in ordinary prose writing.

A common error in speech and in writing is the use of one of the compound personal pronouns (compounded with *-self*) for the simple personal pronouns. The compound personal pronouns have two correct uses, as intensives and as reflexives:

Intensive use: Instead of sending a representative, the President *himself* will attend the dinner.

I can give you a complete account, for I *myself* was there.

Reflexive use: I am ashamed of *myself*.

They dressed *themselves* in a hurry.

Do not use the reflexive pronoun for the simple personal pronoun.

Wrong: The Dean let Jim and *myself* go home for the week end.
Right: The Dean let Jim and *me* go home for the week end.

Wrong: I suspect that he wants Jane and *yourself*.
Right: I suspect that he wants Jane and *you*.

5a. Use the nominative case when the pronoun is the subject of a verb.

Determine the exact use of the pronoun; do not be confused by the position of the pronoun or by parenthetical expressions intervening between it and the verb. Watch especially the case of the pronoun in elliptical clauses of comparison (older than she, poorer than they, etc.).

Wrong: Dorothy is taller than *me*.
Right: Dorothy is taller than *I* [than *I am*].

Wrong: *Whom* did you say brought us these cherries?
Right: *Who* did you say brought us these cherries? [The expression *did you say* is parenthetical. The sentence could read: *Who brought us these cherries — did you say? Who* is not the object of *say;* it is the subject of *brought.*]

Wrong: Give this package to *whomever* opens the door.
Right: Give this package to *whoever* opens the door. [*Whoever* seems to be attracted into the objective case by its position after the preposition *to.* But it is not the object of the preposition; it is the subject of the verb *opens.* The object of the preposition *to* is the entire noun clause *whoever opens the door.*]

Right: Captain Henry, *than whom* there is none more generous, at once offered to take Tom's place. [*Than whom* is an accepted idiomatic form.]

5b. Use the nominative case when the pronoun is a subjective complement after a finite verb.

Wrong: It is *me*. This is *her*. It was *them* who notified the police. It was *us* whom you heard singing last night, Mrs. Casey.

Right: It is *I*. This is *she*. It was *they* who notified the police. It was *we* whom you heard singing last night, Mrs. Casey.

Although the use of "It is me" in spoken English has been bitterly defended by some students of the language, the ordinary college student will do well to say "It is I." If he says *I* instead of *me* whenever he remembers to be correct, common human frailty will save him from being too noticeable among his fellows.

5c. Use the objective case when the pronoun is the direct or indirect object of a verb or a verbal.

No one is likely to make a mistake in the objective case of a pronoun when the pronoun immediately follows the verb or verbal of which it is the object. For instance, no one would say, "I saw *she* at the game." Difficulties arise, however, in two types of constructions:

1. When the pronoun, especially *whom*, is out of its normal order.

Wrong: Jane is the girl *who* we met at the game yesterday.

Right: Jane is the girl *whom* we met at the game yesterday. [*Whom* is the object of the verb *met*, but it is attracted into the nominative by its position before the subject and verb of the clause.]

Wrong: *Who* do you think we saw down town today?

Right: *Whom* do you think we saw down town today? [*Whom* is the object of *saw*.]

2. When the pronoun is the second of two objects.

Wrong: The traffic officer told her and *I* that the road was closed.

Right: The traffic officer told her and *me* that the road was closed.

Wrong: I heard of his inviting Jim and *she* to the dance.

Right: I heard of his inviting Jim and *her* to the dance.

5d. Use the objective case when the pronoun is the object of a preposition.

Here again, trouble arises not when the pronoun immediately follows a preposition, as in "I was with *her* (not *with she*), but when the pronoun comes before its preposition or when it is the second of two objects.

Wrong: *Who* are you going with to the dance?
Right: *Whom* are you going with to the dance? [*With whom* are you going?]

Wrong: Just between you and *I*, he is a hopeless dancer.
Right: Just between you and *me*, he is a hopeless dancer.

Wrong: I know that the teacher intended her remarks for Janet and *I*.
Right: I know that the teacher intended her remarks for Janet and *me*.

A common error in speech and in writing occurs in connection with a pronoun that is linked with a noun in the objective case, as with "of we students" or "for we men."

Wrong: Several of *we* girls decided to go home for Christmas.
Right: Several of *us* girls decided to go home for Christmas.

5e. Use the objective case when the pronoun is the assumed subject or the complement of an infinitive.

Right: She thought Oswald to be *me*.
       We want *him* to be our chairman.
       A girl whom I believed to be *her* waved to me from a passing car.

5f. Use the possessive case when the pronoun expresses possession.

Remember that the personal pronouns form the possessive without the apostrophe. Possessive pronouns used to modify nouns are classed as adjectives; used in the predicate (see page 33) they are classed as pronouns.

Wrong: The furniture is *their's*, but the house is *our's*.
Right: The furniture is *theirs*, but the house is *ours*.

Wrong: Will you take care of the canary, please? It's a long time since *it's* cage has been cleaned.

Right: Will you take care of the canary, please? It's a long time since *its* cage has been cleaned.

Note carefully the difference between *it's*, which means *it is*, and *its*, which is the possessive form of *it*.

Use the apostrophe with the indefinite pronouns, such as *somebody, anybody, nobody, other, one, someone, anyone, everyone.*

Right: Everybody's business is *nobody's* business.
       Someone's hat fell into the water.
       Was the hat *yours?* I thought it was *somebody else's.* [See *else, adj.,* in *Webster's New International Dictionary.*]

5g. Use the possessive case when the pronoun introduces or modifies a gerund.

Right: We were told about *his* running away from home.
       I cannot understand *their* staying so late.

In these sentences the verbals *running* and *staying* are gerunds. A gerund is used as a noun — as subject, as complement, or as object of a preposition. When the verbal is a participle, however, the objective case is correct.

Right: We watched *them* playing a game of tennis. [Them in the act of playing.]
       Their handling of the delicate problem was tactful. [Here the subject of the verb is *handling,* a gerund.]

With nouns introducing or modifying gerunds, usage varies. There are situations in which the possessive is desirable; there are others in which it is difficult or clumsy, and therefore gives way to the objective. (See George O. Curme, *Syntax,* pp. 485–491.)

Right: I never did approve of *John's* running off to South America.
       Everybody was amazed at the *story* being released by the censor.
       I do not like the idea of *girls* marrying before they are out of school.
       The very thought of so many *officers* being murdered horrifies everyone.

5h. Make a pronoun agree with its antecedent in number, gender, and person.

Be careful about words like *each, every, each one, everyone, everybody, nobody, either, person, type, sort, kind*. These words are singular and therefore require singular pronouns. *Neither* is usually singular; some writers will occasionally use it in the plural sense. *None* is construed as either singular or plural, depending on the sense intended. See also sections 4e and 55.

Wrong: Every person in the room rose to *their* feet.
Right: Every person in the room rose to *his* feet.

Wrong: Nobody likes to have *their* name misspelled.
Right: Nobody likes to have *his* name misspelled.

Ordinarily, do not use *he or she, his or her, him or her* when the singular number is demanded and both sexes are involved. The best usage demands *he, his,* and *him.*

Undesirable: I should like every person in the audience to sign *his or her* name to this petition.
Better: I should like every person in the audience to sign *his* name to this petition.
Wrong: I should like every person in the audience to sign *their* name to this petition.

The correct idiom when one refers to more than two persons is *one another* instead of *each other.*

Undesirable: The Dionne quintuplets resemble *each other* greatly.
Preferred: The Dionne quintuplets resemble *one another* greatly.

In modern usage, the relative pronoun *who* is used to refer to persons and occasionally to animals, but *whose* may refer to persons, animals, or things, especially when *of which* produces an awkward construction. The relative *which* is used to refer to animals, things, and ideas. The relative *that* may refer to both persons and things.

Right: My mother, *who* is ill, remained in Florida. It is a problem *that* will not be solved in our time. He spoke a few words *which* we could not understand. I do not like a dog *whose* ears have been clipped.

Except in the most formal writing, American usage prefers *he* and *his* when *one* is the antecedent.

Formal: One must not lose one's temper when one is being criticized.
Preferred: A person must not lose his temper when he is being criticized.

Right: If one were to read between the lines, he would quickly detect the irony in Swift's calm proposal.

Pronouns used in apposition are in the same case as their antecedents.

Right: The three leaders — you, Harry, and I — will meet in the library.
Mother had told us — him and me — to meet her at Clark and Broadway.

5i. Use either a singular or plural pronoun to refer to a collective noun, depending upon whether the noun designates the group as a whole or the members of the group.

Be consistent. Your construction may be either singular or plural but not both. See section 4g.

Inconsistent: The band *is playing their* best selection now. [The verb is singular and the pronoun is plural.]
Consistent: The band *is playing its* best selection now.

Inconsistent: The team *is* now on the floor, taking *their* practice shots at the basket. [Verb and pronoun indicate a shift in number.]
Consistent: The team *are* now on the floor, taking *their* practice shots at the basket. [*The team* is thought of as being more than one person.]

5j. In writing that is more or less formal, do not use the pronouns *you* or *they* in the indefinite sense.

The indefinite *you* is widely used in the informal, familiar styles ranging from the purely colloquial to the semi-formal of serious magazine essays. It is objectionable in formal writing, such as most scientific books and essays, histories, books and essays dealing seriously with public affairs, sociology, economic questions, the arts, and a hundred or so other subjects. It is objectionable in student papers which the instructor has assigned as practice essays on the formal level. With some students it has become a pest — a weed — that hinders their cultivation of the resources of the English language.

They and *it*, although not so often misused as *you*, also need to be watched. See also section 57b.

In the following sentences the examples marked "colloquial" are not wrong on the informal level; they are, however, inappropriate and objectionable in formal writing.

Colloquial: If you think only of yourself, you will never become popular.
Formal: A person who thinks only of himself will never become popular.

Colloquial: They do not allow hunting in the national parks.
Formal: Hunting is not allowed in the national parks.

Colloquial: It says in the morning paper that another revolution has broken out in Central America.
Formal: The morning paper reports the outbreak of another revolution in Central America.

In expository themes, it is ordinarily best not to address the reader directly, using the imperative mood.

Inappropriate: Take Germany for an example.
Better: Let us take Germany as an example. *One may take* Germany as an example.

EXERCISES

Exercise 1, Case of pronouns. In the following sentences tell whether each pronoun, here italicized for your convenience, is used as the subject of a verb, as the complement of a verb or verbal, or as the object of a preposition.

1. *Who* did *you* think could have managed *it* without the danger of hurting someone's feelings?
2. If Mary, Helen, and *I* get the lunch ready, *some* of *you* boys should be able to provide the transportation.
3. Two of *you* girls get up and play a set against Roger and *me*.
4. Mother wants to know *whom you* were talking with when *you* failed to answer *her*.

5. If *it* was *they who* sent *us* the pears, why did not Bob and *she* say something about *them* last night?

6. Do *you* think that Graham should marry *her* if *she* is taller than *he?*

7. *I* do not care to know *whom you* are against; *I* am interested in knowing *whom you* are for.

8. If *everyone* mentions the bill to *whoever* shows any interest in *it*, *we* shall gradually gather enough votes to pass *it*.

9. *I* wonder *who* could have spread the vile gossip about Jane and *me*.

10. *Nobody* remembered to bring *his* dictionary except *you* and *her*.

Exercise 2, Case and number. In the following exercise correct every error in the use of pronouns. Give the rule which applies to each correction.

1. Is Chamberlain the one who they expect to win in the next election?

2. Salem will be satisfied; they will retain the capital.

3. "Farmers have to watch the source of their income," I explained. "He can grow only one crop every two years."

4. Many women purchase goods with the intention of returning or exchanging it the next day.

5. Donna is one girl whom I am sure will never become uninteresting.

6. How can anyone in their right mind think that Sarah is prettier than me?

7. If some of we girls will please stop talking, everyone will be able to find their places, and the meeting will proceed.

8. "Yes, it is her," Gracie thought; "it is the same woman who I saw getting on the train."

9. The watch will be awarded to whomever gets the most votes.

10. The best course for you and I is to deny everything they say.

Exercise 3. Correct every error in each of the following sentences. Find the rule which governs each correction.

1. He was the first man to invent an airplane, but he destroyed it because he thought that someone would hurt themselves trying to fly it.

2. When Mary and Belle meet a friend who they have not seen for several days, they proceed to tell them all the neighborhood gossip.

3. Everybody seemed to be having the time of their life.

4. I cannot understand why college girls come walking into the stands wearing expensive fur coats and all that goes with it.

5. Before the patient went into my father's office, I asked their name and got their card from the file.

6. Everybody must keep their books closed until I give the signal to begin.

7. Professor Jenkins told her and I that he did not assign a theme for Monday.

8. After all, everyone has personal handicaps and limitations that they must overcome.

9. If the team plays its first game tomorrow, why aren't they out on the field practicing their plays?

10. In early Roman times, they showed little interest in enhancing their personal appearance.

Exercise 4. Some of the following sentences are correct. Mark them with a C. In the others, correct every error in pronoun or reference that you find.

1. Mother wants you and she to try Blank's; Madge, Jane, and myself will look in the Emporium.

2. Do you suppose that eight men in one tent never grow tired of one another's company?

3. Harry and James looked at one another in surprise.

4. If every man and woman in this city will buy every bond that he or she can afford, they will help themselves as much as they help their country.

5. It's strange that Mary's leaving college has caused no comment.

6. Miss Wilson's singing of the ballad of Rodger Young did not please everybody, for that is a song that only men should try to sing.

7. The words may be your's, Clara, but the thoughts are his.

8. When Mrs. Cox revealed her plans to Mr. Cox and I, she did not say who she was leaving in charge of the shop.

9. If I were they, I should not hesitate to say whom I wanted for the office.

10. At the first table the master of ceremonies seated the president, three visiting professors, and I.

ADJECTIVES AND ADVERBS

6. Use the correct form of the adjective or the adverb.

Adjectives have no characteristic form. Most adverbs have the distinctive ending *-ly*. Many adverbs, however, have no distinctive ending, and some adjectives have the *-ly* suffix which is characteristic of adverbs. Hence arises the student's confusion.

Some of the common adverbs not ending in *-ly* are *here, there, where, why, very, too, then, when.*

Certain adverbs have the same form as the corresponding adjectives. In the following sentences notice carefully that each adverb modifies a verb or an adjective or another adverb, whereas each adjective modifies a noun.

Examples:	(Adverb)	(Adjective)
close	Come close.	That was a close decision.
deep	Dig deep.	He dug a deep well.
early	Come early.	He was an early riser.
far	You are not far wrong.	He came from a far country.
fast	Run fast.	It was a fast game.
hard	Hit it hard.	The problem was hard.
high	Throw it high in the air.	He spoke in a high voice.
just	He just entered.	He is a just man.
late	He came late.	One student was late.
little	His work is little known.	I had a little sleep.
loud	Do not shout so loud.	His voice was loud.
low	Speak low.	I have a low opinion of him.
near	She came very near.	That was a near escape.
quick	Come quick.	He is a quick thinker.
right	Do it right.	That is the right answer.
slow	Go slow.	It is a slow train.
straight	He can't see straight.	Walk in a straight line.
well	He played well.	He is now a well man.

Some adverbs have two parallel forms. When the two forms convey the same meaning, as in *slow — slowly*, there is a tendency to use the *-ly* form in the more formal types of speech and writing. When the two forms convey different shades of meaning, your only help is a gradual acquaintance with accepted English idioms.

Examples:

late — lately	He came late.	Lately he has not been prompt.
high — highly	Aim high.	He was highly thought of.
near — nearly	Don't go near.	He is nearly there.
loud — loudly	Speak louder.	He protested loudly.
right — rightly	He did right.	He was rightly indignant.

256

Some adjectives which have the *-ly* suffix characteristic of adverbs are: an *early* bird, a *likely* story, a *lively* kitten, a *kindly* person, a *friendly* community, an *only* child.

6a. Do not use an adjective in place of an adverb or an adverb in place of an adjective.

The use of an adverb for an adjective, except in the predicate position (see section 6b), is usually due to pure carelessness; the use of an adjective for an adverb, however, is a common error. To avoid the error, you must remember the function of each of the two parts of speech: an adjective modifies a substantive, that is, it names a quality or a condition; an adverb names the manner of an action.

Wrong: He did not do *good* in his last examination.
Right: He did not do *well* in his last examination.

Wrong: Mary did not take her study of grammar *serious* enough.
Right: Mary did not take her study of grammar *seriously* enough.

Wrong: We *sure* appreciated her kindness.
Right: We *surely* appreciated her kindness.

Wrong: Yes, I am doing *fine*.
Right: Yes, I am doing *very well*.

6b. After verbs like *become, appear, seem, prove, remain, look,* and the verbs pertaining to the senses, like *smell, taste, feel,* be careful to use an adjective subjective complement instead of an adverb.

Wrong: If you remain *quietly*, we shall begin the concert.
Right: If you remain *quiet*, we shall begin the concert. [The adjective *quiet* modifies *you*. It means, "If you *are* quiet."]

Wrong: This water tastes *badly*.
Right: This water tastes *bad*. [*Bad* tells a quality of water, not the manner of tasting it.]

Wrong: The rose smells *sweetly*.
Right: The rose smells *sweet*. [The sentence means, "The rose *is* sweet." The adjective *sweet* tells a quality of a rose; it does not indicate the manner of smelling.]

Wrong: Lowell ranks *highly* as an essayist.
Right: Lowell ranks *high* as an essayist. [Lowell *is* high.]

6c. Avoid awkward, illogical, or misleading comparisons.

Adjectives and adverbs form the comparative degree either by adding *-er* to the positive or by using *more* or *less* with the positive degree. They form the superlative by adding *-est* to the positive or by using *most* or *least* with the positive degree. Some adjectives and adverbs are compared irregularly. See also Parts of Speech, pp. 33–34, and *Adjective* and *Adverb*, sec. 9. The choice of the form used depends entirely upon euphony.

Positive	Comparative	Superlative
ADJECTIVES:		
strong	stronger	strongest
noble	nobler	noblest
	or more noble	most noble
famous	more famous	most famous
beautiful	more beautiful	most beautiful
good	better	best
bad	worse	worst
ADVERBS:		
quick	quicker	quickest
happily	more happily	most happily
well	better	best

It is awkward, not grammatically wrong, to use forms like *famouser, beautifuler,* or *beautifulest;* it is wrong to use *badder* or *weller.* In formal writing, it is usually considered undesirable to use comparative and superlative forms of adjectives naming absolute qualities, as, for instance, *most perfect, most unique.* In formal writing one may find such approximations as *most nearly perfect* or *most nearly unique,* but in speech and in informal writing such forms as *straightest, blacker, most universal, most perfect,* and *most unique* are common.

In modern English it is undesirable to combine two forms to produce a comparative or a superlative.

Undesirable: That is the *most unkindest* thing that you could have said.
Better: That is the *most unkind* thing that you could have said.

Undesirable: His fame reached the *more remoter* districts of the country.
Better: His fame reached the *more remote* districts of the country.

Use the comparative form of the adjective when referring to two persons or things.

Wrong: Betty Jane is the *prettiest* of the two girls.
Right: Betty Jane is the *prettier* of the two girls.

6d. Avoid the double negative.

In the English language the usual negative is *not*. Adding another negative to *not* in the same sentence produces what is called a "double negative." It is not true that one negative tends to cancel out the other, or that two negatives produce an affirmative; whenever used, it is used with the intention of making the negation more emphatic. Although the double negative was once common in all levels of speech and writing, it has survived only in the lower levels of spoken English, in such expressions as "I don't want nothing from nobody," or "I ain't got no friends nowhere." In student writing the trouble arises with such words as *hardly*, *scarcely*, and *but*, which are negative in force.

Wrong: For a few moments he *couldn't hardly* speak.
Right: For a few minutes he *could hardly* speak.

Wrong: I do *not* doubt *but* that I shall be terrified when the test comes.
Right: I do not doubt that I shall be terrified when the test comes. [Omit *but*.]

Wrong: Most girls *cannot help but like* attentions from men.
Right: Most girls cannot help liking attentions from men. [Omit *but* and change *like* to *liking*.]

6e. In formal writing avoid the awkward use of a noun as an adjective.

The use of a noun in the adjective function is a common thing in the English language. Consider such forms as: a *bird* dog, a *house* cat, an *ivory* tower, a *silk* dress, a *leather* shoe, a *flower* pot, a *paper* sole, the *horse and buggy* doctor, the *city* streets, the *Chicago* fire. Occasionally, however, such a construction is better rephrased.

Awkward: The Elm Street paving and widening project was discussed.
Better: The plan to pave and widen Elm Street was discussed.

Awkward: The principal speaker was the University of Minnesota law school dean.
Better: The principal speaker was the dean of the law school at the University of Minnesota.

EXERCISES

Exercise 1, Recognition. In the following sentences, is the italicized word an adjective or an adverb?

1. After playing four sets of tennis I feel *tired*.
2. It was a most *generous* and *friendly* act.
3. That is a *likely* tale, Charlie, but were you *there?*
4. Mr. Maser looks *well*. He slept *well* last night, and this morning he ate a *hearty* breakfast.
5. I knew I had played it *wrong* as soon as I finished my swing.
6. The *early* worm suffers a *just* punishment for getting up *early*.
7. Does not Homer Smith look *proud* and *pleased?*
8. The clouds are drifting in *very low* today.
9. *Lately* there have been *several* attempts to float the ship *again*.
10. Marjorie, as usual, arrived *late* for the party.

Exercise 2, Correct forms. Correct the error in the form or use of the adjective or adverb in each of the following sentences.

1. Which is the oldest, Harry or George?
2. After life's fitful fever, he sleeps good.
3. They sure are hungry, are they not?
4. The quarterback is usually smaller and lighter than any man on the team.
5. The speaker was the Junction City Chamber of Commerce secretary.
6. Wait for me, Bob; my theme is near finished.
7. Better move fastly if you want to get there by night.
8. After working steady for several hours, we got out to stretch our legs.
9. His pictures have been muchly admired by the critics.
10. Mr. Nelson thinks that I am not taking my work serious enough.

Exercise 3, Correct forms. In each of the following sentences select the correct form of the adjective or adverb.

1. The teacher's comments made me feel (cheap, cheaply).
2. The batter protested (loud, loudly) against the decision.
3. I am sorry, sir; I got up (late, lately) this morning.
4. My uncle feels (some, somewhat) better today.
5. Although my uncle seems to be in perfect health, he really has not felt (good, well) for a long time.
6. The trip cost (considerable, considerably) more than I had expected.
7. The room would have been pleasanter if she had arranged the furniture (different, differently).
8. Do you realize how (bad, badly) things look for us?
9. The whistle of the train sounds (loud, loudly) on a cold morning.
10. The troops (couldn't hardly, could hardly) wait for the order to advance.

VERB FORMS

7. Use the correct form of the verb.

Cultivate the habit of looking up troublesome verbs in your dictionary. The following examples show the manner in which the principal parts of verbs are indicated in *Webster's New International Dictionary:*

rise; *past tense* ROSE; *past part.* RIS'EN; *pres. part. & verbal n.* RIS'ING.
raise; RAISED; RAIS'ING.
lie; *past tense* LAY; *past part.* LAIN; *pres. part. & verbal n.* LY'ING.
lay; LAID; LAY'ING.
sit; *past tense* SAT; *past part.* SAT; *pres. part. & verbal n.* SIT'TING.
set; *past tense & past part.* SET; *pres. part. & verbal n.* SET'TING.

The principal parts are the basis of all the changes in the form of a verb. Principal parts of *take:* took, taken, taking.

INDICATIVE MOOD, ACTIVE VOICE
Present Tense

Singular	*Plural*
I take	we take
you take	you take
he takes	they take

INDICATIVE MOOD, ACTIVE VOICE — *Continued*

Past Tense

Singular	*Plural*
I took	we took
you took	you took
he took	they took

Future Tense

I shall take	we shall take
you will take	you will take
he will take	they will take

Perfect Tense

I have taken	we have taken
you have taken	you have taken
he has taken	they have taken

Past Perfect Tense

I had taken	we had taken
you had taken	you had taken
he had taken	they had taken

Future Perfect Tense

I shall have taken	we shall have taken
you will have taken	you will have taken
he will have taken	they will have taken

INDICATIVE MOOD, PASSIVE VOICE

Present Tense

I am taken	we are taken
you are taken	you are taken
he is taken	they are taken

Past Tense

I was taken	we were taken
you were taken	you were taken
he was taken	they were taken

Future Tense

Singular	*Plural*
I shall be taken	we shall be taken
you will be taken	you will be taken
he will be taken	they will be taken

Perfect Tense

I have been taken	we have been taken
you have been taken	you have been taken
he has been taken	they have been taken

Past Perfect Tense

I had been taken	we had been taken
you had been taken	you had been taken
he had been taken	they had been taken

Future Perfect Tense

I shall have been taken	we shall have been taken
you will have been taken	you will have been taken
he will have been taken	they will have been taken

SUBJUNCTIVE MOOD, ACTIVE VOICE

Present Tense

if I take	if we take
if you take	if you take
if he take	if they take

Past Tense

if I took, etc.	if we took, etc.

Perfect Tense

if I have taken, etc.	if we have taken, etc.

Past Perfect Tense

if I had taken, etc.	if we had taken, etc.

SUBJUNCTIVE MOOD, PASSIVE VOICE

Present Tense

if I be taken	if we be taken
if you be taken	if you be taken
if he be taken	if they be taken

SUBJUNCTIVE MOOD, PASSIVE VOICE — *Continued*

Singular	*Plural*
Past Tense	
if I were taken, etc.	if we were taken, etc.
Perfect Tense	
if I have been taken, etc.	if we have been taken, etc.
Past Perfect Tense	
if I had been taken, etc.	if we had been taken, etc.

IMPERATIVE FORMS: take, be taken
INFINITIVE FORMS: to take, to have taken, to be taken, to have been taken
GERUND: taking, having taken, being taken, having been taken
PARTICIPLE: taking, taken, having taken, being taken, having been taken

Most of the illiterate errors in the form of the verb arise from the student's failure to look up and learn the principal parts.

Wrong: After he had *throwed* it at me, I just let it *lay* where it *had fell.*
Right: After he *had thrown* it at me, I just let it *lie* where it *had fallen.*

Wrong: The men *drug* the carcass to their camp and *hanged* it up out of reach of prowling coyotes.
Right: The men *dragged* the carcass to their camp and *hung* it up out of reach of prowling coyotes.

7a. Use the correct tense of the verb.

Tense is that property of a verb that indicates the time of its action. The names of most of the tenses — present, past, future — are self-explanatory. Several distinctions, however, need further explanation:

1. The perfect tense shows that an act was completed, but it does not specify when:

Right: Yes, I *have taken* a course in English grammar.
   They *have been taught* not to run across the street.

2. The past perfect tense shows that an act was completed before some other specified act or time.

Right: I *had registered* for the course before I spoke to him.

He was trying to put into practice some of the principles which he *had been taught.*

The following cautions will help you to avoid most of the common errors in tenses of verbs:

1. Use the tenses which show the correct relation of time between the main verb and subordinate verbs. Make the verbs in subordinate clauses conform to the tenses of verbs in the main clauses.

Wrong: Yesterday I told my teacher that I *have written* my essay.
Right: Yesterday I told my teacher that I *had written* my essay. [The past perfect must be used because the writing had been completed before the time of his telling the teacher.]

Wrong: We started for home so that our fond parents would not suspect that anything out of the ordinary *took* place.
Right: We started for home so that our fond parents would not suspect that anything out of the ordinary *had taken* place. [The time of "taking place" was before that of "starting."]

2. Be careful to use the correct tense of infinitives and participles. Notice in the following examples that the time indicated by the verbal is always in relation to the time expressed by the main verb.

Wrong: I was delighted *to have received* your invitation.
Right: I was delighted *to receive* your invitation. [In other words, his delight took place at the same time as the receiving of the invitation, not at some time afterwards.]

Wrong: He probably intended *to have returned* the book, but he forgot.
Right: He probably intended *to return* the book, but he forgot.

Wrong: *Working* hard all day, Jim was tired when evening came.
Right: *Having worked* hard all day, Jim was tired when evening came. [The time of "working" came before the time of "being tired."]

3. In telling a story, do not shift from the past to the present and from the present to the past unless there is a real change in time. See also section 57. Occasionally a writer uses what is called the "historical present," by which he aims for greater life and vividness in telling events which happened in the past. This device can easily be abused. Do not attempt it unless you use it in a whole section of a narrative.

4. Be careful not to leave off the ending *-s* of the third person singular of the present tense, or the *-ed* of the past tense of the weak verb.

Wrong: He *insist* that he is ill, but I do not believe him.
        I *ask* him last night to lend me his notebook.
Right: He *insists* that he is ill, but I do not believe him.
        I *asked* him last night to lend me his notebook.

5. Use the present tense to indicate that something is habitual, characteristic, or permanently true:

Right: The speaker said that honesty *is* the best policy. [Meaning that it still is.]
        The county agent told my father that potatoes *grow* best in sandy soil.

7b. Use the correct form of the subjunctive in certain situations that clearly call for the subjunctive.

If you study the conjugation of the verb *to take*, you will see that the subjunctive form differs from the indicative only in a few forms, mainly in the third person singular of the present tense. The verb *to be* is a special problem. The problem may be simplified by saying that the subjunctive of *to be* uses:

1. "be" in all forms of the present tense
2. "were" in all forms of the past tense
3. "have been" in all forms of the perfect tense

The only uses of the subjunctive with which a student need concern himself in his speech and writing are:

266

1. In *if*-clauses expressing doubt or impossibility of the condition (usually referred to as "condition contrary to fact").

Subjunctive: If he *were* heavier, he would be more useful to the team.
　When I entered, I could hear him shouting at his secretary, and I could not help wondering if that *were* his usual manner.
　Were he alive, he would be proud of his son.

2. In *that*-clauses expressing a wish, request, or command:

Subjunctive: The colonel requested that the delegates *be* treated with all military courtesy.
　The committee demanded that he *come* to a decision immediately.
　We recommend that he *take* the entrance examination.

3. In main clauses to express hope, wish, or prayer, in more or less traditional and stereotyped patterns:

Subjunctive: Heaven *help* the working girl.
　Long *live* the King!
　"The subjunctive *be* hanged!" exclaimed the weary student.
　The peace of quiet gardens *be* with you.

7c. Use the correct form of *shall* and *will*.

In modern informal speech most persons use *will* and *would* (or the contractions *I'll, he'll, I'd, you'd*) for all persons. Careful usage still observes the following distinctions:

1. Use *shall* for the future tense in the first person, both singular and plural; use *will* for the future tense in the second and third persons.

Simple futurity: I *shall* go to New York. You *will* find me at home. He *will* be twenty-one next June. She *will* come later. They *will* meet you at the train.

2. To express a promise, determination, or assurance, use *will* in the first person, and *shall* in the second and third persons.

Assurance: I *will* go to New York in spite of your warning. They *shall* not pass! You *shall* give me the money.

3. In asking questions, a speaker adds a note of formality to his question by using the form which he anticipates in the answer.

Formal: *Will* you return my book tomorrow? I *will.*
        Shall he spoil our plans? He *shall* not.
        Shall you be old enough to vote? I *shall.*

4. To express a habitual or customary action, use *would* in the first, second, and third persons.

Right: I *would* sit on the banks of a stream all afternoon.
     He *would* go for long walks in the morning.
     You *would* wander off when you knew that your mother wanted you at home.

5. *Should* is often used in the sense of *ought*, although in some sentences *ought* may imply a slightly stronger obligation.

Right: You *should go* to the meeting. [You *ought to go* to the meeting.]
     His papers *should have been returned* to him. [His papers *ought to have been returned* to him.]

7d. Do not overuse the passive voice.

The active verb form is more common in speech and writing, more vivid, and more emphatic than the passive. The passive voice, however, has its legitimate uses: the object, or recipient, of the action of the verb may be more important than the doer; the doer of the action may not be known; or the writer may wish to place the emphasis on the recipient instead of upon the doer. It is not the passive voice that is objectionable — it is the *wrong* use of it.

Weak: A good time was had by all.
Better: Everybody had a good time.

Weak: Your kind letter was received by me.
Better: I received your kind letter.

Weak: A fishing trip was suggested by my father.
Better: My father suggested a fishing trip.

More objectionable than the "weak passive" (see section 65) is the careless shift from one voice to the other in the same sentence or in the same group of sentences.

Confused: One girl may be writing a letter; a book absorbs the attention of another. As usual someone sat in her chair sound asleep. Constant whispers could have been heard by the lecturer.

Consistent: During the lecture, one girl is writing a letter; another is reading a book. As usual someone sits sound asleep. Several girls are whispering constantly.

EXERCISES

Exercise 1, Principal parts. With the help of your dictionary find the principal parts of the following verbs. List the form given, the past tense, the past participle, and the present participle or gerund; as, *begin, began, begun, beginning.*

blow	drive	leave	sink
break	eat	lose	slay
bring	fly	prove	smite
burst	get	ride	spring
choose	go	ring	sting
dive	grow	rise	swim
do	lead	set	take
drink	lend	shake	throw

Construct sentences in which you use the past tense of each of the verbs.

Exercise 2, Verb forms. Some of the following sentences are correct. You should be able to identify them. In others the verb is incorrect. Make all necessary corrections:

1. I left it laying where it had lain all day.
2. The drouth will probably raise the price of wheat.
3. Have courage, young man; the whole world lays before you.
4. The murderer was hung at six o'clock yesterday morning.
5. I am tired; I have drove hard since early this morning.
6. All the refuse has rose to the surface of the pool.
7. When I heard that, you could have slayed me with a feather.
8. All the pears were shooken off the tree by the strong wind.

9. Please raise your voice if you want to be heard.
10. Have you wrote your theme yet, George?
11. No, I have took pains to do a good piece of work this time.
12. All right, George; I'll set down and wait until you shall finish it.
13. Jones will probably try to raise hogs on his farm.
14. He was so tired that he laid on the couch all evening.
15. I think that you shouldn't have hanged the picture in this room.
16. You will catch cold if you set on the grass.
17. The principal asked me to set down just as I was raising to speak.
18. He was caught in the act of setting the garage afire.
19. When a hen cackles, the important question is, "Is she laying or lieing?"
20. Bobby was so frightened that his hair seemed to raise up.

Exercise 3, Tenses. If you find any mistakes in tenses in the following sentences, make the necessary corrections.

1. They seemed pleased to have been asked to go with us.
2. The doctor said that cancer is not a contagious disease.
3. I should have liked to have visited the Horner Museum.
4. We intended to have seen the Bonneville Dam on our way to Portland.
5. We were all surprised to receive the news of your marriage.
6. Having lost my job, I decided to enter the state university.

Exercise 4, Shall and will. Judging the following sentences according to the standards of formal usage, select the correct forms from those given in parentheses.

1. Professor Brown (shall, will) be thirty on his next birthday.
2. The new director has promised that no one (shall, will) go hungry.
3. We (shall, will) be pleased to investigate your record.
4. I must insist that everyone (shall, will) have his essay ready by eight o'clock tomorrow morning.
5. Nancy (should, would) usually put off her work until it was too late.
6. You have my promise. I (shall, will) return.
7. "(Shall, Will) you go to the President's reception?" "I shall."

Exercise 5, The subjunctive. In the following sentences select the correct forms from those given in parentheses.

1. Mrs. Brown acts as if she (was, were) angry, but I know that she is really flattered.

2. If I (was, were) a man, you could not say that to me.
3. I wish it (was, were) possible to read the whole essay to you.
4. The senator moved that the motion (be, is) laid on the table.
5. May I ask that the consideration of my case (is, be) postponed until tomorrow?
6. I wish I (was, were) in San Francisco now.
7. If this (was, were) my dog, I (should, would) keep him locked up.
8. If I (was, were) they, I (should, would) feel flattered.
9. If I (was, were) the owner of half that dog, I (should, would) sell my half.
10. If Tom (was, were) my son, I (should, would) spank him.
11. I knew Tom so well that I could not help wondering if that (was, were) his first mistake.
12. I wish that my mother (was, were) here to help me.
13. He acts as if he (was, were) pleased, but I know that he is disappointed.
14. If I (was, were) the chaperon, I (should, would) ignore the whole incident.
15. The committee recommends that he (postpones, postpone) his matriculation.

CONJUNCTIONS

8a. Use the co-ordinating conjunction that will express the exact relationship between co-ordinate sentence elements.

Every student knows that *and*, *but*, and *for* are co-ordinating conjunctions — a bit of exact but fragmentary information that may actually hinder him in the development of variety and flexibility in writing. If you become conscious of the monotonous series of *and*'s, *but*'s, and the colloquial *so*'s in your papers, you may find help through the study of the following examples. The conjunctions *and*, *but*, and *for* are quite legitimate. You must not think that their use is an error. There are many other conjunctions, however, which may express more exactly what you mean. It does not matter at this moment that some of them are called conjunctive adverbs instead of conjunctions.

I can enjoy classical music *and* jazz.
I can enjoy *both* classical music *and* jazz.

Call your dog home, *or else* I shall notify the sheriff.

Sarah *and* I have not read the current best seller.
Neither Sarah *nor* I have read the current best seller.

He means well, *but* he is always unlucky.
He means well, *only* he is always unlucky.

The new freshman can write poetry *and* play football.
The new freshman can write poetry *as well as* play football.

In that crisis he showed courage *and* resourcefulness.
In that crisis he showed *not only* courage *but also* resourcefulness.

I do not believe that they are lazy *and* ignorant.
I do not believe that they are lazy, *still less* that they are ignorant.

She is much older than I, *but* she fascinates me.
She is much older than I, *and yet* she fascinates me.

You must observe the correct usage in punctuation with co-ordinating conjunctions. The conjunctions *and, but, for, nor, or,* when introducing a co-ordinate clause within a sentence, require a comma before the conjunction, except when the clauses are short and closely related in meaning. The more formal the style of writing, the more careful must be the punctuation. The conjunctions *yet* and *so* (*so* belongs in speech and very loose, informal writing) usually take a comma. See section 20.

The so-called conjunctive adverbs *therefore, moreover, however, nevertheless, likewise, hence, also, besides, notwithstanding, accordingly* — if they are used at all — require a semicolon before the conjunction if the conjunction stands at the beginning of a clause within a sentence. Remember, however, that you will have to read several hundred pages of modern prose before you find a sentence in which a conjunctive adverb *begins* a co-ordinate clause. In present-day expository prose the conjunctive adverbs are almost invariably tucked away within the clause. There, as interrupters, they are set off by commas. See section 21.

Any of the conjunctive adverbs may be used to begin a sentence. They are frequently so used in modern writing.

Here are some of the connecting words which may be used for variety in sentence structure. See also "Transitions," pp. 90–100, and section 60.

accordingly
after all
again
also
and also
and moreover
and likewise
and yet
as also
as well as
at times
all the same

besides
but then

*conversely

else
even

finally
first
firstly
for all that
for that reason
further
furthermore

however
indeed

in the first place
in the second place

later
let alone
likewise

meanwhile
moreover
much less

namely
nevertheless
not to mention
notwithstanding

only
on the other hand
on the contrary
on that account
or else

rather

secondly
still
still less
still more

then

yet

8b. Avoid some of the common errors in the use of subordinating conjunctions.

Although the connectives discussed here have gained wide currency in loose, informal speech, they are still avoided, in the senses indicated, by writers of both formal and informal expository prose.

1. *like* for *as if, as though, as*

Wrong: He acts *like* he was hungry.
Right: He acts *as if* he were hungry.

Wrong: Hold your club *like* your coach held it.
Right: Hold your club *as* your coach held it.

2. *as* for *like*

Wrong: She talks *as* a foreigner.
Right: She talks *like* a foreigner.

3. *except* for *unless*

Wrong: They refuse to begin work *except* you agree to raise their pay.
Right: They refuse to begin work *unless* you agree to raise their pay.

4. *without* for *unless*

Wrong: He will not come out *without* you put down your rifle.
Right: He will not come out *unless* you put down your rifle.

5. *while* for *although, whereas, and, but*

While, in exact formal usage, is a subordinating connective of time.

Inexact: While in many respects I am fond of Jane, her conceit irritates me.
Better: Although in many respects I am fond of Jane, her conceit irritates me.

Inexact: Jim is intelligent, *while* his brother is stupid.
Better: Jim is intelligent, *but* his brother is stupid.

Inexact: A married man must support his family *while* a single man has only himself to think of.
Better: A married man must support his family, *whereas* a single man has only himself to think of.

6. *because* for *for*

In formal usage, *because* introduces a dependent clause giving the reason for the fact stated in the main clause; *for* introduces a co-ordinate clause telling why the writer knows that the fact stated is true. In informal usage the distinction between *because* and *for* is fading.

Right: That boy made an "A" in the course because he worked hard.
      That boy made an "A" in the course, for I see that he looks happy.

7. *if* for *whether*

In formal usage, *whether* is used to introduce an indirect question used as a noun clause. *Whether* is more likely to be used when followed by *or*.

Formal: Mrs. Winston asked *whether* he would come to the cabin party.
Informal: Mrs. Winston asked *if* he would come to the cabin party.

9.   GRAMMATICAL TERMS

Absolute. An expression grammatically independent of the rest of the sentence. See sec. 54 and Phrases, p. 47.

The work having been finished, we returned to the camp.

Adjective. A word used to limit or describe a noun or pronoun. See Parts of Speech, p. 33, and sec. 6. The main classes of adjectives are:

1. Descriptive: a *new* hat, a *large* man, a *stern* father.
2. Pronominal: *my* hat, *her* man, *their* father.
3. Demonstrative: *this* book, *that* horse, *these* lessons.
4. Interrogative: *whose* book? *which* lesson?
5. Indefinite: *some* woman, *any* teacher, *either* book.
6. Articles: *a* boy, *an* apple, *the* room.
7. Numeral: *one* apple, *five* cents, the *first* lesson.

Adjective clause. A subordinate clause used like an adjective. See Clauses, pp. 50–53. It modifies a substantive.

Our ranch, *which is small but well managed,* returned a profit last year.
George, *who is older than Sally,* spoke first.

Adverb. A word used to modify a verb, another adverb, or an adjective. See Parts of Speech, p. 34 and sec. 6. Adverbs may indicate:

1. Place: Please remain *outside.*
2. Manner: He returned *quickly.*
3. Time: You may go *now.*
4. Degree: The dinner was *very* good.
5. Affirmation or negation: *Yes,* he is here. *No,* do *not* go.

Adverb clause. A clause used to modify a verb, an adjective, or an adverb. See Clauses, pp. 51–52. An adverb clause may indicate:

1. Time: *When he arrives*, give him this money.
2. Place: He worked best *where the difficulties were greatest.*
3. Cause: He left school *because he had to find a job.*
4. Purpose: He came to college *in order that he might meet the right people.*
   The troops rested *so that the supply train could overtake them.*
5. Result: The troops rested *so that the supply train was able to overtake them.*
6. Condition: *If he asks questions*, deny the whole story.
7. Concession: *Although Father is old*, he is active and strong.
8. Manner: Try to dance *as Dorothy does.*
9. Comparison: Dorothy is more graceful *than you are.*

Adverbial objective. A substantive used adverbially.

He went *home*. He walked three *miles*.

Agreement. A correspondence between pronoun and antecedent in person, number, and gender (see sec. 5); between subject and verb in person and number (see sec. 4).

Antecedent. A word, phrase, or clause to which a pronoun refers. See sec. 55.

England expects every *man* to do *his* duty.
He returned the money, which is the least he could do.

Appositive. A word placed beside another word and denoting the same thing or person.

Harold, the older *boy*, recommended *archery*, his favorite *hobby*.

Article. The words *a* and *an* are the indefinite articles; the word *the* is the definite article. Articles are used as adjectives.

Auxiliary. A verb is called auxiliary, or helping, when it helps to make a form of another verb. The auxiliary verbs are *be*, *have*, *shall*, *will*, *should*, *would*, *can*, *could*, *may*, *might*.

But I *do* know. He *was* called. I *shall* return soon. He *might* like it.

Cardinal number. The numbers *one, two, three, four,* etc. See Ordinal numbers.

Case. The relation, or the form indicating it, between nouns, pronouns, and adjectives and other words in the sentence. In English the three cases are nominative (subjective), objective, and possessive. For the case forms of the personal pronouns see sec. 5. Nouns have the same case form in the nominative and the objective. For the possessive case of nouns and indefinite pronouns see sec. 23.

Clause. A group of words containing a subject and a predicate. Clauses that make independent assertions are independent or co-ordinate. Clauses that depend on some other part of the sentence are called dependent or subordinate. See also Noun clauses, Adjective clauses, Adverb clauses.

> *Independent:* The dogs barked, and the children shouted.
> *Dependent:* Mary, *who is now fourteen,* attends junior high school. [adjective]
>
> > *If it rains,* the game will be postponed. [adverb]
> > *What he planned to do* will never be known. [noun]

Collective noun. A noun naming a collection of individuals by a singular form. See sec. 4g.

Common noun. See Noun.

Comparison. The inflection of an adjective or an adverb to indicate degree. The three degrees are positive, comparative, and superlative. For examples see sec. 6.

Complement. A word used to complete the sense of a verb. A complement may be a direct object, an indirect object, a subjective complement, a double object, an objective complement, or a retained object. The first three on this list are the most common. See Complements, pp. 37–39.

> *Direct object:* The pitcher threw the *ball.*
> *Indirect object:* Tell *me* your name.

Subjective complement: Herbert is a good *boy*. [noun]
Herbert is *weary*. [adjective]
Double objects: Ask the *man* his *name*.
Objective complement: They made him their *leader*.
Retained object: They were given their *wages*.

Complex sentence. A sentence containing one independent clause and at least one dependent clause. See p. 40.

Compound sentence. A sentence containing two or more independent clauses. See p. 43.

Compound-complex sentence. A sentence containing two or more independent clauses and at least one dependent clause. See p. 43.

Concrete noun. See Noun.

Conjugation. The inflectional forms of a verb. For the conjugation of the verb *take* see pp. 261–264.

Conjunction. See Parts of Speech, p. 34, Conjunctions, sec. 8.

Conjunctive adverb. See Parts of Speech, pp. 34–35, Conjunctions, sec. 8, and the Semicolon, sec. 21.

Construction. The grammatical function of a word in the sentence.

Co-ordinate. Of the same rank; equal in rank, not subordinate.

Copula, copulative verb. A verb used to link subject with complement, to show the relation between subject and complement. It does not express action. The copulative or linking verbs are *is, was, were, seems, feels, tastes, smells, sounds,* and the like. A linking verb does not take an object. It is followed by a subjective complement (which see). The verb is, in effect, a sign of equality: it indicates that the subject either is the same thing as the complement or that it has a quality named by the complement. See sec. 6b.

Howard *was* a soldier.
The bread *is* very stale.
It tastes *sour*.
The air *smells* sweet.

Correlative conjunctions. Conjunctions that are used in pairs. See Parts of Speech, pp. 34–35.

> *Examples:* either ... or, neither ... nor, both ... and, not only ... but also.

Dative case. A case form not found in English.

Declension. The inflectional forms of nouns or pronouns. See sec. 5.

Demonstrative pronoun. A pronoun which points out what it refers to. The demonstrative pronouns are *this*, *that*, *these*, *those*. See Pronoun.

Direct address. A construction in which a speaker or writer addresses a second person directly.

> *Father*, let me have ten dollars.
> In that case, *Mary*, I shall be delighted to take you home.

Direct discourse. The words of a speaker quoted exactly as they were spoken. In indirect discourse the thought or substance of the speaker's words is given. See sec. 24.

> She said, "My brother is coming back from Germany."
> She said that her brother was coming back from Germany.

Ellipsis (elliptical expressions). The omission of words necessary to grammatical completeness. An expression in which some words are implied or understood. The most common form is the adverbial clause of comparison. For the common error resulting from a misuse of elliptical clauses, see Dangling Modifiers, sec. 54.

> She is taller *than I* [*am tall*]. (Note the case of the pronoun in such a clause.)

Expletive. A word used to fill out or to introduce. The most common expletives are *it* and *there*.

> *It* is true that he never told a lie. [The real subject of the verb is *that he never told a lie*.] *There* are three men in the room now. [Three men are in the room now.]

Finite verb. A verb form capable of making a predication or an assertion, as distinguished from the non-finite forms — the gerund, the participle, and the infinitive.

Gender. There are three genders in English — masculine, feminine, and neuter. Some nouns and pronouns have special forms to indicate gender: actor, actress; host, hostess; he, she, it.

Genitive. The possessive case. In English, possession may also be expressed by an *of*-phrase: Robert Frost's poems; the poems of Robert Frost. Note the occasional use of the double genitive (possessive): no son of mine, this life of ours, some friend of Mother's.

Gerund. A verbal used as a noun. A gerund, like the present participle, usually ends in *-ing*. For the various forms of the gerund, see the conjugation of the verb *take*, section 7a. A gerund, since it is partly a verb, may take adverbial modifiers and complements; since it is partly a noun, it has the functions of a noun and can be modified by adjectives. See Verbals, pp. 35–37, for the various uses of gerunds.

Gerund phrase. A gerund with its complements and modifiers.

Idiom. An expression peculiar to a language. See sec. 37.

> *Examples:* make a clean breast of it, take kindly to, make no bones about, do away with.

Indefinite pronoun. Pronouns that do not designate a definite or particular person or thing. Some indefinite pronouns are: anybody, any one, anything, somebody, some one, everybody, another, one, none, some, something, either, neither. See Pronoun.

Indirect discourse. See Direct discourse.

Indirect object. See Complement.

Infinitive. A verbal form usually preceded by the sign *to*. The sign is occasionally omitted. The infinitive has two tenses, present and perfect. Since the infinitive is partly a verb, it may take complements and adverbial modifiers. It may be used in the sentence as a noun, as an adjective, or as an adverb. See Verbals, pp. 35–37.

> *Noun: To work* is *to pray.* [Subject and subjective complement.]
>> He wanted *to see* the game. [Object of verb and takes an object.]
>> I heard *him* [*to*] *say* he would come. [Sign omitted. Also note that *him* is the assumed subject of the infinitive.]
>
> *Adjective:* I have a right *to challenge* your statement. [Modifies *right*.]
> *Adverb:* Harold came *to see* me. [Adverb of purpose modifying *came*.]

Infinitive phrase. An infinitive with its complements and modifiers.

Inflection (inflexion). The change of form which a word takes to show case, gender, number, tense, person, mood, etc.

Intensive pronoun. See Pronoun.

Interjection. An exclamation like *oh, alas, ah, fiddlesticks*, which is grammatically independent of the rest of the sentence. See Parts of Speech, p. 35.

Interrogative pronoun. See Pronoun.

Intransitive. See Verb.

Linking verb. See Copula.

Modal auxiliary. Auxiliary verbs like *shall, will, may, might.* See Subjunctive, sec. 7b, and Shall and Will, sec. 7c.

Mood or mode. The form of the verb which indicates the manner in which the action it denotes is conceived, as fact, assumption, volition, possibility, etc. The three modes in English are indicative, imperative, and subjunctive. See the conjugation of the verb *take*, sec. 7.

Nominative absolute. The noun or pronoun used in an absolute expression. See Absolute.

Nonrestrictive clause. A clause which adds information about a word it modifies but does not help to identify or to point out a certain thing or person. For examples and proper punctuation, see sec. 20a.

Noun. A word which names a person, an object, a quality, etc. A common noun names any one of the members of a class or group of persons, places, things, qualities, ideas, etc. Common nouns are not capitalized. (*Examples:* man, cat, courage, city, advice, ocean.) A proper noun names some particular person, place, or thing. Proper nouns are capitalized. (*Examples:* Clara Olson, Washington Avenue, Carleton College, New York, Civil War.) A collective noun names a group by using a singular form. (See sec. 4.) An abstract noun names a quality or a general idea. (*Examples:* service, loyalty, darkness.) A concrete noun names something that may be perceived by one of the senses. (*Examples:* finger, bread, smoke, fog, song, wind.) See Parts of Speech, pp. 32–33.

Noun clause. A dependent clause used as a noun. For examples and uses, see Clauses, pp. 50–51.

Number. There are two numbers — the singular, indicating one, and the plural, indicating more than one.

Object. See Complement.

Objective complement. See Complement.

Ordinal numbers. Numbers indicating order or succession, such as *first, second, third,* etc.

Parenthetical expressions. Sometimes called Interrupters. An expression that interrupts the flow of a clause or sentence. For the correct punctuation of parenthetical expressions see sections 20g, 25, and 27.

Parse. To explain the use of a part of speech in a sentence.

Participle. A verbal used as an adjective and occasionally as an adverb. A participle cannot be used to make a complete clause or a sentence. Since it is partly a verb, it may take complements and be modified by adverbs. Since it is partly an adjective, it may modify a noun or pronoun and be modified by adverbs. For the various forms of a participle, see sec. 7. For the uses of a participle, see Verbals, pp. 35–36. See also Dangling Modifiers, sec. 54.

Participial phrase. A participle with its complements and modifiers.

Parts of speech. The classification of words according to the function they perform in the sentence. The parts of speech are noun, pronoun, verb, adverb, adjective, preposition, conjunction, interjection. For examples and uses, see Parts of Speech, pp. 32–35.

Passive voice. See Voice.

Person. Changes in the form of pronouns and verbs which indicate the speaker (first person), the person spoken to (second person), and the person spoken about (third person).

Example: I am, you are, he is.

Personal pronoun. See Pronoun.

Phrase. A group of words, less than a clause or a complete sentence, used as a single part of speech. See Phrases, pp. 45–49.

Predicate. In a sentence, the verb and its modifiers and complements.

Predicate adjective. The adjective form of the subjective complement. See Complement. *Examples:* The man is *old*. Your hat looks *beautiful*. I am *sure*.

Predicate complement or **subjective complement.** The adjective or noun used to complete a copulative (See Copula) or linking verb. For a list of linking verbs, see sec. 6b.

> *Examples:* Her voice sounds *loud*. The air smells *fresh*. [adjectives]
> They are *artists*. Both men had been *soldiers*. [nouns]

Predication. Any assertion consisting of a subject and a finite verb.

Preposition. The part of speech which shows the relation between its object and some other word in the sentence. See Parts of Speech, p. 34.

> *Examples:* about, above, across, around, at, before, behind, below, beneath, beside, between, beyond, by, despite, during, for, from, in, into, over, through, to, under, until, up, with, within, without.

Prepositional phrase. A phrase consisting of a preposition, its object, and any modifiers that may be present. See Phrases, pp. 45–47.

> *Examples:* across the burning sands, behind the victorious army, into the oven.

Principal parts of a verb. The forms of a verb from which the complete conjugation may be derived. The principal parts are: the present infinitive, the past tense (first person singular), and the past participle. See sec. 7 for examples and for complete conjugation of a verb.

Progressive tenses. Verb forms which show the action as going on at the time indicated by the verb. The tenses are made up of some form of the verb *be* and the participle of the verb used.

> *Examples:* She *was eating* her breakfast. I *had been reading* a book. I *shall be working* in the garden. He *was being taken* for a ride.

Pronoun. A word that takes the place of a noun. Pronouns are classified as follows:

> *Personal:* I, you, we, he, she, it, they.
> *Demonstrative:* this, that, these, those.
> *Relative:* who, which, that, what, whoever, whatever.
> *Interrogative:* who, which, what.
> *Indefinite:* any, anyone, some, someone, nobody, etc.
> *Intensive:* myself, yourself, etc.
> *Reflexive:* myself, yourself, etc.
> *Possessive:* mine, ours, yours, his, hers, theirs, its.

Most grammarians consider the last three classes — intensive, reflexive, and possessive — as personal pronouns. See Parts of Speech, p. 33, and sec. 5.

Proper noun. See Noun.

Restrictive clause. See Nonrestrictive clause. See also sec. 20a.

Retained object. See Complement.

Sentence. For definition and classification (simple, complex, compound, compound-complex) see "The Sentence," chapter 2.

Sentence modifier. Modifiers, usually adverbial, used to modify the *idea* of a sentence rather than any one word in it.

> *Examples: Unfortunately*, you took the wrong train.
> *Yes*, you may take another piece of cake.
> *Certainly*, that is what I said.

Strong verb. A verb that forms its principal parts by a change of vowel and not by addition of *-ed*, *-d*, or *-t*.

> *Examples:* begin, began, begun
> eat, ate, eaten
> go, went, gone
> grow, grew, grown

Subjective complement. See Predicate complement.

Subjunctive mood. The mood of supposition, hope, wish, condition, concession. See Mood. See also sec. 7 for rules governing the use of the subjunctive.

Subordinate clause. See Clauses, pp. 50–52.

Subordinating conjunction. See Parts of Speech, pp. 34–35, and sec. 8.

Substantive. A general name for any word or group of words that may be used as a noun. Substantives are nouns, pronouns, gerunds, infinitives, and noun clauses.

Substantive clause. A clause used as a noun.

Syntax. The part of grammar which deals with the relationship of words to each other in the sentence.

Tense. The property of a verb which indicates the time of the action or state. There are three kinds of time — present, past, and future. To indicate variations of the three kinds of time there are a number of tenses: present, historical present, future, present progressive, perfect, past perfect, future perfect, etc. For a complete conjugation of a verb, indicating the most common tense distinctions, see sec. 7.

Transitive verb. See Verb.

Verb. A part of speech which asserts an action, a condition, or state of being. A verb may be either transitive or intransitive.

A transitive verb is one that takes an object. An intransitive verb is complete without the addition of an object. The copula, or copulative verb, a special kind of intransitive verb, is followed by a subjective complement. See Copula, Complement, Predicate Complement. Some verbs may be used in either the transitive or the intransitive sense.

Transitive: He *hit* the ball. She *wore* a new hat.
Intransitive: She *talks* in her sleep. Ducks *swim.* Flowers *grow* in her garden.
Copulative or *Linking:* He *is* an honest man. She *seems* happy.

Verbal. See Parts of Speech, pp. 35–37; also Gerund, Infinitive, Participle.

Vocative. A case form in Latin showing the person addressed. English has no special case form to correspond.

Voice. The characteristic of a verb, shown by its form, which tells whether the subject acts (active voice) or is acted upon (passive voice).

Active voice: Mary *brought* a dictionary to class.
George *ate* an apple.
Peter *wrote* a theme.
Passive voice: A dictionary *was brought* to class by Mary.
An apple *was eaten* by George.
A theme *was written* by Peter.

Weak verb. Sometimes called a regular verb. A verb that forms its principal parts by adding *-ed*, *-d*, or *-t*. See Strong verb.

Examples: walk, walked, walked
burn, burned, burned (burnt)

THE MANUSCRIPT

10a. Use the kind of paper that is recommended by your English instructor.

Most English departments require composition students to use regulation typewriter paper (about $8\frac{1}{2} \times 11$ inches in size), unruled if the themes are typewritten, ruled if the themes are handwritten.

10b. (1) Write legibly.

If you write by hand, make your handwriting easy to read. Write with a good pen and use black or dark blue ink. Do not use red, violet, or green ink. Form all letters distinctly, especially those that might be confused with similar letters. Dot your *i's* and cross your *t's*. Do not decorate your letters with unnecessary loops or flourishes.

(2) Type legibly.

If you use a typewriter, see that the ribbon is fresh and the type clean. Adjust your margins properly. (See sec. 10e.) Always double-space your typing. Space five spaces for paragraph indentations, one space between words, and two spaces after the end punctuation of a sentence. If you must delete material in typing, type over it with a capital "M." If you must cross out any considerable portion of your material, type your page over again.

Never begin a line with a punctuation mark, such as a comma, a period, a question mark, an exclamation point, which belongs at the end of the preceding line.

10c. Label your themes correctly.

Use the method of labeling themes that is recommended by your instructor. Follow his instructions exactly. If themes are to be handed in on flat, unfolded sheets of paper (the method preferred by all publishers), the right place for the name, the page number, and the theme number is the upper right-hand corner of each page. Of course you should never write on the back of the paper. To a printer, paper has only one side.

10d. Be careful about the correct placing and capitalization of the title.

Write the title on the first line of the first page only, or about two inches from the top of the sheet. Center the title on the page. Capitalize the first word and all important words in the title. The usual practice is to capitalize all nouns, pronouns, verbs, adverbs, adjectives, and prepositions that stand last or contain more than five letters. Do not underline the title or enclose it in quotation marks. Do not use a period after it, but you may use a question mark or an exclamation point if the sense of the title calls for either of these marks. Leave a space of about an inch between the title and the first line of your theme. Do not repeat the title on succeeding pages of your essay.

10e. Leave margins of an inch at the top and at the left of each page.

Do not crowd your words at the right or at the bottom of the page. Some instructors like a wide margin at the right as well as at the left of the page so as to have room for comments and corrections. After the first page, begin writing on the first line.

10f. Indent the first line of each paragraph.

Do not indent a line unless you are beginning a paragraph. Do not leave a blank space at the end of any line except the last one in a paragraph.

If you are quoting verse — a fairly uncommon occurrence in compositions — center your quotation on the page and follow the line arrangement of the poem from which you are quoting. If the quotation does not end a paragraph, begin the next line of your own composition flush with the left margin.

10g. Draw a horizontal line through words which you want deleted. In typing, it is customary to "M" out material which you do not wish to appear. See 10b.

Never use parentheses or brackets to delete or cancel a word. See section 27 for the correct function of these marks. Parentheses are used to enclose parenthetical material; brackets are used for words added by the person quoting someone else's writing. If you want to insert a correction in your text, mark the point of insertion with a caret $(\wedge)$ and write the inserted material above the caret.

10h. Revise your manuscript carefully.

Make every correction indicated or suggested by your instructor. If your instructor refers you to a rule in this handbook, first study the rule carefully to see how it applies to your error. Then, in red ink, draw a horizontal line through the word or words that you want to cancel, and in the space above, between the lines, write the revised version. Copy the rule on the back of the sheet. If your instructor indicates by a note or a comment in the margin that some part of your paper is confused, undeveloped, poorly phrased, inadequate in detail or evidence, or illogical, rewrite the section criticized. Whenever the revision is short, you may write between the lines. When you rewrite a number of sentences or paragraphs, however, you should first make your corrections, in red ink, on the face of your manuscript, and then recopy the entire page.

If you rewrite or recopy a page or an entire theme, be sure to return both versions to your instructor.

10i. In preparing copy for the printer follow the style manual of the publication for which you are writing.

Adequate general directions for the preparation of copy may be found on pages 1272 and 1273 of *Webster's Collegiate Dictionary*, fifth edition.

Very few students will have occasion to prepare copy for the printer. If you are fortunate enough to have some work accepted for publication, remember that a paper good enough to be praised by your instructor is usually ready for the printer. Your copy is, of course, typed and double-spaced. Beyond that about all that you can do is to check spelling, punctuation, and capitalization.

If you want to know the most common proofreaders' marks, look on page 1273 of the same dictionary.

TITLES

11a. Italicize (underline once in manuscript) titles of books, newspapers, periodicals, bulletins, and pamphlets. See also sec. 16.

Some publishers use quotation marks with titles of books; a few set book titles in capitals. It is now the general practice to use capitals instead of italics for book titles in business correspondence. In most formal writing, however, the practice is to use italics.

Use quotation marks for chapter headings, titles of short stories and poems, and titles of magazine articles, especially when it is necessary to distinguish between the whole book and one of its parts.

Right: He spent the summer reading Woollcott's *While Rome Burns*.
   The short stories I like best in Maugham's *East and West* are "Rain," "The Letter," and "The Force of Circumstance."
   We bought a copy of *Harper's Magazine*.

The name of a city which forms a part of the title of a newspaper is usually not italicized.

Right: We subscribed for the Minneapolis *Tribune.*

11b. A good title should be brief, accurate, and interesting.

Do not write long and involved titles. A title is not a topic sentence, nor is it a complete summary of what you have written. A good title should be truthful; that is, it should direct the reader's attention to what he may expect from the theme, but it must not promise more than the theme can deliver. A good title should be interesting; it should serve as a bait, a lure to interest the reader in the paper.

Wordy: My Impressions of the Emotions of a College Freshman During the First Week of College
Better: Six Days in a Daze

Vague: An Interesting Incident
More precise: My Battle with Ants

11c. Capitalize the first word and all important words in the title.

Capitalize all nouns, pronouns, verbs, adjectives, adverbs, and prepositions that stand last or are more than five letters long. The articles *a, an,* and *the,* which are used as adjectives, are capitalized only when they begin titles. The sign of the infinitive *to* is capitalized. See sec. 10d.

11d. Use quotation marks to enclose titles of short poems, short stories, essays, articles in magazines and newspapers, pictures, and subdivisions of books. See sec. 11a.

Right: The chapter in *Anthony Adverse* entitled "The Crew Goes Ashore" is very interesting.
"The Blue Boy" hangs in the Huntington gallery.
"The Man Who Was" is a short story by Kipling.

EXERCISES

Exercise 1. The following are titles of papers written in freshman English composition. Keeping in mind the three principles — brevity, truth, and interest — try to improve these titles.

1. Why I Like to Play Football
2. My Conception of an Ideal Roommate
3. A Description of an Interesting Character
4. Why I Like to Live in a Large City
5. The Various Ways in Which Persons Commit Suicide
6. What I Expect to Get out of My College Education
7. How the Freshman English Course Could Be Improved

Exercise 2. Correct the following sentences by the proper use of capitals, italics, and quotation marks.

1. Her best short stories, three men and a girl, katinka, and the case of peter patchin, were first printed in the centerville journal.
2. After you left last night, I picked up O. Henry's roads of destiny and read the enchanted profile, the passing of black eagle, and friends in san rosario.
3. The current issue of the reader's digest gives in condensed form articles from such magazines as esquire, the saturday evening post, the american mercury, harper's magazine, and the yale review.

CAPITALS

12a. Capitalize the first word of every sentence, of a group of words understood as a sentence, of a direct quotation, and of a line of poetry.

Right: The delegates have left San Francisco.
Do you think they will return?
Not now. Later, perhaps.
He said, "Try to get some sleep."
The question is, Shall the people rule?

> And this same flower that smiles today
> Tomorrow will be dying.

Do not capitalize the first word of an indirect quotation, of a direct quotation that is fragmentary or structurally a part of the sentence in which it stands, or of the part of a direct quotation which follows expressions like *he said* unless this begins a new sentence.

Wrong: He said He would try to get some sleep. [Indirect quotation.]

He talked a long time about his comrades "Hid in death's dateless night."

"I believe you," the Dean replied, "But I can do little for you."

Right: He said he would try to get some sleep.

He talked a long time about his comrades "hid in death's dateless night."

"I believe you," the Dean replied, "but I can do little for you."

For the proper capitalization of a title see sections 10d and 11c.

12b. Capitalize proper nouns and adjectives.

A proper noun names some particular person, place, or object; a common noun names one of a class of persons, places, or objects. See Nouns, pp. 32–33.

1. Names of persons and places: Joseph Conrad, Chicago, Harry, University of Chicago, Dr. Jones, France, Poland, New Zealand.
2. Names of political and geographic divisions if used in the proper sense: Dominion of Canada, Union of South Africa, the Middle West, the Orient. [But *not:* a union of states, a dominion, a republic].
3. Names of historic epochs or events: World War II, Armistice Day, the Middle Ages, the Renaissance.
4. Names of races and languages: English, French, Indian, Latin, Jewish, Negro.
5. Derivatives of proper names if used with a proper meaning: Miltonic, Russian literature, German poetry, Macedonian.
6. Names of organizations: Elks, Masons, the Beavers, Bureau of Engraving and Printing, the Bears, Red Cross.
7. Religious terms: Catholic, Protestant, the Almighty, Christianity.
8. Personifications: O wild West Wind, thou breath of Autumn's being.
9. Days of the week: Sunday, Monday, Tuesday, etc.

See also sec. 12e for distinctions between a word used as a proper noun and the same word used as a common noun.

12c. Capitalize any title when it is used preceding a proper name, or when it is used as a substitute for the proper name.

A title following a name is capitalized only when it is intended to indicate high respect or distinction.

Right: President Roosevelt; the President; King George; Dean Smith; Governor Snell; ex-President Hoover; Chairman Thomas; Captain Simms; the Governor; Cordell Hull, Secretary of State; Ralph Jones, chairman of the nominating committee; Theodore H. Busby, professor of mathematics.

Abbreviations after a name, such as *Esq., Jr., Sr., M.A., Ph.D., LL.D., D.D., F.R.S.,* are usually capitalized.

12d. Capitalize the pronoun *I*, the vocative *O* (but not the exclamation *oh*), *B.C.* and *A.D.*, and usually *No.* (for *number*) and *A.M.* and *P.M.* (for *in the morning* and *in the afternoon*).

12e. Do not capitalize common nouns unless they are used in the proper sense.

1. Capitalize *North, East, West, South,* the *Middle West* only when these words refer to geographical divisions. Do not capitalize these words when they refer to points of the compass.

2. Capitalize *University of Wisconsin, Albany College,* etc., only when these are names of particular institutions. Do not capitalize *a university, my college,* etc., when these words are used as common nouns.

3. Capitalize the names of particular studies or courses, such as *Mathematics 37, Contemporary Literature 271.* Do not capitalize the names of studies when they are not used in the sense of specific courses, as *geology, history, engineering, forestry, home economics, law, educational psychology.* Remember, however, that names of races and languages are always capitalized, as *English language, French literature, Latin words, Indian songs.*

12 MECHANICS

4. Capitalize *Mother*, *Father*, and occasionally *Brother*, *Sister*, *Uncle*, etc., only when these words stand for the name of some individual. Do not capitalize these words when they are used as common nouns, as *my father*, *her old mother*, *my youngest brother*, etc.

EXERCISES

Exercise 1. In the following sentences correct the errors in the use of capitals and supply capitals where they are necessary.

1. He registered for mathematics, latin, and english literature.
2. H. C. Brown, professor of french, returned to center college after a summer in the south.
3. "Golf is one of those games," remarked the chairman of the Committee, "In which the score is often improved by a good lie."
4. The members of the Committee were dean Rogers, captain Holt, and colonel Williamson.
5. Last Summer I took a short course in Psychology at the university of southern California.
6. My class in Psychology 232 meets every monday, wednesday, and friday at eight o'clock.
7. He failed to graduate from High School; his Father died, and his Mother could not afford to send him to College.
8. After I had learned something about Mechanics in the army, I decided to enter the university of Michigan and register for courses in Engineering.
9. After christmas I shall return to the West and resume my profession of Nursing.
10. "What do you have at eight o'clock on monday, History 201 or that new course in russian culture?" inquired my adviser.

Exercise 2. Before each of the following statements write C if the statement is correct and W if the statement is wrong.

_____ 1. Capitalize the first word of an indirect quotation.
_____ 2. Always capitalize "Oh" but never "O."
_____ 3. Always capitalize Mother but not Father.
_____ 4. Do not capitalize the names of seasons.
_____ 5. Do not capitalize the days of the week.
_____ 6. Capitalize the points of the compass when they refer to directions.
_____ 7. Capitalize any title when it is used preceding a proper name.

_____ 8. In referring to studies, it is correct to say, "I am taking two courses in English history."

_____ 9. "I am enrolled in Sociology 201," is correct, but "I am enrolled in a course in Sociology," is incorrect.

_____ 10. "I attended a high school in Boston," is right, but "I attended Grant High School," is wrong.

NUMBERS

13a. In formal writing spell out numbers that can be expressed in a few words, preferably in not more than two or three words.

For the use of the hyphen with compound numbers see sec. 26b.

Right: He earned *sixteen hundred* dollars last year.
Harry is only *twenty-one* years old.
The price was *two and a half* dollars.

13b. Do not begin a sentence with a figure.

If the number can be easily written out, do so. If it cannot, change the sentence so that the number does not stand at the beginning.

Wrong: 27 students were awarded special honors.
Right: Twenty-seven students were awarded special honors.

Wrong: $12,375 was paid for a purebred Holstein bull, a record price in this county.
Better: A purebred Holstein bull sold for $12,375, a record price in this county.

13c. Use figures for the following:

1. Dates. Do not use *st, nd, rd, th* with the day of the month.

Undesirable: He was born on January sixth, eighteen hundred and seventy-eight.
Preferred: He was born on January 6, 1878.

297

2. Street and room numbers.

Right: Please take this note to Dr. Hathaway, who lives at 224 Elm Street. If he is not at home, you will find him in West Hall 308.

3. Page numbers.

Right: Read the discussion in chapter 4, page 231.

4. Decimals and percentages.

5. Several numbers occurring in the same paragraph or section.

Right: These systems are at distances ranging from 100,000 to 1,500,000 light years, their diameters range from 4,000 to 45,000 light years, and the total luminosities from 20 to 500 million times the luminosity of the sun.

Notice in the last example that commas are used to separate figures into groups, for clearness and convenience in reading. Commas, however, are not used in dates, serial numbers, page numbers, and telephone numbers.

Right: The total number of ballots returned was 2,376,344.
October 15, 1946 (*not* 1,946).
Bryant 9944 (*not* 9,944).
Policy No. 332254 (*not* 332,254).

In ordinary writing do not express a sum in both figures and words.

EXERCISE

Exercise 1. In the following sentences encircle the numbers which should have been written out in words.

1. Helen paid $17.00 for her new hat.
2. About 2000 students responded to the appeal.
3. My sister is only 2 years older than I, but she is 6 inches taller.
4. There are 6 brothers and 2 sisters in my family.
5. On his 85th birthday he sold his business and bought a house at 235 Maple Street, where he lived until his death at the age of 90.
6. 4 years ago he rented a small shop at 324 Michigan Avenue.
7. The first bid was $3.50. Then in a spirited contest the bids were rocketed upward: $7.50, $10.00, $25.00, and finally $75.

8. During the three years that the camps have been in existence, over 100,000 men have been given employment.

9. Last summer I earned $350. Of that sum $75 went for tuition, $25 for books, $50 for clothes, and the rest will have to take care of my board and rent for the next 3 months.

10. On the 3rd day of November a heavy snow blocked all roads in the valley.

ABBREVIATIONS

14a. Avoid the use of abbreviations in formal writing.

The following abbreviations are customary and appropriate at all levels of writing:

1. *Dr., Mr., Mrs., Messrs.,* when used before proper names;

2. *Jr., Sr., Ph.D., D.D., LL.D.,* when used after names;

3. *A.D.* (*Anno Domini*), *B.C.* (*before Christ*), used with dates only when necessary for clearness. Note that the date precedes *B.C.* and follows *A.D.*

Example: Augustus was born in 63 B.C. and died in A.D. 14.

The following are not abbreviated in formal writing:

1. *Reverend* and *Honorable.* These titles must not be used with surnames alone. They should be followed by the first name, or initials, or the appropriate title. If preceded by *the*, these words are not abbreviated.

Formal: The Reverend George M. Donaldson, the Reverend Dr. Donald-son, the Honorable Elihu Root.
Less formal: Hon. Elihu Root, Rev. George M. Donaldson.
Rude: Rev. Donaldson gave the convocation address.

2. Professor, President, Governor, Senator, etc.

3. Names of months and days of the week.

In informal writing of many kinds, some abbreviations are customary.

1. The connectives *i.e., e.g., viz., cf., etc.,* but *that is, for example, namely, compare, and so forth* when a more formal effect is desired.

2. Names of government agencies: *TVA, OWI, PWA,* etc.

3. *No.* (*number*), in technical and business writing.

Avoid the following crudities in both speech and writing: *lab., prof., lit., comp., ag., convo., chem., phys. ed., stenog., soph., libe.*

For a complete list of abbreviations and their meaning, consult any recent edition of a good dictionary. Use the same authority in determining the correct punctuation and use of capitals with abbreviations.

14b. In ordinary writing, both formal and informal, except in footnotes, bibliographies, addresses, and tabulations, spell out:

1. Names of countries and states.

2. Names of months and days of the week.

3. *Number, volume, chapter, page, and, street, avenue, manufacturing, company, mountain, Christmas.*

4. Christian names.

Crude: My chem class meets every Mon., Wed., and Fri.

Wm. & Chas. found jobs with a mfg. concern on Union Ave.

The U.S.A. was represented at the peace conference.

On the 1st of Sept. we took a trip to the mts.

The Co. for which I worked has a branch office on a st. near the docks.

I shall go home Xmas and return in Feb.

Right: My chemistry class meets every Monday, Wednesday, and Friday.

William and Charles found jobs with a manufacturing concern on Union Avenue.

The United States was represented at the peace conference.

On the first of September we took a trip to the mountains.

The company for which I worked has a branch office on a street near the docks.

I shall go home for Christmas and return in February.

EXERCISES

Exercise 1. Correct the errors in the use of abbreviations in the following sentences.

1. Henry Lawler, prof. of chemistry, Dr. I. R. Jones, and Rev. Stockman represented the U of Iowa at the dedication ceremonies.
2. I have the same prof. for sosh. and ed. sike, but I still have not learned his name.
3. World War I began in 1914, A.D.
4. Our leader was Mister Ford, a graduate of the U of Wisconsin.
5. The U is my alma mater, but I prefer to attend the basketball games at Central Hi.
6. My roommate registered for two lab courses this term.
7. At the first convo of the year the entertainment was provided by a committee representing the soph class.
8. The sophs. and the frosh battled it out this a.m.
9. On our way to Texas we stopped in L.A. to enjoy some of the unusual weather that I always seem to find in Cal.
10. I enjoy my lit. course because the prof. has a good sense of humor.

Exercise 2. What do the following abbreviations mean? Consult your dictionary. Where did you find a list of abbreviations?

1. AAA	9. CCC	17. TVA
2. A.E.F.	10. D.A.	18. S.P.C.A.
3. anon.	11. D.S.C.	19. RFC
4. A.W.O.L.	12. f.o.b.	20. U.S.S.R.
5. B.L.	13. F.R.S.	21. U.P.
6. B.P.O.E.	14. I.O.O.F.	22. TNT
7. B.T.U.	15. G.A.R.	23. Sc.D.
8. S.J.	16. dial.	24. l.c.

SYLLABICATION

15a. Avoid the awkward division of a word at the end of a line of handwritten or typewritten manuscript.

An uneven right-hand margin is usually preferable to a number of divided words, especially short words. Words of one syllable should never be divided. Words of two or more syllables should never be so divided that a single letter either ends the line or begins the next line.

15b. If you find it necessary to divide a word, make the division between syllables, and place a hyphen at the end of the line, not at the beginning of the next line.

16 MECHANICS

If you are not sure of the correct syllable division, consult your dictionary. Few writers, other than lexicographers, ever master completely the rules for syllable division.

EXERCISE

Exercise 1. Study the following list. Before each word write:

1. if the word contains only one syllable
2. if the word contains more than one syllable but is too short to be divided in typewritten manuscript
3. if the word may be divided in typewritten manuscript

_____ 1. through	_____ 11. mediocrity
_____ 2. hour	_____ 12. meaty
_____ 3. convocation	_____ 13. obey
_____ 4. rhythm	_____ 14. thrifty
_____ 5. enough	_____ 15. observatory
_____ 6. extraordinary	_____ 16. ivy
_____ 7. architecture	_____ 17. grown
_____ 8. science	_____ 18. cosmopolitan
_____ 9. regimentation	_____ 19. sulphathiazole
_____ 10. dreamed	_____ 20. groove

ITALICS

To indicate that a word should be italicized, draw a single straight line under it.

16a. Italicize titles of books, plays, newspapers, magazines, musical compositions, works of art, and names of ships and aircraft.

Use quotation marks for chapters or subdivisions of books, titles of short stories, magazine articles, newspaper articles, and short poems. For examples see sections 11a and 11d.

16b. Italicize unnaturalized foreign words and phrases.

It may be difficult for you to know whether or not a certain foreign phrase has been Anglicized. A dictionary will help you.

302

In *Webster's Collegiate Dictionary*, for instance, you will find parallel bars before foreign words that are used frequently in English but which are not completely Anglicized.

Italicize		Do not italicize	
ante meridiem	*élan*	ad valorem	décolleté
beau geste	*fait accompli*	apropos	dilettante
bon vivant	*faux pas*	attaché	ensemble
bourgeoisie	*mise en scène*	billet-doux	ex officio
casus belli	*ne plus ultra*	bona fide	nom de plume
comme il faut	*nisi*	chargé d'affaires	patois
coup d'état	*rara avis*	clientele	prima facie
de facto	*sang-froid*	crèche	résumé
déjeuner	*tabula rasa*	cul-de-sac	viva voce

16c. In formal writing, italicize words, letters, or figures when they are referred to as such.

In informal writing quotation marks are more commonly used for this purpose. For examples refer to the section on page 76 quoted from Robertson's *Development of Modern English*.

Formal: We realize the humorous intention when somebody invents from the noun *swashbuckler* a verb to *swashbuckle,* or to *buttle* and *cuttle* from *butler* and *cutler,* but it is not so well known that the same process (probably with the same humorous intent behind it) gave us such sober words as *burgle, sidle, edit, grovel, beg,* and *greed.* — Owen Barfield, *History in English Words.*

Thus words like *sapolio, oleomargarine, brillo,* a name for steel wool used in polishing, *fermillac,* fermented milk, *sozodont,* the name of a tooth powder, and dozens of others like these betray at least a moderate degree of familiarity with the classical languages. — George P. Krapp, *The Knowledge of English.*

Informal: He used *infect* [or "infect"] in place of *inflict* ["inflict"].
Dot your *i's* and cross your *t's.* Your *3's* and *8's* are alike.
Dot your "i's" and cross your "t's." Your "8's" and "3's" are alike.

16d. Italicize (underline) a word or phrase to which you wish to give particular emphasis.

The use of italics for emphasis is a privilege that must be resorted to circumspectly.

If you want to examine a sample of an older style, look up an old edition of Poe or Carlyle. It was once the fashion for an author to shout and scream at the reader in capitals and italics. At present it is permissible to use italics for emphasis only when the sentence would not be immediately clear without italics. The following sentences are not examples of bad writing; they are merely illustrations of an older fashion.

Great is the combined voice of men; the utterance of their *instincts*, which are truer than their *thoughts:* it is the greatest a man encounters, among the sounds and shadows which make up this World of Time. He who can resist that, has his footing somewhere *beyond* Time. — Thomas Carlyle.

But, as *you* draw near, the woman raises her wasted features. Would Dom-rémy know them again for the features of her child? Ah, but *you* know them, bishop, well! Oh, mercy! what a groan was *that* which the servants, waiting outside the bishop's dream at his bedside, heard from his labouring heart, as at this moment he turned away from the fountain and the woman, seeking rest in the forests afar off. Yet not *so* to escape the woman, whom once again he must behold before he dies. — Thomas De Quincey.

BIBLIOGRAPHY

17a. Select a simple form and use it consistently.

A bibliography is a list of writings relating to a given subject or author. It may be a complete directory of all published information relating to a subject, or a selected list of books and articles which the ordinary reader might find useful, or simply a list of the printed sources which the writer has used, since a student may compile a bibliography without ever intending to write an essay based on the source material he has collected.

For information dealing with the construction of a bibliography consult the section dealing with the preparation of the research paper, pages 198–202.

The following are two forms which have been widely used in non-technical and non-scientific papers. Use the one which your instructor recommends.

FORM A (the University of Chicago Press style)

The "Chicago style," as it has often been called, is recommended by many authorities. See *A Manual of Style*, published by the University of Chicago Press in 1937.

FOR GENERAL REFERENCE BOOKS:

"Philately." Encyclopedia Americana, 1932, XXI, 736–739.

Thorndike, Edward Lee. "Intelligence Tests." Encyclopaedia Britannica, 1942, XII, 460–461.

FOR BOOKS:

Greenough, James Bradstreet, and George Lyman Kittredge. Words and Their Ways in English Speech. New York: Macmillan Co., 1901, 1923.

Marshall, Bruce. The World, the Flesh, and Father Smith. Boston: Houghton Mifflin, 1945.

FOR MAGAZINE ARTICLES:

Green, Z. E. "English Literature in the Rural High School," Peabody Journal of Education, XII (May, 1935), 270–275.

Pardee, J. T. "Appalachians Offer Gold Possibilities," Engineering and Mining Journal, CXXXVI (April, 1935), 183.

"New Swiss Oil Recovery Process," Chemical Industries, XXXIV (January, 1934), 48.

FOR BULLETINS:

Tracy, Samuel Mills. "Grape Growing in the South," Farmers' Bulletin, CXVIII (1900), U.S.D.A.

FOR NEWSPAPER ARTICLES:

"Comment on C Content of Lima Beans," New York Times, April 18, 1937, sec. 12, p. 8, col. 4.

FORM B (a simplified form)

Notice these differences between the "Chicago style" and the simplified form:

1. Each reference is treated as a unit, the three parts (author, title, and the facts of publication) being separated by commas, not by periods.

2. Every figure is labeled, so that there is never any doubt as to which figure means *volume*, which *number*, which *section*, and which *pages*.

3. Since most periodicals have discarded the clumsy Roman system of numbering, all numbers are in Arabic numerals.

4. The date of a magazine article follows the volume and page references, since it is merely supplementary information.

FOR GENERAL REFERENCE BOOKS:

"Philately," Encyclopedia Americana, 1932, vol. 21, pp. 736–739.

Thorndike, Edward Lee, "Intelligence Tests," Encyclopaedia Britannica, 1942, vol. 12, pp. 460–461.

FOR BOOKS:

Greenough, James Bradstreet, and George Lyman Kittredge, Words and Their Ways in English Speech, The Macmillan Company, New York, 1901, 1923.

Marshall, Bruce, The World, the Flesh, and Father Smith, Houghton Mifflin Company, Boston, 1945.

FOR MAGAZINE ARTICLES:

Green, Z. E., "English Literature in the Rural High School," Peabody Journal of Education, vol. 12, pp. 270–275 (May, 1935).

Pardee, J. T., "Appalachians Offer Gold Possibilities," Engineering and Mining Journal, vol. 136, p. 183 (April, 1935).

"New Swiss Oil Recovery Process," <u>Chemical Indus-</u>
<u>tries</u>, vol. 34, p. 48 (January, 1934).

FOR BULLETINS:

Tracy, Samuel Mills, "Grape Growing in the South,"
<u>Farmers' Bulletin</u>, No. 118 (1900), U. S.
Department of Agriculture.

FOR NEWSPAPER ARTICLES:

"Comment on C Content of Lima Beans," The New York
<u>Times</u>, April 18, 1937, sec. 12, p. 8,
col. 4.

FOOTNOTES

**18a. For your footnotes use a form which is brief but abso-
lutely clear.**

Footnotes may be used to identify and acknowledge material
used in the body of the essay, to give additional information which
does not fit into the text, to quote in detail what has been merely
referred to in the text, or to define or explain some term used in
the text. Most undergraduate papers use footnotes for the first of
these purposes only.

To identify footnotes place an Arabic numeral immediately
after and a little above the material referred to. Place the same
number before your footnote. Do not use a period after the figures. Number all of your footnotes consecutively from the beginning to the end of your paper or begin numbering with number
one on each page. Either method is acceptable. For most undergraduate papers, the system of placing footnotes at the foot of
the page is the preferred system. Use it unless you are told otherwise.

A footnote which refers to a source used is like a bibliographic
item (see section 17) with two minor changes: (1) the author's
name is given in the normal order; (2) the exact page reference is
added.

A summary of some of the conventions governing footnoting is in order here. For a more complete discussion and for examples, see pages 203–204 in the section on the research paper.

1. Complete information about the source referred to must be given in the first reference to that source (author, title, all facts of publication as in the bibliography). After that, if there is no danger of confusion, a note consisting of the author's last name, the title, and the page is sufficient.

2. When a list of sources used is handed in with the paper, it is usually acceptable to abridge all references, including the first reference to any item, to author, title, and page.

3. Any part of the source which is given in the text of the essay need not be repeated in the footnote.

18b. Use abbreviations in footnotes whenever you can do so without sacrificing clearness.

The following abbreviations are permissible in footnotes:

Ibid., in the same place.
Op. cit., in the work referred to.
Loc. cit., in the place mentioned.
Id., the same.
p., pp., page, pages.
vol., vols., volume, volumes.
l., ll., line, lines.
col., column.
sec., section.
ff., following (pages).
cf., compare, see.

Ibid., or *ibidem* (pronounced ĭ-bī′dĕm), may be used to show that the footnote refers to the same source as the footnote immediately preceding. If the reference is not to the same page as in the preceding footnote, *ibid.* must be followed by the exact page reference. The author's name should never be used with *ibid.*

Op. cit. (*opere citato*, ŏp′ĕ-rē sī-tā′tō) is used with the author's last name and the page reference to show that the footnote refers to a work already cited but not to the one immediately preceding. If more than one work by that author is being used, the footnote must give the author's name and the title of the work. If works by two or more authors with the same surname are in the bibliography used, each author must be properly identified by his initials.

Loc. cit. is not frequently used in present-day writing. When used, it means almost the same thing as *op. cit.*

In ordinary writing it is better to use English words in place of the abbreviations of their Latin equivalents. See section 14. Write *for instance* or *for example* instead of *e.g.*, *that is* instead of *i.e.*, *and so forth* instead of *etc.* In footnotes, however, abbreviations are convenient.

The purpose of punctuation is to help make clear the meaning of written or printed language. In learning how to punctuate correctly, you must not forget two guiding principles. The first of these is that correct punctuation depends upon an understanding of the grammatical relation of the parts of the sentence. The other is that punctuation rules are a set of conventions, which, like the conventions of social etiquette, of play, or of business, make communication between people easy and natural. If punctuation marks are to facilitate understanding of what is written, the same marks must always be used for the same sort of sentence construction. In other words, the reader must understand at once what each mark is doing in the sentence. The following rules represent the most widely accepted practice in ordinary writing.

As writing grows more informal, a corresponding loosening of punctuation conventions is permissible.

PERIOD, QUESTION MARK, EXCLAMATION POINT

(THE PERIOD)

19a. Use a period after a declarative or an imperative sentence, or after an indirect question.

Right: Revenge is a kind of wild justice.   [Declarative.]
Please leave the room quietly.   [Imperative.]
Our teacher asked us how many books we had read.   [Indirect question.]

19b. Use a period after an abbreviation.

For a list of abbreviations permissible in ordinary writing see section 14. For a complete list of abbreviations and their meanings see *Webster's Collegiate Dictionary*, fifth edition, pages 1175–1181. Use the period after such common abbreviations as *Mr., Mrs., Dr., St., Ave., Jr., Sr., a.m., p.m., A.D., B.C.* Do not use a period after the letters standing for certain recently created governmental agencies: *TVA, CCC, RFC, NRA*, nor after *MS* (manuscript).

19c. Use periods or "leaders" (usually three within a sentence, four at the end of a declarative sentence) to indicate the omission of words from a quoted passage, or pauses and hesitations in dialogue.

Examples:

The souls of emperors and cobblers are cast in the same mould. . . . The same reason that makes us wrangle with a neighbor causes a war betwixt princes. — Montaigne.

"You think I go about staring at nothing," she remarked. . . . "Not a bit of it! I have been planning all sorts of things. . . . I have been thinking how I could get to Germany. . . . Or one might catch them in Switzerland. . . . I've had all sorts of plans. They can't go guarded for ever. . . ." — From H. G. Wells, *Mr. Britling Sees It Through*.

(THE QUESTION MARK)

19d. Use a question mark after a direct question.

Right: Can you understand him? Did he say anything to you?
Who said we couldn't win this game?

A question mark may be used to end each of a series of elliptical phrases or clauses which may be read as a single sentence.

Right: Will he respond to your arguments? or your threats? or your tears?

A question mark is used to punctuate a sentence which ends with a quoted question.

Right: After we landed we learned, with a tremendous surge of pride, that as the waters rose around them, those green troops, soldiers from

far northwestern states mostly, stood in ranks on the canted decks singing a popular song of the war, "Where Do We Go from Here, Boys?" — Irvin S. Cobb.

Right: The question is no longer, Shall we have unemployment compensation, but rather, What form of unemployment compensation shall we adopt, and What unit of government shall be intrusted with its administration? — John Gilbert Winant.

A single question mark is used after a double question, that is, a quoted question following a question. See also section 24g.

Right: Did he say, "How many?"
Who said, "When do we eat?"

A question mark within parentheses may be used to indicate doubt or uncertainty as to the preceding figure or fact.

Right: Lucien Botha was born in 1779 (?) and died in 1859.

The use of a question mark to indicate irony is not sanctioned by reputable practice. It should be avoided in serious writing.

Poor: We returned from a most enjoyable (?) hunting trip.

A question mark is often used after commands or requests phrased as questions if a formal effect is desired, but a period for a less formal effect.

Formal: Will the staff please assemble in the auditorium at four o'clock this afternoon?
Less formal: Will you return the proof at your earliest convenience.

(THE EXCLAMATION POINT)

19e. Use an exclamation point after an expression of strong feeling.

Use the exclamation point with caution and discretion. Your tendency will be to use it too often. Words like *yes, no, oh, well, alas, surely,* and the like, when beginning a sentence, are usually followed by a comma. If *oh* introduces an expression of strong feeling, put the exclamation point at the end of the expression. Never use more than one exclamation point after an exclamation.

Right: "Great guns!" he shouted in consternation.
He actually said that!
Oh, this is unspeakable!

The days wore on, and yet got nowhere. . . . Time had simply come to a standstill! He had never seen the like; this was worse than the deadest lay-up in Lofoten! — O. E. Rölvaag.

"I know a lady who was told by a Jesuit that it might be her vocation to be the best-dressed woman in every room she walked into as long as she did it to the greater glory of God, so boo!" Elvira said. — Bruce Marshall.

EXERCISE

Exercise 1. In the following sentences supply periods, question marks, and exclamation points where they are necessary.

1. Oh, it does not matter much what he will do
2. "What book are you reading?" Dora inquired
3. Have you talked with Dr. I R Smith this morning
4. No but I asked Mrs. Reed whether she had seen him
5. Did you ask, "When is Rockwell coming home"
6. "Gee What an idea," my brother exclaimed in disgust
7. The question now is, Shall we fail the world again as we did in 1918
8. That is what Mr. Brown wrote — 1730 Washington Ave, not Washington St
9. Did he ask how many wanted to repeat the lesson
10. He wanted to know how many the classroom could hold

THE COMMA

The best way to master the uses of the comma is to learn and to apply the rules. The rules of punctuation are the codified practice of writers, the English "common law," as it were, of written communication. The rules reflect what writers have been doing; in other words, in punctuation, as in everything else connected with English speech and writing, usage comes before rules. Practically all of the possible uses of the period, the question mark, the exclamation point, the semicolon, the hyphen, the dash, and quotation marks are definitely determined by custom. About nine-tenths of all the possible uses of the comma are determined by custom and covered by rules. Most of your punctuation, therefore, can be done by rule.

But comma rules must, at times, be interpreted with a little common sense. It is true, for instance, that writers place a comma after an introductory clause or phrase if they feel that this sentence element is not an integral part of the main clause, that is, it is not closely restrictive, but no rule, only common sense, can tell you when this clause stops being restrictive and becomes not restrictive. Whenever in a few punctuation situations there is difference in practice, you must fall back on common sense.

Punctuation also has another function, a rhetorical one. The comma — and, to a certain extent, the semicolon — may be used to indicate subtle differences in meaning, degrees of pause or emphasis in reading, or rhetorical balance or contrast of ideas. The important fact still remains, however, that the student who hopes to make punctuation an artistic resource must first learn the rules.

20a. Use commas to set off nonrestrictive clauses. Do not use commas to set off restrictive clauses.

If the distinction between restrictive and nonrestrictive clauses is not already clear to you, think of restrictive clauses as "identifying" or "pointing-out" clauses. A restrictive clause helps to locate or identify its antecedent. It says to the reader, "I mean this particular person, object, or thing, and no other." It is close to its antecedent in meaning, so close that it cannot be separated from it by a comma. A nonrestrictive clause does not identify or point out. It merely gives additional information about its antecedent. (See also page 51.)

Restrictive: We have decided to hire a woman *who knows how to cook.* [The clause says that we have decided to hire a particular kind of woman, one with ability to cook, and no other kind.]

Nonrestrictive: We have decided to hire Mrs. Williams, *who knows how to cook.* [The name identifies the woman. The clause merely adds information.]

Restrictive: The boy *who has a hobby* will never be lonely. [Not any boy, but this particular kind of boy.]
  Please bring me the book *which you see lying on my desk.* [That particular book and no other.]

Nonrestrictive: We were introduced to Ben Ross, *who asked us to go salmon fishing with him.* [The name has identified the person; the clause does not need to identify or point out.]
  Astronomy, *which is the study of the heavenly bodies,* is a fascinating subject. [Astronomy identifies itself. It does not need a clause to tell which particular astronomy.]
  My father, *who had not heard the question,* shook his head in silence. [A person has only one father.]

The same rule applies to adverbial clauses, with an added proviso that adverbial clauses opening a sentence tend to be felt as nonrestrictive and that adverbial clauses closing a sentence tend to be restrictive. (See section 20f.)

Restrictive: He had spent the money *before his father died.*
  Our navy will not be scrapped *when peace is declared.*
  I studied engineering *because I wanted to help my father in his work.*

Nonrestrictive: *If that was not an apology,* I do not know what it was.
  While we have been absorbed in our play and our business, the world has been steadily drifting toward chaos.

Participial phrases may be either restrictive or nonrestrictive, depending on the meaning intended.

Restrictive: The boy *standing near the door* is waiting to register.
  A book *written by that author* is sure to be interesting.

Nonrestrictive: *Raising his rifle quickly,* he fired at the moving object.
  Tom Nolan, *standing there near the door,* is waiting to register.

20b. Use a comma to separate co-ordinate clauses joined by *and, but, for, nor, or,* except when the clauses are short and closely related in meaning. (See section 8b.)

A writer is safe to apply this rule rather strictly in formal writing and to relax its application progressively as the level of writing

315

becomes more and more informal. Journalistic writing discards the comma between co-ordinate clauses. On the formal level, the general practice is to omit the comma when the subject of the clauses does not change. If there is any other clearly defined practice to help the beginning student, it is that the comma is obligatory before *for* and recommended before *but*.

> *Right:* After a time a farmer offered to help us, and we went into his machine shed to get a chain. [The subject changes.]
> He explained that he was sorry, but he found that he could think better if he walked about the room. [Same subject. The conjunction is *but.*]
> I know that his novels are interesting, for I have read them all.
>
> I could look back into America and see its beginnings, but I could also see other beginnings that never grew, and then I thought I saw why it was so lonely and lopsided and aggressive. — John Hyde Preston.
>
> The old life was lonely and hard, but it bred a strong individualism. — James Truslow Adams.

20c. Use commas to separate words, phrases, or clauses in a series.

A series may consist of words, phrases, or clauses. A series must have at least three members; usually the last two are joined by *and* or *or*. In formal writing a comma is required before the conjunction. In informal writing there is a progressive tendency to discard the comma before the conjunction, except for clearness, as the writing grows less formal. In journalistic writing, the comma is regularly omitted.

> *Right:* A university is not made up of a stadium, a library, science laboratories, and recitation halls. [Nouns.]
> Everywhere you may see the same nearly flat country, the same fields and crops, the same rough wooden fences, and the same solitary farmhouses. [Series of objects with modifiers.]
> The thief pried open a window, entered my bedroom, and stole my watch and purse. [Series of predicates.]

No youthful radiant beauty of features, no grace and style of a Parisian dress, no certificate of a ring, no premature initiation into the mysteries, could save her from the appearance of a raw fool whose foolishness had been her undoing. — Arnold Bennett. [Series of subjects with modifiers.]

20d. Use commas to separate consecutive adjectives preceding the noun they modify when the adjectives are co-ordinate in meaning.

The comma is correct only when the adjectives are co-ordinate — that is, when each of the adjectives refers directly to the noun. When an adjective modifies the whole idea that follows it, it is not separated from it by a comma. If you can substitute *and* for the comma, the comma is correct. Note that in the following examples, it would be natural and correct to say "a surly and treacherous and cruel fellow," but it would be unnatural to say "a lazy and old fellow."

Right: Bones was a surly, treacherous, cruel fellow.
Henry was a lazy old fellow.

It was a raw, blustery night. [Raw *and* blustery.]
The smithy stood under the spreading chestnut tree. [*Spreading* modifies *chestnut tree*, not *tree*.]

A safe practice is to omit the comma with numerals and with the common adjectives of size and age.

Examples: the little old lady, a large red-haired girl, four tiny black dots.

20e. Use the comma to separate words and phrases that might be incorrectly joined in reading.

This rule applies to the following types of situations:

1. When the conjunctions *for* and *but* might be mistaken for prepositions.

Confusing: The coyote must have turned for the dog seemed to hesitate a moment. [Must have turned for the dog?]
The men slid down the ropes but one sailor seemed to be caught in the rigging. [Slid down the ropes but one sailor?]

Right: The coyote must have turned, for the dog seemed to hesitate a moment.

The men slid down the ropes, but one sailor seemed to be caught in the rigging.

2. When a noun might be mistaken for the object of a verb, verbal, or preposition before it.

Confusing: After washing the men filed into the dining tent.

Before starting to eat Father bowed his head in prayer.

Above the sun burned a dull red; below the sand radiated heat like a furnace.

Right: After washing, the men filed into the dining tent. [*Not:* After washing the men.]

Before starting to eat, Father bowed his head in prayer. [*Not:* Before starting to eat Father.]

Above, the sun burned a dull red; below, the sand radiated heat like a furnace. [*Not:* Above the sun . . . or below the sand.]

20f. Ordinarily, use the comma to set off a modifier which precedes a main clause, especially when the introductory element is long and not closely connected with the main clause in meaning.

In punctuating modifiers that precede the main clause you must depend on your good sense as well as on rules. You must decide whether or not the sentence will be clearer with the introductory modifier set off. Length of clause alone will not tell you when to use a comma and when not to use it. Frequently very short clauses are set off for emphasis. In general, if you feel that the introductory element is nonrestrictive, put a comma after it. The following distinctions will help you.

1. Use a comma when you begin with a fairly long nonrestrictive adverbial clause.

Right: In so far as the school can rely upon the genuine merits of America, there is no need to associate the teaching of American patriotism with the inculcation of false standards.

Although the candidate is honest and patriotic, we do not believe he is practical enough.

Until our communities are ready to undertake the sort of community planning that leads to garden cities, it will be empty eloquence to talk about the future of American architecture. — Lewis Mumford.

If, as I have said, the things already listed were all we had had to contribute, America would have made no distinctive and unique gift to mankind. — James Truslow Adams.

2. Use a comma to set off a beginning participial phrase modifying the subject or an absolute phrase before the subject.

Right: Having listened to his story, the judge nodded and then dismissed the case.

The excitement being over, the students returned to the classroom.

3. Set off introductory prepositional phrases only when they are definitely nonrestrictive, such as transitional phrases.

Right: In the first place, he is usually the last man to leave the office.

About three years ago his father decided to move to England.

During the concert a little dog kept howling dolefully.

In another way Dr. Brown breaks away from the academic tradition.

4. In writing below the formal level, do not use a comma after a short introductory clause.

Right: When he gives us a test he usually leaves the room.

If the boy comes I shall tell him to look for you in your shop.

20g. Use commas to set off parenthetical elements (interrupters), or words, phrases, and clauses used to explain, to qualify, or to emphasize. (See also 25 and 27.)

In a sense, several of the sentence elements discussed under other rules are "interrupters" in that they tend to break or interrupt the normal flow of a sentence, but strict classification is not here important. The parenthetical elements dealt with here may be roughly classified as follows:

1. Conjunctive adverbs (see sections 8b and 21d), such as *however*, *therefore*, *moreover*, *furthermore*, when they are used within the clause. These words are more appropriate in a formal than in a colloquial style. And in any style, an epidemic of *moreover's* and *furthermore's* is as bad as a plague of *and's* and *but's*.

Right: An institution, *therefore*, may fail because its standards are too high.
In truth, *however*, it was probably not known until after the French Revolution.

2. Directive and qualifying words and phrases. Some of the most common of these, such as *also, perhaps, indeed, too, at least*, may, in informal writing, be considered as close modifiers and therefore not set off by commas. Others are usually set off.

Right: My theory, *unluckily*, was disproved by the events that followed.
He would become, *in short*, a problem child of the worst kind.
He will, *by so doing*, bring greater happiness to himself and his family.
Indeed, two of them actually did escape from the island.

3. Parenthetical clauses. Most of these are parenthetical comments, but some are adverbial clauses which break into the sentence flow.

Right: This, *I suppose*, is the essence of morality.
No teacher can give you an education; he can only, *as it were*, point in the direction of it.
Our interpretation of his motives is, *I think*, totally unfair.

Adverbial: If you must take risks on the lake, see to it that, *whenever storm warnings are up*, you at least have a life preserver with you.
These men, *if they are not subjected to the authority of political institutions*, will lead us into disaster. — Alexander Meiklejohn.

20h. Use commas to set off appositives.

An appositive, or a word in apposition, is used to limit or qualify the meaning of another word, to add to its meaning, or to emphasize it. Most appositives are nonrestrictive and should therefore be set off by commas.

Right: Mr. Walker, *the grocer*, has just sold his business. [Simple appositive.]
Her language, a terrifying *mixture* of bad grammar and slang, irritated and fascinated her teachers. [Appositive with modifiers.]
The three boys made the hazardous journey down the Snake River canyon, an *exploit* which called for unusual courage and resourcefulness. [An appositive to a whole idea.]

As he neared Fourth Street, another man, *a new one*, sprang up suddenly before him, *a short, heavy-set fellow*, stepping out of the shadows and striding directly toward him. — Robert M. Coates. [Notice how the use of appositives may add to sentence variety.]

Cooper, *an aristocrat in temper*, was a stickler for his social rights, *the right to consideration*, *privacy*, *respect*, and he was often at war with himself, for his tastes and prejudices were by no means in harmony with his conscience and convictions. — Van Wyck Brooks.

But do *not* use commas with many common expressions in which the appositive and its substantive are so close that they are felt as a unit.

Examples: My brother John, Henry the Eighth, the word *appositive*, your son James, my Aunt Caroline, William the Conqueror, the novelist Hawthorne, etc.

Participles and occasionally adjectives may be placed for greater emphasis after the words they modify. When so placed they are said to be in the appositive position and are therefore set off by commas.

Right: Our plan, *sound in principle and proved in practice*, will bring greater prosperity to our community.
They were like a ballet of spinsters, *elderly but flippant*, standing in affected attitudes with the simpering graces of a bygone age.

A growl, *low and distant like the roll of a train on a faraway bridge*, began to stir in his throat. — Wolcott Gibbs.

This style, *so elegant and so simple*, was to mark all of Irving's work, *the sign of his cheerful good nature and transparent good taste* . . . — Van Wyck Brooks. [Adjectives in the appositive position and then a substantive appositive.]

Appositives may be enclosed within parentheses or set off by dashes to indicate a greater degree of separation, if such a distinction is proper. (See sections 25 and 27.)

Right: It is this power over background — a power which Mr. Brooks has gained from an intense absorption of every book, document, journal, letter available to him about early America — that makes this history so rich. — Henry Seidel Canby.

Winnowing — generally the task of women — was done by throwing the grain and chaff into the wind, so that the chaff might be blown away. — Barnes and Ruedi, *The American Way of Life.*

The citizens of the United States are assured, under the Constitution, of the rights to personal security, liberty, equality before the law, trial by jury and "due process of law" (that is, the accused has a right to know of what he is accused), and freedom of worship, press, speech, and assembly. — Barnes and Ruedi, *The American Way of Life.*

Appositives are often introduced by such words as *that is, namely, such as, for instance, for example,* and the like. In long, formal sentences these words may be preceded by a colon or a semicolon. In ordinary writing, both formal and informal, *namely, that is, for example,* and *for instance* are usually preceded and followed by commas. *Such as* is not followed by a comma.

Right: Short prepositions, such as *in, on, to, for,* are not capitalized in titles.
There is only one proper thing for a driver to do when the army mule dies, namely, cut the harness and pull the cart himself.

20i. Use commas to set off substantives used in direct address.

Right: George, let me tell you what I did last night. [To begin a sentence.]
Come here, *my child,* and talk to me. [Within the sentence.]
"Please change places with me, *Helen,*" I requested. [With quotation marks.]

20j. Use commas to set off mild exclamations, sentence adverbs, and the responsives *yes* and *no* when they begin sentences.

Right: Well, I don't know what to tell him.
Oh, it does not matter.

Certainly, I will have my report ready on time.
Unfortunately, the third transport ship received a direct hit.
Yes, the second essay is due tomorrow.
No, I shall not go to the game this afternoon.

20k. Use commas to set off an explanatory clause like *he said* when it breaks into a sentence of dialogue. (See also 24h.)

Right: "All the same," she said, "it is just as well to be on the safe side."
My father answered, "Throw it away, then." [Dialogue guide begins the sentence.]
"It is a rough trail," the guide explained. "Walk slowly, and watch out for falling rocks." [Dialogue guide at end of sentence and before second quoted part.]
"I am sorry," replied Baker; "I did not mean to be rude." [With semicolon in compound sentence of dialogue.]

20l. Use commas to indicate transposed or contrasting sentence elements.

Right: She will pick up a book, not any special book, but just to feel a book in her hand.
Inequality, by arousing jealousy and envy, provokes discontent.
The mistakes of our opponents, not our organization or planning, won the election for us.

20m. Use commas to set off geographical names, dates, and addresses.

Right: Barbara Lee, who was born on Friday, September 13, 1908, has never been superstitious about the number thirteen.

If you will address the package to Harry Tweed, 67 Stark Street, Yorktown, Nevada, the orderly will leave it at the post office.

Granville Stanley Hall was born in Ashfield, Massachusetts, on February 1, 1844, a farm boy who attended the district school, the local academies, and finally was graduated from Williams College, in 1867, with the conviction that he belonged in the ministry. — Oscar Cargill.

Son of James O'Neill, the actor who "cleared fifty thousand" season after season in *Monte Cristo*, Eugene O'Neill was born in the Barrett House, on Broadway at Forty-Third Street, New York, on October 16, 1888. — Oscar Cargill.

20n. Do not use unnecessary commas. Avoid the following common mistakes in the use of the comma.

1. Do not use a comma to separate a subject from its verb.

Wrong: That our candidate was fighting a losing battle, was only too evident.

Right: That our candidate was fighting a losing battle was only too evident.

2. Do not use a comma to separate a verb from its complement.

Wrong: My favorite sports are, fishing, golf, and swimming.

Right: My favorite sports are fishing, golf, and swimming.

3. In a series of simple adjectives, do not place a comma between the last adjective and the word it modifies.

Wrong: The scout was a tall, cadaverous, ungainly, fellow.

Right: The scout was a tall, cadaverous, ungainly fellow.

4. Do not put a comma after a co-ordinating conjunction joining two clauses.

Wrong: A war to save democracy was fought twenty years ago, but, democracy is still in danger.

Right: A war to save democracy was fought twenty years ago, but democracy is still in danger.

5. Do not put a comma before a co-ordinating conjunction joining two words, two simple phrases, two subjects, or two predicates.

Wrong: From his pocket he fished out an old pipe, and a pouch of tobacco.
Right: From his pocket he fished out an old pipe and a pouch of tobacco.

Wrong: Before she left the room she stopped to powder her nose, and to pat her hair.

Right: Before she left the room she stopped to powder her nose and to pat her hair.

Exception: Compound elements of a sentence, such as compound subject, compound predicate, compound direct object, etc., if long and variously modified, are separated by a comma for the sake of clearness.

Example: A man walked into the lobby of the hotel that stands on the corner of Main Street and Seventh Avenue at four o'clock last Thursday afternoon, and with an air of secrecy approached a group of men who were sitting in the corner around a table that was covered with books and papers.

EXERCISES

Exercise 1. Punctuate each nonrestrictive clause in the following sentences.

1. Her eyes remained fixed upon the glistening beach which they had left.
2. We took our problem to our company commander who seemed too young to be wearing a uniform.
3. A quick last look for errors in spelling which many typists fail to give the letter may mean the difference between a good and a hopeless letter.
4. Naturally I addressed myself to the man who was seated next to me.
5. Chess which most of the older boys considered to be a form of mild insanity was his favorite recreation.
6. We looked up at the blue clusters of wild grapes which hung among the foliage of the elms.
7. I fancied that my father who was a country doctor was a sort of medieval knight going about on errands of mercy.
8. Through my bedroom window which was left open all summer I caught the faint breath of orange trees in blossom.
9. The play was written by A. A. Milne who is also the author of some delightful stories for children.
10. A good hunting dog which every boy in town aspired to possess could be purchased for a few days of hard work in the harvest fields.

Exercise 2, Compound sentences. Punctuate each of the following sentences. Decide whether to use a comma, a semicolon, or no mark at all. Be able to justify your decision.

1. The folk songs of the South are interesting but many of them are not of native origin.
2. I had worked with him for three seasons and I can understand how he feels about giving up his job for a college education.

3. He was quick and spry for a man of his age and he seemed to love the heat.

4. One sergeant I despised for I thought that he was trying to break my spirit.

5. She was naturally a sentimental old soul but none of the boys could interpret her apparent sternness.

6. Grayson had never fought any one before he closed his eyes and swung his fists wildly.

7. One boy I shall never forget for he once saved my life at the risk of his own.

8. The boys did the chores about the barns and the girls helped in the kitchen.

9. They have no choice they must conform or they are expelled from the institution.

10. It was a day's job to cut down the tree and it took a four-horse team to drag it away.

Exercise 3, Words in series. In the following sentences insert commas where they are necessary.

1. Their lives may be darkened by financial losses family disputes or personal bitterness.

2. It is only as we become older mellower less violent and more tolerant that we begin to value the art of conversation.

3. The battle raged all over the bathroom until Moppet was finally washed dried brushed and perfumed.

4. All her life she had been petted humored and spoiled; she did not know the meaning of unselfishness or co-operation.

5. She gloried in her reputation of being the most untamable unpredictable and generally impossible girl in Bennington.

6. With a sigh she dropped the package into the cold murky swirling waters.

7. They regretted the colorful pageantry of football contests the festive evenings in fraternity houses and the stimulation of human contacts which they had learned to enjoy in college days.

8. A tall gaunt moody-looking man at the door bared his teeth in a mechanical grin.

9. Their scientific knowledge was devoted to making guns poison gas bombing planes and submarines for the purpose of killing their fellow men.

10. No one could understand how this motley group of third-rate artists futile poets and frustrated esthetes had accepted him so completely as one of their kind.

Exercise 4. Supply every missing comma and tell what rule governs its use.

1. A crackling cheerful fire awaited us.
2. Mr. Brown who is our next-door neighbor is very ill.
3. Although the boy could neither read nor write English his diction was surprisingly cultured and dignified.
4. Of all the Smiths in the city we were trying to find the Mr. Smith whose first name was John.
5. My aunt lives at 230 University Avenue Southeast Minneapolis Minnesota.
6. We knew that the game had started for the students were cheering wildly.
7. Tall slender girls should not seek the company of short fat men.
8. Before starting to work Father carefully removed his coat folded it and laid it on a stump.
9. Lillian Foster the girl with the red hair spoke to me just as we left the room.
10. Becoming tired of fighting the boys suddenly found a victim in Styx a big white cat who belonged to our neighbor.

Exercise 5, All uses of the comma. Punctuate by rule. Tell what rule governs every comma that you use.

1. At the desk sat a girl who gave us more cards to fill out.
2. The men were all hungry tired and resentful.
3. According to the proverb the best things are the most difficult.
4. The robins have returned but there is still snow on the ground.
5. Be not careless in deeds nor confused in words nor rambling in thought.
6. Having devoured the cookies and ice cream the boys bashfully shuffled out eager to engage in affairs more important to boys.
7. At noon we camped where a full-grown river bubbled out of the lava rock.
8. Before putting the dog inside Father gave him a bone to comfort him.
9. A tall stately lady approached our booth and smiled at us.
10. The president of our class George Baker called me that same afternoon.
11. Jane gathered the flowers for her mother was busy making an apple pie for dinner.
12. Oswald who could not remain quiet for more than two minutes finally slipped from his chair and ran out of the room.
13. Before starting to clean the maid shook out the dust mop.
14. Privates corporals and sergeants must arise and stand when an officer enters the barracks.

15. He seemed a harmless old fellow but the excited red-faced woman pointed a monitory finger at him.
16. Universal's stupendous colossal million-dollar four-star production was a complete failure.
17. He swam rode and hunted but his vacation was still not a success.
18. Part of his nervousness I dare say arises out of his feeling of superiority to us.
19. If I should be asked for examples of short-sighted policy I should mention these three.
20. After the game the students tore down the goal posts broke them into small pieces and took the pieces home for souvenirs.

THE SEMICOLON

21a. Use a semicolon between the clauses of a compound sentence when they are not joined by one of the co-ordinating conjunctions. See sections 2 and 3.

Do not use a semicolon to cut off a phrase or a dependent clause from the main clause.

In weight, a semicolon is more than a comma and less than a period. The period separates complete sentences. The semicolon separates complete clauses within a sentence. Its frequent use marks a dignified, formal style, and for this reason the presence of many semicolons in a light, informal paper should be viewed with suspicion.

The frequency with which writers of serious expository essays or articles use semicolons may be judged from the following table. A count of commas and semicolons found on five representative pages of each writer revealed the following:

	Commas	Semicolons
James Truslow Adams	106	9
George Santayana	143	25
Howard Mumford Jones	113	10
Louis Untermeyer	82	14
Pearl Buck	180	1
Fortune Magazine	163	12
A "Profile" from the *New Yorker*	117	1

Examples:

We have, during this time, learned many things; we have become acquainted with college routine; we have become an integral part of a new society.

When the busman takes his proverbial holiday he takes a bus; when a sailor gets a holiday he hires a rowboat; when an anthologist has a holiday he thinks of another anthology. — Louis Untermeyer.

The college is primarily not a place of the body, nor of the feelings, nor even of the will; it is, first of all, a place of the mind. — Alexander Meiklejohn.

What concerns me is that the intelligent people — the leading people, the people who have brains and whatever we possess of culture and very often of means — they do not read; or if they do, they read too often digests of books and essays and stories rather than the works themselves. — Pearl Buck.

The Unwelcome Man is a much more intense book than *Moon-Calf*, yet the objectivity Dell attained is here altogether lacking; not only is the subject matter adolescence, but the point of view is still adolescent. — Oscar Cargill.

Students are often urged to use semicolons before the conjunctive adverbs *therefore, however, hence, accordingly, moreover, nevertheless, furthermore,* and *consequently.* More practical and more realistic advice would be, "Do not write compound sentences in which the second clause begins with one of these conjunctive adverbs. Modern writers do not write sentences of that sort. Hide the connective within the clause and enclose it in commas." If no conjunction remains between the clauses, the rule about semicolons still applies.

21b. Use a semicolon between the clauses of a compound sentence joined by a co-ordinating conjunction when the clauses are long and when they contain other punctuation, or when you desire a more distinct pause than the comma would give.

You should interpret this rule in terms of sentences written by professional writers. The presence of two or three commas in a short compound sentence does not justify a semicolon. Neither should you assume that you can cut off a dependent clause by a semicolon merely because you desire "a more distinct pause." Use commas with subordinate clauses if any punctuation is necessary.

Examples:

German merchantmen, as well as German warships, were driven from the seas; and the British navy enforced, with growing stringency, a virtual "blockade" of German seaports and interfered more and more with neutral trade with Germany. — Carlton J. H. Hayes.

But for our purpose the fact is of little importance, for it is the ideals of a people rather than the geography they have outgrown that determine their destiny; and in Kansas, as has been well said, "it is the ideas of the Pilgrims, not their descendents, that have had dominion in the young commonwealth." — Carl Becker.

The old view of government as the natural field of an hereditary aristocracy has been definitely relegated to the museum of historic antiquities; and it is certainly difficult not to feel that the scale of life today is for the average man ampler than at any previous time. — Harold J. Laski.

21c. The semicolon may be used to show balance or contrast between co-ordinate sentence elements.

This use of the semicolon is infrequent. The normal function of a semicolon is to separate clauses in a compound sentence when no co-ordinate conjunction is used. When a writer experiments with semicolons, he is usually working on a "show piece." Now, of course, it is great fun to try these exhibition sentences once in a while. You might try to imitate the following samples.

Examples:

The world embraces not only a Newton, but a Shakespeare; not only a Boyle, but a Raphael; not only a Kant, but a Beethoven; not only a Darwin, but a Carlyle. — John Tyndall.

Our direct intuitions of Nature tell us that the world is bottomlessly strange: alien, even when it is kind and beautiful; having innumerable modes of being that are not our modes; always mysteriously not personal, not conscious, not moral; often hostile and sinister; sometimes even unimaginably, because inhumanly, evil. — Aldous Huxley.

At the same time there must be great emphasis upon truth and honesty; upon Aristotle's four great humanist ideals, temperance, fortitude, wisdom, and justice; and upon consideration for those with whom one shares this earth in common. — Frank Snowden Hopkins.

EXERCISES

Exercise 1. Assume that the following sentences are from an informal autobiographical sketch. Determine the punctuation you should use in the places marked by brackets. Would you use commas, semicolons, or no marks at all?

1. I have lived on a Wisconsin farm for eighteen years [   ] and I cannot imagine a more normal or a more average American life.
2. My father and mother are average middle-class Americans [;] we live in an average sort of house [   ] and we have an average sort of ideas and interests.
3. My father was born and reared in a little town in Norway [   ] now he is an important man in a little Norwegian town in Wisconsin.
4. Father still speaks English with a strong Norwegian accent [   ] his children [   ] however [   ] speak an American English which is the same in California or Wisconsin or New Jersey.
5. What education I got [   ] I took without question from average teachers in an average American high school [   ] fortunately [   ] however [   ] my teachers knew enough to insist that lessons had to be learned [   ] and duties had to be done.
6. They were probably good teachers [   ] in spite of their lack of "progressive" ideas [   ] for among the graduates of our high school there are a number of doctors, scientists, college professors, and even a much-decorated war hero or two.
7. We have no big industries in our little town [   ] neither do we have tenements or slums or gangs of criminals.
8. In the summer the boys played baseball, went swimming in the creek, rode bicycles into the country, or hunted and fished [   ] we had no country club set, no organized playground, and few dances and parties.
9. My father was the local dealer in Chrysler-made cars [   ] my present interest in mechanical engineering was [   ] consequently [   ] developed early through my attempt to remake wrecks into ambulatory jalopies.

10. My home town is not the best in America [   ] but I am sure it is far from being the worst [   ] in it, as in countless other American towns, one may find happy and useful citizens.

Exercise 2. The following sentences are taken from a formal research paper on "Freedom of Speech." Decide whether to use commas, semicolons, or no marks whatever in the spaces marked by brackets.

1. Opinions should never be restricted simply because they are despised [   ] the right of free speech should be questioned only when it affects the immediate safety of the nation.
2. Neighbor should never be set against neighbor [   ] hysteria, above all, should be kept under control.
3. The preservation of free speech is not only a matter of abstract legal rights [   ] it is also a matter of giving the listeners a chance to analyze and to reply.
4. "I detest what you say [   ] but I will fight with my life to preserve your right to say it."
5. To preserve the right of free speech there must be people who treasure and value this right [   ] people who are not excited by wild stories [   ] and who can remain clear headed when others are hysterical.
6. Americans should realize that freedom of speech did not just happen [   ] for the history of free speech is stained with the blood of martyrs.
7. The authors of the First Amendment said very little about its exact meaning [   ] there are bits of evidence [   ] however [   ] which lead us to assume that the words were meant in a wide and liberal sense.
8. Some people would interpret the free speech clause to permit anyone to say anything at any time [   ] Chief Justice Oliver Wendell Holmes [   ] on the other hand [   ] believed that false and malicious utterances were unlawful.
9. Mobs organized to whip, shoot, and kill all dissenters were common [   ] and violence became so severe that President Wilson twice called on the nation to stop it.
10. It is true that there are fanatics who preach ideas as poisonous as strychnine [   ] but the true friend of free speech will not interfere if he has faith in the average citizen's good sense.

Exercise 3. Look through a collection of essays recommended by your instructor and bring to class ten sentences in which semicolons are used. Try to determine the reason for using each semicolon. Would commas have served the purpose just as well in some instances? Why were not commas used?

THE COLON

22a. Use the colon to introduce a long and formal quotation, an enumeration or a list of particulars, or a formal explanation.

The colon is a formal mark. It should not be used before a series introduced informally. In ordinary formal context, writers usually hold to the rule that what precedes the colon must be a complete sentence, but in lists and tabulations the colon is used after the verb introducing the list. In other words, a comma or no mark at all is used before a series if the series is part of a sentence.

Poor: My favorite amusements are: dancing, golfing, and attending movies.

Right: My favorite amusements are dancing, golfing, and attending motion pictures.

After a colon it is customary to use a capital letter when the list that follows consists of a complete sentence or of several sentences; a small letter is used when what follows the colon is a part of the same sentence.

Examples:

Clearing his throat, the speaker began as follows: "We look before and after, and we see, through the half-drawn folds of time. . . ."

His faults are these: an uncontrollable temper, inexperience, and a lack of interest in his work.

There are, by the way, three sorts of created beings who are sentimentally supposed to be able to judge individuals at the first glance: women, children, and dogs. — Arnold Bennett.

He must, we are sure, feel and know the steady progress of the morning: a crosstown car establishing its characteristic crescendo, a hose being played in a doorway after a hot summer night, the eight-o'clock greeting of a saw in a picture-framer's shop nearby. — "City Rhythms," from *The New Yorker*.

22b. Use a colon between two clauses if the second supplements, amplifies, or interprets the first.

Examples:

By destroying all his illusions, man's intellect has devised a painful dilemma for him: he can neither go back to a state of relative ignorance nor can he cling to his faiths and repress his doubts merely because it would be desirable to do so. — Oscar Cargill.

Men had only to follow reason and self-interest: something not themselves, God and Nature, would do whatever else was necessary for *r*ighteousness. — Carl L. Becker.

22c. Observe the following special uses of the colon: after a formal salutation of a letter; between the hour and minute figures of clock time; between the title of a book and the subtitle; in Biblical references.

Examples: Dear Madam:
At 8 : 45 a.m.
English Fundamentals: A Handbook and Practice Leaves.
Luke 4 : 5–13.

EXERCISE

Exercise 1. In each of the following sentences determine whether or not the colon is used correctly.

1. The following are the chief uses of radar: 1. To detect . . .
2. Her worldly goods consisted of: the clothes she wore, one lipstick, and $3.67 in a tiny coin purse.
3. The schedule has been changed so that class bells will ring at 7 : 50, 8 : 30, 9 : 10, and 10 : 50.
4. Among the various types of life insurance contracts, the following are the most important: 1. the ordinary life policy, 2. the endowment policy . . .
5. Three vital questions in connection with any student government are: 1. Are there free elections? 2. Who makes the rules? 3. Who enforces the rules?

Exercise 2. Get a copy of *Harper's Magazine* or *The Atlantic Monthly.* Copy five sentences in which colons are used and bring them to class for discussion. Try to determine why the colon was used in each case. Could semicolons have been used for some of the colons?

THE APOSTROPHE

23a. Use an apostrophe and -s to form the possessive of a noun, singular or plural, which does not end in -s.

Right: A man's hand, men's suits, a child's hat, children's shoes, a horse's neck, my mother-in-law's house, George's books, Nolan and Clark's store, Sears and Roebuck's catalogue.

But when two or more names joined by *and* are represented as joint owners of something, the last name alone takes the possessive form with the apostrophe.

Right: We shopped at Meier and Frank's store. Nancy and Sally's mother is in town today. Will you please stop at Larson, Jones, and Marshall's antique shop on Third Street?

Usage sanctions such group possessives as *the Queen of England's hats,* but it is just as well to dodge an awkward expression by saying *the hat which belongs to Mr. Snell, the Governor of Oregon* instead of wondering whether it should be written *Mr. Snell, the Governor of Oregon's hat* or *Mr. Snell's, the Governor of Oregon, hat.*

23b. Use the apostrophe alone to form the possessive of a plural noun ending in -s.

Right: Foxes' tails, boys' clothes, ladies' hats, the Smiths' house.

23c. Use the apostrophe with -s to form the possessive of singular nouns ending in -s, if the resultant form is not unpleasant or difficult to pronounce; otherwise use the apostrophe alone.

Right: Keats's or Keats' poems, James's or James' hat, Jones's or Jones' office, for goodness' sake, Demosthenes' orations, Jesus' words.

23d. Use an apostrophe with -s to form the possessive of indefinite pronouns. Do not use the apostrophe to form the possessive of personal pronouns.

Right: One's, another's, everybody's, nobody's, somebody's, anybody's.
Wrong: Your's, her's, their's, our's.
Right: Yours, hers, theirs, ours.

The possessive of the pronoun *it* is *its*. *It's* means *it is*.

23e. Use an apostrophe to indicate the omission of letters or figures.

Right: Doesn't, isn't, o'clock, the class of '46, I'll, it's (for *it is*).

23f. Use an apostrophe and -s to form the plurals of figures, letters, and words referred to as words.

Right: You have not dotted your *i*'s or crossed your *t*'s.
Your *m*'s, *n*'s, and *u*'s look alike.
He used too many *and*'s, *so*'s, and *but*'s in his theme.
Be careful not to make your 3's look like 8's.

EXERCISES

Exercise 1. Insert apostrophes wherever they are necessary in the following sentences.

1. At seven oclock the doors of the boys dormitory swung open, and a crowd of noisy youngsters trooped out.
2. Rogers shop is advertising a sale of ladies dresses and boys and girls non-rationed shoes.
3. "Arent you going to call this a days work?" asked the masons assistant.
4. A few minutes after twelve oclock it was announced that the drive had missed its goal by five per cent.
5. If its not too much to ask, will you remember to bring your roommates dictionary to class?
6. I agreed with the deans remark that ones religion was ones own private affair.
7. Its true, isnt it, that everybodys business is usually nobodys business.

8. "Your kitten seems to be limping," said Marions mother. "Will you see if its leg is hurt?"
9. The Joness dog killed one of the Davises chickens.
10. Its two oclock; Ill be late for the meeting of the class of 27.

Exercise 2. Draw a circle about every word in which the apostrophe is incorrectly used. Above the word write the corrected form.

1. This sweater is Helen's; your's is upstairs in your closet.
2. Its time for my ten-oclock coffee. Have you had yours?
3. Everybodys garden is doing well this spring. How is their's?
4. If you like Keat's poems, Im sure that youll enjoy Amy Lowell's.
5. Sally's in Nolans store looking for some ladie's dresses.

Exercise 3. Write the possessive singular and the possessive plural of each of the following:

Example: girl girl's girls'

1. woman
2. attorney
3. man
4. veteran
5. professor
6. Smith
7. Powers
8. Atkins
9. soldier
10. player

QUOTATION MARKS

24a. Use double quotation marks to enclose a direct quotation.

Right: "I did not hear you," Dorothy replied. "I was in the other room." George said, "I saw him enter this building."

Do not leave out one set of quotation marks.

Quotation marks come in pairs, one set at the beginning and one set at the end of every quoted part.

Wrong: "Oh, how can I tell? he objected. What's the good of asking me that now?"

Right: "Oh, how can I tell?" he objected. "What's the good of asking me that now?"

If a quotation consists of several sentences, place the quotation marks at the beginning and at the end of the entire quotation. Do *not* enclose each sentence in quotation marks.

Right: George replied: "Yes, that is his weakness. I have pleaded with him; he only laughs at me. I have appealed to his sense of honor, but he is too selfish to see the rights of others."

If a quotation consists of several paragraphs, begin each paragraph with quotation marks but place them at the end of the last paragraph only. Remember that this convention applies to a continued speech by one person. In writing dialogue, use a separate paragraph for every change of speaker. Short descriptive, narrative, or explanatory passages may be paragraphed with dialogue, especially if they are placed between sentences of dialogue spoken by the same person.

24b. Do not put quotation marks about an indirect quotation.

Wrong: The teacher asked "how many had their themes ready."
Right: The teacher asked how many had their themes ready.

24c. Use single quotation marks to enclose a quotation within a quotation.

Examples:

Mary replied, "The dean said to me, 'No report has reached this office.' "

"If the good Lord should tell me I had only five minutes to live," said Justice Oliver Wendell Holmes, "I would say to him, 'All right, Lord, but I'm sorry you can't make it ten.' " — Quoted in Catherine Drinker Bowen's *Yankee from Olympus.*

24d. Use quotation marks to enclose words spoken of as words or slang expressions used in formal writing, to call attention to a word used in a special sense, or to set off phrases borrowed from other writers and used in your own work.

Italics are used to mark words spoken of as words when the style of writing is formal. In informal writing, quotation marks are more common. See also section 16c.

Examples:
She thought that I should have written "preying" mantis instead of "praying" mantis.

National greed has disguised itself in mandates to govern "inferior" races. [To indicate that he is using somebody else's word and that he does not think these races are inferior.]

Need leads the "small fry" to rob and steal, in the same way that greed causes the "big shots" to go in for organized crime and racketeering. — Barnes and Ruedi, *The American Way of Life.* [Slang used in formal writing.]

When defining words, you should put their meanings in quotation marks.

Example: The word *indomitable* means "unconquerable."

Avoid sprinkling your writing with quotation marks. Remember that quotation marks do not excuse or justify slang. They merely call attention to it. If you are sure that some slang expression is more vivid or more eloquent than respectable English, use it in informal writing, by all means, but use it without shame or apology. And do not use quotation marks for proverbs or for phrases so familiar that they have become common property.

Examples:
After life's fitful fever he should be left to sleep in the soil he gave his life to free. ["Life's fitful fever" is too well known to require quotation marks.]

In his quiet way, he went about his work without any great ado, and valued his good name among his friends above great riches. [The words are from the Old Testament — "A good name is rather to be chosen than great riches" — but they are now common property.]

24e. Place the comma and the period inside the quotation marks.

This rule is a printers' convention. The period and the comma are the two marks that occupy the lower half of a line of print;

all the other marks, the colon, the semicolon, the question mark, and the exclamation point, stand the full height of the line. To have a comma or a period trail out beyond quotation marks looks bad. Remember the convention: periods and commas are *always* placed inside quotation marks.

Right: "Yes," she repeated. "Marriage is not a word; it is a sentence."
Louis Untermeyer once said that "violet," "laughter," and "willow" are three of the most musical words in the English language.

24f. Place the question mark, the semicolon, the colon, and the exclamation point inside the quotation marks if they belong to the quoted part; if they do not, place them outside the quotation marks.

Right: Did you hear him say, "I won't go"? [The quoted part is a declarative statement. The question mark belongs to the entire expression, which is a question.]
"Well, I like that!" she exclaimed in anger.
"It is as much a trade," says La Bruyere, "to make a book as it is to make a clock"; in short, literature is largely a matter of technique. — Irving Babbitt. [Notice that the semicolon is not part of the quotation. It belongs to the entire sentence.]

24g. For introductory or explanatory phrases (like *he said*) with dialogue use the marks of punctuation which the structure of the sentence calls for. (See also 20k.)

Right: "Sister," she replied sweetly, "did you ever hear of Cleopatra?"
"Howard!" a voice called from the garden.

She continued breathlessly: "They are going to fight. I heard them shouting and cursing at each other. Please do something, Father...." [The colon introduces several sentences of dialogue. A comma is often used for the same purpose.]

"The price is not a matter of profit," he said, stiffly; "it is a matter of principle." [Notice the semicolon to separate co-ordinate clauses in a compound sentence of dialogue. Most writers use a period and a following capital letter instead of a semicolon in this sort of construction.]

You must be careful not to use a comma before a quotation that is woven into the sentence or before a title in quotation marks. The general practice is not to use a comma before a quoted part that is less than a sentence.

Examples:

That led him to see and to say that judges "have other motives for decision, outside their own arbitrary will, besides the commands" of the lawmakers, so that "the only question for the lawyer is, how will the judges act?" — Jerome Frank.

It is doubtful if adolescents since the time of Byron have repeated any poems (without compulsion) as frequently or as enthusiastically as the youth of the 'twenties recited "My candle burns at both ends" and "Safe upon the solid rock. . . ." — Oscar Cargill.

EXERCISES

Exercise 1. In the following sentences supply missing quotation marks and correct any that have been incorrectly used or placed. Some of the sentences may be correctly punctuated as they stand.

1. "A little fresh air will not hurt them, replied Mrs. Sullivan. It's the smoke that gets them after a time."
2. "Where are you going"? she asked. Are you looking for Gail?"
3. "The message is important — in a way", Dorothy replied. "Let us try the Western Union office at the hotel".
4. He departed for the country from which "no traveler returns."
5. "I want to take my hair down, she said, and have a heart-to-heart talk with myself."
6. It was his luck to find all thrilling episodes "continued in our next," until he began to feel like a tramp peering into the back windows of college life.
7. "I wonder who that man is," she said to herself. He seemed hurt by what I said."
8. The speaker inquired "how many had voted the Republican ticket at the last election."
9. A college man who wants to "be in the swim" must "work up a line."
10. "Tolstoy was lost in the creative mood when he made, 'Natasha,' 'Pierre', and 'Anna'," said Galsworthy in an address entitled, "On Expression."

Exercise 2. Look through an issue of some magazine of the better kind and bring to class five examples of unusual uses of quotation marks. Look for broken or elliptical sentences and for sentences which are part quoted matter and part not quoted.

Exercise 3. Find an essay about language or words. Your instructor may save you time by directing you to one. Bring to class five examples of words referred to as words, or of slang expressions enclosed in quotation marks. You may find that in one essay words referred to as words are always italicized; in another essay they are always enclosed in quotation marks. Which do you find to be true in the essay you examine?

THE DASH

25a. Use the dash to indicate a sudden, abrupt break in thought or structure.

On the typewriter use two hyphens, without a space between them and the word before and after, to indicate a dash.

Right: This song—how many remember it?—once swept the country.
He asked me—but I cannot repeat his words.
"I wish—I wish you'd let him know—please do—it was an accident." [In dialogue to give the effect of hesitation.]
"I don't know whether she would like—" [Speech abruptly broken off.]

25b. Use the dash for an explanatory or parenthetical phrase or clause that breaks into the normal flow of the sentence.

Three kinds of marks may indicate parentheses — the comma, the dash, and marks of parenthesis. The degree of separation indicated by these marks varies from the lightest, for which commas are used, to the most definite and most formal, for which marks of parenthesis are used.

Examples:

"The West" — there were successively many of them — unlike the colonial America, was of almost limitless extent and wealth. — James Truslow Adams.

Directly we go wrong — directly, that is to say, we cease to act in a way of which society approves — conscience begins to nag. — C. E. M. Joad.

And New Orleans — or rather the Creole quarter of New Orleans, for the rest of the city is commonplace — is delicious, suggesting old France and Spain, yet a France and Spain strangely transmuted in this new clime. — James Bryce.

25c. Use the dash to introduce or to set off a long, formal appositive or a summary.

Examples:

The American frontier is sharply distinguished from the European frontier — a fortified boundary line running through dense populations. — Frederick Jackson Turner. [An appositive with added explanatory comments.]

That train of reasoning is what logicians call a syllogism, and has all its various parts and terms — its major premise, its minor premise, and its conclusion. — Thomas Henry Huxley. [A series of appositives.]

The dash may occasionally be found before such words as *namely* and *that is* introducing an appositive. See also section 20h.

Example:

Also you find out about the queer fade-away, the slow curve, the fast in- and out-shoots that seemed to be timed almost as delicately as shrapnel, to burst, or rather break, just when they will do the most harm — namely, at the moment when the batter is swinging. — Paul Gallico.

A dash may be used before such words as *all* and *these* introducing a summary, or summarizing appositive, after a series.

Examples:

Teas, dances, new clothes, blind dates — all these should be part of your freshman year.

Regional survey and regional service — these are the chief ingredients for a responsible citizenship. . . . — Lewis Mumford.

25d. Do not use dashes indiscriminately for other marks of punctuation.

A dash-spattered theme or letter marks its author as a gushing school-girl, breathless with emotion, pouring out words with little time for stuffy rules of punctuation! Do not be a "Breathless." Save the dash for its special function so that it will have force when it is used.

THE HYPHEN

26a. Use hyphens with two or more words forming a compound adjective before a noun.

Examples: A worn-out metaphor, a heaven-sent blessing, a high-school girl, a double-bottomed boat, a red-hot poker, a foul-smelling pipe, a long-delayed answer, a heart-to-heart talk, an old-fashioned woman, a wide-open door, a dark-blue sea, the well-known scientist, in up-to-date condition, a ten-foot pole, a six-by-eight sheet, a two-thirds majority.

When a compound modifier consists of two or more words with a common beginning, use the following style:

Examples: the fast in- and out-shoots, a two- or three-inch block.

Do not hyphenate compound modifiers used in the predicate; compounds consisting of two proper nouns; compounds in which an adverb ending in -ly is used.

Examples: The poet was well known. His information was up to date. The horse responded to the softly spoken command. He is a United States citizen. He inspected several New Jersey schools.

26b. Use hyphens with compound numbers from twenty-one to ninety-nine.

Examples: Fifty-five men, twenty-seven dollars, seventy-three cents. One hundred and twenty-nine.

Fractions, when used as modifiers, are hyphenated. Otherwise, no hyphen should be used between the numerator and denominator if either part already contains a hyphen. Such simple fractions as *one half*, *two thirds*, etc., are usually written without a hyphen.

Right: The resolution must be passed by a two-thirds majority. Three twenty-fifths, one thirty-seventh.

26c. Use hyphens with the following classes of words:

1. With the prefixes ex-, self-, but rarely with other prefixes: ex-soldier, ex-president, self-starter, self-adornment.
2. To avoid doubling a vowel or tripling a consonant: pre-existence, re-enter, re-echo, semi-independent, semi-invalid, shell-leaf, skill-less, bell-like, co-operative (also coöperative).
3. With groups making or containing prepositional phrases: son-in-law, father-in-law, man-of-war.
4. To prevent confusion with similar words: re-form (*cf. reform*), re-cover (*cf. recover*), re-create (*cf. recreate*).

When in doubt as to the correct form of a compound, consult *Webster's Collegiate Dictionary*, fifth edition.

EXERCISE

Exercise 1. With the aid of a dictionary determine which of the following are written solid, which with a hyphen, and which separate.

1. all right	15. by law
2. all American team	16. dining room
3. all inclusive examination	17. drug store
4. any body	18. every body
5. any how	19. every thing
6. any time	20. every time
7. any more	21. every where
8. anti Fascist	22. eye opening answer
9. anti typhoid	23. eye shade
10. air driven pump	24. foot ball
11. air base	25. full back
12. base ball	26. good night
13. book store	27. good by
14. by pass	28. half crazed animal

29. half intoxicated man
30. half back
31. half cousin
32. in as much as
33. note book
34. north east
35. one armed paper hanger
36. out doors
37. post office
38. quarter back
39. re written theme
40. score board
41. score card
42. some thing
43. some body
44. sharp tempered
45. text book
46. un balanced
47. under graduate
48. upper class man
49. week end trip
50. well chaperoned dance

PARENTHESES, BRACKETS

(PARENTHESES)

27a. Use parentheses to enclose material that is supplementary, explanatory, or interpretive.

The general principle to follow in the use of parenthetical marks is that commas set off material which is fairly close to the thought of the sentence (see section 20g); dashes set off material which is more loosely connected (see section 25b); and marks of parenthesis are used to indicate the most distant parenthetical relation. This principle is not always observed by all writers. A study of a group of modern essays will probably reveal that some writers seldom use parentheses, others use them frequently but logically, and still others use them when the mood comes upon them. But the privilege of being moody and irrational in punctuation is denied to young writers.

Right: Houston was born in Cairo (Illinois, not Egypt) in 1897.
She brought with her a reputation for originality, or eccentricity, or downright willfullness (whatever one wished to call it).
There is really nothing (except the salary) that attracts me to my present occupation.
The pruned rose plant (see fig. 7) will have more under ground than above.

If other marks of punctuation are necessary with parentheses, place the comma, the semicolon, and the period after the second parenthesis; place a question mark or an exclamation point before it, if the mark belongs to the parenthetical element; otherwise after it.

Right: Everyone listened attentively (imagine falling asleep during one of his sermons!).

When George brought me the orchids (it was George, wasn't it?), I realized that my destiny had arrived.

27b. Do not use parentheses to show that you want to cancel or cross out any part of your writing. Draw a line through the part that you want to cross out.

If you use parentheses with the intention of crossing out words, you will mislead your reader, who will assume, with good reason, that these words are to be read as part of the sentence.

Wrong: Public utilities are (monopolies) industries which serve the public.

Right: Public utilities are ~~monopolies~~ industries which serve the public.

(BRACKETS)

27c. Use brackets to enclose corrections, interpolations, and supplied omissions added to a quotation by the person quoting.

Right: Santayana says, "Religion lay on him [Dickens] like the weight of the atmosphere, sixteen pounds to the square inch, yet never noticed nor mentioned."

The President [Harding] offered him an appointment in the diplomatic service.

The battle began on the 6th [5th] of August, 1916.

EXERCISES

Exercise 1. Look through a copy of a good magazine and bring to class five sentences in which parentheses or brackets are used. Try to determine the exact reason for the presence of these marks.

Exercise 2. Write five sentences of your own in which you use parentheses.

SPELLING

Let us extend a word of encouragement to the poor spellers. The inability to spell is not an inherited disease. It is not due to malnutrition or to improper functioning of one of the ductless glands. It is indeed a curse, but the curse can be lifted by proper incantations — one is almost tempted to say by the use of proper spells! If you are a bad speller, you must begin by refusing to admit defeat, for spelling *can* be learned.

You can learn how to spell by observing the following directions:

1. Memorize the spelling rules and use them constantly.

2. Whenever your attention is called to a misspelled word, look it up in a good dictionary and learn to pronounce it by syllables. Some of your trouble with spelling comes from an incorrect pronunciation of words. Keep a list of the words that you misspell. Review this list frequently.

3. Whenever you look up a word in a dictionary, copy it carefully, forming each letter as plainly as you can. Some of your trouble with spelling comes from your bad handwriting. It is possible that you have used illegible handwriting as a shiftless substitute for learning how to spell.

4. After you have tried to photograph the word on your mind, write it from memory on a sheet of paper. Check your spelling with the correct spelling.

5. Whenever you misspell a word, look through the spelling rules to see what rule might have helped you to remember the correct spelling.

PRONUNCIATION

28. Pronounce words correctly.

The following is a brief list of words misspelled because of incorrect pronunciation:

Right	Most common error	Right	Most common error
accidentally	(accidently)	literature	(literture)
athlete	(athelete)	occasion	(ocassion)
athletics	(atheletics)	optimistic	(optomistic)
arctic	(artic)	particular	(paticular)
barbarous	(barbarious)	perform	(preform)
boundary	(boundry)	perseverance	(perserverance)
candidate	(canidate)	perspiration	(prespiration)
disastrous	(disasterous)	practically	(pratically)
dissatisfied	(disatisfied)	probably	(probally)
February	(Febuary)	quantity	(quanity)
formerly	(formally)	recognize	(reconize)
government	(goverment)	representative	(represenative)
hindrance	(hinderance)	sophomore	(sophmore)
history	(histry)	strictly	(strickly)
interesting	(intresting)	surprise	(supprise)
introduce	(interduce)	temperament	(temperment)
laboratory	(labratory)	tragedy	(tradegy)

FINAL –E

29. A word ending in silent -e generally drops the -e before a suffix beginning with a vowel, but it retains the -e before a suffix beginning with a consonant.

Drop -e

admire	+ ation	=	admiration
admire	+ able	=	admirable
allure	+ ing	=	alluring
arrange	+ ing	=	arranging
arrive	+ ing	=	arriving
believe	+ ing	=	believing
care	+ ing	=	caring

Drop -e

come	+ ing	=	coming
deplore	+ able	=	deplorable
dine	+ ing	=	dining
desire	+ ous	=	desirous
explore	+ ation	=	exploration
fame	+ ous	=	famous
imagine	+ ary	=	imaginary
imagine	+ able	=	imaginable
love	+ able	=	lovable
lose	+ ing	=	losing
move	+ able	=	movable

Retain -e

arrange	+ ment	=	arrangement
care	+ ful	=	careful
force	+ ful	=	forceful
hate	+ ful	=	hateful
like	+ ness	=	likeness
move	+ ment	=	movement

But after *c* or *g*, if the suffix begins with *a* or *o*, the *e* is retained to preserve the soft sound of *c* or *g*.

advantage	+ ous	=	advantageous
change	+ able	=	changeable
courage	+ ous	=	courageous
notice	+ able	=	noticeable
outrage	+ ous	=	outrageous
peace	+ able	=	peaceable
service	+ able	=	serviceable

IE OR EI

30. In words with *ie* or *ei* when the sound is long *ee*, use *i* before *e* except after *c*.

i before e

achieve	cashier	piece	shriek
apiece	field	pierce	siege
belief	fierce	priest	thief
believe	frieze	relieve	wield
brief	grief	retrieve	yield
besiege	niece	reprieve	
chief	pier	shield	

except after c

| ceiling | conceive | deceive | receipt |
| conceit | deceit | perceive | receive |

Exceptions: either, neither, financier, weird, species, seize, leisure.

These may be remembered by arranging the words in a sentence: "Neither financier seized either species of weird leisure."

Another group of troublesome words which end in the long *ee* sound may be easily remembered by memorizing the entire list:

1. Only one word ends in "sede": supersede

2. Three words end in "ceed": exceed
proceed
succeed

3. The rest end in "cede": accede
cede
concede
intercede
precede
recede
secede

FINAL CONSONANT

31. **In words of one syllable and words accented on the last syllable, ending in a single consonant preceded by a single vowel, double the final consonant before a suffix beginning with a vowel.**

drop [word of one syllable]+ed [suffix beginning with a vowel]=dropped.
control [accented on the last syllable] + ed [suffix] = controlled.
benefit [not accented on last syllable] + ed [suffix] = benefited.
confer [accented on last syllable] + ed [suffix] = conferred.
confer [notice the shift in accent] + ence [suffix] = conference.
defer [accented on last syllable] + ed [suffix] = deferred.
defer [notice the shift in accent] + ence [suffix] = deference.

Suffix begins with a vowel

(One syllable)

brag	— bragging	man	— mannish
cram	— cramming	plan	— planning
drag	— dragging	snap	— snapped
din	— dinning	sin	— sinning
drop	— dropped	stop	— stopped
cut	— cutting	quit	— quitting
bid	— bidding	rob	— robbed
flag	— flagged	stab	— stabbed
get	— getting	whip	— whipped
clan	— clannish	glad	— gladdest

(Accent on last syllable)

admit'	— admitted	equip'	— equipped
begin'	— beginning	commit'	— committee
commit'	— committed	occur'	— occurrence
concur'	— concurring	submit'	— submitted
confer'	— conferring	compel'	— compelled

(Not accented on last syllable)

prefer	— preference	benefit	— benefited
refer	— reference	profit	— profitable
happen	— happened	marvel	— marvelous

Suffix begins with a consonant

glad	— gladness	sin	— sinful
fat	— fatness	equip	— equipment
man	— manhood	profit	— profitless

FINAL —Y

32. A noun ending in -y preceded by a consonant forms the plural in *-ies;* a verb ending in -y preceded by a consonant forms its present tense, third person singular, in *-ies.*

(*Ending in* -y *preceded by a consonant*)

baby, babies	sky, skies	fairy, fairies
marry, marries	copy, copies	fly, flies

(Ending in -y preceded by a vowel)

attorney, attorneys	valley, valleys	delay, delays
destroy, destroys	enjoy, enjoys	chimney, chimneys

Note: Some other rules for forming plurals are:

1. For most nouns, add *-s:* boys, girls, houses, ideas, aches, pains.
2. For nouns ending with a sound similar to *s,* add *-es:* birches, foxes, boxes, classes.
3. For nouns ending in *-f, -fe, -ff,* use *-s* or *-ves:* chief, chiefs; staff, staffs, staves; wife, wives; sheriff, sheriffs; elf, elves.
4. For nouns ending in *-o,* add *-s* or *-es:* solo, solos; echo, echoes; potato, potatoes; motto, mottos, mottoes; tomato, tomatoes; alto, altos.
5. Some nouns have irregular plurals: foot, feet; mouse, mice; goose, geese; ox, oxen; woman, women; axis, axes; basis, bases; datum, data; locus, loci; formula, formulas, formulae.

These last five rules are less useful to the student than the systematic use of a dictionary and memorizing plurals as one masters a new word.

SIMILAR FORMS

33. Learn the distinction in meaning between words similar or identical in sound.

accept: to take something offered; to agree to; to approve; to believe as true.
except: to leave out; to exclude.

accent: emphasis or stress; to stress.
ascent: climbing; a way sloping up.
assent: to agree; agreement.

admittance: permission to enter a place. [*W.D.S.* 23.] [1]
admission: admitting to rights and privileges; the price of being allowed to enter.

affect: to influence; to pretend; to assume. [*W.D.S.* 30–31.]
effect: to perform; make happen. "They effected an escape."

---

[1] All references to *Webster's Dictionary of Synonyms.*

all ready: everyone is ready. "They were all ready."
already: by this time. "They had already eaten breakfast."

altar: a place of worship. "They knelt before the altar."
alter: to change. "Do not alter a single word in my report."

ante: before. "antebellum"
anti: against; opposed to. "anti-aircraft; antifreeze; antitoxin"

bole: trunk of a tree.
boll: the pod of a plant.
bowl: a hollow dish.

breath: air drawn into lungs. "We need a breath of fresh air."
breathe: to take a breath. "We cannot breathe in this room."

capital: chief; important; leading city; resources.
capitol: the State building.

censure: blame; condemn; criticize severely.
censor: to oversee morals and conduct; to examine and make changes.

charted: mapped or diagramed. "The Arctic is still not fully charted."
chartered: hired; granted certain rights. "We chartered a boat."

cite: to quote or use as an example. "Can you cite another instance?"
site: location. "This is a good site for our new church."
sight: vision; to see. "At last we sighted land."

continually: frequently repeated. [*W.D.S.* 195–196.]
continuously: with an unbroken flow.

coarse: rough; crude. "coarse food; coarse manners; coarse sand"
course: direction; path; series; order. "a course of study; of course"

complement: that which completes. "subjective complement"
compliment: praise; a polite and flattering lie. "He paid her a compliment."

choose: to pick out, select. "Do you think he will choose me?"
chose: past tense of *choose*. "They chose a new secretary."

consul: government official appointed to look after foreign business
    interests.
council: a group; an assembly. "the city council"
counsel: advice; one who advises; a lawyer. "Give her good counsel."

detract: take away. "Her hair detracts from her beauty."
distract: draw away; disturb. "Do not distract my attention."

device: a contrivance, machine; a trick. "a new device for harvesting beans"
devise: to invent; to plan or work out. "to devise a scheme"

354

eminent: distinguished. "the eminent statesman"
imminent: about to happen. "War is imminent."

fain: eager; willingly; pleased.
feign: pretend. "She feigned complete surprise."

farther: distance in space. "We shall go no farther." [*W.D.S.* 331.]
further: in addition to; progress in time, quantity, degree.

formally: in a formal manner. "He was formally installed in office."
formerly: in the past. "Formerly, he had been a sailor."

healthy: possessing health. "He looks like a healthy boy." [*W.D.S.* 406.]
healthful: giving health. "We live in a healthful climate."

hoards: stores; collections. "The police found hoards of stolen jewels."
hordes: crowds; groups of nomads. "The barbarian hordes were attacking again."

imaginary: existing in the imagination. "Her life is full of imaginary troubles."
imaginative: having imagination; able to imagine. "She wrote an imaginative poem."

implicit: absolute; implied. "implicit obedience to orders; an implicit displeasure."
explicit: distinctly stated; definite. "He gave us explicit directions."

incredible: unbelievable. "Your story is incredible."
incredulous: unwilling to believe. "He was incredulous when I told my story."

informant: one who gives information.
informer: one who accuses or complains.

intrinsic: essential; inherent. "its intrinsic value"
extrinsic: not essential; external.

irrelevant: not to the point. "His question is irrelevant."
irreverent: lacking reverence or respect. "His actions are irreverent."

per cent: part of a hundred. "fifty per cent"
percentage: rate or proportion. "A large percentage of automobiles have faulty brakes."

principal: chief; most important; chief teacher. "the principal occupation; the principal of the school"
principle: a truth; a belief; a scientific rule. "He is a man of high principles."

rend: to tear apart; to disturb. (rend, rent, rent, rending)
rendered: make; give; represent; play or sing. "She rendered a selection."

respectfully: with respect. "Speak to your teacher respectfully."
respectively: each in turn or in order.

stationary: not movable; not changing. "a stationary engine; a stationary enrollment."
stationery: writing materials.

straight: not curved; upright; continuous; direct. "Come straight to the point."
strait: narrow; strict; restricting. "a strait jacket; a strait passage."

Please note that this is merely a check list for quick reference. It will not take the place of a dictionary.

EXERCISES

Exercise 1. In each space at the left write in pencil the complete word as indicated.

_____ 1. love + able

_____ 2. notice + able

_____ 3. care + ful

_____ 4. courage + ous

_____ 5. deplore + able

Exercise 2. On a sheet of paper copy the following words, filling in the blanks with either *ei* or *ie*.

bes—ge	s—zed	w—rd	conc—ve	shr—k
dec—ve	s—ge	spec—s	ach—ve	financ—r

Exercise 3. In the space before each sentence write the number of the correct spelling.

_____ 1. He was (1. benefited   2. benefitted) by a change of diet.

_____ 2. The teacher (1. snaped   2. snapped) her fingers at me.

_____ 3. Gentlemen, what is your (1. preference   2. preferrence)?

_____ 4. Everyone (1. prefered   2. preferred) to remain indoors.

_____ 5. That was a (1. marvelous   2. marvellous) performance.

____ 6. I do not believe in (1. craming   2. cramming) for a test.

____ 7. He was (1. confering   2. conferring) with the captain.

Exercise 4. Write the plurals for the following:

_____ valley   _____ army   _____ baby

_____ lady   _____ attorney   _____ monkey

Exercise 5. From each of the following groups select the correct form.

____ 1. Please (1. wait on   2. wait for) me while I comb my hair.

____ 2. Every boy eats plenty of (1. healthy   2. healthful) food.

____ 3. We bought some paper at the (1. stationery   2. stationary) store.

____ 4. You must exclude all (1. irrelevant   2. irreverent) material.

____ 5. All we could get was an upper (1. berth   2. birth).

____ 6. "The (1. decent   2. descent) is arduous," said Milton.

____ 7. He had a torso like the (1. boll   2. bowl   3. bole) of a tree.

____ 8. Is this the (1. cite   2. sight   3. site) of the new church?

____ 9. All letters are (1. censured   2. censored) by the captain.

____ 10. The actor was surrounded by (1. hordes   2. hoards) of women.

SPELLING LIST

34. The following is a list often misspelled by college students. Memorize ten of these words every day.

1. abbreviate	11. accustom	21. all right
2. absence	12. achievement	22. alley
3. absorption	13. acknowledge	23. allies
4. absurd	14. acquaintance	24. always
5. accept	15. acquitted	25. almost
6. accidentally	16. across	26. although
7. accommodate	17. additionally	27. altogether
8. accomplish	18. address	28. alumna (ae)
9. accompanying	19. affect	29. alumnus (i)
10. accumulate	20. aggravate	30. amateur

31. among
32. amount
33. analysis
34. analyze
35. angel
36. angle
37. annual
38. answer
39. apartment
40. apology
41. apparatus
42. apparent
43. appearance
44. appropriate
45. arctic
46. argument
47. arising
48. arithmetic
49. arrangement
50. artillery
51. ascend
52. association
53. athlete
54. athletics
55. attendance
56. audience
57. auxiliary
58. awkward
59. bachelor
60. balance
61. balloon
62. banana
63. barbarous
64. battalion
65. becoming
66. beggar
67. begging
68. beginning
69. believing
70. benefited
71. biscuit
72. boundaries

73. brilliant
74. Britain
75. Britannica
76. bureau
77. burglar
78. business
79. busy
80. cafeteria
81. calendar
82. candidate
83. can't
84. capital
85. capitol
86. career
87. carburetor
88. cemetery
89. certain
90. changeable
91. changing
92. chaperon
93. characteristic
94. chauffeur
95. choose
96. chose
97. clothes
98. coarse
99. column
100. coming
101. commission
102. committed
103. committee
104. comparative
105. compelled
106. competitive
107. complement
108. compliment
109. compulsory
110. concede
111. conceivable
112. confidently
113. confidentially
114. conference

115. conferred
116. connoisseur
117. conqueror
118. conscience
119. conscientious
120. conscious
121. consciousness
122. continuous
123. controlled
124. convenient
125. courteous
126. criticism
127. criticize
128. curiosity
129. cylinder
130. dealt
131. debater
132. deceive
133. definite
134. describe
135. description
136. despair
137. desperate
138. desert
139. dessert
140. dictionary
141. difference
142. dilapidated
143. dining room
144. disagree
145. disappear
146. disappoint
147. disastrous
148. discipline
149. dissatisfied
150. dissipate
151. divide
152. doctor
153. dormitory
154. during
155. ecstasy
156. eighth

157. eligible
158. eliminate
159. embarrass
160. eminent
161. emphasize
162. employee
163. encouraging
164. engineer
165. enthusiastic
166. equipped
167. equivalent
168. erroneous
169. especially
170. exaggerated
171. exceed
172. excellent
173. except
174. exceptionally
175. exhaust
176. exhilarate
177. existence
178. experience
179. explanation
180. extraordinary
181. extremely
182. familiar
183. fascinate
184. February
185. fiery
186. finally
187. financier
188. foreign
189. forestry
190. formally
191. formerly
192. forty
193. fourth
194. frantically
195. fraternities
196. friend
197. gauge
198. ghost

199. generally
200. government
201. governor
202. grammar
203. grievous
204. guard
205. guidance
206. handkerchief
207. harass
208. having
209. height
210. hindrance
211. hoping
212. humorous
213. hypocrisy
214. illiterate
215. imaginary
216. imagination
217. immediately
218. impromptu
219. incidentally
220. incredible
221. indefinitely
222. independence
223. indictment
224. indispensable
225. inevitable
226. infinite
227. ingenious
228. ingenuous
229. innocence
230. innocuous
231. inoculate
232. instance
233. instants
234. intellectual
235. intelligence
236. intentionally
237. intercede
238. interesting
239. irrelevant
240. irresistible

241. itself
242. knowledge
243. laboratory
244. laid
245. legitimate
246. liable
247. library
248. lightning
249. likely
250. liquefy
251. literature
252. loneliness
253. loose
254. lose
255. lying
256. maintain
257. maintenance
258. maneuver
259. marriage
260. mathematics
261. mattress
262. meant
263. merely
264. millionaire
265. miniature
266. minute
267. mischievous
268. misspelled
269. murmuring
270. muscle
271. naive
272. naturally
273. necessary
274. neither
275. nevertheless
276. ninety
277. ninth
278. noticeable
279. nowadays
280. oblige
281. obstacle
282. occasion

283. occasionally
284. occur
285. occurred
286. occurrence
287. omitted
288. omission
289. oneself
290. opportunity
291. optimistic
292. origin
293. original
294. outrageous
295. paid
296. pamphlet
297. parallel
298. paralysis
299. parliament
300. participle
301. particularly
302. partner
303. pastime
304. peaceable
305. perceive
306. perform
307. perhaps
308. permissible
309. perseverance
310. personal
311. personnel
312. perspiration
313. physically
314. picnicking
315. planned
316. pleasant
317. politics
318. possession
319. practically
320. prairie
321. precede
322. precedence
323. preceding
324. preference

325. preferred
326. prejudice
327. preparation
328. presence
329. presents
330. prevalent
331. principal
332. principle
333. privilege
334. probably
335. proceed
336. professor
337. pronunciation
338. propeller
339. prove
340. quantity
341. questionnaire
342. quiet
343. quite
344. rarefy
345. really
346. receive
347. recognize
348. recommend
349. reference
350. referred
351. regard
352. religious
353. repetition
354. representative
355. respectfully
356. respectively
357. restaurant
358. rhythm
359. rhythmical
360. ridiculous
361. sacrilegious
362. sandwich
363. saxophone
364. schedule
365. secretary
366. seize

367. sense
368. separate
369. sergeant
370. severely
371. siege
372. similar
373. simultaneous
374. soliloquy
375. sophomore
376. specifically
377. specimen
378. speech
379. stationary
380. stationery
381. statue
382. stature
383. statute
384. stopping
385. stretch
386. strictly
387. studying
388. successful
389. superintendent
390. supersede
391. surprise
392. syllable
393. temperament
394. temperature
395. their
396. there
397. they're
398. thorough
399. throughout
400. together
401. tragedy
402. tries
403. truly
404. Tuesday
405. unanimous
406. undoubtedly
407. unnecessary
408. until

409. using
410. usually
411. vilify
412. village

413. villain
414. weather
415. weird
416. whether

417. writing
418. wholly
419. women
420. you're

USE OF THE DICTIONARY

Every college student should own a good desk-size dictionary. When he has occasion to consult an unabridged dictionary, he should use either *Webster's New International* or the Funk and Wagnalls *Standard*. Copies of these are usually to be found in the reference room of the college library.

For desk use the following dictionaries are usually recommended: *Webster's Collegiate*, the Funk and Wagnalls *College Standard*, the *Winston*, and *Macmillan's Modern Dictionary*. In this section all references are to *Webster's Collegiate*, fifth edition.

35. Use your dictionary intelligently to get the following information:

1. *The exact meaning of a word.*

Webster's Collegiate uses the historical order in arranging meanings; most of the others give the most common meanings first. If a word has several meanings, the meanings are grouped and numbered. A word may mean different things under different conditions. You should be careful, when looking up a word, to select the meaning which fits the context and the occasion. See *Webster's*, "Explanatory Notes," sec. 6, p. xxiii.

2. *The correct spelling of a word.*

When two permissible spellings are given side by side, the preferred one is given first: *among, amongst; program, programme.* When two spellings are given in different places in the vocabulary, the preferred form carries the etymology and definitions: *gauge, gage.*

3. The correct pronunciation of a word.

In *Webster's* the word is respelled in parentheses, after the word, in the Webster phonetic alphabet. A brief key to this alphabet is printed at the bottom of every two pages facing each other. See the specimen page from *Webster's.*

One of the main errors in pronunciation is the wrong placing of the accent. Practice pronouncing the following words aloud:

a CU men	acumen	EX qui site	exquisite
a DULT	adult	fi NANCE	finance
a WRY	awry	FOR mi da ble	formidable
as PIR ant	aspirant	in EX o ra ble	inexorable
CAS u al ty	casualty	IN fa mous	infamous
COM bat ant	combatant	ir REP a ra ble	irreparable
con DO lence	condolence	LAM en ta ble	lamentable
CU li nar y	culinary	PREF er a ble	preferable
DEC ade	decade	re COURSE	recourse
DES pi ca ble	despicable	su PER flu ous	superfluous

4. The source or etymology of a word.

In Webster's the etymology is given in brackets before the definition.

inoculate, from *in + oculare,* "to furnish with eyes." Hence when you inoculate a person, you put an eye into him.
recalcitrant, from *recalcitrare,* "to kick back," hence stubborn like a mule.
bowery, from the Dutch word *bouwer,* a farmer, very remote from the modern Bowery.

The following words have unusually interesting origins. Some of these you will have to get from an unabridged dictionary: bedlam, boycott, broker, calico, curfew, daisy, dollar, exhume, lunacy, panic, sandwich, sinister, saxophone, tawdry, thug, vandal.

5. The usage label of a word.

Learn how to use these usage labels, such as *slang, colloquial, archaic, obsolete, vulgar, poetic,* etc. Learn how to read these labels intelligently. The same word may be marked *colloquial* or *slang*

Apostle, whose name is attached to the Fourth Gospel, three Epistles, and the Book of Revelation. **b** (1) The Gospel of John, (2) One of the three Epistles of John.

John Bull (bool). The English nation personified; the English people; also, the, or a, typical Englishman.

John Doe (dō). Law. The fictitious lessee acting as plaintiff in the common-law action of ejectment. Hence, a fictitious name for a party, real or fictitious.

John-Do'ry (dō'rĭ; 70); pl. **John Dorys** (-rĭz). Also **John Do'ree** (-rē). [John + doree, dory, the fish.] A marine fish constituting a family (Zeidae); specif., a common yellow to olive European food fish (Zeus faber), or an allied Australian fish (Zeus australis).

John Han'cock (hăn'kŏk). An autograph signature; — from the legibility of the handwriting of John Hancock.

John'ny-cake' (jŏn'ĭ-kāk'), n. [For journey cake.] U.S. A bread made of Indian meal, flour, eggs, milk, etc.

John'ny-jump'-up', n. Also **Johnny jumper**. a Any of several American violets, as the bird's-foot violet. b U.S. The wild pansy.

John'son-ese' (jŏn'sŭn-ēz'; -ēs'), n. The diction or literary style of Dr. Samuel Johnson, or one formed in imitation of it; — used derogatorily of stilted or pompous style.

John-so'ni-an (jŏn-sō'nĭ-ăn; 58), adj. Pertaining to, or resembling, Dr. Samuel Johnson or his style; derogatorily, pompous; inflated. — n. A follower or copier of Dr. Johnson. — **John-so'ni-an-ism** (-ĭz'm), n.

joie' de vi'vre (zhwä' dē vē'vr'). [F.] Literally, joy in living; hence, zest; keen enjoyment of the pleasures of life.

join (join), v. t. [OF. joindre, fr. L. jungere to yoke, join.] **1.** To connect physically; to unite; to fasten or put together; to couple. **2.** To unite in association, specif., in marriage; to associate oneself with; as, to join the church. **3.** To combine or unite in time, effort, action, consideration, or other immaterial manner; as, to join prayers. **4.** To assemble in a body or group; as, to join forces. **5.** To accept, or engage in, as a contest; as, to join battle. **6.** Colloq. To be adjacent to; adjoin. **7.** Geom. To connect by a line, esp. by a straight line. — v. i. **1.** To come together so as to be connected; to unite; to form a union. **2.** Now Rare. To engage; to join battle.

Syn. — **Join**, combine, unite, consolidate, amalgamate agree in denoting the association, with varying degrees of closeness, of two or more objects. **Join** may express connection of any degree or closeness. **Combine**, rather more than unite, keeps in mind the elements associated; **unite** lays slightly greater emphasis on the resulting unity; as, the combined forces of the allies; the regulation unity, a united family. **Consolidate** emphasizes the compactness or stability arising from the association of the parts; **amalgamate** emphasizes the closeness of their union; as, to consolidate two railroads; an amalgamation of races. — Ant. Separate, sever, disconnect, part.

join the colors. To join a service, as the army or navy.

joint'ress (join'trĕs; -trĭs), n. Law. A woman who has a jointure.

joint stock. Stock or capital held in company; capital held as a common stock of fund.

joint'-stock' com'pa-ny. Law. A company or association, consisting of a number of individuals organized to conduct a business for gain, with a joint stock, the shares owned by any member being transferable without the consent of the rest.

join'ture (join'tụr), n. [OF., fr. L. junctura, fr. jungere to join.] **1.** Obs. A joining; union. **2.** Law. The joint tenancy of an estate, or the estate so held. Obs., except specif.: Orig., an estate settled on a wife to be taken by her in lieu of dower.

joint'weed' (joint'wēd'), n. U.S. An American polygonaceous herb (Polygonella articulata), with jointed, almost leafless stems, and spikelike racemes of small white flowers.

joint'worm' (-wûrm'), n. The larva of any of several small chalcid flies (genus Harmolita, family Eurytomidae), which attack the stems of grain and cause gall-like swellings.

joist (joist), n. [OF. giste, fr. L. jacēre to lie.] a Any of the small timbers or beams ranged parallelwise from wall to wall in a building to support the floor, or the laths or furring strips of a ceiling. b U.S. A stud or scantling about 3 by 4 inches in section.

F Floor; J, J, J Joists.

joke (jōk), n. [L. jocus joke, jest, game.] **1.** Something said or done to excite a laugh; something witty or sportive; jest; witticism. **2.** Something said or done in sport and not seriously. **3.** A laughingstock; as, he is a joke. — Syn. See JEST. — v. i. To do something as a joke; to be merry; to jest. — v. t. To make merry with, to rally; banter; as, to joke a comrade. — Syn. Sport, rally, banter. — **jok'ing-ly** (jōk'ĭng-lĭ), adv.

jok'er (jōk'ẽr), n. **1.** One who jokes; a jester. **2.** a Political Cant. An apparently harmless clause inserted in a legislative bill to render it inoperative or uncertain in some respect without arousing opposition at the time of its passage. **b** Hence, an unsuspected clause in a document, or the like, which nullifies or greatly alters its apparent terms. **3.** Card Playing. An extra card now usually made to accompany the regulation pack. When used, it has special privileges; thus, in euchre it is the best trump.

jole (jōl). Var. of JOWL.

jol'li-er (jŏl'ĭ-ẽr), n. Colloq. One who jollies, flatters, etc.

jol'li-fi-ca'tion (jŏl'ĭ-fĭ-kā'shŭn), n. [Jolly + -fication.] Colloq. A merrymaking; jovial festivity.

—n. Act of joining; place or point of junction.

join'der (join'dēr), n. [F. *joindre*, inf. as n.] **1.** Act of joining; a conjunction. **2.** *Law.* A joining of parties as plaintiffs or defendants in a suit. **b** Acceptance of an issue tendered. **c** A joining of causes of action or defense.

join'er (join'ēr), n. **1.** One who or that which joins. **2.** One whose occupation is to construct articles by joining pieces of wood; a mechanic who does the woodwork (as doors, stairs, etc.) necessary for the finishing of buildings.

join'er-y (-ĭ), n. Also **joiner work.** Art or trade of a joiner; the work of a joiner; also, things made by a joiner.

joint (joint), n. [OF. *joint, jointe*, fr. L. *junctus*, past part. of *jungere, junctum*, to join.] **1.** The part, or the arrangement of the parts, where two bones of an animal's body, or parts of an invertebrate's body, are joined esp. so as to admit of motion; hence, a part in a plant where branches give off. **2.** The part or space included between two articulations, knots, or nodes. **3.** Specif., any of the large pieces of meat as cut for roasting. **4.** The place or part where two others or parts are joined or united; junction; as, a *joint* in a pipe. **5.** *Slang.* A gathering place; loosely, any establishment, resort, etc. **6** *Geol.* A fracture in rock, smaller than a fault and not accompanied by dislocation.

—*adj.* [OF., past part. of *joindre*.] **1.** Joined; combined; specif., *Law*, of the lives of two or more persons, united in time; concurrent. **2** Common to two or more; as: **a** Involving the united activity of two or more. **b** Shared by, or affecting, two or more; specif., in diplomacy, designating an action or expression in which two or more governments unite (dist. from *identic*). **3** United, joined, or sharing with another or with others; acting together; as, *joint* creditor; *joint* debtor. **4** *Parl. Practice.* Of or pertaining to the two branches of a legislative body; as, a *joint* committee.

—*v. t.* **1.** To unite by a joint or joints; to fit together. **2.** To separate the joints; cut up into joints, as meat. **3.** To provide with a joint or joints; to articulate.

joint account. *Banking.* A bank deposit account owned jointly by two or more persons.

joint'ed (join'tĕd; -tĭd), *adj.* Having joints.

joint'er (join'tēr), n. **1.** One who or that which joints; esp., any of various tools used in making joints. **2.** *Agric. Mach.* A triangular-shaped edged attachment to a plow beam for covering trash in plowing.

joint'ly, *adv.* In a joint manner; together; unitedly.

jol'li-fy (jŏl'ĭ-fī), *v. t. & i.*, -FIED (-fīd); -FY'ING. *Colloq.* To make, or to be, jolly.

jol'li-ty (jŏl'ĭ-tĭ), *n.; pl.* -TIES (-tĭz). **1.** State or quality of being jolly; gaiety. **2.** *Brit.* A festive gathering. — Syn. Mirth, joviality, hilarity.

jol'ly (jŏl'ĭ), *adj.*; JOL'LI-ER (-ĭ-ēr); JOL'LI-EST. [OF. *joli, jolif,* joyful, merry.] **1.** Full of spirits; joyful. **2.** Full of life and mirth; jovial; merry. **3.** Expressing or inspiring mirth. **4.** *Colloq.* Splendid; pleasant; also, large; strong. — Syn. See JOCULAR. — **jol'li-ly,** *adv.* — **jol'li-ness,** *n.*

jol'ly, *n.; pl.* JOLLIES (-ĭz). **1.** *Brit. Sailors' Slang.* A marine. **2.** *Colloq.* Something said or done to keep a person or people in good humor or quiet. **3.** *Slang, Eng.* A social meeting for mirth and good cheer. — *v. t.*; JOL'-LIED (-ĭd); JOL'LY-ING. *Colloq.* To encourage to feel pleasant or cheerful; — often implying a bantering spirit; hence, to poke fun at; rally. — *v. i.* **1.** To be or act jolly. **2.** *Colloq.* To jolly a person or people.

jolly boat. *Naut.* A boat of medium size belonging to a ship, used for general rough or small work.

jolt (jōlt), *v. i. & t.* **1.** To shake with short, abrupt risings and fallings, as a carriage moving on rough ground; to jar; boxing, a jarring blow. — **jolt'er,** *n.*
—*n.* A butt, knock, or blow; a sudden shock or jerk; in

Jo'nah (jō'nà), *n.* [Heb. *Yōnāh*, lit., dove.] **1.** *Bib.* A Hebrew prophet, who, during a tempest sent by God because of his disobedience, was cast overboard from his ship, swallowed by a great fish, and remained in its belly three days before being cast out. **2.** The book of the Old Testament that tells his story.
3. One who brings ill luck.

Jon'a-than (jŏn'à-thăn), *n.* [Heb. *Yōnā-thān*.] *Bib.* Son of Saul, and friend of David.

Jon'a-than, *n.* *Hort.* A late autumn variety of red apple.

jon'gleur' (zhôn'glûr'; jŏng'glēr), *n.* [F. See JUGGLER.] In medieval France and Norman England, an itinerant minstrel who recited or sang by way of entertainment, as at courts.

jon'quil (jŏng'kwĭl; jŏn'-; still by some, jĭng'kwĭl), *n.* [F. *jonquille*, fr. Sp. *junquillo* jonquil, reed, dim. of *junco* a rush, fr. L. *juncus*.] A bulbous plant (*Narcissus Jonquil,* (⅜) *jonquilla*) of southern Europe and Algeria, with long, rushlike leaves, and yellow or white, single or

āle, chāotic, cāre, ǎdd, ǎccount, ärm, ȧsk, sofá; ēve, hēre, ĕnd, ẽvent, ēnd, silĕnt, makẽr; īce, Ĭll, charÍty; ōld, ōbey, ôrb, ŏdd, sŏft, cŏnnect; fōod, fŏŏt; out, oil; cūbe, ûnite, ûrn, ŭp, circŭs, menü;

By permission. From Webster's Collegiate Dictionary
Fifth Edition
Copyright, 1936, 1941, by G. & C. Merriam Co.

in one sense; it may be acceptable on all levels of usage in another sense. The word *pinch*, for instance, is labeled *slang* only in the sense of *to steal* or *to arrest*.

Find, in *Webster's*, the usage label for each of the following:

blitz	crack down	jive
boloney	dither	spunky
corny	in the groove	tote

6. Grammatical information.

Your dictionary will give you full information about the plurals of nouns and the principal parts of verbs. In *Webster's*, inflectional forms are given when they are irregular or present difficulties of spelling or pronunciation. For example, no information is given about the plurals of *handkerchief*, *book*, *house* because it is assumed that these words form their plural in the normal way. But after *index* you find two plurals, *indexes*, *indices;* after *deer* you find the information that the plural is also *deer;* after *ox* you find "*pl.* OXEN, *rarely* OX." Similarly, you find no information about principal parts after a verb like *talk*, which is regular, but after *blow* you find BLEW; BLOWN; BLOWING.

7. Correct idioms.

The *Webster's Collegiate* gives fewer idioms than the *International*, it is true, but it gives enough to interest any student. Here are a few samples: fight shy of; hang together; lay by the heels; lay hold of; take stock; take the floor; work one's passage.

EXERCISES

Exercise 1. Look up the meaning of each of the following words. In what different senses is each of these words commonly used?

aggravate	fellow	nice
homely	irony	curious
criticize	hobby	minute

Exercise 2. Look up each of the following. In the spaces provided write *1* or *2* to show, respectively, if the first or the second form is the preferred spelling.

_____ theater or theatre		_____ judgement or judgment	
_____ good-by or good-bye		_____ advisor or adviser	
_____ today or to-day		_____ mould or mold	
_____ enrolment or enrollment		_____ dramatize or dramatise	
_____ honor or honour		_____ chlorin or chlorine	
_____ sulfur or sulphur		_____ colour or color	

Exercise 3. Determine the preferred pronunciation of each of the following.

either	coupon	decile	literature
neither	italics	column	vehement
suite	garage	vagary	precedence

THE RIGHT WORD

36a. Use the right word.

The right word for you — and for every writer — is the word which does exactly what it has been told to do. Every word that you write is, in a way, an accredited ambassador sent from your mind to the mind of another person. It has an obligation placed upon it, but, at the same time, it must serve you under many handicaps. Since it is but a word — a symbol, a coin, and not the thought or sense image that is in your mind — it cannot *convey* what is in your mind to the mind of another. It has merely the power to suggest, to call forth, something which is already in his mind. Once a word goes out as your messenger, it begins to function independently. You lose control over it. It does its work in terms of its own reputation, its family history, its background. Its reputation, moreover, like the reputation of a person, is not something it carries with it like a halo. It exists in the mind of the person to whom it delivers your thought. Let us illustrate. "What that man writes is poetry," you say. "Ah — poetry!" thinks your reader. "That means exaltation of the spirit, melody, nobility of sentiment, beauty!" "Oh — poetry!" thinks another. "That means he is confused, inflated, high flown, hard to understand!"

Recently there has been a revival of interest in semantics, the ancient science of meanings. One fact which the new semanticists have stressed especially is that words have a tendency to acquire emotional meanings. Now it is quite proper that they do, for language is the medium through which we express emotions as well as thoughts. The point that these semanticists are making, however, is that emotionally colored words interfere with straight thinking and the ability of language to evoke ideas. Consider such words and phrases as *liberty, democratic forms of government, justice, a fair trial, freedom of speech, communist, progressive,* and so on. Do these words mean the same thing to us and to our friends in Europe?

We speak of certain attributes of words — their denotation and their connotation. The **denotation** of a word is its actual, literal meaning. The word *mother* means "a female parent, especially one of the human race." The word *bread* means "dough made from the flour or meal of grain, moistened, raised, kneaded, and baked." But when you see the word *mother* on this printed page, does it mean the same to you as *a female parent?* When you say, "Give us this day our daily bread," are you actually thinking of "dough or meal, moistened, raised, kneaded, and baked"? The difference lies not in words themselves but in their power to call up associations and experiences. This power to suggest associated images or emotions we designate by another label — **connotation.** What the word *mother* calls up in your mind we cannot know exactly; nor can you foretell, when you use the word, what it will call up in the mind of any of your readers. You cannot foretell *exactly,* yet you do know, by drawing upon the fund of common human experience, that the word *mother* ordinarily suggests love, unselfish devotion, a home, warmth, kindness — all pleasant associations. There are other words, like *rat, snake, traitor,* which ordinarily call up unpleasant associations. But "a female parent" — these are cold, sterilized words.

Choose your words with care, with due regard for their literal as well as for their associated meanings. Your dictionary through the definitions, the synonyms, and the illustrations of correct use, will help you find the exact meanings of words. What the dictionary cannot tell you, you must learn through reading, listening, and living.

The whole subject of the "meaning of meaning" can easily float up into the clouds of metaphysics, yet for the beginner there are a number of common-sense guides which are distinctly helpful.

1. Words associated with everyday living have more emotional power than scientific terms or literary terms. Both have their place in writing. If you are aiming at exact scientific exposition, you should use one type; if you want to give power to your words, you should use the other.

2. Specific words usually carry more associated meanings than do general words.

3. Concrete words usually call up emotions quicker than do abstract words. Note the following contrasted groups of expressions:

Homely words	*Bookish words*
Marriage, a bed, breakfast, my son, our church, a lie, to eat, to dig, to plow.	Matrimony, a couch, the matutinal meal, a male descendent, a religious organization, prevarication, to devour, to delve, to cultivate.

Specific words	*General words*
An armchair, a smock, a carving knife, a frying pan, murder, a welder, a violet, our old black cat.	Furniture, apparel, cutlery, kitchen utensils, a crime, an industrial worker, a flower, an animal.

Concrete words	*Abstract words*
She served him like a dog; my mother hummed a lullaby; a splinter of shrapnel ripped open his right arm; he was drunk as a lord.	The faithfulness of an animal, the harmony of music, a misfortune of battle, extreme intoxication.

And now that we have learned the constructive principles involved, we should ask whether there are any specific traps to avoid. Here again your dictionary should be your friend in helping you to guard against the following common errors in the use of words:

1. Words used in the wrong sense because they are confused with other words similar in sound but different in meaning.

Wrong: She was so *credible* that she would believe anything.
Right: She was so *credulous* that she would believe anything.

Wrong: The Camp Fire girls went out in a *charted* launch.
Right: The Camp Fire girls went out in a *chartered* launch.

Wrong: Tom was severely *censored* for his editorial.
Right: Tom was severely *censured* for his editorial.

See section 33 for a list of words similar in form but different in meaning. Here are a few more that are frequently confused:

allusion: an indirect reference. "No one understood his allusion." A person "alludes" to something indirectly; he "refers" to it directly.
illusion: a false appearance; a false belief. "Love is an illusion."

alternate: a substitute or double. "I have an alternate method to suggest."
alternative: an option or choice. "His orders gave us no alternative."

contemptible: deserving contempt. "He is a contemptible person."
contemptuous: showing contempt. "His attitude toward us was contemptuous."

disinterested: unprejudiced; without bias.
uninterested: without interest; indifferent.

infer: to draw a conclusion from facts.
imply: to hint or suggest. [See *Webster's Dictionary of Synonyms*, p. 449.]

ingenious: clever; skillful.
ingenuous: innocent; frank; open.

proposal: something proposed or suggested; an offer. [See *W.D.S.* 659.]
proposition: a formal statement for discussion or debate.

sensual: base; lustful. [See *W.D.S.* 738.]
sensuous: pertaining to or perceived by the senses.

2. Words twisted out of their customary meaning.

Wrong: Three grimy urchins were gazing *awfully* at General Clark.
Right: Three grimy urchins were gazing *with awe* (*in awe*) at General Clark.

Wrong: Peggy set out to clean her *disheveled* room. [Refers to hair.]
Right: Peggy set out to clean her *untidy* room.

3. Words so used that they produce unintentional humor.

Poor: Finally, at midnight, I sat down to *learn my history.*
Better: Finally, at midnight, I sat down to *study my history lesson.*

Poor: A college teacher should not at all times be a *sober* person, but he should wear a smile and occasionally tell a joke.
Better: A college teacher need not be *solemn* at all times; occasionally he may smile or crack a joke.

4. Vague, blanket words, such as *factor, proposition, point of view, line, majority,* and so on.

Poor: Weather conditions are excellent this spring *in the line of* truck gardening.
Better: Truck gardeners have had excellent weather this spring.

Poor: An orchestra was an *essential factor* because in such a large hall no other source could make the music be heard.
Better: In such a large hall only an orchestra could play music loud enough to be heard.

36b. Use words that are in keeping with the subject of your paper, with the occasion, and with the readers you are addressing.

Some of the papers that you write are formal; some are informal. When you write a serious discussion of a serious subject, you must use language that is dignified but not pretentious or affected. Every intelligent person has different styles of writing at his command just as he has clothes appropriate for different occasions. The words you choose should be appropriate. They should not attend a formal dinner in sweater and slacks, or a football game in tails and white tie. Students of writing often assume that writing is hedged in by too many "dont's." Perhaps there *are* rules and conventions, just as there are conventions and decencies which govern human intercourse everywhere else — at the dinner table, on a streetcar, at a dance, at a football game, in business. A writer's good sense is his best rule of conduct. In scientific writing, technical words are appropriate. In everyday informal writing, everyday informal language is best.

Inappropriate in formal writing:

After that but one practicable course presented itself to the Progressives, and that was *to gang up with* the Democrats. [to collaborate with.]

We must have enough faith in our institutions to believe that they can *stand the gaff* of a world war. [withstand the effects.]

Even during the war the British government refused to *do away with* the right of free speech in England. [abolish.]

Inappropriate in informal writing:

When I came back three years later I was surprised at his *decrepitude*. [I was surprised to see how worn and feeble he was.]

We paused just long enough *to pen a brief epistle* to our mother. [to write a short letter.]

EXERCISES

Exercise 1. Find the synonyms which the *Roget Dictionary of Synonyms and Antonyms* gives for the following words: work, handsome, beautiful, dull, strenuous, keen, large, interesting.

Exercise 2. Find *Webster's Dictionary of Synonyms* in your college library. Bring to class a report of what this book has to say about each of the following pairs: ability and capacity; effective and effectual; proposal and proposition.

Exercise 3. Pronounce each of the following words in turn. First try to determine whether your general reaction is pleasant or unpleasant. Then write down a number of words which come to your mind. In this manner you will come close to understanding what is meant by connotation.

1. snake	5. teacher	9. smoke
2. cheap	6. cowboy	10. lady
3. uniform	7. radical	11. altar
4. Sunday	8. shepherd	12. foreigner

Exercise 4. In each of the following groups write *F* above the word most appropriate in formal writing, and *I* above the word most appropriate in ordinary informal writing.

1. Apparel, duds, garb, clothes, habilament.

2. Repast, nutriment, food, sustenance, grub, victuals.

3. Marriage, matrimony, nuptials.

4. Adversary, foe, antagonist, enemy.

5. To imbibe, to carouse, to drink, to quaff, to tipple, to booze.

Exercise 5. In the following sentences point out and correct the errors in the use of words.

1. School functions are a seldom source of recreation.
2. The expedition transversed the jungle in thirteen days.
3. Through this exercise their ankles are slenderized and their arches strengthened.
4. I was able to piece together small bits of information and to make an exacting statement about its purpose.
5. The new homes are owned by the white-collar workers, which includes clerks through store owners.
6. His dog spent the majority of the day sleeping in the shipping room.
7. Soon his resolve to study will melt under such detractions as radio music or loud talk in the smoking room.
8. He was best known for his ability to assume endless "cokes" at the campus "coke bar."
9. Johnny may be the clown of his fraternity house and a perfect grudge at home.
10. This book deals with the humor side of publishing.
11. My roommate takes a sadistic delight in pointing out my fallacies.
12. Three long years in the army changed my point of view on life.
13. The outer epidermis of her face was loricated with incalculable numbers of freckles.
14. There are many factors in college which contribute toward a reconversion of one's attitude toward success.
15. The customs of college life outrule many silly high-school pranks.
16. She comes from a rich family situated somewhere in Florida.

17. He is the sort who will keep working unrelentlessly until he collapses.
18. Of course there were rumors that the Dean would overthrow this new college activity.
19. He is constantly experimenting with hybridizing cacti, hoping to render a new variety in that field.
20. A happy social life and a benefiting occupation are two of the goals I have set out for myself.

IDIOMS

37a. Use the correct English idiom.

An idiom is an expression peculiar to a language. An idiom may be (it is not always so) irrational, untranslatable, even ungrammatical. How can one, literally, *pick a quarrel* with a person who is *beside himself with anxiety?* How can one translate "How do you do?" into French or German? Because idioms are created out of the day-to-day living of ordinary men and women, they are themselves alive, pungent, racy. They are truly the heart of the language. But it is highly misleading to say, as has often been said, that idiomatic speech is that used by cultivated Englishmen. Many idioms border on slang; many of the idioms now accepted as part of the language were roundly denounced by cultivated but squeamish English gentlemen of a former day.

You must not think that the study of English idiom concerns itself with a few illogical phrases like those just mentioned, or with a score or so of verbs that must always be used with certain prepositions. Vizetelly and De Bekker in *Idioms and Idiomatic Phrases* [1] list 498 pages of idioms. You cannot memorize all the idioms in the English language. At best you can cultivate a different attitude toward idiomatic speech — an attitude of curiosity and understanding.

Many idiomatic phrases have grown up around the verbs of everyday living — to go, to do, to get, to make, to take. Notice the following idioms. Some of them are still restricted by convention to speech or informal writing; some of them are correct in any kind of writing.

[1] Funk and Wagnalls Company, New York, 1923.

To do:

I am *done for*. (vanquished, ruined)
We shall *do away with* poverty. (abolish)
He *did* himself *proud*. (distinguished)

To make:

She *made faces* at her mother. (grimaced)
He *made free* with my money. (squandered)
He *made good*. (succeeded)
He *made off* with the jewels. (escaped)
I cannot *make out* what he is saying. (understand)
Please *make sure* of it. (be certain)

To go:

He *goes in for* gardening. (indulges)
He'll *go to the dogs*. (to ruin)
It *goes without saying*. (is self-evident)

To take:

He was *taken aback*. (surprised)
Take it from me. (believe)
She *takes after* her mother. (resembles)
Take hold of the rope. (grasp)
Take him *in hand*. (deal with)
Take him *down a peg*. (humble)

To get:

She will *get along*. (succeed)
The dean will *get wind of it*. (hear)
The fish *got away*. (escaped)
He will *get on with* mother. (be on friendly terms)

A study of the following list will help you avoid a few common mistakes in the use of idiom. The expressions in the first list are all under suspicion for some reason or other. Some are common in speech, but most of them are objectionable in the sort of writing

375

you will do in college. (The numbers in parentheses refer to the sections in which the expressions are discussed.)

Under suspicion	*Preferred in formal use*
all-around (75)	all-round (*still colloq.*)
all the farther (75)	as far as
all the faster (75)	as fast as
anyplace, anywheres (75)	anywhere
blame it on him (75)	blame him for it
cannot help but laugh (6d)	cannot help laughing
complected (75)	complexioned
different than (75)	different from
equally as bad (75)	equally bad
feel of it	feel it
in back of (75)	behind
inside a year (75)	within a year
near enough that	near enough to
no doubt but that (6d)	no doubt that
nowhere near enough (75)	not nearly enough
off of (75)	off
out loud (75)	aloud
over with (41)	over
remember of (75)	remember
stay to home	stay at home
tend to the sick	tend the sick
try and get it	try to get it
very interested (51)	very much interested
want in (off, out) (75)	want to come in (to get off, to go out)
where are we at? (41)	where are we?

EXERCISES

Exercise 1. In the following pairs select the correct idiom and write its number at the left. Reference: Fowler's *A Dictionary of Modern English Usage,* "Cast-Iron Idiom."

____ 1. entertained to a dinner	2. entertained at a dinner
____ 1. of his own accord	2. on his own accord
____ 1. contented himself with saying	2. contented himself by saying
____ 1. get the upper hand	2. get the better hand
____ 1. to a great measure	2. in a great measure
____ 1. promoted to a professor	2. promoted to a professorship
____ 1. rise equal to the occasion	2. rise to the occasion

Exercise 2. In *Webster's New International Dictionary* find the idioms listed under the following words. Bring these to class for discussion.

have	pick	hand	home	mouth
eat	stand	head	heart	horse
run	hang	foot	word	dog

37b. Use the accepted prepositions after verbs, participles, adjectives and nouns.

The following list will not take the place of an unabridged dictionary. It will serve merely as a check list to put you on your guard. Consult the dictionary for more complete information.

abstain from
accede to
accommodate to (to conform)
accommodate with (to furnish, oblige)
acquiesce in
acquit of
addicted to
adept in
adequate for
adhere to
agree to (a thing)
agree with (a person)
agree in (opinion)
agreeable to
angry with (a person)
angry at (a thing)
apprehensive of (danger)
apprehensive for (one's safety)
averse to
capable of
careless of, about
characteristic of
compare to (for illustration)
compare with (to examine qualities)
concern in (be interested)
concerned for (troubled)
concerned with (involved)

concur in (an opinion)
concur with (agree with a person)
confide in (entrust a secret)
confide to (entrust)
conform to, with
consist in, of
contend for (to argue)
contend with (opposition)
contrast with
desire for
desirous of
desist from
devoid of
differ about
differ from (things)
differ with (a person)
different from
disagree with
disdain for
dissent from
distaste for
empty of
envious of
expert in
foreign to
guard against
hint at
identical with

independent of
infer from
initiate into
inseparable from
jealous of
laugh at, over
mastery of (a subject)
mastery over (self)
need of, for
negligent of
obedient to
oblivious of
part with, from
plan to
prefer to
preparatory to
prerequisite to
prior to
proficient in
profit by
prohibit from
protest against

reason with
regret for
repugnant to
resemblance between, to
responsible for, to
revel in
rewarded for, by, with
sensible of
sensitive to
separate from
subscribe to, for
substitute for
superior to
sympathize with
tamper with
treat of, with
try to
unconscious of
unmindful of
variance with
vexed at, with
vie with

EXERCISE

Exercise 1. Point out and correct the errors in idiom in the following sentences.

1. Tomorrow night the Beavers will vie against the Spartans on the local basketball floor.
2. All the girls are planning on attending the game.
3. He was acquitted from all charges of negligence.
4. Can we blame her for being desirous for beauty and happiness?
5. I am sorry to differ from you about its usefulness.
6. Are we prohibited against attending any dances?
7. He was always an expert on the use of language to deceive.
8. Unmindful to the noise, he continued reading his newspaper.
9. She expressed a distaste against vulgar speech.
10. How can anyone be angry at her?

GOOD USE

38. In formal writing avoid the frequent use of colloquialisms; in any kind of writing avoid all crude, trite, or dull slang.

Your choice of words is governed by common-sense standards of appropriateness and good taste. As we have seen, you choose the language level at which you wish to express and communicate your thoughts. If your occasion is informal, you write in an informal, easy manner. If you are writing a dignified, formal discussion of a serious subject, your words, by established tradition, must meet certain tests. A word is said to be "in good use" if it is in present use, in national use, and in reputable use. It is in good use if it belongs to our time and age, not to the past; if it is accepted and used throughout the entire country; if it is recognized and accepted by educated men and women.

The following definitions and discussions may help you to decide what kinds of words you should use and what kinds you should avoid.

Slang has been defined as a kind of made-to-order language, characterized by extravagant or grotesque fancy or humor. Greenough and Kittredge, in *Words and Their Ways in English Speech*, speak of it as "a peculiar kind of vagabond language, always hanging on the outskirts of legitimate speech, but continually straying or forcing its way into the most respectable company." But they also add, "in fact, slang may be called the only living language, the only language in which these processes [growth of the language] can be seen in full activity." And this, although not strictly accurate, is a passable definition. It is also true that slang expressions, like weeds after a shower, sprout into life quickly, but most of them also die quickly. Reputable words, like a forest of redwoods, may grow for a thousand years, and although there may be less violent activity in a redwood than there is in a weed, it also is alive.

Here are a few examples to reinforce our definition. The following are labeled slang in *Webster's New International Dictionary:*

savvy, hooey, to neck, scram, a gat, to take the rap, jalopy, jive, gripe, trigger man, corny.

Colloquialisms are not wrong in themselves. They are expressions correct in conversation, in informal speeches and writing, or in familiar letters, but not in formal writing. There has been much pedantic nonsense taught college students about colloquialisms. As Professor Kittredge has pointed out, every educated person uses colloquial English, and, what is very important to remember, he uses it correctly if he uses it appropriately. He uses formal English correctly when formal English is more appropriate, when he dresses up in his literary clothes, as it were. Your practical problem will be to determine when an occasion is formal and when it is informal. It might be a safe rule for you to guard against too free and informal a style, to err a little on the side of formality and dignity. And then it is just possible that your written English is stiff, prosy, and barren because you are afraid to use the language that is natural to you. If this is true, remember that it is better to write forcefully and informally than to write with stiff and ineffective formality.

Here are a few expressions marked *colloq.* in *Webster's New International Dictionary:*

to go in for, to go west (to die), *to get ahead of* (to surpass), *to fix one's hair, to get away with* (to carry off, to defeat), *to fire* (to eject forcibly), *a fish story, to make no bones about it, to take a brace, to take the road, to walk into* (to attack), *to set one's cap for, I'll, haven't, shan't, exam, lab, dorm, thusly.*

Provincialisms, often called localisms or dialectal expressions, are to be avoided in formal writing because, theoretically, these words run the risk of not being understood outside their native district. The warning against provincialism has become a bit of traditional futility, since newspapers, magazines, the radio, and the motion pictures have made known the speech of even the most isolated and backward regions. We may not ourselves use *I reckon, out of kilter,* or *you-all,* but we certainly know what these expressions mean. The provincialisms which are not generally understood very few college students will be tempted to use.

A word is **obsolete** if it is no longer in use. A word is **archaic** if it is too old-fashioned to be generally used. Here are a few examples of words or special meanings that have fallen by the wayside: *consecute* (to follow closely), *whilom* (formerly), *smug* (a blacksmith), *sim* (to simmer), *homespun* (a rustic person), *to face* (to brag), *a fellow* (a partner). The average college freshman will find little occasion to worry about archaic words in his vocabulary.

Words that are in some way twisted out of their proper use and form are given such names as vulgarisms, barbarisms, and improprieties. Fortunately for the student who is more interested in effective writing than in linguistic classifications, these terms, perhaps having succumbed to the diseases they sought to cure, are now more or less obsolescent. One dictionary, for instance, uses the words *impropriety, neologisms, obsolete, provincial* in a definition of *barbarism*, and quotes *burgle, undoubtably,* and *lab* as examples. Then in the vocabulary it labels *burgle* as *humorous, undoubtably* as *obsolete* except as *dialectal* and *illiterate,* and *lab* as *colloquial.*

Any student who is interested in words will find it profitable to look through some of the following books:

FOR POPULAR READING:

Barfield, Owen, *History in English Words,* George H. Doran Company, New York, 1924.

Greenough, James B., and George Lyman Kittredge, *Words and Their Ways in English Speech,* The Macmillan Company, New York, 1901, 1923.

Herbert, A. P., *What a Word!* Doubleday, Doran and Company, New York, 1936.

McKnight, George H., *English Words and Their Background,* D. Appleton and Company, New York, 1923.

Smith, S. Stephenson, *The Command of Words,* Thomas Y. Crowell Company, New York, 1935.

FOR THE SCHOLARS:

Fowler, H. W., *A Dictionary of Modern English Usage,* Oxford, 1926.
Kennedy, Arthur G., *Current English,* Ginn and Company, Boston, 1935.

Krapp, George Philip, *The Knowledge of English*, Henry Holt and Company, New York, 1927.

Robertson, Stuart, *The Development of Modern English*, Prentice-Hall, Inc., New York, 1934.

Smith, Logan Pearsall, *Words and Idioms*, Houghton Mifflin Company, Boston, 1925.

A DICTIONARY OF SLANG:

Berrey, Lester V., and Melvin Van Den Bark, *The American Thesaurus of Slang*, Thomas Y. Crowell Company, New York, 1942.

CONCRETENESS

39. Use the concrete and specific word in preference to the abstract and general.

A concrete noun names something that can be perceived through any of the senses, such as *stove, robin, fog, shoe, coffee, smoke, clatter, ice*. An abstract word names a quality, as *virtue, devotion, enmity*. General words name classes or groups; specific words name the individual objects, actions, or qualities which compose the groups. Thus *weapon* is a general noun; *rifle, bayonet, bolo, dagger* are specific kinds of weapons. *Move* is a general verb; *stride, amble, fly, trot, glide, drift* are all specific forms of *move*. The adjective *bright* is general; *dazzling, sparkling, luminous, shiny* are more specific forms of brightness.

Abstract and general words, it is true, are necessary in a language; we must have them to express abstract qualities and general ideas. The principle, however, will serve you well, as your danger will be the too frequent use of general words. And even when you are expressing a general idea or an abstract concept, you can make it clearer by means of concrete example or illustration. Here are a few examples:

General and ineffective:
The soldier was wounded while performing an act of heroism.

Specific and concrete:
Private Tony Dombrowski had three machine-gun slugs rip through his back while he was dragging his wounded sergeant to the safety of a shell hole.

Ineffective:
He removed his shoes and walked along more comfortably in his bare feet.

More vivid:
He leaned down and untied the laces, slipped off first one shoe and then the other. And he worked his damp feet comfortably in the hot dry dust until little spurts of it came up between his toes, and until the skin on his feet tightened with dryness. — John Steinbeck, *The Grapes of Wrath.*

Ineffective:
We drove happily through the countryside, admiring the beautiful scenery along the road.

More vivid:
As the horse's back rose and fell gently, like a ship, between the shafts, the countryside slipped past — misted woods, glimpses of park land, a grey mansion with tall chimneys, terraces and glasshouses, amongst the steaming trees. — A. J. Cronin, *The Green Years.*

Ineffective:
We noticed a girl sitting in a chair and crying.

More vivid:
She was sitting deep down in the chair, with her knees high up and pressed together, while her head was cast down on her lap and her two hands held a handkerchief to her eyes. And her body heaved spasmodically as she sobbed. — Liam O'Flaherty, *Spring Sowing.*

EXERCISES

Exercise 1. Find several specific words for each of the following general words.

tree	building	furniture	to hit
ship	clothing	vehicle	to clean
grass	bird	slow	to oppose
animal	road	to laugh	to play

Exercise 2. Construct sentences in which you give concrete examples of each of the following abstract terms:

thoughtfulness	modesty	loyalty
fear	hope	pleasure
horror	delight	speed
dullness	gratitude	friendliness
humility	thoroughness	efficiency

Exercise 3. Try to determine which word in each of the following groups is the most specific:

1. Bird, ptarmigan, grouse, large bird.
2. Rodent, animal, small animal, rat, pack rat.
3. Ship, vessel, sailing ship, schooner, merchant ship.
4. Bad, depraved, wrong, sinful.
5. Superior, good, healthful, adequate.

Exercise 4. Rewrite the following sentences, making them more specific and concrete.

1. Various objects littered the table.
2. A woman was carefully cleaning the kitchen.
3. The girl's features were unattractive.
4. The man was armed with a dangerous weapon.
5. The bright-colored shrubs contrasted with the dark foliage of the trees.
6. My sister expressed her displeasure.
7. The morning air was sweet with the songs of many birds.
8. A moving vehicle passed him at high speed.
9. As he passed the house, a dog barked at him.
10. He seated himself upon the nearest article of furniture.

VIVIDNESS

40. Select words which give life and freshness to your style.

If you avoid dull, colorless, and trite expressions, if you avoid worn-out slang, if you avoid general and abstract words, you may have, instead of a vigorous and lively style, a head full of negative rules that will keep you from saying anything at all. Mere avoidance of dullness does not create a vivid style. But you do have positive and practical aids as well as negative cautions:

1. Use nouns which are exact and which call up definite sense images. This is just another way of saying that specific words are more vivid than general words. When you say, "I heard a bird singing," your words may call up a definite sense image in the mind of your reader — or they may not — but you do not know what that image is. If instead of "bird" you say "meadow lark" or "hermit thrush," your reader will at least make an effort to recall the song of the meadow lark or the hermit thrush. Whenever you use a specific noun, you make it easy for your reader's mind to create a specific image. You do more than suggest images by your words; you direct the picture making that goes on in your reader's brain.

2. Use adjectives that are bold, vital, alive — adjectives that carry their heads high and strut as if they were proud to be on your pages. You may overwrite, it is true, but overwriting is a sin that may in time lead to a freer style. Your teacher can prune luxuriant eloquence, but what can he do for you if you offer him merely a few spindly, anemic plants? What are some of these anemic adjectives in your vocabulary? You say, "That was a *good* lecture," when you mean that it was *witty, stimulating, eloquent, instructive, entertaining*, or *informative*. You say, "She is a *nice* girl," when you mean that she is *friendly, sympathetic, generous, vivacious, modest, talented*, or *conventional*. What adjectives can you find that are more vivid than *pleasant, dull, swell, big, easy, hard?* A book of synonyms will help you find them.

3. Use verbs that carry in themselves the descriptive force of a modifying adverb. A verb-adverb group may often be replaced more effectively by a single verb. Study the following examples:

He ran quickly. (He fled, sprinted, trotted, rushed, surged.)
He was breathing rapidly. (He was panting, blowing, wheezing, puffing, gasping.)
He cut through it. (He pierced it, sliced it, tore it open, split it, ripped it open.)
He threw it down violently. (He hurled it, flung it, heaved it, pitched it.)

4. Use specific instead of general verbs. Study the following examples. Notice that some verbs are general; they name the

action but they do not describe the manner of the action. Other verbs are descriptive.

He moved toward the door. (He crept, crawled, strolled, sidled, inched, drifted, flitted toward the door.)
He spoke several words. (He whispered, roared, shouted, hissed, mumbled, muttered several words.)
We put it on the wagon. (We tossed, lifted, pitched, threw it on the wagon.)
He got on the horse. (He scrambled, leaped, jumped, vaulted on the horse.)

5. Use figures of speech to give vividness and concreteness to your style.

Similes and metaphors will help you present your facts and ideas with the aid of pictures. Every figure of speech uses a picture, an image. Hence it is concrete. Try to get a few figures of speech into everything that you write. Disregard the old warning, so often directed at students, not to force figures when figures will not come of their own accord. It is true that effective figures are natural and spontaneous — at least they must seem so, no matter what creative pains their author went through in producing them. But you will never learn how to use figures unless you wheedle and coax and even bully them into life while you are learning to write. After a time, when you are more sure of yourself, you will be able to create a natural, unforced, spontaneous, and appropriate figure of speech in a half hour of grim mental struggle. Whatever you do, be not tempted to use a worn or trite figure. Forced or spontaneous, let it be your own.

The following are the most commonly used figures of speech:

1. A simile is an expressed comparison, usually with *like* or *as*.

The water lay gray and wrinkled like an elephant's skin. — Nancy Hale.

She barged in with the children like a bomber escorted by fighters. — Margaret Halsey.

When her husband entered she looked up, and her lips curved and parted; her eyelids fluttered twice or thrice — a movement remindful (Poesy forgive us!) of the tail-wagging of a faithful dog — and a little ripple went through her like the commotion set up in a weeping willow by a puff of wind. — O. Henry.

2. A metaphor is an implied comparison.

Youth is a blunder; manhood a struggle; old age a regret. — Disraeli.

Life is a tale told by an idiot.

Love is a delightful day's journey.

3. Personification gives to inanimate objects the qualities of a person.

The mountains reached up their bulky shoulders to receive the level gallop of Apollo's homing steeds, the day died in the lagoons and in the shadowed banana groves. . . . — O. Henry.

The sun sharpened its light across a razor edge of hills. — Allis McKay.

A log in the fire was singing to itself, as if the sound of summer rustlings and chirpings had been stored away in its sap. — Sarah Orne Jewett.

4. Hyperbole is poetic exaggeration or overstatement.

Was this the face that launched a thousand ships,
And burnt the topless towers of Ilium?
Sweet Helen, make me immortal with a kiss!
          — Christopher Marlowe.

5. Metonymy and synecdoche, two very similar figures, name an object by sign, by a part for the whole, by material for the object.

The following are common examples: *sheepskin* for *diploma*, a good *table* for *food*, *pigskin* for *football*, *redcoat* for *soldier*, *skirt* for *girl*, etc.

For more examples of figures of speech and a discussion of unsuccessful attempts at figurative language, see section 59.

WORDINESS

41. Avoid wordiness.

If you are curious about the prolix hierarchy of wordiness, investigate the following words in an unabridged dictionary:

pleonasm, redundancy, verbosity, verbiage, prolixity, diffuseness, cir-cumlocution, and *periphrasis.* These various children of Father Wordiness were known by name to the college students of your grandfather's day. It is not recorded anywhere that as a result they wrote less wordily.

But what advice can be given to the student who is more interested in good writing than in classifications of bad writing? To say, "Do not write in circles," is not enough. To say, "Write simply and directly," may be misleading. When are words unnecessary? What is meant by writing simply and directly? A style rich in concrete detail is not wordy. Mere length is not wordiness. A short story is not better than a novel merely because it is shorter. A good essay might possibly be compressed to a few sentences, but in the process all life would be squeezed out of it. The first, and perhaps the final, bit of advice, then, must be: "Use as many words as you need, but be sure that every word is doing its work, carrying its proper load of meaning, and helping its neighbors with their loads. Keep the workers. Throw out the loafers."

For a discussion of "Weak and effective repetition," see section 62; for a discussion of "Conciseness," see section 66.

Certain obvious types of wordiness are illustrated in the following:

1. Repetition of the same word or of words with the same meaning:

Wordy: Jane is the sort of girl *with* whom a boy likes to be *with.*
Scholarship *alone* is not the *only* thing that counts.

2. The double (pleonastic) *that* before a clause:

Wordy: I felt *that* if he said another word *that* I would scream. [Omit the second one.]

3. Roundabout expressions (circumlocution or periphrasis):

Wordy: The reason why I came to college was on account of the fact that I lost my job in the shipyards. [reason — on account of — the fact that]

4. The double negative (see section 6d):

Wordy: There is*n't hardly* any risk in flying. [*Hardly* is negative.]

A type of wordiness which is illustrated in the paragraph given below is harder to correct. In this kind of writing, wordiness results from fuzzy, confused thinking. Like the knight in the story, the student has leaped on his horse and galloped off in all directions. If you are guilty of confused and obscure writing like this, do not try to revise by crossing out words. Make a fresh start. Outline what you intend to say. Jot down your main ideas. Arrange them in a satisfactory order. Then express them as simply and directly as you can.

THE UNKNOWN

To be kind, intelligent, fair, cheerful, tolerant, patient, and be endowed with the technique, are those qualities, which made compact, will make an ideal English professor. When he stands before us on his feet for almost an hour, we form our certain opinions. While he is standing there looking at us he has a very kind expression on his face and is also very neat and clean. Those things we only know by looking at him but we must come to class many times, in order that we may know the real English professor. When he first speaks to us so that we may understand clearly what he is talking about and knows his subject well, we may quickly form an opinion on his intellectual powers. And, when the day comes before leaving for a game, and everyone is excited and conducting themselves so, the professor will grin and bear it.

EXERCISES

Exercise 1. Underline the wordy spots in the following sentences. Then make the necessary corrections.

1. There followed eighteen equally as successful concerts everywhere all over the country.
2. From this moment on my most enjoyable times that I have ever experienced in my life were presented to my enjoyment.
3. After meeting up with two other boys, we returned back to the drug store.
4. Is it perfectly all right to endorse this check on the back?

5. She had a set rule for almost everything that she did and for anything on which she had made up her mind it was very hard to convince her otherwise.

6. The main reason for the domestic troubles in my family is on account of money and financial troubles.

7. Jones is chiefly interested in the line of mathematics, physics, chemistry, and etc.

8. My grandmother she didn't think I should ought to study English.

9. She had got along perfectly all right and she couldn't hardly read a word.

10. I thought that if I could not take chemistry that I would not have the necessary prerequisites for pharmacology.

Exercise 2. Outline the paragraph quoted above. First write a compressed paraphrase of it. Then expand this to a full-length paragraph by means of added concrete details and examples.

TRITENESS

42. Avoid trite expressions.

A trite phrase is one that has been rubbed smooth and thin through long use. Trite phrases are also called hackneyed phrases or clichés. When they were new they were effective. Some of them were apt, witty, felicitous; some began life as figures of speech. Because they were good they suffered, and now they are used only for humor or irony.

The following list will put you on your guard:

aching void	beat a hasty retreat
acid test	beggars description
after all has been said	better half
all in all	better late than never
all work and no play	blissfully ignorant
a long-felt want	blushing bride
among those present	bolt from the blue
ardent admirers	bountiful repast
arms of Morpheus	breathless silence
as luck would have it	briny deep
at a loss for words	budding genius
at one fell swoop	busy as a bee

by leaps and bounds
caught like rats in a trap
checkered career
cheered to the echo
clear as crystal
conspicuous by his absence
course of true love
devouring element
discreet silence
doomed to disappointment
downy couch
drastic action
dull, sickening thud
each and every one
easier said than done
equal to the occasion
fair sex
familiar landmark
favor with a selection
festive occasion
few and far between
filthy lucre
goes without saying
great open spaces
grim reaper
gridiron warriors
hands across the sea
holy bonds of matrimony
in all its glory
in the last analysis
irony of fate
justice to the occasion
last but not least
long-felt want
lonely sentinel
mantle of snow
meets the eye
method in his madness

monarch of all he surveys
mother nature
motley crowd
nipped in the bud
none the worse for his experience
none the worse for wear
no sooner said than done
partake of refreshments
pleasing prospect
powers that be
presided at the piano
proud possessor
psychological moment
reigns supreme
riot of color
replete with interest
rendered a selection
ripe old age
sadder but wiser
shadow of the goal posts
silence reigned supreme
single blessedness
specimen of humanity
sweat of his brow
sumptuous repast
sweet girl graduate
table groaned
tired but happy
vale of tears
venture a suggestion
watery grave
wee small hours
wends his way
where ignorance is bliss
with bated breath
words fail to express
worked like a Trojan
wrought havoc

EXERCISES

Exercise 1. Hand in a list of trite expressions found in your college newspaper. You will find many of them on the sports page.

391

Exercise 2. Hand in a list of trite expressions which you have overheard in the conversation of your friends and acquaintances.

Exercise 3. Write a paragraph in which you try to use as many trite expressions as you can. Use the list in this section. Then rewrite the paragraph in a more fresh and effective style.

FINE WRITING

43. Avoid the pompous and inflated style which is known as "fine writing."

"Fine writing" is not, as you might think, good writing. It is flowery, artificial, overdone writing. In an effort to be literary, the writer loads his style with too many adjectives, with big words, trite figures of speech, and tags from foreign languages.

A certain type of "fine writing" called "jargon" (in the sense made famous by Sir Arthur Quiller-Couch in his essay "On Jargon") consists of the use of vague, high-sounding words in place of the more exact words which the writer was unwilling to find. If you are addicted to jargon, read Sir Arthur Quiller-Couch's *On the Art of Writing*, G. P. Putnam's Sons, New York, 1916.

The jargon of newspaper writers also goes under the name of "journalese." See the definition of "journalese" in *Webster's New International Dictionary*.

EXERCISE

Exercise 1. Simplify and strengthen the following sentences:

1. At the tender age of fourteen he left his paternal domicile to espouse the life of the wayfarer over the briny deep.
2. The modern young lass of today is steadily ascending rung by rung to the status formerly held by the sterner sex in the business world.
3. In the case of friendship, before a person can accomplish these other factors that are mentioned, he must first commit himself to the right mental attitude.

4. The youths who had forsaken the shady walks and lawns of their Alma Mater to engage in strife on far-flung battlefields will again be trooping back to seek knowledge in the cloistered seclusion of the campus.

5. In case we had to defend this great nation, which all of us should be proud to be the citizens of, it certainly would help with regard to our morale if we knew the loss by being defeated.

EUPHONY

44. Avoid harsh and unpleasant combinations of sounds.

Euphony means "pleasing or sweet sound." The opposite of "euphony" is "cacophony," which means "harsh or discordant sound." Good prose should be pleasant to the ear when it is read aloud; it should not offend by harsh, jarring, or disagreeable sounds. The best prose has a rhythm, a melody, which, although it must avoid the regular patterns of poetic rhythm, is easily detected by the trained ear. For a further discussion of this subject, refer to the section on "Euphony and Rhythm," pages 62–66.

Most beginning writers must be satisfied with a negative virtue —the avoidance of unintentional rhymes and of unpleasant sounds.

EXERCISE

Exercise 1. Read the following sentences aloud. Then revise them.

1. They were taking their Sunday siestas in the shade of some scraggly trees that grew in the square. [Note the hissing sounds in *Sunday, siestas, shade, some, scraggly, trees, square.*]

2. In the gloom of the living room several silent pledges were sitting awaiting their doom. [Note the awkward rhyme of *room, gloom, doom,* and the *s* sounds in *silent, pledges, sitting.*]

3. The silent soldier stood silhouetted against the sunset sky.

4. The infuriated bear bared his teeth at the yelping hounds.

5. Under similar conditions superior scholarship is essential.

6. It would be best to first baste the waist and skirt together.

LOGICAL COMPLETENESS

SENTENCE UNITY

45a. Write complete, unified sentences.

A sentence is unified if it expresses one complete thought. The reader of the sentence must feel that all its parts are closely and logically related to its main thought. The sentence, however, is not a formula or an unchangeable pattern. On the contrary, it is a unit of such variety and flexibility that no rule, only the good sense of the writer, can decide when "not enough" becomes "complete," and when "complete" becomes "too much."

Obviously, a sentence is "not enough" when it is not grammatically complete, that is, when it does not have an expressed or implied subject and verb. For a discussion of the sentence fragment see section 1, pages 227–233. The following fragments illustrate this fault:

Not enough to make a sentence:

Roger walked with a noticeable limp. Probably a result of carelessness in setting a broken bone. [Correct by using a comma instead of a period. The second part of this is merely an appositive, not a sentence.]

The laws of this peculiar community were made by officers of the church. The president of the church presiding over the law-making assemblies. [Correct by combining these two parts. The second part is an absolute participial phrase, not a sentence.]

As I sit here in my room, looking out with windowless eyes, I can hear a variety of sounds. Sounds which convey to me the realization that others, more fortunate than I, are finding life a pleasant experience. [The second part is an appositive. Use a dash instead of the period.]

394

45b. Do not include in the sentence any words, phrases, or clauses which have no direct bearing on the principal thought of the sentence.

A sentence may have "too much" in several ways. Two unrelated ideas of the same weight and importance may be thrown together to make a compound sentence. For a discussion of this fault see section 46. A sentence may appear bulging and baggy from having too many related minor details thrown into it. For a discussion of the overloaded sentence see section 48. In this section we are discussing the sentence which is weak because the writer tossed in some unrelated detail which happened to pop into his mind as he was writing.

Unrelated details:

My uncle, short of temper and of breath, eighty years old at this time and weighing two hundred pounds, swore angrily at the tramp. [The swearing may be related to "temper" but not clearly to his weight and his age.]

The destructiveness of the termite, which is an insect with almost human instincts for social organization, is very great. [The relative clause has nothing to do with the termite's ability to do harm.]

After the Spanish Civil War, free speech, which is guaranteed to every American by our Constitution, was suppressed by the Franco regime. [If this is about Spain, the reference to America is merely thrown in.]

Unified:

My uncle, a short-tempered man, swore angrily at the tramp.

The destructiveness of the termite is very great.

After the Spanish Civil War free speech in Spain was suppressed by the Franco regime.

EXERCISE

Exercise 1. Determine which of the following groups of words are sentence fragments. Correct them by supplying the missing elements.

1. The government also helping to establish nursery schools where the children of working mothers may be left.
2. The houses, neat and in good repair, fringed by fresh green lawns and artfully placed shrubbery.

3. The principal provision of the new decree being that children over twelve, charged with stealing, murder, or violence, were to be brought before a criminal court.

4. His keen dark eyes sparkling as he greets his customers with a broad smile.

5. A reactionary government being unable to cope with the problems of the post-war world.

6. Having lost the election, the Prime Minister resigned and retired to his country estate to "keep pigs."

7. Although there is no proof that filtrable viruses resemble bacteria.

8. Although it was known as early as 1894 that a filtrable virus caused a disease of tobacco plants, not much attention was paid to that fact.

9. Thus contributing to the congestion, noise, and confusion of the city.

10. Which button to press and which lever to pull remained a mystery to her as long as she worked in the shop.

FAULTY CO-ORDINATION

46a. Do not unite unrelated ideas in a single compound sentence.

A sentence may lack unity because the thoughts in it have no possible relation to each other, but it may also lack unity because the thoughts *seem* unrelated.

Unrelated facts:

Luther Burbank was born in Lancaster, Massachusetts, on March 7, 1849, and the work of this remarkable man makes an interesting story. [Both facts relate to Burbank, it is true, but the relationship is not close enough. Make two sentences out of this.]

The story is about the Welsh coal miners and I liked it very much. [This is a type of immature sentence often found in college papers. Did the writer like the story *because* it was about coal miners?]

Bob Cavendish is the student-body president, and he is tall and dark and has a pleasant smile for everyone. [If there is any relationship of facts implied, it might be this: "Bob Cavendish was elected president of the student body because he is tall and dark and has a pleasant smile for everybody." Or it might be this: "Tall and dark Bob Cavendish, the man with a smile for everyone, is our student-body president."]

The women were short and stocky, with straight black hair, and they did all the hard work on the plantations. [This is a bad mixture of details. The writer is throwing facts together because he does not know what to do with them. The sentence should be broken up.]

46b. Do not join a series of loose, straggling sentences. Break them up into compact units.

The weakness of a long, straggling sentence does not lie in its length alone, nor in its co-ordination either, if that is done skillfully. A long sentence may be highly effective because of its easy flow and rhythm. The following long sentences are good. The first one, by Sally Benson, is built on a pattern of parallel clauses, each one adding to the single effect of the whole. The second and third, by E. Arnot Robertson, also are carefully patterned, with parallel phrases worked in to aid the forward movement.

Effective long sentences:

They came loaded with mementos of their sordid pasts; they hung Dutch curtains at the kitchen windows; they put cribs or painted breakfast sets in the half-rooms and radios in the bookshelves; and the garden, which was meant to look like a bit of green from another world, was noisy with the blare of music when the windows were open and smelled of cooking. — Sally Benson, "People from Out of Town." *The New Yorker*, Jan. 30, 1943. Permission *The New Yorker*, Copyright 1943, The F.–R. Publishing Corporation.

London, sprawling over so many miles, was impossible to miss for the bombers: if they were not picking their targets in detail there was no need for them to come low enough for the few guns or searchlights to matter; and the people knew it. It was disturbing beyond expression, the emanation of close-packed, controlled fear from millions of human beings cowering in shelters, in cellars, keeping up a fine pretence of indifference in their own homes, nervously carrying on with gaiety or trying to sleep, if they were workers who must sleep, with vaselined cotton wool in their ears, or their bedclothes over their heads, or their windows closed in the stuffy night; striving to shut out the noise of death which was all they could shut out. — E. Arnot Robertson, *The Signpost*. By permission of The Macmillan Company, publishers.

Ineffective, straggling sentences:

When I was a little girl, I did not care for motion pictures, but as I grew into high-school age I began to go every week and now that I am out of high school I do not go so often and I am more particular about the quality of the pictures that I see.

The girls persuaded me to go to a stag dance and the hour finally came, but as I entered the dance floor and walked along the sidelines and looked the place over I found it to be very crowded and noisy.

In my sophomore year the teacher thought that we needed more drill in creative writing, which was the same course we had had the previous year, but in my junior year we did not have any English course but instead spent two terms studying literature.

The cure for the disease of the straggling sentence is "subordinate and divide," — subordinate what seems to be of secondary importance, and divide if you cannot subordinate.

Revised sentences:

My taste in motion pictures has developed through three stages: a complete indifference to them in my childhood, a movie-a-week phase in my high-school days, and my present discriminating enjoyment of a few of the best.

Several girls persuaded me to accompany them to a stag dance. As we entered the dance hall I noticed with distaste that the floor was crowded and noisy.

My high-school training in English consisted of a two-year course in creative writing, the second year a repetition of the first, and a year's study of literature.

46c. Do not co-ordinate elements which are subordinate in thought.

Too much co-ordination is a sign of immaturity, in thinking as well as in writing. A child will say, "We had a birthday party, and Bobby and Jackie came to the party, and we had ice cream, and we played games." A mature person will not assume that all ideas, details, or facts are of the same importance or that they should be expressed on the same level. He knows that some thoughts are of first importance, that others are supporting or explaining details, and he will write sentences that show the proper relationship of one part of the sentence to another.

Poor: The Caldwell family opened the first rough trail and soon other settlers were coming in.

Better: Soon other settlers were coming in over the first rough trail which the Caldwell family had opened. [Use an adjective clause.]

Weak: The Smithsonian Institution is constantly working for a better understanding of nature for man's benefit, and it gets little or no publicity.

Better: The Smithsonian Institution is constantly working, with little or no publicity, for a better understanding of nature for man's benefit. [Use a prepositional phrase.]

Weak: Queen Mary was easily shaken by passions. They were both passions of love and passion of hatred and revenge.

Better: Queen Mary was easily shaken by passions — passions of love and of hatred and revenge. [Use appositive.]

Weak: I dreaded opening the door of his office, but it was only for a few days.

Better: For a few days I dreaded opening the door of his office. [Use prepositional phrase.]

Weak: There are changes in government and no one knows what they will be.

Better: No one can anticipate what changes in government will take place.

Weak: It was early morning and there was a fog and so I crawled out and made my way to the beach.

Better: Concealed by the fog of early dawn, I crawled out and made my way to the beach. [Use a participial phrase.]

46d. Do not destroy the unity of a compound sentence by using the wrong connective.

If your instructor refers you to this section, he is saying to you, "You are too fond of *and, but, so,* and *while.* You co-ordinate too much and too inaccurately." See also "Conjunctions," section 8.

Poor: Sulfanilamide is often toxic *while* penicillin is absolutely harmless. [*While* should not be used in formal writing to mean *but* or *whereas.* *While* means *at the same time as.*]

Susan is never out of trouble *and* she is always happy. [There is a contrast implied here. Say *and yet she is* . . . or subordinate.]

My roommate is always borrowing my clothes *and* he never remembers to return them. [Use *only* instead of *and* to express the exact relationship between the two ideas.]

The British needed to keep open their route through the Suez Canal *so* they decided to hold Malta at all costs. [Subordinate the first clause. You will never find *so* used as a connective in formal writing and only rarely in informal writing. It is common only in a very loose, unstudied sort of speech. Avoid it altogether in writing.]

. EXERCISES

Exercise 1. Some of the following compound sentences must be separated; some should be improved by subordinating one of the co-ordinate clauses. Before each sentence in which the ideas are obviously unrelated write *1*. Before those in which the relationship between the clauses can be improved by subordination, write *2*. Then show what subordination you would use.

——— 1. I spent three years fighting our war as an infantryman and now I find college life slow and unexciting.

——— 2. They knew that the war was over so they did not care what they did.

——— 3. His hair is gray and he usually wears gaudy ties.

——— 4. I waited for a truck for about thirty minutes and then I heard an ambulance siren in the distance.

——— 5. Queen Elizabeth was as efficient as any man who ever ruled England and she is supposed to have had red hair.

——— 6. The office was small and it accommodated only three girls.

——— 7. The beach is crowded and there is much noise.

——— 8. Classic architecture is severe and plain in outline and it has been used in the Supreme Court Building in Washington.

——— 9. Unemployment is a serious problem in the modern world and it has been caused largely by the introduction of automatic machinery.

——— 10. Karl Marx has been called the father of scientific socialism and he was born in 1818.

——— 11. Mrs. Cline is a tall, grey-haired woman, and she is the mother of three grown boys, and she teaches a course called Family Relations.

_____ 12. Many city homes no longer know what family life is, and the family is the most important of our basic social institutions.

_____ 13. Some people think that the scientific and technological studies are as important as the social studies, but that is a serious mistake.

_____ 14. His only political experience came from a term as justice of the peace in a small town in Indiana, and he once owned and managed a hardware store.

_____ 15. Criminal law has many defects and no one knows it better than Judge Black.

Exercise 2. Each of the following sentences may be improved by proper subordination. Subordinate one of the clauses by using the connective indicated before the sentence.

although   1. Protection against smallpox was known as far back as 1798, but there are still many people who are attacked by the disease.

after   2. We stood in line for an hour, and then we were told that we could get a reservation in three days.

which   3. The girls had left their dishes in the kitchen sink, and I was trying to wash them and put them away.

if   4. Enforce the regulations we have now and we shall not need any new regulations.

where   5. Europeans think of America as a land of plenty, and anyone can find wealth and happiness in it.

after   6. The British army had lost all its equipment at Dunkirk, and there was only a single armored division left to protect the home island.

which   7. We have wasted our natural resources, but we should have protected and conserved them.

although   8. The dry prairie land will drift away in dust storms, but it is still being plowed for profitless wheat farming.

because   9. The voters have taken little interest in the city schools, and now the schools are faced with another financial crisis.

if   10. The educational program may succeed, but it has to have more than mere financial support from every citizen in Chicago.

Exercise 3. Use an appositive to subordinate one of the clauses in each of the following sentences.

1. I met Helen at Seaside; she is the girl with whom I am rooming now.
2. Every college knows three kinds of students; they are the scientists, the artists, and the followers.

46 LOGICAL COMPLETENESS

3. The oldest daughter was preparing supper; she was the provider and homemaker of her little family and she was only fourteen.
4. An older man managed our club, and he listened to our complaints and judged our disputes.
5. Something was learned from the League of Nations; it was a failure but a failure with noble purposes.

Exercise 4. Subordinate one of the clauses in each of the following sentences by reducing it to a prepositional or verbal phrase.

1. There were many architects who advocated revolutionary changes in structure, and Frank Lloyd Wright deserves special mention.
2. He tried to force the British people to support his reactionary domestic policies and he lost his position as the head of the government.
3. Ethiopia was in great peril and she was abandoned to her fate by the League of Nations.
4. One has only to study the minority problems in India and then one can easily sympathize with Britain's attitude.
5. The people of Teschen were predominantly Polish and they did not like to be subject to Czechoslovakia.
6. He found an interesting detective story in the library and he sat down and read it while he waited.
7. I left the door of the safe unlocked and took the leather bag of coins and walked down the street toward the bank.
8. The boy who preceded me had once made a mistake; he had taken the money out of the safe and then he had locked the door.
9. In the night some curious strangers had investigated and the lock of the safe was blown into the next room.
10. He was the football coach for fourteen years, and his teams did not lose a single game to the state university.

Exercise 5. Each of the following sentences is weak because of too much co-ordination. Improve each sentence by division, or by reducing a main clause to a subordinate clause or to a phrase.

1. There were angleworms in the soil under my feet, and they were going about in nature's way to cultivate and to enrich it.
2. America is faced with its gravest danger and that is the danger of indecision in a world crisis.
3. Fred is only nineteen years old, and he is a junior in the school of forestry.
4. He is a total abstainer from alcohol, and his marriage he calls a success, and he dedicates his books to his wife.

5. Heavy breathing announces that someone is sleeping, and my brother has come home at last.
6. We have never had a foreign policy and we have never needed one.
7. His programs are always interesting, and consist of selections of his own choice.
8. One of my presents was a model lamp post, it stood about six inches high and was made of cast iron.
9. Mrs. Hall was about six feet tall, and she outran a few of the men in a footrace.
10. The word *propaganda* has of late acquired a sinister meaning; originally it meant a "spreading of the faith."

FAULTY SUBORDINATION

47a. Do not subordinate the principal thought of the sentence.

Subordinating the principal thought of the sentence — a fault which is often given the name of "upside-down subordination" — occurs when the writer does not take the trouble to think of what he is saying. The sign of it is usually a "when" clause.

Wrong: One day I was pulling weeds in our garden when I saw two timber wolves near the corral.
Right: One day, as I was pulling weeds in the garden, I saw two timber wolves near the corral. [The important thought is certainly that he saw the wolves, not that he was weeding the garden.]

Wrong: We were nearing the dock when our boat overturned.
Right: Just as we were nearing the dock our boat overturned. [The overturning of the boat is more important than the time or the place.]

47b. Avoid writing sentences with overlapping dependence.

A series of phrases or clauses so written that each depends upon the preceding usually produces an awkward sentence. Rewrite the sentence.

Poor: I had heard the warning so often that I was so used to hearing it that I failed to realize that it was important.
Better: Repeated warnings had dulled my appreciation of their importance. The warnings had been repeated so often that I failed to realize their importance.

47c. Do not use the wrong subordinating connective.

If you are referred to this section, you should also read sections 8 and 60. This section deals with a few connectives that are often misused in student writing. They are *like, while, because, as, without, where*. See also 46d.

Wrong: The men looked *like* they had had nothing to eat for weeks.
Right: The men looked as if they had had nothing to eat for weeks.

Wrong: He had always been a Conservative *while* his son was a member of the Labor Party.
Right: He had always been a Conservative but his son was a member of the Labor Party.

Wrong: Because Churchill lost the election is no proof that he is unpopular.
Right: The fact that Churchill lost the election is no proof that he is unpopular.
or: Churchill's loss of the election cannot be taken as proof of his unpopularity.

Wrong: I do not know *as* I deserve the reward.
Right: I do not know *whether* (or *that*) I deserve the reward.

Wrong: The striking miners will not return to the mines *without* they are given an increase in wages.
Right: The striking miners will not return to the mines *unless* (or *until*) they are given an increase in wages.

Wrong: I had read in a magazine *where* a dead man had been brought back to life.
Right: I had read in a magazine *that* a dead man had been brought back to life.

Wrong: While I do not dislike literature, I prefer the sciences.
Right: Although I do not dislike literature, I prefer the sciences.

EXERCISES

Exercise 1. Point out the errors in the following sentences. Some of the sentences may be correct. You are to determine which are incorrect and to make the necessary corrections.

1. I had trudged about a mile into the woods, when I came upon a grassy hollow.
2. I was with General Patton's army in Germany when the war ended.
3. The crowd cheered madly although everyone saw that Merril was running like he was tired.

4. We heard the first of a series of concerts of the Minneapolis Symphony Orchestra.
5. One of the reasons why this picture impresses me is because it follows the plot of the novel very closely.
6. Santa Claus has no significance any longer other than a person who is forever giving things away.
7. I was dozing lazily by a trickling stream when I heard the tinkle of a distant bell.
8. I am not sure as I want to hear the rest of the story.
9. The famous violinist was struck by a truck as he was trying to cross Broadway.
10. We had the ball on their three-yard line when the game ended.

Exercise 2. Underline the incorrect connective in each of the following sentences. Write the correction in the space before the sentence.

_____ 1. I felt like I was in a world by myself.

_____ 2. Thousands of Chinese children will starve without we send them food.

_____ 3. I read in the morning paper where the strikers had returned to work.

_____ 4. It seemed like the truck would not travel fast enough.

_____ 5. The man was a habitual drunkard while his wife was a splendid woman.

_____ 6. While the book is no doubt instructive, it is long and dull.

_____ 7. The two men looked like they had been drinking heavily.

_____ 8. Because he talks about music is no evidence that he appreciates it.

_____ 9. The bridge began to creak and groan like it were going to break under our weight.

_____ 10. I am not sure as I have any right to be in college.

OVERLOADED SENTENCES

48. Do not destroy the unity, as well as the order and clearness, of your sentences by overloading them with details.

Analyze the following sentences. What is the writer trying to say? How many thoughts is he trying to express at one time?

48 LOGICAL COMPLETENESS

Confused:

Military training teaches a person to stand up straight and walk with his head up; this helps in future life because it becomes a habit and so many people have the bad habit of walking stooped and this leads to poor health and poor appearance.

Military science teaches also common courtesies, not only to your superior officers but to everyone to whom courtesy is due; for instance when you enter offices, or the courtesies you should use when you are using firearms while hunting or shooting in the presence of another person.

The feed mixture usually contains rolled wheat, rolled barley, ground corn, and oil meal, mixed according to the time and age of the calf; the amount of corn meal does not vary in proportion, but rolled wheat and barley are very good body and fat builders and they are fed to a great extent at first.

If you write sentences like these, your remedy is to go back to the first principles of thought communication: say one thing at a time; say it as simply and clearly as you can; say it so that it cannot be misunderstood.

Let us try to dissect these sentences in order to discover what the writer tried to say.

Revised:

Military training teaches a person to stand erect and to walk with his head up. [That is enough for one sentence.] Good posture [Is that what the writer meant by "this" and "it"?] becomes habitual. It leads directly to better health and better appearance.

Military science also teaches common courtesy, not only to officers superior in rank but also to everyone. [Are there some persons to whom "courtesy is not due"?] For instance, it teaches one how to enter an office, or how to handle firearms with safety to others. [The two examples are so badly chosen that no sentence can make them apt or congruous.]

The feed mixture usually contains rolled wheat, rolled barley, ground corn, and oil meal, the proportions of the mixture depending on the age of the calf. [By "time" did the writer mean the time of the year?] The proportion of corn meal remains constant, but since rolled wheat and barley are good body and fat builders [This is still an awkward expression.] they are used in larger proportions than oil meal when the calf is young.

406

EXERCISE

Exercise 1. Reorganize and rewrite the following sentences. Discard details that do not belong here. Simplify the sentences; make them absolutely clear.

1. Such things as the vast amount of people and the way they dress is the first thing the freshman notices, then he compares other places where he has been, and starts to feel a gratifying relief coming to him, for he realizes he has seen this many people before at the little county fair.

2. The average country boy that comes to college is quite familiar with what college life will be like, for he has read all the literature that he could acquire upon the matter, although it is always joked and talked about his surprises and disillusionments which arrive in his awkward path of acquiring an education.

3. My future will lead me into every type of condition, and I must be able to adapt myself to each of them.

4. My tendency to waste time inspires the professor to give threatening advice or criticism to this cause, but when I am scolded my opinions become hard toward him just as any other boy in the class.

5. We improve our reckoning by understanding all phases or sides of every subject dealt with; whether it be amusements, business, studies, or social life; thereby making the most logical decisions.

CHOPPY STYLE

49. Avoid expressing in short, choppy, co-ordinate sentences a group of ideas subordinately related to each other.

Correct the fault by combining related ideas and subordinating those that are of secondary importance.

Poor: The performance was over. I arose to go out. I was so nervous that I had to sit down on a chair. Soon I grew calm again.

Better: After the performance was over, I arose to go out, but I was so nervous that I had to sit on a chair until I became calmer.

Poor: Back of the grandstand are the stables. The stables are long, rambling, one-story barns. Each barn is divided into box stalls. Each stall is enough to accommodate one horse.

Better: The stables, situated behind the grandstand, are long, rambling, one-story barns, each barn divided into stalls large enough to accommodate one horse apiece.

EXERCISE

Exercise 1. Improve the following groups of sentences by combining related ideas and subordinating where subordination will express the thought more accurately.

1. I did not like the idea of reading a whole book of poems. But I read Sandburg's *Chicago Poems* and I liked them. They seemed a man's kind of poems. They were good pictures of life in a great city.
2. One of the boys had an old car. We went to Waldport in it. There we stayed at a cottage. The cottage belonged to the father of one of the boys.
3. The people of the world have always dreamed of peace. But they have never done much about it. Now at last it seems that something definite has been done to form a world organization.
4. Everyone should see Multnomah Falls. If he is driving along the Columbia River Highway, he will never regret stopping to see the falls. It is a sight one could never forget. There are many charming and beautiful falls along the highway. I truly believe none exceeds Multnomah in beauty.
5. Then we were on our way. I felt very important. I was going on my first vacation alone. Our first stop was Portland. We stayed there over night. Early next morning we started for Pendleton.

COMPARISONS

50a. Make your comparisons logical and complete. Use enough words to make your statement compare the things that you intend to compare.

Written English, especially formal written English, requires a logic, a precision in comparisons which is often lacking in loose, informal speech. In informal speech certain elliptical or illogical comparisons have become idiomatic; these idioms, however, are still unacceptable in writing.

1. In formal writing do not omit *than* or *as* in a double comparison.

Not acceptable in formal usage: Agriculture is now as important, if not more important than mining.
The improved Sherman tank is as good, if not better than anything the Germans can produce.

Logical but awkward: Agriculture is now as important as, if not more important than mining.

The improved Sherman tank is as good as, if not better than anything the Germans can produce.

The last two examples illustrate what is often called the "suspended construction." Some writers use it; others object to it on the score of awkwardness. It can easily be avoided.

Logical and smooth: Agriculture is now as important as mining, if not more so.

The improved Sherman tank is as good as anything the Germans can produce, if not better.

2. Do not omit one term of a comparison.

Misleading: I admire him more than Scott.

The United States helped Russia more than England.

Clear: I admire him more than I admire Scott (*or* more than Scott does).

The United States helped Russia more than England did (*or* more than we helped England).

3. Do not omit *other* after *than* or *as* in comparing two members of the same class.

Misleading: Buckley is heavier than any man on the team. [If Buckley is not on the team, this sentence is clear. If he *is* a member of the team, he cannot be heavier than himself.]

Clear: Buckley is heavier than any other man on the team.

or: Buckley is the heaviest man on the team.

4. In pointing out the superlative member of a class or group, do not use *any* or *other;* use *all*.

Illogical: I like E. Arnot Robertson's *The Signpost* the best of any novel I have read this year. [*Any* means "one." It cannot be the best of one.]

Logical: I like E. Arnot Robertson's *The Signpost* the best of all the novels that I have read this year.

or: I like . . . *The Signpost* better than any other novel. . . . [Notice that this is comparative, not superlative.]

Illogical: E. E. Cummings is the most interesting of all the other American poets.

Logical: E. E. Cummings is the most interesting American poet.

or: E. E. Cummings is more interesting [comparative] than any other American poet.

5. Finish your comparisons so that you will not seem to be comparing something that you do not intend to.

Misleading: The salary of an English teacher is lower than a lawyer. [Are you comparing salaries, or are you comparing salary and lawyer?]

Logical: The salary of an English teacher is lower than that of a lawyer. [In your desire to escape awkwardness you should not say, "An English teacher earns less than does a lawyer." If you want to be accurate in fact as well as logical in expression, you could say, "An English teacher earns more than does a lawyer, but he gets less."]

Illogical: The duties and responsibilities of a traffic officer are more complex than a game warden.

Logical: The duties and responsibilities of a traffic officer are more complex than those of a game warden.

50b. Do not leave a comparison unfinished unless the missing term of the comparison can be easily supplied by the reader.

Undesirable: It is easier to remain silent when attacks are made upon the things one loves. [Easier than what?]

Students who live in a dormitory do better work. [Better than who?]

Better: It is easier to remain silent when attacks are made upon the things one loves than to risk criticism by defending them.

Students who live in a dormitory do better work than those who room in private homes (*or* who live in fraternity houses).

In simple statements, in which the comparison is easily understood and supplied by the reader or listener, usage permits the unfinished comparison. Comparisons like this are correct: "It is always better to tell the truth. Her explanation is simpler." Uncompleted superlatives, like "He is the darlingest man!" or "This food is *so* good!" or "We had the best time," although appropriate enough in school-girlish conversation, are not acceptable in serious writing.

EXERCISE

Exercise 1. Revise the following sentences. Make the comparisons complete and logical.

1. The methods used in college English courses are very different from high school.
2. His step was as light as many middle-aged men.
3. Wilson is the best passer of any quarterback in the Middle West.
4. *The Bridge of San Luis Rey* is the most popular of any of Thornton Wilder's novels.
5. Girls are probably better at flattering their teachers than the best of the male efforts.
6. On Saturday night more men study their lessons than girls.
7. Browning is more intellectual than any poet in the Victorian era.
8. My theme is as good if not better than the theme which the teacher read to us.
9. Although he was not thirty when he died, his poems were better known than many older writers.
10. I admire a business leader more than a college professor.

WORDS LEFT OUT

51a. Do not leave out words which are necessary for clearness.

Some students are fond of a telegraphic style, which they carry over from informal speech to formal writing. Writing requires a completeness and a precision of expression which speech often ignores. It is better to be generous with words than to leave the reader guessing.

The following are some of the common sins of omission in writing:

1. Omission of prepositions with expressions of time.

Not proper in writing: Evenings we usually go for a swim. [Say *during the evening.*]

Winter term a new course in chemistry will be offered. [Say *during the winter term.*]

The day when honors are announced there is much suspense. [Say *on the day.*]

2. Misleading omission of *that*.

Misleading: I soon observed nearly all the women, especially the young and pretty ones, were carrying strange little baskets. [Did he observe the women, or did he observe *that* the women were carrying baskets?]

He told me his family had all been killed in one of the first air raids on England and that he had developed an unreasoning hatred of all Germans. [The parallel structure requires *that* before the first clause as well as before the second. See section 56. Write: He told me *that* his family . . .]

3. Omission of a part of a verb or verb phrase.

Illogical: The patient was given an anesthetic and the instruments made ready. [Say *were made ready*, because *patient* is singular, and the verb following it cannot be understood with *instruments made ready*.]

His ideas were progressive and adopted without debate. [Repeat *were*. The two verbs are not parallel. The first *were* is used as a main verb; the second *were* is an auxiliary verb, or a part of the verb phrase *were adopted*.]

4. Omission of words which would make a parallel series intelligible.

Confusing: He is about fifty-nine years old, gray hair, and very distinctive features.

Necessary words supplied: He is about fifty-nine years old. He has gray hair and very distinctive features.

5. Nouns or verbs understood in a double capacity.

Illogical: Winterset is one of the best, if not the best play I have ever seen. [One of the best play or plays?]

Some men never have and never will understand generosity.

Improved: Winterset is one of the best plays I have ever seen, if not the best. Some men never have understood generosity and never will understand it.

6. The omission of *much* after *very* in a passive verb phrase.

Objectionable: All the people were very surprised by the attack.
The delegate seemed very impressed by what he saw.

Acceptable: All the people *were very much surprised* by the attack.
The delegate *seemed very much impressed* by what he saw.

51b. In formal writing avoid the exclamatory *so, such,* or *too*.

Complete the thought, or use some intensifier like *very, certainly, surely, exceedingly, extremely* in place of *so, such,* or *too*.

Not acceptable in formal writing: The French major was so surprised!
The explanations of the Japanese delegates were too unconvincing.
Everybody had such a good time.

Completed: The French major was so surprised that he could only blush and stammer.
The explanations of the Japanese delegates were too unconvincing to carry much weight with Cordell Hull.
Everybody had such a good time that the party did not break up until midnight.

51c. Do not leave out the preposition necessary to complete an idiomatic expression.

Incomplete: This is a good time to show your faith and devotion to your country. [Say *faith in*.]
Customers have neither respect nor faith in a merchant who cheats. [Say *respect for*.]

For a more complex sentence in which idiomatic prepositions are used with precise care, see the following sentence taken from Galsworthy's essay on drama, page 85:

This third method requires a certain detachment; it requires a sympathy with, a love of, and a curiosity as to, things for their own sake; it requires a far view, together with patient industry, for no immediately practical results.

EXERCISE

Exercise 1. Supply the missing words in the following sentences. Rearrange the wording wherever it is necessary.

1. All the students were very interested in what the speaker said.
2. The unhappy veteran finds none of the girls has even heard of the battles in which he risked his life.
3. A fraternity house or a dormitory is a question which many freshmen have to answer.

413

4. For these reasons, lumbering has and is contributing greatly to our economic stability.
5. Debating has definitely made me more self-reliant, more friends, and more wrinkles in my gray matter.
6. Instead of playing bridge or other forms of recreation, she spent her time studying her biology.
7. He was one of the first, if not the first man to dream of flying across the North Pole.
8. The convocation speaker was such a tiresome talker.
9. The women of the town were very interested in his plans for a new library.
10. The prisoner protested tearfully that he was innocent and he was being mistaken for someone else.

AWKWARDNESS AND OBSCURITY

52. Do not write sentences which are confused, awkward, illogical, or obscure.

An awkward and confused sentence may occasionally be a sign of slovenly thinking, but it is probably more often a result of haste and carelessness in writing. A confused sentence may have several faults: the central thought may be lost in a tangle of modifiers; the thoughts may not be arranged properly; the words used may be inexact, ambiguous, or inappropriate; several constructions may be telescoped into one. See also section 58. Correct a muddled sentence by rewriting it. Express your thoughts as simply and directly as you can.

Confused and obscure:

My belief is that if more emphasis was stressed in college on extemporary speaking, the graduating student would be better prepared to face people of social prominence and college professors.

The word "laureate" comes from the Greeks when they used laurels to crown certain people.

The fact that it is a gigantic crater formed suddenly by an eruption of volcanic nature has been determined.

In high school not much need for correct punctuation and principles is stressed, but in college punctuation and correct forms are closely criticized.

Muskrats work on the dikes before we get to them by burrowing through between two ponds and thus connect them when their contents are supposed to be kept separate.

Revised:

I believe that colleges should stress courses in extemporary speaking in order to give college graduates more confidence and social ease.

The word "laureate" comes from the language of the ancient Greeks, who used a laurel crown as a mark of special honor.

Scientists have determined the fact that a volcanic eruption had formed the gigantic crater.

Correct punctuation and the principles of good writing are stressed more in college courses than in high-school courses.

Muskrats burrow tunnels through the dikes between the ponds. Through these openings the water flows from one pond to another.

EXERCISE

Exercise 1. Revise the following sentences:

1. By doing something one does not want to do and doing it regularly is a reason why military training develops a man's will power.
2. Living alone in a twelve-room house finds Mrs. Blank busy with card clubs, social calls, jig-saw puzzles, and favorite books.
3. The position at the throttle of a huge steam locomotive has struck many a boy's fancy to become an engineer on just such a locomotive.
4. All around the hall were benches, but most of the old women sat on the ground, for there was no floor, smoking long pipes filled with a mixture made of bark which gave off a peculiar yet pleasant odor.
5. Fifteen years ago my father bought a farm with no intention of making it our present home, then five years ago we did.
6. When some question which seemed silly to him but was asked in earnestness by the questioner, his square chin became perceptibly more square, and his voice, which for all ordinary conversation had a slight lisp, suddenly became a harsh growl like that of a lion as he squelched the boy who was seeking for knowledge.
7. The causes of my present difficulties in English is not because of poor teachers in high-school years, but of the fact partly because I have been out of school so long I have forgotten most of the rules, and partly because of lack of attention and interest to explanations by my high-school teachers.
8. It is fatal for diamond smugglers to try to smuggle jewels again and again.
9. In swimming one must move fairly rapidly his feet in a down and up position in order to keep balance in the water.

10. One must move hands in various positions depending upon style of swimming one wished to perform.
11. Some girls who desire to be a nurse may be sympathetic only in a mental sense and wish to help by alleviating the mental strain of the situation.
12. My trouble in college English seems to be my inability to pick out the proper places for commas, quotation marks, and semicolons, where should be placed, and where used, although it has become more simple for me all the time due to constant effort.
13. One may be completely worn out, and the world may seem a place of shrunk souls, and having risen in the morning the future and coming tasks may be slain with the least resistance to man's efforts.
14. Memorizing of poems, great authors, and most important works of each, the remaining two years literature was a main topic, although theme writing played quite a major part also.
15. The music consisted of an odd-shaped drum and wooden horns, which in comparison to music of today the rhythm was very poor.

PROPER ARRANGEMENT

53. Do not destroy the clearness of a sentence by improper arrangement of sentence elements.

Since the English language is not a highly inflected language, the meaning of an English sentence depends to a large extent on the arrangement of words in the sentence. The reader naturally assumes that the parts of a sentence which are placed next to each other are logically related to each other. You must therefore be careful to arrange words in a sentence in such a way that the meaning of the sentence will be clear on the first reading. The rule which will guide you may be stated in two parts: (1) place all modifiers, whether words, phrases, or clauses, as close as possible to the words they modify; (2) avoid placing these elements near other words they might be taken to modify.

1. Adverbs, such as *almost, ever, nearly, merely, only, scarcely,* and *not.*

Misplaced: He *merely* said it because he did not stop to think.
Right: He said it *merely* because he did not stop to think.

Misplaced: Every student cannot win honors in college. [This means that nobody can.]

Right: Not every student can win honors in college. [This means that some can and others cannot.]

Misplaced: The canteen only contained about two cups of water.
Right: The canteen contained only about two cups of water.

Misplaced: Harry *almost* weeded the whole garden this morning.
Right: Harry weeded *almost* the whole garden this morning.

2. Phrases.

Misplaced: He began to lose his desire to reach the summit *after a time.* [Does it refer to *to reach* or *began to lose?*]
Clear: After a time he began to lose his desire to reach the summit.

Misplaced: I was dressed and ready to start climbing *within an hour.* [Does it refer to *being dressed* or to *starting to climb?*]
Clear: Within an hour I was dressed and ready to start climbing.

Misplaced: Every girl was really sorry to have the trip end *for more reasons than one.*
Clear: For more reasons than one, every girl was really sorry to have the trip end. [Refers to *being sorry*, not to *the trip ending.*]

3. Clauses.

Misplaced: When you were a child do you remember all the interesting toys you had? [Does the clause refer to *remember* or to *toys you had?*]
Clear: Do you remember all the interesting toys you had *when you were a child?*

4. Squinting modifiers.

Modifiers so placed in a sentence that they may be understood with either the preceding or the following words are called squinting modifiers. As a rule, it is better not to try to cure the fault by means of punctuation.

Squinting: Because we covered more ground with a tractor *in six days* we finished plowing the field.
Clear: Because we covered more ground with a tractor, we finished plowing the field *in six days.*

Squinting: As we pulled into the service station *with the help of a lady attendant* we found our position on the map. [Putting a comma after *station* is not a satisfactory correction.]

Clear: As we pulled into the service station, a lady attendant helped us to locate our position on the map.

Squinting: As we drove westward *every now and then* the blinding rays of the sun shone into our eyes. [Putting a comma after *westward* is a makeshift correction. It does not eliminate the confusion entirely.]

Clear: As we drove westward, the blinding rays of the sun *frequently* shone into our eyes.

5. The split infinitive.

Placing an adverbial modifier between the sign *to* and the verb of an infinitive results in what is traditionally known as the "split infinitive." The split infinitive is no longer considered one of the seven deadly sins of college composition — if it ever was. It is not true that the parts of an infinitive are inseparable. But since a split infinitive still causes many persons discomfort, if not actual suffering, it is better for the student not to split his infinitives too rashly or promiscuously. A good rule to follow is this: place the adverbial modifier between *to* and the verb of an infinitive only when such an arrangement is necessary to avoid an awkward phrase.

Split infinitive: A writer should remember to not carelessly split his infinitives.

Better: A writer should remember not to split his infinitives carelessly.

6. In general, do not separate words that normally belong near each other, such as subject and verb, verb and object, the parts of a verb phrase, substantives and adjective modifiers, and substantives and appositives.

Awkward: The explorers had, after many adventures and much suffering, reached the headwaters of the Salmon River. [Verb *had reached* separated by long phrase.]

Before it became dark, the stragglers caught up with the main party, tired, wet, discouraged. [Adjective modifiers separated from the word they modify.]

Justice Holmes, in a brilliantly written interpretation of the Four-teenth Amendment, dissented. [Subject and verb split by a long phrase.]

Improved: After many adventures and much suffering, the explorers had reached the headwaters of the Salmon River.

Before it became dark, the tired, wet, and discouraged stragglers caught up with the main party.

Justice Holmes dissented in a brilliantly written interpretation of the Fourteenth Amendment.

7. Ordinarily it is better to avoid the suspended construction, that is, two verbs, two prepositions, etc., having a common object. This construction is grammatically correct; many good writers use it, but some object to it. See 51c.

Awkward: Our parents are interested in and anxious about our welfare.
Smoother: Our parents are interested in our welfare and anxious about it.

Awkward: He approves and loses no opportunity to promote the spread of democracy.
Smoother: He approves of democracy and loses no opportunity to promote its spread.

EXERCISES

Exercise 1. Watch for misplaced adverbs in the following sentences. Place them where they belong.

1. I can recall the incident as if it had happened almost yesterday.
2. Everybody is not interested in classical music; some people only like jazz.
3. The men had almost washed all the dishes before the women arrived.
4. It was the coldest spring we have had ever.
5. The football team has only won two out of the seven games played this fall.
6. He did not play football in high school and has only taken an interest in it since he came to college.
7. All vegetables are not planted at the same time.
8. Many people think that we are merely in school to have a good time.

9. All persons cannot get along with each other or to appreciate one another's ideas.
10. Our room would be even considered too small for one person

Exercise 2. Point out the misplaced element in each of the following sentences. Correct each sentence. Do not use punctuation as a means of correcting an error.

1. Twenty years ago girls used to come to school where I was principal without any stockings on.
2. I shall attempt to explain the function of the least known, to one who does not play the game, section of the football team.
3. Their activity and progress in recent years have surprised the world.
4. At one time I remember that she had three engagement rings.
5. Masefield has many ideas about things that are different.
6. We were finally settled in seats that cost twice as much as we had paid for our tickets when the play began.
7. He usually has a lapful of food at the close of the dinner which he brushes to the floor to be stepped on by some other boarder.
8. If you should disturb her by coming in late, you will hear that she was awakened for the next three months.
9. There is a telephone at the end of the counter which is constantly in use.
10. Freshman English courses are taught by instructors who are required to have at least a master's degree in most colleges.
11. He would tell me to look up words I could not spell in the dictionary.
12. A crowd gathers to sorrowfully gaze upon the destruction of the magnificent structure.
13. He finally had to prove that his rival was a coward in order to hold his wife.
14. The pleasant, merry-faced girl seems exactly like a pansy with its upturned face to the sun.
15. To mention going for a ride in the car in front of her is almost fatal.
16. Wood can be kept for a long time without danger of rotting in the woodshed or the basement.
17. A year later I went to several classes with five or six other children conducted by our minister.
18. The freshmen only have to wear their green caps one year.
19. Why do they spend all their money, time, and effort to please a man with a new dress and a fingerwave?
20. The new laboratory at Dairen has found new uses too numerous to mention for the soy bean.

DANGLING MODIFIERS

54a. Avoid dangling verbal phrases.

The careless use of verbal phrases results in an error usually known as "the dangling modifier." A phrase is said to dangle if it is not tied to something it modifies.

Correct the error by supplying the word to which the phrase should refer or by changing the phrase to a clause with a subject and a predicate. Do not try to correct the error by moving the phrase to another position in the sentence. The results of transplanting are seldom happy.

The following are types of dangling verbal phrases:

1. The participle or gerund.

Dangling: Being in a hurry to finish my exercise, several dangling modifiers were left uncorrected in my essay. [The reader associates *being* with *modifiers*. Who was in a hurry? Certainly not the modifiers. Correct the sentence by supplying the word to which *being* refers.]

Better: Being in a hurry to finish my English exercise, I left several dangling modifiers uncorrected in my essay.

or: As I was in a hurry to finish my English exercise, I left several dangling modifiers uncorrected in my essay.

The test of a dangling phrase is very simple: ask "Who or what is doing what the verb of the sentence states?" If the answer is in the sentence, the phrase does not dangle. This test applies also to a special kind of phrase called an absolute phrase. An absolute phrase consists of a noun and its modifying participle. It is a complete and independent unit of speech, related to the rest of the sentence in thought but not in structure. An absolute phrase does not dangle.

Absolute phrases: The day's work being over, we returned to town.
The guests having arrived, Mother went to the door.

Dangling: Last year, after graduating from high school, my father put me to work in his office. [Who graduated from high school? Father? Correct the sentence by supplying the word to which *graduating* may refer.]

Better: Last year, after graduating from high school, I went to work in my father's office.

or: Last year, after I had graduated from high school, my father put me to work in his office. [Correct the error by changing the phrase to a clause with a subject and a predicate.]

2. The dangling infinitive.

Dangling: To appreciate this poem, it must be read aloud.
Correct: To appreciate this poem, one must read it aloud.
or: If one wishes to appreciate this poem, he must read it aloud.

Dangling: To enjoy outdoor sports, sensible clothing must be worn. [Who or what enjoys sports? The clothing?]
Correct: To enjoy outdoor sports, one must wear sensible clothing.

3. The dangling phrase of result.

Dangling: I helped my mother wash clothes this morning, thus causing me to miss my English class. [Who caused me to miss the class?]
Correct: I missed my English class this morning because I had to stay at home to help my mother wash clothes. [Correct by rewriting the phrase.]

Dangling: I sold my automobile for three hundred dollars, thereby giving me enough money to pay my debts. [What gave me enough money? Not the automobile or the three hundred dollars.]
Correct: I sold my automobile for three hundred dollars — enough to pay my debts. [Change the phrase to an appositive.]
or: The sale of my automobile for three hundred dollars brought me enough money to pay my debts.

54b. Do not write a sentence with a dangling elliptical clause.

A clause is said to dangle when its understood subject is different from the subject of the main clause, or when the subject is not understood at all. Correct the error by supplying the missing words in the clause.

Dangling: When cooked till tender, remove the meat from the oven. [The subject of the sentence is *you*, but the understood subject of the clause must be *meat*.]
Correct: When the meat has been cooked until it is tender, remove it from the oven.

Dangling: His foot was injured while swimming in Wild Cat Hole. [Was his foot swimming?]

Correct: His foot was injured while he was swimming in Wild Cat Hole. [Supply the understood subject and verb of the elliptical clause.]

54c. Avoid writing sentences with any sort of expression, like a phrase or an appositive, that is not easily understood with the rest of the sentence.

Illogical: A gentleman farmer, his wardrobe ranges from faultlessly tailored suits to four-buckle rubber boots. [The expression *a gentleman farmer* seems to be in apposition with *wardrobe.*]

Revised: As he is a gentleman farmer, his wardrobe ranges from faultlessly tailored suits to four-buckle rubber boots.

Illogical: After five years in a city school, a country school presents many problems in adjustment. [One naturally associates the opening phrase with *a country school.*]

Revised: A person who has spent five years in a city school encounters many problems in adjustment when he goes to a country school.

Certain idiomatic phrases, especially those that express a general action and those that serve as directive and transitional links, are exceptions to the rule. These are phrases like *generally speaking, taking everything into consideration, providing, looking at,* and so forth.

EXERCISES

Exercise 1. This exercise should help you to distinguish between verbal phrases used correctly and verbal phrases that dangle. Mark the sentences with danglers and make the necessary corrections.

1. Driving across the state, many beautiful lakes were seen.
2. Many beautiful lakes were seen driving across the state.
3. Driving across the state, we saw many beautiful lakes.
4. Working fourteen hours every day, he soon finished the plowing.
5. He soon finished the plowing by working fourteen hours every day.
6. Upon engaging him in conversation, his interest in music is revealed.
7. Upon engaging him in conversation, he reveals his interest in music.
8. When engaged in conversation, his interest in music is revealed.

9. When only six years old, my father took us to Canada.
10. Being only six years old, my father took us to Canada.
11. When I was only six years old, my father took us to Canada.
12. To be a success in the business world, good manners must be used.
13. The janitor having resigned, we swept the office ourselves.
14. Having refused to resign, the principal was summoned before the school board.
15. In order to get a certificate, two years of work must be done.
16. When almost boiled, remove the pan from the large burner and set it in the warming oven.
17. Looking out over the crowd and noticing my father, my voice failed me.
18. Being frightened, my legs trembled and my throat was dry.
19. I was frightened, thus causing my legs to tremble and my throat to be dry.
20. I took the last biscuit from the plate, thereby committing another social error.

Exercise 2. Underline the dangler in each of the following sentences and then reconstruct the sentence. Do not try to correct a dangler by moving it to some other part of the sentence.

1. Once seen, no one will ever forget its exalted beauty.
2. Besides being interesting you will gain much valuable information about the life in Borneo.
3. Warm and happy in their bunk beds, the girls' faces in the candlelight resemble the faces of mischievous little elves.
4. After climbing into the pajamas, the next step is the brushing of the hair.
5. Upon reading further, the article suggested the proper warmth-giving undergarments for a ramble in the snow.
6. One of the first things noticed when entering the room is a collection of Varga girls.
7. At the age of sixty-seven I find that Mrs. Blank has a rare sense of humor.
8. When delivering fuel by truck, wet weather makes driving miserable.
9. Being before the present housing shortage, tenants were very critical of apartment houses without elevators.
10. Looking out the window for the first time, my mouth fell open and my eyes almost popped out of my head.
11. When mixed thoroughly, the next step is to add the fat to the milk and flour.

12. Upon entering, my attention was immediately drawn to the end of the room.
13. This takes us far enough away from the city's lights and noises to enjoy the quiet of the country.
14. The children plan and decorate in their own way, thus giving them an opportunity for self-expression.
15. Upon arriving in this country from Slovenia, the language and customs of the people were strange to him.

Exercise 3. Some of the following sentences are correct; some contain danglers. You are to pick out the faulty sentences and to correct them.

1. Being unaccustomed to rowing, my arms ached and my heart raced violently.
2. After much fumbling in my pockets, I finally produced a coin.
3. When conversing with her teachers, her remarks were modest and dignified.
4. While on the rocks, a small stone was dislodged and started to roll toward us.
5. A person can discover many opportunities to meet interesting people vacationing at the seaside.
6. Not having had a profound event in my life, it is rather difficult for me to find a subject on which I could write a profound English theme.
7. While coming home from Elgin one night, the starter switch on the car went out of order.
8. After becoming interested in the sport of fishing, one can easily make at home all the fishing tackle except line, hook, and spinners.
9. Meals must be taken regularly, allowing no eating between meals.
10. Knowing she was an expert stenographer, my mind would seem to be a blank when taking dictation from her.
11. While lathering his upper lip, Bob's nervousness will often lead him to insert a portion of the soap into his mouth.
12. As chairman of the decorations committee, it became my assignment to dream up some kind of ornament suitable to the occasion.
13. I have found that in living with a group of girls many adjustments have to be made.
14. Being the first child, my father and mother were both pleased and excited.
15. As foreman of the unloading gang, my instructions were to keep the street and sidewalks unobstructed at all times.
16. After a sleepless night recalling war memories, weariness and intense nervousness make the entire day a nightmare.

17. On interviewing him, the question arose as to why he had chosen Russia for his particular field of study.
18. This past year has left a deep impression on me, for as president of the group my responsibility made me see all that a group can do for one of its members.
19. If a person does not have to face the sun, he will not squint, thus getting a more natural picture.
20. When taking pictures of buildings or landscapes, the sun is usually behind the person taking the picture.

REFERENCE OF PRONOUNS

55a. Do not let a pronoun refer to an antecedent that is vague, or remote, or implied.

As a rule, pronouns should have definite antecedents and should be placed as near their antecedents as possible. The meaning of the sentence should be unmistakable on the first reading. If the reader has to hesitate, if he has to look back to find the substantive to which a pronoun refers, the sentence is a poor one.

Indefinite: I can remember that we met many people, but I did not enjoy *it* very much. [To what does *it* refer?]

Clear: I can remember that we met many people, but I did not enjoy the reception very much. [Supply the word for which *it* stands.]

Indefinite: My mother was a school teacher; therefore it is no wonder that I have chosen *that* as my profession. [The antecedent of *that* is only vaguely implied.]

Clear: My mother was a school teacher; therefore it is no wonder that I have chosen teaching as my profession.

Misleading: Each damaged article is marked in such a way that *it* cannot be erased. [The reader is confused because *it* seems to refer to *article*.]

Clear: Each damaged article is marked in such a way that the mark cannot be erased.

Indefinite: We enjoyed our stay at the Newport Hotel. *They* provide comfortable rooms and excellent food. [*They* seems to refer vaguely to the persons who operate the hotel.]

Clear: We enjoyed our stay at the Newport Hotel, which provides comfortable rooms and excellent food.

It is usually awkward to have a pronoun refer to an antecedent in a subordinate position. The reader will instinctively associate a pronoun with the most prominent substantive in the clause he has just read. The result is confusion — possibly a momentary confusion but still an undesirable one.

Confusing: Men have lounged and crouched around their fires; they have been the companions of their dreams and meditations. [The reader will hesitate when he comes to "they have," because he will assume that the subject of the sentence is still "men."]

Clear: Men have lounged and crouched around their fires — the companions of their dreams and their meditations.

or: Men have lounged and crouched around their fires, since fires have been the companions of their dreams and meditations.

55b. Do not write a sentence in which the pronoun might be understood to refer to more than one antecedent.

Ambiguous: He crossed his other leg, took out a handkerchief from a back pocket, wiped his forehead, blew his nose, and carefully and methodically folded and replaced it. [Does *it* refer to *nose?*]

Clear: He crossed his other leg, took out a handkerchief from a back pocket, wiped his forehead, blew his nose, and then carefully and methodically folded the handkerchief and replaced it.

Ambiguous: Almost all of the merchants know their customers and they are in the habit of calling them by name.

Clear: In a small town everyone knows everyone else so well that even the merchants usually address their customers by name.

Ambiguous: At the breakfast table, Dorothy told Mary that she had committed a bad social error. [Who had committed the error? Dorothy or Mary?]

Clear: At the breakfast table, Dorothy accused Mary of committing a bad social error.

It is neither customary nor necessary to resort to an explanatory antecedent in parentheses after a pronoun.

Poor: Father told the doctor that he (Father) did not think that the war would greatly affect his (the doctor's) profession.

Better: Father said to the doctor, "I do not think that the war is going to affect your profession very much."

55c. In formal and serious writing, do not use the pronouns *you* **and** *they* **in the indefinite sense.**

The indefinite *you* and *they* are common in speech and in many forms of informal writing. They are not appropriate in formal writing. For a fuller discussion of this usage see section 5j.

Colloquial: When saluting, you must stand up straight and bring your right hand up smartly to the visor of your cap.

Formal style: When a soldier salutes, he must stand up straight and bring his right hand up smartly to the visor of his cap.

Colloquial: They do not have fraternities in many colleges in the East.
Formal: Fraternities are not permitted in many colleges in the East.

Colloquial: In the army, you do not ask; you do what you are told to.
Formal: In the army, a soldier does not ask; he obeys.

Colloquial: They say that Mrs. Dill has applied for a divorce.
Formal: There is a rumor that Mrs. Dill has applied for a divorce.

55d. Do not use *this, that,* **or** *which* **to refer vaguely to an idea implied or suggested but not clearly expressed in the preceding clause or sentence.**

A pronoun may have a clause or a sentence for its antecedent; it may even refer to a thought expressed by a part of the preceding sentence. As long as the reference is unmistakable, the sentence is clear. But the careless writer may fall into the habit of stringing together a series of "this," "that," and "which" clauses without troubling himself about either clearness or exactness. Whenever the writer suspects the clearness or definiteness of an antecedent, he should try to summarize the general idea of the clause referred to by using some expression like *this fact, this condition, a fact which,* and so forth. If the result is still unsatisfactory, he should rewrite the sentence.

Notice that the references are entirely clear in the following sentences.

Clear: I have given up smoking. That should please my mother.
So you have decided to support my candidate. This is indeed a surprise.
Father suggested that I keep the money, which I did without a protest.

429

Now notice the vague references in the following.

Vague: After locking the beasts in the barn, I went to bed and slept soundly, which is one of the effects of hunting cows. [The writer evidently means "sound sleep," but *which* could refer to two other things in the sentence.]

Clear: After locking the beasts in the barn, I went to bed and slept soundly, for sound sleep is one of the effects of hunting cows.

Vague: If a girl suspects that her roommate needs help or a friendly word of encouragement, she should do it before it is too late. [Do what?]

Clear: If a girl suspects that her roommate needs help or a friendly word of encouragement, she should offer assistance before it is too late.

Vague: The fish are kept alive and fresh in glass tanks, and it also attracts people, which helps the business considerably. [What do *it* and *which* refer to?]

Clear: The fish are kept alive and fresh in glass tanks. The display of live fish helps business by attracting people to the place.

55e. Avoid the awkward use of *same, such, above,* and *said* as reference words.

These words are used as reference words in legal or technical writing; in ordinary writing they should be avoided, not because they are incorrect but because they usually lead to awkwardness of expression. Use one of the common pronouns (it, them, this) or the name of the thing to which you refer.

Poor: I stood there holding the monkey wrench and oil can in my hands. The foreman ordered me to return the same to the engine room.

Better: I stood there holding the monkey wrench and oil can in my hands. The foreman ordered me to return the tools to the engine room.

Poor: The significance of said decision is not yet fully comprehended.

Better: The significance of the decision referred to is not yet fully comprehended.

Poor: Please return same to me by bearer.

Better: Please return it [or name the object] to me by the bearer of this note.

Poor: The above is a complete refutation of their arguments.

Better: These facts completely refute their arguments.

55f. Make a pronoun agree with its antecedent in number, gender, and person.

For a discussion of the agreement of pronouns and antecedents, see "Pronouns," section 5.

Wrong: I advise every beginner to purchase the best instruments they can afford. [*Every* is singular and therefore must be followed by a singular pronoun.]

Right: I advise every beginner to purchase the best instruments he can afford.

Wrong: When an orchestra becomes successful, their success reflects upon the type of leadership they have had. [You must be consistent. If you begin by considering *orchestra* as singular, you must continue to refer to it as one unit.]

Right: When an orchestra becomes successful, its success reflects the kind of leadership it has had.

55g. Do not begin an essay with a reference to the title.

If the title is the same as the subject of the first sentence, it is better to repeat the words of the title. For instance, if your title is "Trout Fishing," do not begin your paper, "This has always been my favorite sport." Say, "Trout fishing has always been my favorite sport."

EXERCISES

Exercise 1. In each of the following sentences underline the pronoun or pronouns with faulty reference. Rewrite each sentence so as to correct the error.

1. The dean's duties are that of a mother.
2. Dynamite is placed on the rock, and after breaking the rock it is loaded into cars to be taken away.
3. Although one would think that he lives on excitement, they would be mistaken.
4. The soil here is sandy and loose, which makes it easy digging.
5. We often see peculiar resemblances between people and animals. Many times it is not meant to be uncomplimentary, and this is one of those instances.

6. When a person first meets her, they notice that she has a scar over her right eye.
7. We built many bridges over small swamps which kept us constantly occupied.
8. He seldom reprimands us for anything, but when he does, it is always taken seriously.
9. At the reception everybody was introduced to the dean of the school in which they were enrolled.
10. Peace and a disarmament program should go hand in hand, for without one the world cannot have another. This was one of the failures of the League of Nations.

Exercise 2. Cross out every pronoun with a faulty reference. Write your correction above the pronoun which you have crossed out.

1. The Chamber of Commerce has exerted their influence in favor of a new recreational center.
2. When I was a little girl, most mothers thought that a Dutch bob was the style for their little girls' hair, and mine was no exception.
3. Potato growing is the second largest industry in the county, and these workers also flock into town for their Saturday night celebration.
4. They were unable to finish their education, which will create a problem after the war.
5. Every workman who had a grievance was told to bring the same to the personnel office.
6. As my father is an engineer, it is natural for me to choose that as my life work.
7. In some places the untouchables are required to wear a bell in order to give others proper warning of his approach.
8. Of course the performance was widely advertised, and it served its purpose well.
9. India has resented British domination since it was first imposed upon them.
10. For years America has heard his symphonies, but they have not heard much about the composer himself.

Exercise 3. Point out the vague or faulty reference in each of the following sentences. Then rewrite each sentence so as to correct the error.

1. The machine stands about waist high to the operator, which is about three and a half feet high.

2. Her day is so full that seldom does she have time for letter writing. I do not miss them, for I know that she would write if she could.
3. Some students try many courses to see which one he is interested in.
4. Oftentimes when a person has been away, they are ill at ease among old acquaintances.
5. He joined the Merchant Marine two years ago and has seen numerous strange places in that time.
6. If I have been introduced to someone who does not appeal to me, it is likely that I'll not greet them when I see them on the street.
7. The orchestra was usually composed of a violin, a banjo, and a mouth harp. Occasionally they were fortunate enough to secure the services of an accordion.
8. During the last bond drive, Centerville was the first town in the state to reach their quota. Not only did they reach the top but they also passed it.
9. John can bake beautiful rolls. One needs only to express a doubt as to his ability and they will be rewarded with a pan full of delicious rolls.
10. Her wheat-colored coat is thrown over a straight-backed chair which gives the room a lived-in appearance.
11. With practice one can judge a person by the dogs they own and by the way the dogs behave.
12. However, the South African fields no longer have the monopoly of the supply of diamonds that it once had.

PARALLELISM AND CORRELATIVES

56a. Use parallel structure for sentence elements that are co-ordinate in rank.

It is not true that every series of words, phrases, or clauses, or any combination of these elements, must always be expressed in parallel form. Occasionally an attempt to produce complete parallelism in structure results in a stilted and artificial writing which some critics refer to as "schoolmarm" English. The student writer, however, will seldom be guilty of too much structure. Any rule which helps him to design and build good sentences is a good rule. The rule may be restated in this form: a noun should be followed by another noun, an infinitive by an infinitive, a phrase by a phrase, and a clause by a clause. See also pages 59–62.

Illogical: Our English instructor asked us to close our books, to take pen and paper, and that we were to write a short theme.

Parallel: Our English instructor asked us to close our books, to take pen and paper, and to write a short theme. [A series of three infinitive phrases.]

Illogical: Few of the leaders anticipated the bitterness of the strike or how long it would last.

Parallel: Few of the leaders anticipated the bitterness or the duration of the strike. [Noun followed by another noun.]

Illogical: It had never occurred to me before to thank God for the blessings I already had and that there were worse afflictions in this world than broken friendships.

Parallel: It had never occurred to me before that I should thank God for the blessings I already had and that there were worse afflictions in this world than broken friendships. [One *that* clause followed by a second *that* clause.]

A particular form of error in parallel structure — an error in grammar, too, for that matter — is the use of an "and which" or "and who" clause in a sentence which does not contain a preceding "which" or "who" clause.

Faulty: He is a man of wide experience and who is also very popular with the farmers.

Parallel: He is a man of wide experience and also great popularity among the farmers. [Cancel the "and who."]

Faulty: I am interested in electronics, because it is a new field and which offers interesting opportunities to one who knows science.

Parallel: I am interested in electronics, which is a new field and which offers interesting opportunities to one who knows science. [Change the first clause to a "which" clause.]

or: I am interested in electronics, because the field is new and full of interesting opportunities for the person who knows science. [Cancel the "which" clause and make a different sort of parallel.]

56b. Avoid the false parallel, that is, using parallel structure for ideas that are not parallel.

Illogical: I finally realized that my daydreaming was not making me beautiful, slender, or friends. [The three words seem to depend on *making me*, but two of them are adjectives and one is a noun. They are not logically parallel.]

Better: I finally realized that my daydreaming was not making me beautiful and slender or bringing me friends.

Illogical: She has black hair, blue eyes, and is very fair.
Parallel: She has black hair, blue eyes, and a very fair complexion. [Make it a series of three nouns.]

Awkward: She has black hair, blue eyes, and wears glasses. [This is undesirable because the three elements are not co-ordinate. They should not be made to seem co-ordinate.]
Logical: She has black hair and blue eyes, and she wears glasses. [Put *and* between the two which are similar. Put the third into a separate clause.]

56c. Use correlatives only before sentence elements that are parallel in form.

The correlatives are *both . . . and, either . . . or, neither . . . nor, not only . . . but also*, and *whether . . . or*.

Wrong: You are either mistaken or I am.
Right: Either you are mistaken or I am. [Either you or I.]

Wrong: Unselfish people not only are happier but they are more successful.
Right: Unselfish people are not only happier but also more successful. [The parallel words are *happier . . . more successful*.]

Wrong: Our guide was undecided whether to continue on the trail or if we should return to our camp.
Right: Our guide was undecided whether to continue on the trail or to return to the camp.

EXERCISES

Exercise 1. In each of the following sentences underline the parts that should be expressed in parallel form. Then rewrite each sentence.

1. It is easy for one ski to twist across the other and breaking your leg or pulling your knee out of joint.
2. Joe, the habitual drunkard, portrayed a person tired of life and love and yet he had a soft spot in his heart.
3. Deer not only drink at the same time each day but at the same place.
4. A person of this type shows traits of dreaminess, impoverishment of personality, moody, unsocial, and irritable.

5. This teacher not only made me realize the importance of friendship but also how one can benefit from wanting to know and understand people.
6. The average motorist, in order to avoid accidents, must not only watch where he is going, but he must also watch where other people are going.
7. Chipmunk burrows have two openings, one for general use and there is also another that can be used in case of emergency.
8. The reckless driver will pass cars on hills, on curves, or when the approaching traffic is so heavy that it is not safe to pass.
9. In the evening we would play baseball, pitch horseshoes, or some other type of outdoor game.
10. We try to teach them how to get along with people, table manners, good habits, and how to get the most from life.

Exercise 2. Rewrite the following sentences so that correlatives are used logically.

1. The sign informed us that neither was loitering permitted nor could we smoke on the premises.
2. Their leaders are not only clever but they are also unscrupulous.
3. "Either you may take your dividends now or leave them with us to draw interest," said the agent.
4. The natives are both afraid and they are suspicious also.
5. They do not know whether to hide or if they should co-operate with us.
6. Your answer is neither clever nor is it sensible.
7. His students are still wondering whether his advice was meant to be taken seriously or if he was merely joking.
8. The commission must choose a definite course — either to increase the tax levies or borrowing money by selling more bonds.
9. Not only has this policy affected the morale of our soldiers, but also the attitude of the conquered peoples.
10. The wounded veteran neither asked for sympathy nor pity from his friends.

Exercise 3. In each of the following sentences underline the parts that should be expressed in parallel form. Then rewrite each sentence.

1. It is important to analyze these three types of radio broadcasts with a view to purpose, presentation, and how they are sponsored.
2. I am sure that my two years in a military school taught me discipline, respect for authority, and always to be neat in my dress.

3. When I left the army, I did not know whether to go back to college or if I should look for a good job.
4. While in the army the men were careless about bad grammar and they also used much profanity.
5. The military leaders of Japan did not expect the destruction of their navy or that their cities would be bombed.
6. His speech is slow, soft, and it has a monotonous effect.
7. My hobby is an unusual one and which supplies me with not a little spending money.
8. Army officials are asking the wives of officers in foreign service to stay at home and that they must not expect housing accommodations in San Francisco.
9. My work in his office consisted of typing addresses and to answer the telephone.
10. My youngest brother, a high-school lad, is tall, dark, a favorite with the girls, and wears typical "sloppy-Joe" clothes.

SHIFT IN POINT OF VIEW

57a. Avoid an unnecessary and illogical shift in point of view.

One of the most common faults committed by inexperienced writers is shifting from active to passive voice, from past to present tense, from *one* to *you*, from indirect to direct discourse, or from formal to colloquial style. A point of view once chosen should be kept until there is a logical reason for changing to another.

1. Shift from active to passive voice.

Illogical: A roommate is a person who shares your joys and sorrows; shirts and neckties are also shared.

Better: A roommate is a person who shares one's shirts and neckties as well as one's joys and sorrows. [None of the intended humor is lost by the change to the active.]

Illogical: We swept the room carefully, and the furniture and shelves were also dusted.

Better: We carefully swept the room and dusted the furniture and the shelves.

2. Shift in tense — from past to present or from present to past.

Illogical: Elsie asked the doctor about her mother but receives an evasive reply. [This sort of shift, from past to present, must be watched for in narrative accounts.]

Better: Elsie asked the doctor about her mother but received an evasive reply.

Illogical: I begin to get a little curious and stuck my head from under the blanket to see who should be prowling around at that time of the night. [The writer shifts from present to past to future.]

Better: I began to get a little curious and stuck my head out from under the blanket to see who was prowling around at that time of the night.

3. Shift in pronoun, in person or number.

Illogical: You must make yourself interesting to the group that listens to you and are constantly trying to detect your mistakes. [If *group* is used as a singular once, it cannot be used as a plural in the same sentence.]

Better (informal style): You must make yourself interesting to the group that listens to you and is constantly trying to detect your mistakes.

Correct in a formal context: One must always make himself interesting to the group that listens to him and is constantly trying to detect his mistakes.

Illogical: If one's mouth is dry, eat a lump of sugar or chew gum. [Shift from *one* to *you*.]

Better: If one's mouth is dry, one should eat a lump of sugar or chew gum. [It is doubtful, however, if any person who used *one* with such formal precision would chew gum.]

Illogical: If one is careful about their appearance, you may even win a quick promotion. [Shift from *one* to *their* to *you*.]

Correct in colloquial style: If you are careful about your appearance, you may even win a quick promotion.

Formal style: If a person is careful about his appearance, he may even win a quick promotion.

4. Shift in subject.

Illogical: Miller was a great athlete, but studying was not his strong point.
Better: Miller was a great athlete but a poor student.

Illogical: I am taking a course in forestry, although life in the woods does not greatly appeal to me.

Better: I am taking a course in forestry, although I am not especially fond of a life in the woods.

5. Shift from indirect to direct discourse.

Illogical: The girls wonder if their hair is combed or will this dress suit my figure.
Consistent: The girls wonder, "Is my hair combed? Will this dress suit my figure?"
or: The girls wonder whether their hair is combed and whether their dresses are suitable to their figures.
Illogical: He asked us would we find him a room.
Consistent: He asked us to find him a room. He asked us, "Will you find me a room?"

57b. Avoid a shift from one style of composition to another.

In expository writing, which as a rule is serious, avoid the use of slang or colloquialisms, even when you apologize for them by the use of quotation marks. Quotation marks do not justify slang; at best they merely indicate that you know you are using slang.

Inappropriate: The main fault of the League of Nations was that the big shots would not gang up on any large nation that was breaking the peace.
Formal style: The main fault of the League of Nations was that the great powers refused to combine against any one of their group that was breaking the peace.

Inappropriate: The Russian authorities seemed to be steamed up about another attack upon their merchant ships in the Mediterranean.
Formal style: The Russian authorities seemed to be angered (*provoked*) by another attack upon their merchant ships in the Mediterranean.

EXERCISES

Exercise 1. The following are sections from student papers. Rewrite each in the past tense.

1. The door closed with its customary protest, and we stand in the darkness.
   "Hey, quit jiggling my bed. Can't you see I'm trying to sleep?" complained a plaintive voice.

Then at last with groping hands I find my bed. I ease myself into the blankets, but the bed groaned and squeaked its nightly protestation. With the covers pulled snugly around me I prepare to sleep. Then the door admitted another freshman, who in passing, gives my bed another jiggling.

2. A tall, well-groomed man wearing a black pin-striped suit entered the room. He greets the students with a warm smile that made them feel he is a friend as well as an instructor. His deep voice reassured them. His brown sparkling eyes were cheerful and mischievous, and his jet black mustache gave him the air of a comic-opera villain. There isn't a bit of curl in his straight black hair. It is neat and always has the look of just having been combed and brushed.

Exercise 2. In each of the following sentences specify the type of illogical shift that you find — in tense, voice, subject, number, or person. Then make the necessary corrections.

1. The train was two hours late, so Mrs. Smith and I decide to wait in the car.
2. Never before had I operated an elevator, but it surely must be simple because all you had to do was to press a button, which I did.
3. There was just one short half hour of work left. The clerks in the sports department, where I am working, are busy bustling around trying to get rid of the last shoppers.
4. In some cases, when the person was released from prison he committed another crime, and from then on usually leads a life of crime.
5. Many girls who live in the poor sections of the town would profit by becoming a member of a Camp Fire Girls group.
6. We filled out our registration blanks and attended several lectures; also placement tests in English and mathematics were taken.
7. I do not mean that the whole day should be spent on one assignment, but do it carefully and thoroughly.
8. The target was kept moving while the men try to demolish it with a well-placed shot.
9. The twins were not identical; one is larger than the other.
10. There is little enthusiasm shown by the students. However, why should they?

Exercise 3. Identify and correct the illogical shifts in the point of view in the following sentences.

1. When the driver intends to stop, be sure to give the correct signal.
2. Some girls hesitate to come to college because they cannot afford to become a member of a sorority.

3. No matter what one may be discussing with her, she always argues with you.
4. Not all of your time is spent with your roommate, but since a large portion of it is, a roommate that will help one become a better man is almost a necessity in college.
5. When a system of forest management will be worked out whereby irresponsible hunters will be kept out of our forests, the problem of conservation of game is near its solution.
6. Christmas to me is a day to be celebrated because of the very fact that you are alive and well.
7. Holidays are valuable for the mental change one gets. During the day you can rest your mind, and during the night your body is refreshed.
8. If we would try to help other persons instead of worrying about ourselves, we would be much happier. Give the best that is in you and do not hold it back because you think that it is not good enough.
9. We must see ourselves as others see us, and ponder the question, "Do I represent my ideal of the perfect man?" If you do not, can you visualize your shortcomings? If we admit the possession of certain faults, how can you excuse your not overcoming them?
10. I wonder what is the power of salt that causes many to believe that when it is spilled, it will bring you bad luck, or that when it is thrown over one's left shoulder, the future holds something promising for them.

MIXED CONSTRUCTIONS

58a. Avoid an illogical shift from one construction to another.

A "mixed construction" is usually the result of hasty and careless writing. The writer begins one construction, and immediately, without troubling himself to look back at what he has written, continues with another construction.

Mixed: In our basement we found a small wood stove, which upon removing the front, made it resemble a fireplace. [*Which* refers to *stove.* The stove cannot remove its own front, nor can the stove make itself resemble anything.]

Clear: In our basement we found a small wood stove, which we made into a fireplace by removing its front.

In our basement we found a small wood stove. By removing its front, we made it resemble a fireplace.

Mixed: She did not say a word, but took me to the back yard in what seemed to me a bit hurriedly. [The writer has forgotten his original intention.]
He could say either *took me in what seemed a hurried manner* or *took me a bit hurriedly.*]

Mixed: It took us an hour and a half to motor from Portland to Troutdale, a distance, as I said before, was only fifteen miles.
Clear: It took us an hour and a half to motor from Portland to Troutdale, a distance, as I said before, of only fifteen miles.
or: It took us an hour and a half to travel the distance of fifteen miles between Portland and Troutdale.

A common error is the use of an adverbial clause as a noun clause.

Mixed: My main reason for leaving college was because I was offered a good job.
Clear: My main reason for leaving college is that I was offered a good job.
The fact that I was offered a good job was my main reason for leaving college.
I left college mainly because I was offered a good job.

Occasionally a writer will run an independent clause into a sentence in such a way that it appears to stand as the subject of a verb.

Mixed: I had no money was the reason I did not buy it.
Clear: I did not buy it because I had no money.

Mixed: Elsie was disliked by her stepmother was the reason she left London.
Clear: Elsie left London because she was disliked by her stepmother.

58b. Avoid unintentional humor or absurdity in serious writing.

Poor: In my case I apply golf to myself as others apply stamps or antiques to themselves.
I saw a spout of water and I thought it was a whale, but I don't know what kind of fish it was.
To build a good model takes time and patience to have a good model when you are finished.

EXERCISE

Exercise 1. Revise the following sentences.

1. You may notice an old hound lying on the ground and looks as if he were asleep.
2. I believe one reason why she is so ambitious is because her family lives on a farm.
3. We were constantly giving parties that we never asked anyone outside our little group to come.
4. The name "pituitary" was named by Vesalius, who had an erroneous theory of its function.
5. The ladies of a century ago thought it necessary to lead a life of leisure and a disgrace to work.
6. Is it true what they are saying about her?
7. The more advanced one goes into a subject, the more interesting it becomes.
8. Most of their men were down with malaria which was the cause of their failure in Burma.
9. Our first impression being it was something like candy, it tasted sweet but a great deal stronger.
10. The reason Elliott was discharged was on account of there was no more work for him.

MIXED IMAGERY

59a. Do not combine incongruous figures of speech.

In the teaching of writing, warnings against scrambled metaphors may have been given an undeserved and an unfortunate prominence. A mixed metaphor is often a sign of mental vitality. It is surely a lesser literary crime than page after page of dull and uninspired prose. If you scramble two incongruous images, you probably need little more than a hint to show you that your metaphors are inappropriate. It is manifestly absurd to speak of "watering the spark of originality," or "blazing a trail over the sea of knowledge," or of "being blinded by a thirst for revenge." Even Shakespeare spoke of taking up arms against a sea of troubles. If your instructor points out a mixed figure of speech in your writing, laugh over it. He will laugh with you and then "encourage the spark of imagination which the mixed metaphor fore-shadows, water it with drops of kindness and fertilize it with encouragement, so that the springs of originality may blossom forth like a tree and shed their light over many arid pages of prose writing!"

The following samples illustrate what is meant by "mixed imagery."

1. Many high-school athletes think they can ride on their high-school laurels right into a position on the college team. [How can one ride on a laurel?]
2. The future of jazz was at its lowest ebb. [Even were the future not transported to the past, a rare feat in itself, how could a future ebb?]
3. Instead of narrowly pursuing the mechanics of grammar, the clever teacher will often digress into anecdotes which will make the class fairly rock with laughter. [Can "mechanics" be pursued either narrowly or broadly?]
4. A college education enables the graduate to meet the snares and pitfalls of life with a broader point of view.

59b. Do not use inappropriate figures of speech.

Do not, for example, use humorous figures in a serious theme, or prosaic figures in a poetic context.

Inappropriate in a serious paper: The edge of the rising moon, just beginning to show itself above the distant horizon of the prairie, looked like the top of the head of a bald-headed man about to climb over a board fence.

EXERCISES

Exercise 1. What are your comments on the success of the following figures? Which are appropriate in serious writing? Which are obviously meant to be humorous? Which depend on a play on words?

1. The village lay pasted flat on the marsh.
2. Slender poplar trees, evenly spaced, rule off the distance with inky lines.
3. She wore a hat as nondescript as a last-year's bird's nest.
4. Her voice was the thin cry of a quail.

5. The lurid twilight was lanced everywhere with leaping tongues of flame.

6. Its powerful headlight fingered rails and telegraph wires.

7. He played the King in *Hamlet* as if he momentarily expected somebody to play the ace.

8. She clings like a long hair to a wet hand.

9. A witty writer is like a porcupine; his quill makes no distinction between friend and foe.

10. He had an eye like a loose button on an ulster.

11. He was a man of high principle and no interest.

12. Long sentences in a short composition are like large rooms in a little house.

13. He had a face like a smoked herring.

14. His conversation puts a terrific strain on the eyebrows.

15. Lightning stabbed earth's breast with a brilliant blade.

Exercise 2. Use five figures of speech in your next theme.

TRANSITIONS

60. Use connectives and transitions to connect thoughts in a sentence or in a group of sentences.

If your instructor refers you to this section, read also sections 8 and 47c and the section on transitions in the chapter on the paragraph, pages 90–100. There are four main ways of linking ideas — by using conjunctions and transitional words and phrases, by using pronouns, by repeating key words, and by expressing similar thoughts in parallel structure.

1. Conjunctions and transitional expressions.

The following is a brief list of transitional words and phrases. You must not think that this list is complete; neither should you assume that the natural, spontaneous phrases of transition that occur to you as you write are either incorrect or unliterary.

on the other hand	conversely	finally
in the second place	of course	after all
on the contrary	in conclusion	I mean
at the same time	to sum up	indeed
in particular	moreover	next

445

in spite of this	in addition	similarly
in like manner	for example	again
and so again	for instance	I repeat
as I have said	furthermore	and truly
in contrast to this	accordingly	meanwhile

Examples of transitions:

In like manner, all kinds of deficient and impolitic usages are referred to the national love of trade; though, *oddly enough*, it would be a weighty charge against a foreigner that he regarded the Americans as a trading people. — Charles Dickens.

I am not blaming or excusing anyone here. . . . I find, *for instance*, that prejudice, essentially, is worse on the prejudiced than on their targets. — Louis Adamic.

There were then very few regular troops in the kingdom. A town, *therefore*, which could send forth, at an hour's notice, twenty thousand men . . . — Thomas Babington Macaulay.

2. Pronouns referring to antecedents in the preceding sentences.

Examples:

In the summer, Father had his usual two or three weeks of vacation. *These* were spent usually at our cabin in the mountains.

I know a writer of newspaper editorials. *Himself* a liberal, *he* has to grind out a thousand words daily which reflect the ultra conservative policy of the paper for which *he* works. *He* keeps a record like a batting chart. . . . — Stuart Chase.

3. Key words repeated.

Examples:

Nothing in the way of civilization is inborn, as are the forms and workings of our bodies. Everything that goes to make up civilization must be acquired anew in infancy and childhood, by each and all of us. — James Harvey Robinson.

This is all true, of course, but I am unregenerate enough to think that the purpose in studying any language is to speak it and read it. I know from experience that you cannot read a language unless you can speak it. I know that our students are not taught to speak Latin or Greek. I am therefore not surprised that they can read neither language. — John Erskine, "An Education To Be Used." *New York Times Magazine*, Jan. 20, 1939. By permission of the author.

4. Parallel Structure.

Examples:

We had hated the physical suffering and horror of war. . . . We had hated the febrile emotionalism, the propaganda lies and exaggerations. . . . We had hated the intellectual suppressions of war. . . . We had hated war's release of the most primitive passions. . . . We had hated, or thought we had hated, war's complete overriding of the individual. . . . — Walter Millis, *Zero Hour*.

An analysis of the connectives and transitions used in the following paragraph should be helpful.

The human race being what it is, with no two human beings exactly alike, it is reasonable to assume that all gradations of womankind can be found in England, just as in America, or anywhere else. There may be more of one sort and less of another over here, for there are different influences at work. One reason for less pampering, for instance, is that here women greatly outnumber the men, whereas in America the scales are more evenly balanced. Another reason is the natural English thrift, born partly of the fact that the vast majority here live on small incomes. This would also help to explain the scarcity of beautifully dressed women. Even in London they are few and far between as compared to the women of any American city. For one thing, most English women can't afford elaborate wardrobes, and must go in for the sensible and practical clothes. Many of them prefer to, anyway. Also, there are far fewer shops here than in America which specialize in smart frocks at modest prices. And perhaps it is true, as sometimes said by foreigners, that English women have, on the whole, less talent for dressing smartly than the women of America or France. Yet I have often seen an

"Human" repeated.

"One sort" and "another" refer to "gradations."
"Here" refers to "in England."
Directive phrase.
"Here" refers to "in England." Conjunction.
"In America" is repeated.
Refers to "reason."
"Here" is repeated.
Refers to "women."
"Women" repeated.
Directive phrase.
"Women" repeated.
Pronoun. Two connectives. "Here" repeated.
Connectives.

Repetition. Connective phrase. Repetition. Conjunction.

Englishwoman wear dowdy clothes, on a not too shapely figure, with an <u>air of careless good breeding</u> that made her somehow more arresting than many of the Hollywood glamour girls. <u>In fact</u>, <u>that air of good breeding</u> is a characteristic of very many Englishwomen, perhaps because, since 1837, a standard has been set by the reigning Queen. I have noticed <u>it</u> in many walks of life <u>here</u>. My housekeeper has <u>it</u> in abundance. <u>So</u> have most of the <u>women</u> <u>I</u> have observed <u>here</u>.

Connective. Pronoun. Phrase repeated.

Pronoun. "Here" repeated. Pronoun. Conj. "Women" repeated. "Here" repeated.

— James Dyrenforth, "Through Darkest England with Gun and Camera," *The Outpost*, June, 1945.

EMPHASIS BY POSITION

61. Make your sentences more effective by placing the important words in the important positions in the sentence.

The most conspicuous places in the sentence are the beginning and the end. Use these positions for ideas which deserve attention and emphasis. Put your important ideas where they will stand out. Conversely, place less important modifiers and transitional phrases within the sentence.

No writer can consistently rearrange his sentences so as to begin and end them with important ideas. Many sentences are so short that the reader's mind comprehends them as units. In many others the word order is determined by the nature of the English language. For example, we write: "He is a good man. Her son was killed in France. The day's work is done. The President saluted the flag." In sentences like these the question of emphatic position cannot arise.

Whenever possible without sacrificing clearness and smoothness, place explanatory phrases or minor details within the sentence.

Weak: However, the general disclaimed any responsibility for the order.
Better: The general, however, disclaimed any responsibility for the order.

Weak: The student who cheats in an examination is cheating only himself in the final analysis.
Better: The student who cheats in an examination is, in the final analysis, cheating only himself.

Weak: Public speaking should be taught in freshman English I think.
Better: Public speaking, I think, should be taught in freshman English.

Occasionally you may express a thought more effectively by changing your sentence from the loose to the periodic form.

A sentence in which the thought is not complete until the end is called a periodic sentence. The effect of the periodic sentence is one of suspense. Your reader, in other words, is forced to wait for the main idea until after he has comprehended the subordinate details upon which the main idea is based. Not all sentences in English are periodic; a large majority of them, in fact, are loose. It is precisely because of this that an occasional periodic sentence is emphatic.

Study the difference in effect produced by the following:

Loose: Stop talking if you have nothing more to say.
Periodic: If you have nothing more to say, stop talking.

Loose: It is of course impractical to legislate for those who will behave themselves while completely ignoring those who will not.
Periodic: To legislate for those who will behave themselves while completely ignoring those who will not is, of course, impractical.

Loose: The catalytic agents of college life are athletics, forensics, musical organizations, journalism, parties, and dances.
Periodic: Athletics, forensics, musical organizations, journalism, parties, dances — these are the catalytic agents of college life.

Here are two examples of long periodic sentences. Notice in each how suspense is built up by delaying the main statement until the end.

In the almost unique intimacy and good-fellowship of Oxford life, where for the moment men from every nation and every class are living together and surveying the nations of the earth in human and humorous companionship, the Rhodes Scholar, if he has in him the capacity for wisdom, learns the difference between an abstract formula and a living point of view. — Frank Aydelotte, "What the American Rhodes Scholar Gets from Oxford."

To transfer admiration from the thing possessed to its possessor; to conceive that the mere possession of material wealth makes of its possessor a proper object of worship; to feel abject before another who is wealthier — such emotions do not so much as enter the American mind. — Hilaire Belloc.

EXERCISES

Exercise 1. Using the principle of "emphasis by position," improve the following sentences.

1. Her reputation is all that saves her, one might say.
2. We may do some things that are wrong, but we are quite able to take care of ourselves, generally speaking.
3. College students are able to arrange their lives in a satisfactory manner if they are given the chance, in the writer's opinion.
4. The morning newspaper devotes a whole column to the story, I perceive.
5. The new program will include courses in airplane design, according to the Dean of Administration.

Exercise 2. Change the following loose sentences into periodic sentences.

1. Let the women work in offices if they are happy at their jobs.
2. His last remark was that anyone who took hyphens seriously would go mad.
3. The streets are like rivers a few minutes after one of our unusual rains has started.
4. The attack on Pearl Harbor came while the Japanese delegates were in Washington talking soft words of peace.
5. We lost the Philippines before we could recover from the blow.

REPETITION

62a. Give emphasis to a sentence or a group of sentences by repeating important words or the same type of construction.

An obvious form of repetition is illustrated in the following sentences. If used infrequently, it may be made effective.

Examples:

I blew out the light, and presently the only sound that broke the stillness of the night was the drip-drip-drip of the water in the kitchen.

"Boom! Boom! Boom!" replied the guns hidden in the ravine below us.

Soon we heard the steady put-put of his outboard motor.

Note the skillful use of repetition in the following sentences:

Examples:

Wycliffe was, no doubt, a *learned* man. But the *learning* of his day would have *burned* him, had it dared, as it did *burn* his dead body afterwards. — Wendell Phillips.

The nation has been deeply *stirred*, *stirred* by a solemn passion, *stirred* by the knowledge of wrong, of ideals lost, of government too often debauched and made an instrument of evil. — Woodrow Wilson.

It was as *scholars* that you were here; it is to the feeling and life of *scholars* that you return. — George William Curtis.

The effectiveness of a sentence, or of a series of sentences, may be strengthened by repeating the same form of construction.

Examples:

To differ is grotesque and eccentric. To protest is preposterous. To defy is incendiary and revolutionary. — George William Curtis.

Made drunk with the freedom of ideas, college students should charge destructively against all the institutions of a faulty world and all the conventions of a silly one. — Bernard DeVoto.

The life of Man is a long march through the night, surrounded by invisible foes, tortured by weariness and pain, towards a goal that few can hope to reach, and where none may tarry long. — Bertrand Russell.

62b. Avoid awkward repetition.

A word carelessly repeated weakens the effectiveness of a sentence. Careless repetition is frequently associated with wordiness, as may be seen in the following examples. Correct the fault by using synonyms, by using pronouns, or by completely rewriting the sentence.

Poor: I have been asked to write on a subject that has been the subject of controversy among sports commentators for years. That subject, as you have probably guessed, is none other than the question of which is the most interesting, basketball or football.

Better: I shall try to determine which is more interesting to watch — basketball or football.

Poor: A person who has seen each game for the first time would probably prefer the basketball game to the football game because this game is easy to comprehend and can be understood much more quickly.

Better: A person seeing each game for the first time might prefer basketball to football because of its greater simplicity.

EXERCISES

Exercise 1. Find five sentences in which words or constructions are repeated for emphasis. Copy and bring them to your class. Write five sentences in imitation of the five which you have found in your reading.

Exercise 2. Reconstruct the following sentences. Avoid the awkward repetition of words.

1. There are probably many questions which many persons are probably asking about this part of our recent history.
2. Naturally, the amount of time and money that is virtually wasted by college students amounts to a great deal.
3. Since we never had a net for a goal, we used our skates in making a line across the ice, and this line meant the same as a goal to us.
4. My ambition to become a musician was created with the creating of a grade-school band.
5. There are many reasons for a failure in college. Many students are intelligent, but still they do not make high grades for several good reasons. The three most important reasons are as follows.
6. The Spaniards built a large wall, complete with redans, completely around the city to protect it from the fierce Moro pirates.

BALANCE

63. Place similar or contrasted thoughts in balanced constructions.

Balance, like parallelism, uses similarity of structure to show similarity or contrast of ideas. The following examples will make the principle clear:

Examples:

Gush is bad taste, the parade of emotion. Prudery is bad taste, the parade of modesty. Fine writing is bad taste, the parade of elegance. Slang is bad taste, the parade of smartness or knowingness. — Oscar W. Firkins.

Education ought to foster the wish for truth, not the conviction that some particular creed is the truth. — Bertrand Russell.

If they [the Puritans] were unacquainted with the works of philosophers and poets, they were deeply read in the oracles of God. If their names were not found in the registers of heralds, they felt assured that they were recorded in the Book of Life. If their steps were not accompanied by a splendid train of menials, legions of ministering angels had charge over them. Their palaces were houses not made with hands; their diadems crowns of glory which should never fade away! — Macaulay.

EXERCISES

Exercise 1. Rewrite the following sentences so as to express similar or contrasted ideas in balanced form.

1. Young men look to the future, but it is only what has happened that engrosses the attention of old men.
2. A statesman makes the occasion, but a politician is different in that he has to wait for the occasion to make him.
3. Good books are like friends. They are our companions when we are happy. They also give us good advice when things go wrong, and they watch over us when we have had bad luck.
4. A war may be won with great difficulty, but to win a peace is even more difficult.

Exercise 2. Find in your reading five examples of balanced sentences, copy them, and bring them to class.

Exercise 3. Write a paragraph on one of the following topics. Use a number of balanced sentences to show the contrast between the topics.

> Freedom and anarchy
> The liberal and the conservative
> High-school teachers and college teachers
> Sentiment and sentimentality
> Good and bad sportsmanship
> The good teacher and the poor teacher

CLIMAX

64. Whenever you write a sentence which contains a series of elements of varying importance, try to arrange these elements in the order of climax.

It is not often that you have occasion to present facts or ideas in a series of unequal importance, but when you do, you will gain emphasis by arranging them in order from the least to the most important.

Unemphatic: His reward for twenty years of unselfish public service was persecution, exile, and misunderstanding.

Emphatic: His reward for twenty years of unselfish public service was misunderstanding, persecution, and exile.

As a device for increasing the impact of a sentence, climax has lost favor among modern writers. It is still used, especially in oratorical prose, but few writers now strive for it as consciously as did Macaulay, from whose essay on Milton the following examples are quoted. And yet who among us can resist an involuntary turning of his face toward the east when he reads sentences like these?

The very meanest of them [the Puritans] was a being to whose fate a mysterious and terrible importance belonged — on whose slightest actions the spirit of light and darkness looked with anxious interest — who had been destined, before heaven and earth were created, to enjoy a felicity which should continue when heaven and earth should have passed away. . . . For his sake empires had risen, and flourished, and decayed. For his sake the Almighty had proclaimed his will by the pen of the evangelist and the harp of the prophet. He had been rescued by no common deliverer from the grasp of no common foe. He had been ransomed by the sweat of no vulgar agony, by the blood of no earthly sacrifice. It was for him that the sun had been darkened, that the rocks had been rent, that the dead had arisen, that all nature had shuddered at the sufferings of her expiring God!

The rolling thunder of magnificent rhetoric did not die with the death of Macaulay. Read the following from *Time*, the weekly newsmagazine, to realize what balance and climax can do to strictly contemporary writing.

India, among nations, is the ancient of days. Before even China, there was India. Before human memory congealed from legend into record, India loomed from the unimaginable reach of time. Its landscape matched its origins — an immense wedge of the world, vast plains cracked by a too hot sun, vast jungles writhing with growth from too dense rains, vast cities melting under the unflagging onset of oblivion and the soft decay of stone itself, 400 million people pullulating in a too frantic drive to defeat the multiplicity of daily death.

Four thousand miles of all-but-harborless coast and the width of the Arabian Sea and the Bay of Bengal shut off the Indian subcontinent from the western desert world of Semites and the eastern twilight world of Annamese, Cambodians and Malays. Along the north, the highest mountains in the world, the Himalayas, walled off India from the mass of Asia.

Every nation is obsessed with one problem which is the measure of its capacity for greatness: Egypt with immortality; Greece with beauty; Rome with administration and law; France with rationalism; Germany with war; Britain with the freedom of the individual man. India, islanded by sea and land, and haunted by the hourly wanton foreclosure of life by death, looked within and found that its obsession was the soul and its creator, the problem of good and evil. It embodied this vision in one of the world's great faiths (Buddhism) and in religious works of great power (the *Vedas* and *Upanishads*). India, under its squalor and filth, its superstitions and its cruelties, its babble of 75 languages and dialects and hodge-podge of peoples, its lethal famines and lethal wars, was nevertheless the most intensely spiritual area on earth.

In its obsession, it worshipped God under all forms, from inexpressible abstraction to inexpressible obscenity, from the monkeys which defiled villages and ruined precious crops, to the snakes which every year killed 20,000 people. More extreme devotees, the Jains, even placed cloths over their mouths and noses lest they breathe in and kill forms of life too minute for vision but nevertheless God-created. — *Time*, July 16, 1945. Reprinted by permission.

EXERCISE

Exercise 1. Read several good modern essays and bring to class a copy of every sentence in which the device of climax is used.

WEAK PASSIVE VOICE

65. Avoid the use of the passive voice whenever the active voice is more natural and direct.

The passive voice is properly used when the receiver of the action is more important than the doer of the action or the action itself. See also section 7d.

Right: Several priceless old manuscripts were destroyed.
The wounded prisoner was dragged into the trench.

But notice the difference in the following sentences when the active voice replaces the passive.

Weak: Other games are also played by the guests.
Better: The guests also play other games.

Weak: As the top of the stairs is approached, a quickening of the steps of the person is announced by the trembling of the floor.
Better: As the intruder approaches the top of the stairs, the trembling of the floor announces the quickening of his steps.

Weak: The Sunday dinner is a meal at which everyone is present and is enjoyed immensely by all.
Better: Sunday dinner is a meal at which everyone is present and which everyone enjoys.

Weak: Many agonizing minutes are spent by the student in deciding on a subject for a speech.
Better: The student spends many agonizing minutes deciding upon a subject for a speech.

EXERCISE

Exercise 1. Improve the following sentences by changing the verbs from the passive to the active.

1. But his suggestion was received by me with disdain.
2. A last puff is taken, which momentarily illuminates the boy's face, and a glowing arc is noticed when the cigarette is flicked across the lawn.
3. I had heard that the party was to be just a "kid dance," but it was soon found out that it was great fun.
4. With his help the mistake was soon corrected by us.
5. Here and there are heard whispered explanations and giggles.
6. My courses were not given much thought by me.
7. Three women came in, and the question "Are you relatives of the groom?" was asked.
8. A daily trip is made to the attic to wipe the dust from her keepsakes, and then she sheds a tear or two over them.
9. The tractor cannot be driven and the mowing machine manipulated by one man at the same time.

10. In the laboratory all available information is studied by chemists. After this extensive study, experiments are performed. The data are recorded in detail. If no satisfactory results are obtained, another study is carried out, but this time the data obtained from the first trial are included. These trials are carried on until satisfactory results are gained.

CONCISENESS

66. Do not use more words than are necessary for the adequate expression of your thought.

If you are referred to this section, read also "Wordiness," section 41. Then rewrite the sentence to which your instructor objects. It may be that you cannot understand why your instructor thinks your sentence is wordy. If that is true, you must be content to accept his judgment for the present. But continue to study good modern essays. What do you observe? Do modern writers of prose use more words or fewer words than you do to express an idea? Are they wordy — or do they have more to say?

Do not mistake brevity for conciseness. A sentence is not concise if it lacks the words necessary not only for the adequate expression of the idea but also for the effective communication of the idea to the reader. Cutting out words will not always result in conciseness. You may summarize *Anthony Adverse* or *Gone with the Wind* in five hundred words, but can you persuade three million persons to read your five-hundred word summary? Cutting out words in a good essay might also cut out of it those qualities which make it good — strength, variety, maturity, grace, cleverness, even accuracy.

Study the difference in the effect produced by the following pairs of sentences. Notice that the first, although longer, is always clearer, stronger, and richer.

1. Objects, on our first acquaintance with them, have that singleness and integrity of impression that it seems as if nothing could destroy or obliterate them, so firmly are they stamped and riveted on the brain.
2. Our first impressions of objects are the most lasting.

1. The ant and the moth have cells for each of their young, but our little ones lie in festering heaps, in homes that consume them like graves; and night by night, from the corners of our streets, rises up the cry of the homeless — "I was a stranger, and ye took me not in."
2. Insects are more careful about their young than are human beings.

1. When we had done all this, there fell upon us the beneficent and deliberate evening; so that as we sat a little while together near the rakes, we saw the valley more solemn and dim around us and all the trees and hedgerows quite still, and held by a complete silence. — Hilaire Belloc.
2. When we had finished, it was evening; so that we sat a little while near the rakes and looked out upon the quiet valley.

Now study the following sets of sentences. Do you see what is meant by conciseness?

1. Whenever anyone called for someone to help him do some certain thing, Jim was always the first to volunteer and lend his help for the cause.
2. Whenever anyone called for help, Jim was always the first to volunteer.

1. This spirit of co-operation is essential and necessary for anyone to have in order to get along with other people and this is a quality that Jim had what it took.
2. Jim had the spirit of co-operation which is necessary if one wishes to get along with people.

1. Jim was one of those people of whom there are few in this world like him.
2. There are few people like Jim.

1. Lumbering is placed in the upper ten industries in the United States from the standpoint of importance.
2. Lumbering is one of the ten most important industries in the United States.

EXERCISE

Exercise 1. Express the ideas in the following sentences more concisely.

1. The ringing of the alarm clock startled me from the deep depths of slumber.

2. It took very little time for me to realize that it was her quick manner of efficiency that made me think that her manner was gruff.

3. In simple words, the above statement means that people are what they are because of the people with whom they have lived and associated and because of their social environment.

4. In order to broaden the mind on the outlook of life one must mingle with other students and take an interest in social life as well as in studies.

5. From my point of view English ranks first in line with other college subjects in importance and interest.

6. In my opinion the perfect teacher is one who has a pleasing personality combined with a genuine interest in each and every member of the class, an interest which is entirely impersonal in nature.

7. In being an engineer a man associates with all sorts of people in many countries.

8. Upon this occasion the seniors felt all very important and were given the best attention that could be given to anybody.

9. I believe that a good teacher should have an unprejudiced view point of all subjects that might be discussed in his class.

10. Home means to me the idea of finding there an atmosphere which makes me feel at ease and carefree.

VARIETY

67. Make your writing more effective by varying the length and the structure of your sentences.

You may avoid monotony of sentence structure by: 1. not beginning a number of successive sentences with the same word; 2. not beginning a series of sentences with subordinate clauses; 3. not beginning a series of sentences with participial phrases; 4. avoiding the same general sentence pattern throughout a large section of writing.

The principle may be expressed in positive form: mix simple sentences with complex or compound sentences; put a short sentence in the midst of several long ones; occasionally begin a sentence with modifiers instead of with the subject.

Notice the monotony of the sentence patterns in the following excerpts from student papers:

Short sentences beginning with the same word:

He impresses me as a man who enjoys life. He is short of stature and walks with a brisk step. He has heavy white hair, a large head, and strong features. He speaks with an accent that is not too difficult to understand.

Short sentences beginning with a participial phrase:

After cleaning up, we lay down and went to sleep. Upon awakening, we heard a mocking bird singing beautifully. Looking out the window, we could see it perched on a limb of a magnolia tree. Feeling much better by this time, we decided to dress and go out in search of adventure.

Short sentences, all beginning with the subject:

My roommate has some very good traits. She spends most of her study time in the library. She always has her work done, for she is quite studious. She is very good at giving good advice. She keeps me well informed as to the college rules and regulations. She, being a sophomore, knows the students and the professors quite well. She knows each member of the football team personally. She is what is termed a campus "big shot."

Now observe the pleasing variety of sentences in the following paragraph from a freshman paper:

During the scorching summer of 1942 I was invited by Russell Towboat and Mooring Company to work in their confectionery at the ferry boat depot. I was thrilled at the thought. Therefore I asked not what my salary would be, what hours I would work, or what my little task would be — I accepted. My salary was an enormous fifty cents an hour; I worked a split shift, from six to eight in the morning and from three to five in the afternoon; and my task, not at all little, was selling everything from steaming cups of Maxwell House to trip tickets — three for a quarter, nine cents apiece. Worse yet was the fact that I pedaled daily to and from work on an old, broken-down, single-tired Champion. More appropriately should I have been called the champion, for I not only traveled three hilly miles each trip but also lugged along Dad's bulky tire pump for the frequent times that the brittle tires sneezed out their air.

It is not exactly cricket to set beside a competent freshman paper a bit of expert writing by a professional, and yet something can be learned by analyzing the following paragraph. Note that no two sentences begin in the same way. Note also — and this is much more important — that richness and variety are achieved not alone by varying beginnings but more by weaving various details, in phrases, clauses, appositives, into the sentences themselves.

Very different was dapper Mr. Groce, our teacher of English composition and literature, a little plump man, with a keen, dry, cheerful, yet irritable disposition, a sparkling bird-like eye, and a little black mustache and diminutive chin-beard. I suspect that he was too intelligent to put up patiently with all the conventions. Had he not been a public-school teacher, dependent on the democratic hypocrisies of a government committee, he might have said unconventional things. This inner rebellion kept him from being sentimental, moralistic, or religious in respect to poetry; yet he *understood* perfectly the penumbra of emotion that good and bad poetry alike may drag after them in an untrained mind. He knew how to rescue the structural and rational beauties of a poem from the bog of private feeling. To me this was a timely lesson, for it was precisely sadness and religiosity and grandiloquence that first attracted me in poetry; and perhaps I owe to Mr. Groce the beginnings of a capacity to distinguish the musical and expressive charm of poetry from its moral appeal. At any rate, at sixteen, I composed my first longish poem, in Spenser's measure, after *Childe Harold* and *Adonais*, full of pessimistic, languid, Byronic sentiments, describing the various kinds of superiority that Night has over Day. It got the prize.

— George Santayana, *Persons and Places*, Charles Scribner's Sons, New York, 1944. Reprinted by permission.

THE PARAGRAPH

The numbered rules and the discussions in this section are for the convenience of both teacher and student in the process of grading and revising themes. A reference to any of these rules should be an invitation to reread the chapter on paragraph writing, and to study the examples of various types of paragraphs which may be found in it.

THE TOPIC SENTENCE

68. Construct each expository paragraph either with a definite, expressed topic sentence, or with a topic sentence so clearly implied that you could state it without hesitation.

When your instructor refers you to this section, underline the topic sentence of your paragraph in red or write a topic sentence if it is implied in your paragraph. It is quite probable that your instructor is trying to make you see that your paragraph lacks unity, or a close-knit structure, faults which your attention to a topic sentence would help to correct. See also "Unity," section 70.

A succession of paragraphs each beginning with a topic sentence may become monotonous. But monotony of structure is not an adjunct of clearness of thought, and even monotony is better than fuzziness of thought or a hopeless fog. Remember that the position of a topic sentence may easily be varied. It usually comes first, or immediately after the necessary transitional phrases. Frequently the transitional elements are combined with the topic sentence. But the topic sentence may also come last in the paragraph.

In the following selections from papers written by college freshmen, observe how much the supplied topic sentence adds to the clearness and effectiveness of each paragraph.

[The facts surrounding James Smithson and his connection with scientific work are interesting.] Never in his life did Smithson visit the United States. He was born in France in 1765 and was educated at Pembroke College, Oxford, where he received his M.A. degree in chemistry and mineralogy. Later his work as an analytical chemist won him a membership in the Royal Society. His mineralogical specimens, numbering more than 10,000, became the property of the Institution after its founding. He willed his property to his nephew, Henry James Hungerford, and in default of Hungerford's direct heirs, Smithson bequeathed it to the United States for the founding of an institution to bear his name. He died in Genoa in 1829; his body now lies interred in the institution which he hoped would make his name live in unforgotten glory.

[Termites are widely distributed throughout the world.] Living species occur in all the regions except the Arctic and the Antarctic. The African or Ethiopian region is richest in number of species. Termites also occur in the temperate regions of Europe and North America. Certain species have been found as far north as the Quesnal Lake region in British Columbia. Others have been found in Ontario, Canada. These same species have been found at high altitudes in the Rocky Mountains and the Pacific Coast range. To the south, Patagonia seems to be the limit of their distribution.

Refer also to pages 70–90 for examples of various types of paragraphs with expressed topic sentences.

LENGTH

69. Write paragraphs of suitable length.

Rarely do college freshmen write paragraphs that are too long. An occasional long paragraph is not a literary crime. Neither is an occasional short paragraph, for that matter.

If you have three or four paragraphs for every page of your theme paper, your paragraphs are too short. If you split up a five-hundred-word essay into ten or twelve paragraphs, your paragraphs are too short. It follows that the thoughts in your essay are undeveloped, that they are not expressed with the detail necessary to make them clear or impressive or interesting.

If your instructor refers you to this section, rewrite your paper. Start with a plan, or an outline, which calls for a limited number of facts or ideas. Your trouble may be too ambitious a subject. Cut it down to fit your space. Then write a thesis sentence stating your central idea. Write a topic sentence for each paragraph. With these as your guide, proceed to make your paper interesting by means of details, concrete examples, illustrations, comparisons, specific instances, reasons — all those things which transform a skeleton into writing that is alive.

An analysis of paragraphs taken from student papers will make the principle clearer.

Undeveloped paragraph:

The biggest problem that has arisen from this war is the loss of earning power for some individuals who have sacrificed legs, arms, and hands for their country, but some steps have been taken to find a solution for this problem. [This is vague, undeveloped, and unconvincing.]

Rewritten paragraph:

One of the biggest post-war problems, what to do for the veterans whose earning power has been curtailed through loss of arms, hands, or legs, is being solved. One G.I. Joe thought his useful life was ended when he lost an arm from an explosion at Hickam Field. Who would ever want a one-armed mechanic? But the Briggs Clarifier Company hired him upon his discharge from the hospital. His employer said it took five weeks to get the wounded look out of his eyes. Soon his untiring efforts and hard work brought him an adequate income. He became a clerk, later a draftsman, and now he is a service engineer. Another man lost both his hands on Tarawa. Now, equipped with two plastic hands, he is studying to become a hardware salesman.

Undeveloped paragraph:

Happiness cannot be expressed in words. It is something which must be felt to be understood. It cannot be told to someone else. It may consist of various things which mean one thing to one person but nothing to another person. [This is vague and general. It is unconvincing.]

Rewritten paragraph:

Happiness is too intangible a thing to put into words and confine on paper; I can only give examples of the moments when I find it. [Notice how the topic sentence prepares the reader for development by examples.] Happiness may begin on a clear, cold morning, when we burst from the house with shivering and screams about the weather. Then the lawns are fields of white spears; the rooftops are white slopes smothered in fog as the first slanting rays of the sun strike them. Shrill notes of a clarinet being practised sound on the cold air; the lesser sounds blend in — the tramp of uniformed students marching and swearing and singing, the laughter of girls. On these cold mornings happiness comes to sing and purr beneath some radiant warmth inside me, and only meanness can drive it away. Another kind of happiness may come when I dance to one of the Count's wonderful dirges. My body, with that of my partner, is lost in movement and rhythm. My partner is right too, that one with black hair and broad shoulders who sings tenor. Then I feel a gaiety and lightness, and I have a misty satisfaction that I am wearing my new suit, and the bass fiddler is a jolly fat fellow.

Some scrappy paragraphs are the result of the student's failure to think in larger units. The writer fails to determine his central idea, and he fails to recognize his miniature paragraphs as merely parts of his topic idea.

Scrappy paragraphs:

1. Father and Mother marveled at the way my sister Lois and I got along; they still do in fact. They are proud of the family unity we show.

When Lois married, I was as thrilled and happy as she, I am sure. I think I knew better than anyone else what a wonderful wife she would be. Her marriage is an example to me.

Although my sister never attended college, she has encouraged me greatly. I am working to live up to the high standards she set for me, and I am constantly hoping that some day I can in some way repay her.

[Try combining under a topic sentence like this: *My sister Lois has been a companion and an example to me.*]

2. The buzzard usually glides over wooded areas in search for food because a domestic animal is more likely to meet a mishap in the forest than out in a plain pasture. Also one will find buzzards around the sloughs in the summer because the water is drying up and the buzzard will feed on the dead fish.

The buzzard lives in a nest on top of high cliffs and in tree tops.

It is against the law to shoot buzzards because they salvage the animals that have died in the woods through an accident.

[Try combining these three paragraphs under a topic sentence which makes a statement about the feeding and nesting habits of buzzards.]

3. I suppose any mother is happy and proud when her daughters surprise her by cooking a meal. I know that my mother always is. This is one way in which we like to make her happy.

Mother always remembers kindness, whether it be in thoughts and actions, and always forgets the unkindness of others. She appreciates having us cook for her.

[Try constructing a topic sentence about Mother's appreciation of a kind act.]

UNITY

70. Observe the principle of unity in paragraph structure.

A paragraph of exposition is a unit of structure. It deals with one idea, or with one phase of a larger idea. Its unity is destroyed by digressions from the main thought, by the addition of irrelevant details, or by afterthoughts that should have been disposed of earlier in the composition.

Analyze the following paragraphs taken from papers written in a course in English composition.

1. Well-built and comfortable houses can be built for a small amount of money. Any family with small means may build a well-equipped home a short distance from the city limits for less than they could live on in a run-down apartment. Materials for building are also important. Houses are more and more being built with steel frames. The windows are usually steel sashes. The outside may be almost any type — brick, stone, wood, or stucco. [This paragraph breaks in half after the second sentence, since the writer seems to have forgotten his original idea, that families of small means can build inexpensive houses.]

2. Little is known about McGuffey's early theories of education because he failed to write down his sermons and lectures. It is known, however, that he felt the need of a systematic education and textbooks. He liked to do his teaching outside. He would seat his children on logs. He had a log for each subject. The best students would sit at the head of the log and the poorest at the foot. He would often question his students until they could see the truth or falsity of their reasoning. By these methods he encouraged the competitive spirit among his students, and taught them to think logically and speak clearly. He established the tastes of four fifths of the nation's school children in regard to literature, morality, social development, and — next to the Bible — their religion. [The last sentence violates paragraph unity. It is about McGuffey's teaching, but it is not about the particular aspect dealt with by this paragraph. The central topic of this paragraph deals with McGuffey's early ideas about education as they can be known from his methods.]

3. The symphony is at once the most important and the most highly developed and elaborate of musical forms. Years of experimentation are responsible for today's organization of the symphony orchestra. Old instruments have been discarded and new ones introduced. Today there is a definite increase of physical resources, a development of personality, a strengthening and enrichment of the symphony orchestra's voice. The symphony is the most expressive, the most powerful of musical instruments. It is one instrument; it speaks with one voice. The older symphonies are much more sedate and formal in style. They are less richly scored and more repressed emotionally than the later ones. [This paragraph, from a paper based on research in the library, reveals the sort of mental confusion which comes from a partial understanding of the subject. The paragraph speaks not with one voice, but with two. It is a discordant duet. The writer has failed to see that a symphony is not the same thing as a symphony orchestra. The cure for this sort of trouble is more logical outlining.]

4. Life on the farm is an eternal battle against nature. [Topic sentence.] There is always the rush to harvest the crops and to get next year's grain planted before the fall rains start. To get this accomplished the farmer must be out at work by daybreak. Fruits and vegetables have to be gathered before the early frost; hence everyone is bustling around from morning till night. Fall is beautiful when the leaves on the trees change color and then fall off. Winter sends its warming cover over the frozen ground. This causes the animals to hunt for something to eat. There is nothing, so the farmer has to feed them. After his day's work is done, the farmer puts on his slippers, reclines on the davenport in front of the fireplace, and spends a peace-

ful evening reading. Within a few months spring begins with its beautiful flowers and green grass. The cows give more milk so the farmer has more work to do. After the first spring rain, the corn must be cultivated. As summer approaches, the farmer begins to worry for fear that the sun will come up and cook the grain before it is fully developed, or maybe a thunderstorm will come up thus causing his hay crop to rot. [You will say that this is pretty bad. It *is* bad writing. The writer of this has completely forgotten what he had started out to say. Instead of being an "eternal battle," life in this paragraph becomes a pleasant and exciting experience — which it probably is, but that is not what the writer set out to prove. The cure for this sort of muddled writing is a going back to first principles: keep your eye on your main purpose; say one thing at a time.]

If your instructor refers you to this section, you may do one of two things. If the detail which destroys the unity of your paragraph is a minor digression, cross it out. If your paragraph is a muddle of two or more major ideas, select the one idea which you intend to develop and rewrite the entire paragraph.

ARRANGEMENT

71. Arrange the details in your paragraph in the most effective manner.

Study the section on "The Paragraph," pages 90–92, for an understanding of the various ways in which material may be arranged in expository writing. If your instructor refers you to this section, he may wish to suggest one of the following methods as being better than the one you have used. Rewrite the paragraph in conformity with his suggestion.

1. Try presenting your material from "the general to the particular." Most paragraphs of exposition follow this order. The writer states his general idea first in a topic sentence, and then he presents the reasons, details, examples, illustrations, and so on, which make his general statement understandable and convincing.

2. Try the "order of enumeration." In your topic sentence state that your idea may be seen from two points of view, that it has three important aspects, that you are going to use four illus-

trations, that you have two excellent reasons for believing it, and so on. You can see various uses for this method. You should also see that this order may help you to write a clear, compact, and well-organized paragraph.

The following topic sentences from the works of professional writers demonstrate how this method is used:

All social organization is of two forms.
There were also three less desirable results of the Peace Conference.
There are two uses of knowledge.
Among the leading purposes of law today we may list three.

Remember, however, that this sort of beginning gives a formal tone to your writing. Use the device occasionally, when the material of your paragraph is adapted to classification and enumeration.

3. Try the "time order." If details can be arranged in the order of happening, there is no particular advantage to be gained by trying any other arrangement. The order of time (often called the "chronological" order), or happening, produces a clear and orderly paragraph. It is inherently simple, perhaps elementary — but it has the unquestioned virtue of being almost foolproof. It may be used with material that at first glance does not arrange itself in the order of time. For instance, "How To Train a Horse" can become "How I Trained My Horse"; "Academic Freedom" can become "The Historical Development of the Concept of Academic Freedom"; "The Right To Work" can become "How the Notion Grew Up That a Job Is Property."

4. Try using the "inductive order." It may be that your paragraph idea should not be stated bluntly in the first sentence. The reader may not be ready for it. Prepare him for it by using your details, your examples and instances, to guide his thoughts, so that when you are ready to use your summarizing topic sentence he will also be ready to accept it.

USE OF CONCRETE DETAILS

72. Use an adequate amount of concrete detail in developing a paragraph.

The tendency of beginners is to write in generalizations and abstractions. In picturing a scene — "The closing hour at the cafe is always a scene of great confusion." What actually is going on? Why not make us see — hear and smell, too — the various details of that confusion? In criticism — "I like this poem." Why do you like it? Because it makes you think, or because it repeats what you have always believed? Because it irritates you? or because it soothes you? In presentation of character — "My father is an honest man." How is he honest? What does he do that shows honesty? Drag him out on the stage and let us watch him being honest. In discussions of college problems — "College men are more conventional and conservative than college women." Give us examples — many of them. Let us see these college men and women in situations that require choice; let us see how they act and what they think in relation to political questions, to books, to art, to social morality. Give the reader proof. Give him the evidence you have observed.

Here are several excerpts from freshman papers to show how the writers have used details.

Before:

A little old woman came out of the house and slowly made her way down the hill to the water's edge.

After:

An old woman with a face like a crumpled leaf crept out of the grey, weather-worn house that frowned down on the sea from beneath two ragged pines. She was dressed in black, and she carried a small pillow, a book, a red plaid blanket, and a black cotton umbrella under one arm. Leaning heavily on a silver-headed cane while she pricked her quavering way along the slippery, grass-grown path that squirmed over the bluff and down to the sea, she looked like a fairy-tale cricket, a lame one.

Before:

The closing hour at the cafe where I work is always a scene of great confusion. The juke-box is playing, the customers are shouting their orders, everyone is impatient and in a hurry.

After:

The air is blue and suffocating with smoke. Everybody screeches orders at once, and someone wants me to turn up the juke-box because the crowd cannot hear the music. He will probably play either "Minnie the Moocher," which isn't musical or soothing to the nerves, or "Take It Easy," advice which under the circumstances is highly ironic. One of the soldiers, who must have been on the campus for several weeks, wants to know where the Pi Phi house is; another, who is obviously exaggerating, says that he has waited ten minutes for his hamburger. Some helpful soul says, "Just give me anything; I don't care what," or "What do you have that's good?" Someone wonders what kinds of shakes we have, and after I have named all fourteen flavors, says, "I'll take vanilla." At 9:30 we are out of glasses, silverware, and ice cream, and someone has spilled a cup of coffee on the floor. Then the carbonator freezes, and while I am concentrating on defrosting it, a mathematical genius shoves a handful of coins at me and drones, "I want five cents out of this, fifteen out of this, forty out of this, with two nickels change, a hamburger out of this, three shakes from this, and change this bill to three ones, two fifty-cent pieces, two quarters, four dimes, a nickel, and five pennies — have you got that?" A girl who has been lounging in a booth all evening elbows her way to the counter and shouts, "I have to be in by ten. Will you get me six hamburgers to go right away? One with lettuce and no mayonnaise, one with mayonnaise and no lettuce, one with both and mustard, one with nothing but meat, and onions in the other two. I don't know what else they want besides onions. Hurry, please!" Some shrewd thinker will corner me, demanding to know if we don't have some cigarettes hidden under the counter. And then — as suddenly as it came, the mob has vanished, leaving stacks of dirty dishes, whatever silverware could not be used at home, and a quaint little professor to tell us fish stories until long after order has been restored.

Before:

The last appeal of chess is that it is a war game. The men are the soldiers and the different moves are the battles. The pawns are the infantry, and they as usual do most of the hard fighting and get the least credit. The knights and bishops are the officers. The king sits back on his throne and does very little of the fighting.

After:

The last appeal of chess consists of something more vague but just as powerful as the others. Chess is a war game; its men and their moves resemble the picturesque forays of the Middle Ages. With the help of our imaginations let us watch an actual battle. The men are set up on the board. First we see the pawns, or rather foot soldiers, lined up in a row. They must move straight ahead, one step at a time, just like the unmounted warriors of all ages. Our brave little dogfaces will not turn back (in truth, they cannot turn back); they will bear the brunt of the opponent's attack; they are our best defense, the backbone of our small army. Behind them, on either side, are two sturdy castles. Clumsy things are these, with their straight forward moves, but very powerful when handled correctly and strongest when backing up pawns. When hard pressed, we will flee to them for safety. There are the knights. They have a "jumping sort of move" consisting of two squares forward and one to the side. Theirs is the sole ability to leap over other men, and thus in crowded places they have no equal. They will dash in with reckless abandon; destruction follows in their wake. Here are the sly bishops, a tricky pair with tricky diagonal moves — thanks to the capers of the medieval church. They play as important a part in our game as the church did in many of the old wars. In the center sits the king, whom we must protect, for to lose him is to lose the game. In himself he is weak, and once his supporters are gone he will soon fall prey to the enemy. The beautiful queen that sits by his side is far more able to take care of herself. Though she may be captured by the smallest pawn, she is possessed of a tremendous power and a variety of ways to use it. Wars have been won by winsome faces as well as by actual fighting.

APPROPRIATE TONE

73. Give your style the tone which the subject calls for.

The tone which you adopt in your writing is entirely a matter of understanding between you and your reader — in this case your instructor. Writing is a two-ended process — like salesmanship. There is no sale unless someone buys. It is like teaching, too; there is no teaching unless someone learns. When you begin to write, you are accepting an obligation; you agree to communicate your thoughts to your reader, to persuade him or to convince him. If the tone of your communication antagonizes him, you have failed. The following specific warnings may help you to avoid violations of appropriate tone:

1. Do not incorporate facetious remarks in a discussion which is essentially serious and formal.

2. Avoid the use of collegiate slang in a serious discussion.

3. Avoid the use of colloquial abbreviations in writing, even in fairly informal writing. Some of the abbreviations that students are apt to carry over from their conversation to their essays are: *prof* for *professor, exam* for *examination, libe* for *library, chem* for *chemistry, gym* for *gymnasium, frosh* for *freshmen, soph* for *sophomore, dorm* for *dormitory, lab* for *laboratory, math* for *mathematics, sike* for *psychology,* and *sosh* for *sociology!*

4. Avoid a tone of stiff formality in informal discussion. If your subject calls for informal treatment, try to give your writing an air of ease and naturalness, but remember that writing on any level is always just a little more formal than conversation.

5. Avoid the use of technical terms in an article written for popular reading. If you cannot avoid technical terms, translate them into a language understood by everyone.

MATURITY

74. Write in a style suitable to your age.

If you naturally express your thoughts in childish language, it is true that you cannot grow up over night. But you can try to increase your vocabulary, and to vary the structure of your sentences. You can avoid writing a long series of scrappy simple sentences. You can occasionally begin with a phrase or with a clause. You can learn to combine your thoughts and to subordinate the less important ones. It may be that your juvenile style is just a defense reaction: you use a childish style because you are afraid of making mistakes if you attempt a more complex mode of expression. Then the best thing for you to do is to write your first draft freely and naturally, committing, if necessary, all the literary sins in the catalogue. Let no thought of dangling modifiers or vague reference hamper the free flow of your thoughts. But in your revision — that is where you must toil and sweat. Revise and rewrite. Professional writers have rewritten a play or a chapter of a novel fifteen times or more. Why should you hesitate at two or three revisions? Hard writing, someone has said, makes easy reading. And Jonathan Swift has fittingly expressed the toil, sweat, and tears of good writing in these words:

> Blot out, correct, insert, refine,
> Enlarge, diminish, interline;
> Be mindful, when invention fails,
> To scratch your head, and bite your nails.

Good writing may be simple, but it must not be juvenile. Before it can appeal to mature readers it must have positive virtues — strength, vividness, ease, fluency, honesty, clearness, dignity, authority.

A GLOSSARY OF USAGE

75. Consult this list for information about usage.

When you consult this section, first read "Levels of Usage," pages 11–29, and section 38, so that you will understand what is meant by such usage labels as *formal, informal, colloquial,* and *slang.*

The following list of expressions has been prepared for your convenience. You must not look upon it as a comprehensive dictionary of errors in usage. No such comprehensive list is possible, nor would it be desirable were it possible. This list will serve you in two ways: as a quick check list when you are writing your papers, and as a starting point for excursions to the more complete and scholarly discussions in the books which are listed on page 30.

a, an. Use *a* before a word beginning with a consonant sound except silent *h*. Use *an* before a word beginning with a vowel sound.

> a book, a tree, a house, a European country, a union, a utility
> an American, an elephant, an irate man, an onion, an hour

Accept, except. These two words are often confused because of a slight resemblance in sound. Watch your pronunciation of these words. *Accept* means "to receive something offered," "to agree to." *Except* means "to exclude," "to make an exception." See sec. 33.

> The defeated nations must accept (not *except*) our terms.
> We agreed to except (not *accept*) the third problem.

Accent, ascent, assent. See sec. 33.

A.D. *Anno Domini*, for "in the year of our Lord," is properly used with dates in the Christian era only when necessary for clearness. When so used, it precedes the date. Note that *B.C.* "*before Christ*" follows the date.

> He was born 36 B.C. and died A.D, 22.

Ad. This abbreviation for *advertisement* is acceptable in informal conversation, but it is still too new for use in writing or in formal speech.

Admittance, admission. See sec. 33.

Affect, effect. These two words may be confused because of a similarity of sound. *Affect*, as a verb, means "to influence." Its noun use is too rare to be a source of trouble. *Effect*, as a verb, means "to bring about." As a noun, *effect* means "result." See also sec. 33.

> The strike will affect the lumber industry. The effects of the strike will be disastrous.
> The labor board will attempt to effect a compromise.

Aggravate. *Aggravate* means "to intensify," "to increase."

> The terrible heat aggravated her headache.

In recent years *aggravate* has gained wide colloquial currency in the sense of "to irritate," "to annoy." Most writers still use it only in the older sense.

> *Colloquial:* The speaker's mannerisms aggravated everyone.
> *Formal:* The speaker's mannerisms annoyed everyone.

Agree to, agree with. You *agree that* something is true. You *agree to* a proposal. You *agree with* a person. One thing *agrees with* (corresponds with) another. See Idioms.

Ain't, an't. Illiterate for *are not, am not, is not, have not.* If you wish to use a contraction, say *aren't, isn't, haven't,* but not

477

ain't, an't, amn't. The English language has no convenient contraction for *am not.*

Allow. Means "to permit." Do not use for *assert, say, think,* or *believe.*

All-around. The correct idiomatic form is *all-round.* It should be confined to colloquial use.

All right. See *alright.*

All the farther, all the faster, etc. Do not use for *as far as, as fast as,* etc.

> This is as far as (not *all the farther*) we can go today.
> Is this as fast as (not *all the faster*) your car will go?

Allude, refer. *Allude* means to refer to a person or thing indirectly or by suggestion. To *refer* to something means to mention it specifically.

> I shall now take time to refer (not *allude*) to the question of smoking on the campus.
> I shall now take time to speak of (or *to discuss*) the question of smoking on the campus.
> When the teacher spoke of "budding Swifts," every student wondered to whom he was alluding.

Allusion, illusion. See sec. 36.

Already, all ready. *Already,* an adverb, means "by this time," "before this time." All ready, two words, means "entirely ready" or that everyone is ready. See sec. 33.

> The war had already started. The king had already abdicated.
> The men were all ready to embark when the colonel arrived.

Alright. The correct form is *all right.* Used in the sense of *satisfactory, certainly,* or *very well,* it is colloquial. When used merely for emphasis, it is slang.

> *Colloquial:* All right, we shall be glad to save a copy for you.
> *Slang:* We surprised him that time all right.

Altar, alter. See sec. 33.

Alternate, alternative. See sec. 36

Altogether, all together. *Altogether*, an adverb, means "entirely," "completely," "on the whole." *All together* means "in a group."

> It was altogether (not *all together*) too much to expect of so young a child.
> After a long separation, we were all together (not *altogether*) again.

Amount, number. *Amount* refers to quantity; *number* refers to things which can be counted.

> The number of men (not *amount of men*) on the campus has increased.
> The amount (not *number*) of supplies sent to China is great.

Among, between. Use *among* when referring to more than two things or persons. Use *between* when referring to two things or persons.

> The members of the team discussed the play among themselves.
> James and Henry divided the provisions between them.

A.M., P.M. Do not use for *in the morning, in the afternoon.* Use only with the name of the hour.

> This afternoon (not *this P.M.*) the final matches will be played.
> The placement test will be given at 9:30 A.M. in Folwell Hall.

And etc. *Etc.* means "and so forth." *And etc.* would mean "and and so forth." In ordinary writing it is better to write it out. When you do use it, do not spell it *ect*. See *etc.*

Ante, anti. See sec. 33.

Anyplace, any place. Colloquial forms. *Anywhere* is preferred in writing. Similar colloquial forms are *no place* for *nowhere*, *everyhow* for *in every way*, *every place* for *everywhere*, *some place* for *somewhere*.

Anyways. Illiterate for *anyhow, in any case, at any rate, in any event.*

Anywheres, everywheres. Dialect and colloquial for *anywhere, everywhere.*

Apt, likely, liable. *Apt* suggests a habitual or inherent tendency; it may refer to the past, the present, or the future. *Likely* suggests a probability; it refers to the future. *Liable* suggests a chance, a risk of some sort, or a danger. See *Webster's Dictionary of Synonyms*, page 67.

> Mrs. Jones did not mean what she said. She is apt to be irritable because she is not well.
> A cheerful boy is likely to succeed in that occupation.
> You are liable to break your neck if you try to climb that rock.

As. (1) Do not use in place of *that* or *whether.*

> I do not know whether (not *as*) I shall vote this year.
> I cannot say that (not *as*) I care much for his verses.

(2) *As* in the sense of *because* is frowned upon by some writers. It is, however, widely current in speech and in many kinds of writing. It seems to be more appropriate with a clause that begins a sentence than with one that follows the main clause. Fowler, in *Modern English Usage*, page 31, says that there is no objection to causal or explanatory *as*-clauses if they are placed before the main sentence. *Because* and *since* are stronger and more explicit than *as*, which is the least formal of the causal conjunctions. See "because," in *Webster's Dictionary of Synonyms*, page 111.

As . . . as, so . . . as. In negative statements some careful writers prefer *so . . . as* to *as . . . as.* At present, *as . . . as* seems to be established in both speech and writing for both positive and negative statements. For negative statements in a very formal style, *so . . . as* is probably preferable.

> Your promise is as good as your bond.
> A vast army is not so important as a well-equipped air force. [Formal.]

A vast army is not as important as a well-equipped air force. [Less formal.]

At. Do not use, either in speech or in writing, in such sentences as: Where are we at now? Where does he live at? Where at did you stop?

At about. Use either *at* or *about*, whichever is intended. Do not use both.

> We reached Troy at (not *at about*) seven o'clock.
> The guests began to arrive about (not *at about*) nine o'clock.

Auto. A colloquial abbreviation. Do not use in formal writing.

Awful, awfully. Colloquially, these words and *frightful, terribly, shocking, horrible*, and the "frightfully" abused favorite of college students, *disgusting*, are used as mild intensives. They mean little more than an accented *very*. In formal writing *awful* and *awfully* should be saved for their precise meaning, which is used to express something that is full of awe or awe inspiring.

> *Slang:* You are just awful good to me!
> *Formal:* I accept the awful responsibility of carrying on the war.
> The destroyers were tossed about like shells by the awful storm.

Back of, in back of. *Back of* is colloquial for *behind*. *Back of* is defensible in informal writing, but *in back of*, probably suggested by *in front of*, is considered undesirable in both speech and writing.

Badly. Used colloquially for *very much* or *very greatly* with words signifying *to want* or *to need*.

> *Colloquial:* He needs a haircut very badly.
> I want to go badly.
> The Chinese armies need artillery badly.
> *Formal:* The Chinese armies were in extreme need of artillery.
> I wish very much to go.

Balance. Colloquial when used for *the remainder, the rest.*

> *Colloquial:* The balance of the team is stronger than it was last year.
> We played cards the balance of the evening.
> *Formal:* The rest of the team is stronger than it was last year.
> We played cards the rest of the evening.

Bank on. In the sense of *rely upon* it is a colloquial idiom. Do not use in formal writing.

Because. A *because*-clause should not be used as the subject of a verb.

> *Wrong:* Because the work was too hard was my reason for quitting my job.
> *Right:* I quit my job because the work was too hard.

Because of. See *reason is.*

Being as, being that. Dialectal for *since, because.*

> Because (not *being that*) I wore old clothes, he thought I was a tramp.

Beside, besides. According to present usage, *beside* is employed as a preposition meaning "at the side of," as in *Please sit down beside me. Besides* is ordinarily used as an adverb, meaning "in addition to."

Blame on, blame it on. Colloquial.

> *Wrong:* He blamed the error on me.
> *Better:* He blamed me for the error. He said I was to blame for the error.

Between, among. See *among.*

Bunch. Should not be used to mean "several," "a group."

> We saw a group (not *a bunch*) of men standing near the gate.
> Several (not *a bunch*) of us went to the coast last Saturday.

Bust, busted, bursted, burst. *Bust, busted,* and *bursted* are considered dialectal, inelegant, and slangy. But he who has occasion to say that he is *going on a bust* should not make matters worse by saying he is *going on a burst!*

We were delayed by a burst (not *busted*) tire.
The balloon burst (not *bursted*) into flames.

But what, but that. Both should be avoided when a simple *that* is meant.

I have no doubt that (not *but that*) they will come.

Calculate, reckon. Colloquial for *plan, think, expect*.

A dollar will be enough, I think (not *I reckon*).

Can, may. *Can* implies ability. *May* implies permission or possibility.

Colloquial: Mother, can I go now?
Can't we stay up until midnight? No, you can't (instead of the formal *mayn't* or *may not*).
Formal: Sir, may (not *can*) I go now?
The delegate can speak three languages.
If everything goes well, our boys may be home by Christmas.

Can't hardly. To be avoided as a double negative. See sections 6d and 41.

Can't seem to. A colloquial expression for *seem unable to*.

We seem unable (not *can't seem*) to follow his directions.

Cannot help but, can't help but. These forms are widely used colloquially and by some writers in formal writing. Other writers object to these forms. See "Double Negative," sections 6d and 41.

Colloquial: We cannot help but feel proud of our men.
Formal: One cannot help feeling that the Yalta decisions left many matters undecided.

See also George O. Curme, *Syntax*, pp. 252–253.

Cause of. It is illogical to say that the *cause of* something was *on account of.* Complete the sentence with a substantive.

> The cause of my late theme was my having (not *on account of having*) too much work to do.
> The cause of my late theme was the fact that I had too much work to do.

> Both of these sentences are awkward. It may be better to avoid the *cause-of* construction entirely and simply say, "My theme is late because I had too much to do."

Caused by. See *due to.*

Censor, censure. See sec. 33.

Charted, chartered. See sec. 33.

Claim. Claim means "to demand," or "to require." It should not be used for *say, assert, declare, maintain.*

> He says (not *claims*) that he came in before ten o'clock.
> They assert (not *claim*) that all stolen property has been returned.

Company. Colloquial for *guests, visitors, escort.*

Compare to, compare with. *Compare to* means "to represent as similar." *Compare with* means "to examine the differences and similarities of two things." *Compare* is often used without any preposition.

> One may compare some men to wolves.
> One may compare the novels of Dreiser with those of Zola.

Complected. Do not use for *complexioned.*

> I met a dark-complexioned (not *dark-complected*) man.

Considerable. Colloquial when used as a noun. Illiterate when used as an adverb.

> *Colloquial:* He lost considerable by gambling.
> *Formal:* He lost a considerable amount by gambling.

The men were influenced considerably (not *considerable*) by the argument.

Contact. Slang when used to mean "to make a business or social connection."
A more specific verb is preferable, such as *meet, interview, speak to.*

Contemptible, contemptuous. See sec. 36.

Continual, continuous. If a difference exists between the meanings of *continual* and *continuous*, it is that *continual* implies a continued succession or recurrence, and *continuous* implies unbroken continuity. See also sec. 33.

He wrote his play in spite of continual interruptions.
The men advanced toward the continuous roar of distant artillery.

Contractions. In formal and serious writing avoid such contractions as *I'm, I'd, he'll, don't, doesn't, can't,* and so forth. These are correct in speech and in informal writing.

Could of. Illiterate for *could have.*

Couldn't seem to. See *can't seem to.*

Couple. Colloquial for *two, a few, several.*

Colloquial: A couple of men left the theater.
Formal: Two (or *several*) men left the theater.
Right: Only two couples were dancing on the floor.

Criticize. May mean "to find fault with" but may also mean "to judge," "to review." See *Webster's Dictionary of Synonyms,* page 210.

Crowd. Colloquial for *a set, clique.* Watch your pronunciation of *clique* and do not spell it "click."

She became acquainted with the country-club set (not *crowd*).

Cunning. An American colloquialism used to describe attractive children and other small animals. There is no exact equivalent in formal English.

Cute. See *cunning*. It seems futile to rail against *cunning* and *cute*. These words are appropriate enough on the informal levels, and they probably cause little trouble in formal writing.

Data, strata, phenomena. These are plural, not singular forms. The singular forms are *datum*, *stratum*, *phenomenon*.

Date. A colloquialism for everything from a casual meeting to an assignation. It seems a pity that the English language is so poor that it does not have an acceptable word for a concept so important in the life of an undergraduate. After all, a *date* is not exactly an *appointment*, nor an *engagement* — certainly not an *assignation*. Nor could a college girl who brought her "date" to her mother's home find time to speak of him as "the male person with whom I have made a social engagement." *Beau* and *escort* are faintly reminiscent of crinoline and pantalets. And speaking of needed terms, where is the budding philologist or poet who will give us an acceptable expression for "girl friend" and "boy friend"?

Deal. Used figuratively in "a square deal" or "a new deal," but still considered colloquial when used for "a political bargain."

Didn't ought. Similar to *hadn't ought*, which see.

Differ from, differ with. One thing *differs from* another. One person *differs with* another when he disputes or quarrels with him. One may also *differ from* a person when he disagrees with him.

Different than. The correct American idiom is *different from*.

This lad seemed somehow different from (not *than*) the rest.

Disinterested, uninterested. See sec. 36.

Doesn't, don't. The accepted contraction of *does not* is *doesn't.* The contraction of *do not* is *don't.* See also sec. 4.

Harry doesn't (not *don't*) care for golf.

Doubt but what. Colloquial for *doubt that* or *doubt whether.*

I do not *doubt that* (not *doubt but what*) he wrote the letter.
I *doubt whether* he wrote that letter.

Double negative. See sections 6d and 41.

Dove. Colloquial for *dived.*

He dived (not *dove*) into the pool.

Due to, caused by, owing to. *Due to* was originally an adjective. In colloquial usage it is a preposition and is used like any other preposition. In writing, especially in formal writing, there is strong objection to *due to* and *caused by* in any use but adjectival. A simple means of avoiding criticism is to use these expressions only after a verb. When either one begins a sentence, it should be viewed with strong suspicion.

Colloquial: Due to high taxes, many industries are unable to continue.
Formal: Many industries are unable to continue because of high taxes.

Colloquial: Due to an accident, we arrived late.
Formal: We arrived late because we had an accident.
           Our late arrival was due to an accident.

Colloquial: Caused by a rainy season, the crop was a failure.
Formal: The failure of the crop was caused by the rainy season.

Each other, one another. See sec. 5h.

Effect. See *affect.*

Elegant. Should not be used to mean "excellent," "beautiful," "good." *Elegant* means "characterized by elegance," "fastidious," "refined."

That was a delicious (not *elegant*) salad.

Eminent, imminent. See sec. 33.

Enthuse. The correct form is *enthusiastic*.

> Who could become enthusiastic (not *could enthuse*) about this game? She displays great enthusiasm (not *enthuses*) about every new possession.

Equally as good. The *as* is unnecessary. Say *equally good* or *just as good*.

> His plan is equally good (not *equally as good*).
> My theme is just as good (not *equally as good*) as his.

Etc. Et cetera, meaning "and so forth," "and others," "and the rest," should never be used in literary or artistic writing. If you use it in informal writing, never write *and etc*.

Everyplace, everywheres. See *anyplace*.

Exam. Colloquial abbreviations, like *prof., lab., soph., frosh., chem., libe.,* are unacceptable in formal writing and undesirable in informal writing and in formal speech.

Except, accept. See *accept*.

Except. Not at present used for *unless*.

> *Wrong:* I will not go except you go too.
> *Right:* I will not go unless you go too.

Expect. Do not use for *suspect* or *suppose*.

> *Wrong:* I expect that he will be late.
> *Right:* I suspect (or *suppose*) that he will be late.

Extra. Do not use for *very* or *unusually* in formal writing.

> The President has had an unusually (not *extra*) busy day.

Factor. Use with some regard for its precise meaning. It means "a constituent," "a component," "an ingredient." It should not be used to mean "thing."

Farther, further. *Farther* implies a greater distance in space. *Further* implies an addition to previous actions. These are the distinctions made by the most careful writers. In popular usage these terms are used interchangeably. See also sec. 33.

> It can fly farther than the old models. Farther on in the story you will meet the villain.
> Further discussion is useless. I shall not say a word further.

Favor. Do not use for *letter* in business correspondence.

Faze. Colloquial for *disconcert, worry, disturb, bother, daunt.*

Fellow. Colloquial for *a person, a boy, a man, a beau, a sweetheart.* Do not use in ordinary writing.

> Most of the men (not *fellows*) on the campus have volunteered to aid in fire prevention during the summer months.
> I was usually sent off to play when my sister had her sweetheart (not *fellow*) in the living room.

Fewer, less. Use *fewer* when referring to numbers. Use *less* when referring to quantity or degree. See also *amount, number.*

> There are fewer (not *less*) men on the campus than there were last year.
> Most women are earning less than they did three years ago.

Fix. In the sense of *a predicament, to arrange, to repair,* it is colloquial.

> The headmaster was in a predicament (not *fix*).
> Can you repair (not *fix*) my radio set?

Flunk. College slang for *a failure* or *to fail.*

Folks. Colloquial for *relatives,* one's *family.*

For to. Now archaic or illiterate. Omit *for* in such expressions as:

> He went for to buy a new hat.

Funny. Colloquial for *strange, queer, odd.*

> That is an odd (not *funny*) thing for a college professor to say.

Gent. Vulgar for *gentleman.* Say *men's clothes* instead of *gents' clothes.*

Gentleman, lady. It is better to say *man, woman* instead of *gentleman, lady* except when there is an intended distinction between persons of refinement and persons of ill breeding.

Get. *Get to go* for *manage* or *contrive* is dialectal. *Have got* for *have* or *possess* is colloquial.

Gotten. *Got* is preferred to *gotten* as the past participle.

Guess. In the sense of *suppose, think,* it is still objectionable to many people, although many good writers have so used it for five hundred years. Avoid trouble by saying, "I presume," or "I suppose," instead of "I guess."

Had of. Illiterate for *had.*

I wish I had (not *had of*) written my theme yesterday.

Had better, had best, had rather. Correct idiomatic forms. So are *would rather, would best, would better.*

Many Polish soldiers would rather (or *had rather*) remain in England than return to Poland.

Had ought. Illiterate for *ought.*

You ought (not *had ought*) to return his ring. You should return his ring.

Half a, a half. Some persons consider *a half* more proper in formal writing than *half a,* as "He walked a half mile" instead of "He walked half a mile," but Tennyson might object to our rewriting his famous charge like this:

> A half league, a half league,
> A half league onward,
> All in the valley of Death
> Rode the six hundred.

Hanged, hung. Use *hanged* when referring to the death penalty.

> Carter was hanged (not *hung*) for murdering his wife.
> Her wet clothes were hung (not *hanged*) on a stick before the fire.

Hardly, scarcely, only, but. Do not use with another negative. See sections 6d and 41.

> I was so tired that I could (not *couldn't*) hardly move.
> The little animal ventures out (not *does not venture out*) only at night.
> He could (not *couldn't*) scarcely see the man on the dock.

Have got. See *get*.

Healthful, healthy. *Webster's New International Dictionary* states that *healthy* and *healthful* "are interchangeable within certain limits." But in a strict sense, *healthy* means "being in a state of health"; *healthful* means "serving to promote health." People are healthy, but good food is healthful. See also sec. 33.

Home. Colloquial for *at home*.

> The Smiths were at home (not *were home*) when the fire broke out.

If, whether. See section 8b.

Imaginary, imaginative. See sec. 33.

Implicit, explicit. See sec. 33.

In, into. *In* denotes location inside something. *Into* denotes motion from outside to inside something.

> He dived into the water. He ran into the room.
> He was swimming in the pool. He was sitting in his room.

In back of. See *back of*.

Incredible, incredulous. *Incredible* means "unbelievable." *Incredulous* means "not willing to believe." See sec. 33.

Individual, person. *Person* is the word to be used when referring to a human being in general. *Individual* marks off one person or thing specially.

> He is not the right person (not *individual*) for this kind of work.
> In a democracy, we try to do what is best for the citizens in general, but the individual sometimes suffers a hardship.

Infer, imply. See sec. 36.

Informant, informer. See sec. 33.

Ingenious, ingenuous. See sec. 36.

In regards to. The correct idiom is *in regard to*.

Inside of. The *of* is unnecessary. In reference to time, meaning "within," "in less than," the expression is colloquial.

> You are safe inside (not *inside of*) the corral.
> Within (not *inside of*) an hour, every servant had left.

Intrinsic, extrinsic. See sec. 33.

Invite. Do not use for *an invitation.*

> We sent her an invitation (not *an invite*) to the dance.

Irrelevant, irreverent. See sec. 33.

Is when, is where. Do not use as a subjective complement. Do not say: A sonnet is when a poem has fourteen lines. A touchdown is where a man carries the ball over the goal line. Use a noun or a noun clause to complete the sentence.

> A sonnet is a poem of fourteen lines.
> A touchdown is carrying the ball over the goal line.
> A touchdown is scored when a player carries the ball over the goal line.

Its, it's. *Its* is the possessive form of it. *It's* is the contraction of *it is*. Do not confuse the two forms.

Job. Commercial slang when used for *model, design, color.*

Just. A colloquial intensive. Not appropriate in formal writing. Either omit or use *very* or *quite.* See *awful, so* (intensive), *such.*

Kind, sort. The words are singular and therefore should be modified by singular modifiers.

> I do not like this (not *these*) sort of apples.

Kind of, sort of. Colloquial when used to modify a verb or an adjective. Use *somewhat, somehow, rather, in some degree, for some reason, a little.*

> It is still early, but I feel somewhat (not *sort of*) tired.
> She was surprised that I smiled a little (not *kind of smiled*) when she started to cry.

When used correctly, to express a class, *kind of* and *sort of* should not be followed by *a* or *an.*

> He is that kind of (not *kind of a*) doctor.

Lay, lie. Learn the principal parts of these two verbs. Do not confuse them.

> The dog was lying (not *laying*) in the road.
> It had lain (not *laid*) there all morning.
> He had laid (not *lain*) his bundle on the table.

Learn, teach. Do not use *learn* for *teach.*

> My mother taught (not *learned*) me how to cook.

Leave, let. *Leave* means "to abandon," or "to go away." *Let* means "to allow."

> Please let (not *leave*) me go with you.
> Please leave me; I wish to be alone.

Lend, loan. Both correct as verbs.

> Will you please lend me five dollars.
> She loaned me her sweater.

Less. See *fewer, less*.

Liable, apt, likely. See *apt*.

Like, as, as if. Use *as, as if, as though* to introduce clauses of comparison. *Like* should be followed by a noun or pronoun in the objective case. See 8b.

> *Like:* I am like her in my love of music.
> In this crisis let us at least act like men.
> *As, as if, as though:* The war, just as (not *like*) he had predicted, lasted more than five years.
> Let us sing as (not *like*) the birds sing.
> They write as if (not *like*) they knew something.

Line. Like *field, factor*, and *proposition* it should be used with extreme care. In its most popular collegiate use, *line* is number twenty-nine of the fifty groups of meanings given in *Webster's International:* "characteristic form of glib, and often persuasive, address." In that sense it is slang. One hesitates to recommend an adequate literary substitute. In another sense, as in the following examples, it is vague and redundant.

> *Poor:* We bought a few things in the line of groceries.
> *Better:* We bought some groceries.
>
> *Poor:* Have you any interesting books in the line of fiction?
> *Better:* Have you any interesting novels?
>
> *Poor:* He wrote epics and other poems along that line.
> *Better:* He wrote epics and other narrative poems.

Literature. Use accurately. Do not use when you mean *advertising, handbills, circulars*, or *printed folders*.

Locate. A colloquialism for *settle*.

> They settled (not *located*) in Indiana.

Lot, lots of. Colloquial for *many, much, a large number, a large amount, a great deal*.

> There is much (not *a lot*) still to be done.
> Many (not *Lots of*) freshmen did not buy green caps.

Lousy. Avoid using this word as a general term of condemnation. It offends many persons.

Mad. *Mad* means "insane." It is colloquial for *angry*.

> My mother was angry (not *mad*) because I went fishing.

Majority. Do not use with measures of quantity, time, distance. Use *most*.

> Most of the day (not *The majority of the day*) we stood in line and waited.

Might of. Illiterate for *might have*.

Most, almost. *Most* is illiterate for *almost*. *Most* is the superlative form of *much* or *many*. (Much food, more food, most food; many men, more men, most men.) *Almost* is an adverb.

> Almost (not *Most*) all of our men have returned from Italy.
> She is almost (not *most*) as tall as I am.

Neither, or. *Neither* should be followed by *nor; either* should be followed by *or*.

> Neither the British nor the Russians have any interests in that part of the world.
> Either Mr. Jones or I will be there to explain his plans.

Nice. A vague word of mild approval. Avoid in serious writing. In informal speech use only when you mean to be vague and mild.

No good. Colloquial when used for *worthless, useless, of no value*.

> Their efforts to preserve the peace were useless (not *no good*).

Nohow. Illiterate or dialectal. Do not use in writing or serious speech.

Noplace. See anyplace.

Nowhere near, nowheres near. Colloquial for *not nearly.*

> This is not nearly (not *nowhere near*) as much as I expected.

O, Oh. *O* is used with another word, a substantive, usually in direct address. It is always capitalized and is not followed by any mark of punctuation. *Oh* is an exclamation, not capitalized except when it begins a sentence, and is followed by either a comma or an exclamation point.

Off of. The *of* is unnecessary.

> The driver must get off (not *off of*) his high seat in order to find out what is wrong.

Other times. Do not misuse for *at other times.*

Out loud. Colloquial for *aloud, loud, loudly, audibly.*

> He called aloud (not *out loud*) for help.
> He pronounced the words loudly (not *out loud*) so that everyone could hear.

Outside of. Colloquial for *except, besides.*

> No one saw him except (not *outside of*) three small boys who were playing ball in the street.

Over with. In the sense of *finished, ended,* it is colloquial.

Party. Do not use for *person.* See *individual, person.*

> Do you know the person (not *party*) in the next seat?
> The man (not *party*) who telephoned you yesterday called again this morning.

Pep, peppy. Juvenile slang for *energy, high spirits, liveliness, activity.*

Per. Except in technical writing, should be used only with Latin words, such as *diem, annum.* Do not use *per* for *according to.*

> He received five thousand dollars a year (not *per year*).
> We sold the horses according to (not *as per*) your instructions.

Per cent. Not strictly correct as a synonym for *percentage*. Correct after numerals. Do not use the sign % except after figures in technical writing or in tabulations.

> A small percentage (not *per cent*) of them refused to join.
> Over eighty per cent (not *eighty %*, or *80%*) of them were either killed or wounded.

Phenomena. A plural form. The singular is *phenomenon*. See *data*.

Phone. Colloquial for *telephone*. Use the complete word in writing

Photo. Colloquial for *photograph*. Use the complete word in writing.

Piece. Provincial for *a short distance*.

> Will you walk a short distance (not *a piece*) with me?

Plan on. The *on* is unnecessary. The correct idiom is *plan to do*, not *plan on doing*.

> We planned (not *planned on*) a fishing trip.
> We planned to go (not *planned on going*) fishing.

Plenty. Colloquial in such expressions as *plenty good*, *plenty good enough*.

> He was very (not *plenty*) rich. The room is large enough (not *plenty large*).
> There is enough (not *plenty*) wood for another fire.

P.M. See *A.M.*

Poorly. Colloquial for *in poor health, not well, unwell*.

> Aunt Sarah has been in poor health (not *poorly*) all year.

Practicable, practical. *Practicable* means "something possible, feasible, or usable." *Practical* means "useful, not theoretical, experienced." *Practical* may apply to persons, things, ideas; *practicable* may not apply to persons. See *W. D. S.* 639.

Proposition, proposal. *Proposal* implies a direct and explicit act of proposing; *proposition* implies a statement or principle for discussion. Do not use *proposition* loosely to mean "idea, thing, a task, a business enterprise, a problem."

> It is a poor practice (not *proposition*) to study until three in the morning.
> Moving the settlers out of the district was an impractical plan (not *proposition*).

Proven. The preferred past participle of *prove* is *proved*.

> We have proved (not *proven*) that the plan is unsound.

Quite. Means "entirely," "completely," as in *The dress is not quite ready*. Used colloquially, it means "to a considerable extent," as in *Your essay is quite good*.

Quite a few, quite a number, quite a little. All colloquial expressions for *many*, *a large number*, *more than a little*, *a great deal*.

Raise, rear. Linguistic purists still insist that one *raises* corn and *rears* children.

Raise, rise. Two verbs often confused. Learn the principal parts. (I raise my hand; he raised the window; they have raised the flag. I rise in the morning; they rose before I did; they had risen at sunrise.)

Real. Do not use for *really* or *very*.

> His playing was really (not *real*) brilliant.
> It was a very (not *a real*) exciting game.

Reason is because, reason is due to, reason is on account of. All incorrect. Complete a *reason is* clause with a noun or a noun clause. See section 58a.

> The reason he was late was that (not *because*) the roads were blocked.
> The reason for my poor work in English was (not *due to my*) my poor high-school preparation.

Refer. See *allude*.

Remember of. The *of* is unnecessary.

> I do not remember (not *remember of*) his taking the package when he left.

Right. In the sense of *very*, it is dialectal.

> He was a very (not *right*) good speaker.

Rise. See *raise*.

Run. In the sense of *conduct, manage*, it is still considered colloquial.

> He managed (not *ran*) a grocery store.

Same, such. Do not use as a substitute for a pronoun.

> Please repair the camera and ship it (not *same*) to me tomorrow.

Seldom ever, seldom or ever. The correct idioms are *seldom, very seldom, hardly ever, seldom if ever*.

Set, sit. Do not confuse these two verbs. Learn the principal parts. (I set it down; I have set it down. Sit down; I sat down; they have sat down.)

> You may set the cup on the shelf and then sit down.
> I sat on the stool after I had set the cup down.

Shape. Colloquial for *condition*.

> The equipment was in good condition (not *good shape*).

Show. Colloquial for *play, concert, opera, chance, opportunity*.

> We enjoyed the performance (not *show*).
> He tried hard, but he had no chance (not *show*) of winning against Louis.

Show up. Colloquial for *arrive, be present*.

Some. Do not use for *somewhat* or *a little*.

> The patient is somewhat (not *some*) better this morning.
> I worked a little (not *some*) last month.

Someplace. See *anyplace*.

Sort, sort of. See *kind, kind of*.

So. *So* as a co-ordinating conjunction meaning "therefore" is not common in formal writing. It should be avoided as a loose, indefinite connective. See sections 8a and 46a. Even in the most informal writing and speech, *so* is an abused conjunction. It is a poor substitute for carefully built sentence structure.

> *Colloquial:* The Russians were not ready, so they waited until August to declare war on Japan.
> *Formal:* Since the Russians were not ready, they waited until August to declare war on Japan.

So as a subordinating conjunction is used colloquially for *so that* in clauses of purpose.

> *Colloquial:* They flew low so they could observe the results of the bombing.
> *Formal:* They flew low so that they could observe the results of the bombing.
> They flew low in order to observe the results of the bombing.

So as a "feminine intensive" should be avoided in writing. See *awful*.

> My parents were very kind and considerate (not *so kind* and *so considerate*).

Species, specie. Consult the dictionary. *Species*, meaning "kind," "class," has the same form in the singular and plural.

Such. See *awful, so*. *Such* introducing a clause of result is followed by *that*. When introducing a relative clause, it is followed by *as*.

There was such an explosion that it could be felt for twenty miles. Such amendments as you may stipulate will be included in the contract.

Sure. Do not use for *certainly, surely, indeed.*

This is certainly (not *sure*) an interesting story.

Suspicion. Do not use as a verb. The correct form is *suspect.*

We suspected (not *suspicioned*) that something was wrong.

Swell. Colloquial for *stylish, fashionable, smartly clothed.* Slang for *excellent, very good, interesting, enjoyable,* and a host of other words expressing approval or commendation.

We had an enjoyable (not *a swell*) evening.
It is a thrilling (not *a swell*) game.

Take stock in. Colloquial for *accept, believe, put faith in.*

Can we believe (not *take stock in*) his promises?

That there, this here, etc. Illiterate forms. Use *that, this, these, those.*

Very, very much. Do not use *very* for *very much* in a passive verb phrase. See 51a.

They were very much pleased (not *very pleased*).
They seemed very greatly (not *very*) disturbed.

Wait on. Colloquial when used to mean "wait for" or "stay for." Correct in the sense of *attend, perform services for.*

Are you the girl who waited on us?
Will you wait for (not *wait on*) me if I hurry?

Want in, want off, want out, etc. Dialectal forms for *want to come in, want to get off, want to go out,* etc.

Open the door. I think Rover wants to get in (not *wants in*).
I want to get off (not *want off*) at the corner of Sixth and Washington.

Way, ways. *Way* is colloquial for *condition*. *Ways* is dialectal for *distance, way*.

> When we saw him, he was in bad health (not *in a bad way*).
> We walked a long distance (not *ways*) before we rested.

Where at. Do not use for *where*. See section 41.

> Where (not *where at*) is he now?

Whether, if. See section 8b.

While. Do not misuse for *but* or *whereas*. See section 8.

> They ate their K rations while they waited. [Means *at the same time as*.]
> We raise dairy cattle whereas (not *while*) they specialize in growing wheat.

Who, which. Use *who* to refer to people and usually to animals. Use *which* to refer to things and groups of persons regarded impersonally. See section 5h.

> The committee which he had appointed rejected his plan.
> He is no better than our black cat, who also stays out all night.
> He pointed to the two prisoners whom he had brought in.

Without. Illiterate for *unless*. See section 8.

> I will not go unless (not *without*) you go with us.

You all. In Southern speech, *you all* is the plural form of *you*.

Index

All numbers refer to pages.

INDEX

INDEX

Borden, Mary, "Manners," paragraph quoted, 84

Borrowed material, acknowledgment of, *see* Footnotes, 203–204

Both . . . and, parallel structure with, 435

Bowery, etymology of, 363

Brackets, uses of, 347
    to enclose corrections, interpolations, 347
    exercise, 347

Bragg, Sir William, "The Progress of Physical Science," paragraphs quoted, 87–88

Breaking word at end of line, 301

Breath, breathe, defined, 354

Brinser, Ayers, "Don't Plow Us Under," quoted, 108–110

Britannica Book of the Year, described, 179

Bunch, 482

Business letters, 216–220
    body, 219
    closed punctuation in, 217
    complimentary close, 219
    faults to avoid, 222
    heading, 216–217
    inside address, 217–218
    letterheads, 216–217
    open punctuation in, 217
    personal titles in, 218
    salutation, 218–219
    signature, 220
    exercises, 223

Bust, busted, bursted, burst, 482

But, as co-ordinating conjunction, 315
    excessive use of, 399
    in double negative (*cannot help but*), 483
    punctuation with, 315–316

But, and, so, excessive use of, 399

But what, but that, 483

Cacophony, 66, 393

Calculate, reckon, 483

Call numbers, *see also* Card catalogue
    Dewey Decimal system, 175–176
    Library of Congress system, 175–176

Cambridge History of English Literature, described, 183

Canby, Henry Seidel, "The Threatening Thirties," quoted paragraph, 72

Can, may, proper use of each, 483

Cannot help but, can't help but, 483

Can't hardly, double negative, 483

Can't seem to, for *seem unable to*, 483

Capital, capitol, defined, 354

Capitalization, important words in title, 292

Capitals, uses of, 293–296
    abbreviations after names, 295
    days of week, 294
    first word of sentence, 293
    honorary titles with names, 295
    line of poetry, 293
    Father, Mother, etc., used as names, 296
    names of: historic periods, 294
        organizations, 294
        particular studies and courses, 295
        political and geographic divisions, 294–295
        races and languages, 295
    personifications, 294
    pronoun *I*, 295
    religious terms, 294
    vocative *O*, 295
    words not capitalized, 295–296
        common nouns and adjectives, 295
        my *father*, my *mother*, etc., 296
        general names of studies, 295
        points of compass, 295
    exercise, capitalization, 296–297
        capitals, italics, etc., in titles, 293

Card catalogue, uses of, 172–176
    author card, 173
    Dewey Decimal system, 175–176
    Library of Congress system, 175–176
    purpose of catalogue, 172
    subject card, 174
    title card, 174

Cardinal numbers, defined, 277

Caret, for insertions, 290

Case, 246–253
    appositives, 252
    declension of pronoun, 246
    defined, 277
    elliptical clauses, 247
    in prepositional phrase, 249
    nominative, 247–248
        for subject of verb, 247
        for subjective complement, 248
    noun and a participle, 250
    objective, 248–249
        for direct object, 248
        for object of preposition, 249
        with infinitive, 249

INDEX

INDEX

INDEX

INDEX

INDEX

INDEX

quotation marks with, 338–339

Slang, Hamlet's soliloquy translated into, 28

Smell, predicate adjective with, 257

So, as colloquial conjunction, 271–272
  as conjunction, 500
  as feminine intensive, 500
  as co-ordinating conjunction, 34

So . . . as, in negative statements, 480

Some, for *somewhat, a little,* 500

Some place, see *Anyplace,* 479

Sort, sort of, misuse of, 500

Sources, acknowledgment of, *see* Footnotes, 203–204

Spacing in typewritten manuscript, 288

Specie, species, correct use of, 500

Specific words, rich in connotation, 369

Spelling, 348–361
  careful pronunciation an aid to, 349
  checked in dictionary, 362
  compound numbers, 344
  compound (hyphenated) words, 345
  doubling final consonant, 351–352
  dropping final *-e,* 349–350
  formation of plurals, 352
  list of words for study, 357–361
  method of learning, 348
  plurals of nouns in *-y,* 352
  rules for, 349–357
  similar forms, 353–356
  the "seed" words, 351
  use of dictionary for, 362–367
  verbs ending in *-y,* 352
  words with *ie* or *ei,* 350–351
  exercises: application of rules, 356
    choice of correct forms, 356–357
    similar forms, 357
    words in *-y,* 357
    words in *ei* or *ie,* 356

Split infinitive, in modern usage, 419

Squinting modifiers, 418–419

St, nd, rd, th, undesirable with day of month, 297

Standard English, characteristics of, 13–15
  on formal level, 12–15
  on informal level, 15–28
  quoted examples from, 13–14
  see also Levels of usage, 11–30

Statesman's Year-Book, described, 180

Stationary, stationery, defined, 355

Stay to home, for *stay at home,* 376

Straight, strait, defined, 355

Straggling sentences, 397

Strong verb, defined, 286

Student's choice of levels of usage, 28–29

Style, concreteness in, 382–383
  maturity of, 474–475
  relation to personality, 53
  shift in, formal to colloquial, 439
  vividness, 384–387
  wordiness, 387–389

Subject, agreement with verb, 238–244
  diagramed, 37–43, 46–49
  nominative case for, 247
  shift in, 438

Subject of verb, misuse of sentence as, 442

Subjects for themes, 113–142
  autobiographical incidents, 117–119
  autobiographical sketch, 114–117
  directions, processes, organizations, 128–130
  interpretations of home and friends, 119–122
  local color articles, 130–132
  occupations, 122–125
  personal essays, 136–138
  profiles, 125–126
  reading, 126–128
  radio talks, 132–136

Subjects for research papers, 188–191

Subjective complements, defined, 38
  diagramed, 38
  see Complement, 277

Subjunctive mood, defined, 286
  uses of, 266

Subordinating conjunctions, 34
  errors in use of, 273–274
  list of, 273

Subordination in the sentence, faulty, 403–404

Substance: use of details, 160–162

Substantive, defined, 286
  clause, defined, 286

Such, as reference word, 430
  misused, 500

Such as, punctuation with, 322

Superfluous commas, 324
  after co-ordinate conjunction, 324
  between subject and verb, 324
  between verb and complement, 324
  between two words joined by *and,* 324
  with restrictive modifiers, 314–315

Superlative forms, adjective and adverb, 258

524

INDEX

HANDBOOK KEY

GRAMMAR

1 Sentence Fragment	**2** Comma Splice	**3** Run-together Sentence	**4** Subject and Verb	**5** Pronouns
6 Adjectives and Adverbs	**7** Verb Forms	**8** Conjunctions	**9** Grammatical Terms	

MECHANICS

10 Manuscript	**11** Titles	**12** Capitals	**13** Numbers	**14** Abbreviations
15 Syllabication	**16** Italics	**17** Bibliography	**18** Footnotes	

PUNCTUATION

19 Period Question Mark Exclamation Pt.	**20** Comma	**21** Semicolon	**22** Colon	**23** Apostrophe
24 Quotation Marks	**25** Dash	**26** Hyphen	**27** Parentheses Brackets	

SPELLING

28 Pronunciation	**29** Final -E	**30** Ie or Ei	**31** Final Consonant	**32** Final -Y
33 Similar Forms	**34** Spelling List			

WORDS

35 Use of Dictionary	**36** The Right Word	**37** Idioms	**38** Good Use	**39** Concreteness
40 Vividness	**41** Wordiness	**42** Triteness	**43** Fine Writing	**44** Euphony